Chartered Institute of
Management Accountants

CIMA

This book comes with free EN-gage online resources so that you can study anytime, anywhere. This free online resource is not sold separately and is included in the price of the book.

How to access your on-line resources

You can access additional online resources associated with this CIMA Official book via the EN-gage website at: www.EN-gage.co.uk.

Existing users

If you are an **existing EN-gage user**, simply log-in to your account, click on the 'add a book' link at the top of your homepage and enter the ISBN of this book and the unique pass key number contained above.

New users

If you are a new EN-gage user then you first need to register at: www.EN-gage.co.uk. Once registered, Kaplan Publishing will send you an email containing a link to activate your account - please check your junk mail if you do not receive this or contact us using the phone number or email address printed on the back cover of this book. Click on the link to activate your account. To unlock your additional resources, click on the 'add a book' link at the top of your home page. You will then need to enter the ISBN of this book (found on page ii) and the unique pass key number contained in the scratch panel below:

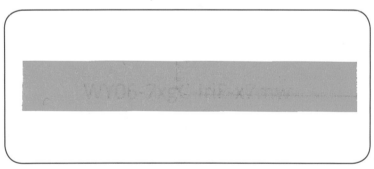

Then click 'finished' or 'add another book'.
Please allow 24 hours from the time you submit your book details for the content to appear in the My Learning and Testing area of your account.

Your code and information

This code can only be used once for the registration of one book online. This registration will expire when this edition of the book is no longer current - please see the back cover of this book for the expiry date.

Existing users

If you are an **existing EN-gage user**, simply log-in to your account, click on the 'add a book' link at the top of your homepage and enter the ISBN of this book and the unique pass key number contained above.

KAPLAN

PUBLISHING

CIMA

Paper F2

Advanced Financial Reporting

Study Text

Published by: Kaplan Publishing UK

Unit 2 The Business Centre, Molly Millars Lane, Wokingham, Berkshire RG41 2QZ

Acknowledgements

We are grateful to the CIMA for permission to reproduce past examination questions. The answers to CIMA Exams have been prepared by Kaplan Publishing, except in the case of the CIMA November 2010 and subsequent CIMA Exam answers where the official CIMA answers have been reproduced.

British Library Cataloguing in Publication Data

A catalogue record for this book is available from the British Library.

ISBN: 978-1-78415-303-8

Printed and bound in Great Britain.

Contents

Introduction

How to use the materials

These official CIMA learning materials have been carefully designed to make your learning experience as easy as possible and to give you the best chances of success in your Objective Test Examination.

The product range contains a number of features to help you in the study process. They include:

- a detailed explanation of all syllabus areas;
- extensive 'practical' materials;
- generous question practice, together with full solutions.

This Study Text has been designed with the needs of home study and distance learning candidates in mind. Such students require very full coverage of the syllabus topics, and also the facility to undertake extensive question practice. However, the Study Text is also ideal for fully taught courses.

The main body of the text is divided into a number of chapters, each of which is organised on the following pattern:

- **Detailed learning outcomes.** These describe the knowledge expected after your studies of the chapter are complete. You should assimilate these before beginning detailed work on the chapter, so that you can appreciate where your studies are leading.

- **Step-by-step topic coverage.** This is the heart of each chapter, containing detailed explanatory text supported where appropriate by worked examples and exercises. You should work carefully through this section, ensuring that you understand the material being explained and can tackle the examples and exercises successfully. Remember that in many cases knowledge is cumulative: if you fail to digest earlier material thoroughly, you may struggle to understand later chapters.

- **Activities.** Some chapters are illustrated by more practical elements, such as comments and questions designed to stimulate discussion.

- **Question practice.** The text contains three styles of question:
  - Exam-style objective test questions (OTQs)
  - 'Integration' questions – these test your ability to understand topics within a wider context. This is particularly important with calculations where OTQs may focus on just one element but an integration question tackles the full calculation, just as you would be expected to do in the workplace.
  - 'Case' style questions – these test your ability to analyse and discuss issues in greater depth, particularly focusing on scenarios that are less clear cut than in the Objective Test Examination, and thus provide excellent practice for developing the skills needed for success in the Management Level Case Study Examination.

- **Solutions.** Avoid the temptation merely to 'audit' the solutions provided. It is an illusion to think that this provides the same benefits as you would gain from a serious attempt of your own. However, if you are struggling to get started on a question you should read the introductory guidance provided at the beginning of the solution, where provided, and then make your own attempt before referring back to the full solution.

If you work conscientiously through this Official CIMA Study Text according to the guidelines above you will be giving yourself an excellent chance of success in your Objective Test Examination. Good luck with your studies!

Quality and accuracy are of the utmost importance to us so if you spot an error in any of our products, please send an email to mykaplanreporting@kaplan.com with full details, or follow the link to the feedback form in MyKaplan.

Our Quality Co-ordinator will work with our technical team to verify the error and take action to ensure it is corrected in future editions.

Icon Explanations

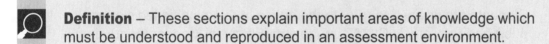 **Definition** – These sections explain important areas of knowledge which must be understood and reproduced in an assessment environment.

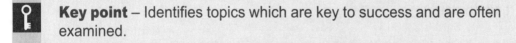 **Key point** – Identifies topics which are key to success and are often examined.

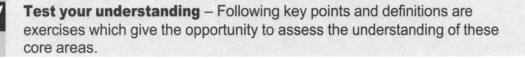 **Supplementary reading** – These sections will help to provide a deeper understanding of core areas. The supplementary reading is **NOT** optional reading. It is vital to provide you with the breadth of knowledge you will need to address the wide range of topics within your syllabus that could feature in an assessment question. **Reference to this text is vital when self studying**.

Test your understanding – Following key points and definitions are exercises which give the opportunity to assess the understanding of these core areas.

Illustration – To help develop an understanding of particular topics. The illustrative examples are useful in preparing for the Test your understanding exercises.

Exclamation mark – This symbol signifies a topic which can be more difficult to understand. When reviewing these areas, care should be taken.

Study technique

Passing exams is partly a matter of intellectual ability, but however accomplished you are in that respect you can improve your chances significantly by the use of appropriate study and revision techniques. In this section we briefly outline some tips for effective study during the earlier stages of your approach to the Objective Test Examination. We also mention some techniques that you will find useful at the revision stage.

Planning

To begin with, formal planning is essential to get the best return from the time you spend studying. Estimate how much time in total you are going to need for each subject you are studying. Remember that you need to allow time for revision as well as for initial study of the material.

With your study material before you, decide which chapters you are going to study in each week, and which weeks you will devote to revision and final question practice.

Prepare a written schedule summarising the above and stick to it!

It is essential to know your syllabus. As your studies progress you will become more familiar with how long it takes to cover topics in sufficient depth. Your timetable may need to be adapted to allocate enough time for the whole syllabus.

Students are advised to refer to the notice of examinable legislation published regularly in CIMA's magazine (Financial Management), the students e-newsletter (Velocity) and on the CIMA website, to ensure they are up-to-date.

The amount of space allocated to a topic in the Study Text is not a very good guide as to how long it will take you. The syllabus weighting is the better guide as to how long you should spend on a syllabus topic.

Tips for effective studying

(1) Aim to find a quiet and undisturbed location for your study, and plan as far as possible to use the same period of time each day. Getting into a routine helps to avoid wasting time. Make sure that you have all the materials you need before you begin so as to minimise interruptions.

(2) Store all your materials in one place, so that you do not waste time searching for items every time you want to begin studying. If you have to pack everything away after each study period, keep your study materials in a box, or even a suitcase, which will not be disturbed until the next time.

(3) Limit distractions. To make the most effective use of your study periods you should be able to apply total concentration, so turn off all entertainment equipment, set your phones to message mode, and put up your 'do not disturb' sign.

(4) Your timetable will tell you which topic to study. However, before diving in and becoming engrossed in the finer points, make sure you have an overall picture of all the areas that need to be covered by the end of that session. After an hour, allow yourself a short break and move away from your Study Text. With experience, you will learn to assess the pace you need to work at. Each study session should focus on component learning outcomes – the basis for all questions.

(5) Work carefully through a chapter, making notes as you go. When you have covered a suitable amount of material, vary the pattern by attempting a practice question. When you have finished your attempt, make notes of any mistakes you made, or any areas that you failed to cover or covered more briefly. Be aware that all component learning outcomes will be tested in each examination.

(6) Make notes as you study, and discover the techniques that work best for you. Your notes may be in the form of lists, bullet points, diagrams, summaries, 'mind maps', or the written word, but remember that you will need to refer back to them at a later date, so they must be intelligible. If you are on a taught course, make sure you highlight any issues you would like to follow up with your lecturer.

(7) Organise your notes. Make sure that all your notes, calculations etc. can be effectively filed and easily retrieved later.

Objective Test

Objective Test questions require you to choose or provide a response to a question whose correct answer is predetermined.

The most common types of Objective Test question you will see are:

- Multiple choice, where you have to choose the correct answer(s) from a list of possible answers. This could either be numbers or text.

- Multiple choice with more choices and answers, for example, choosing two correct answers from a list of eight possible answers. This could either be numbers or text.

- Single numeric entry, where you give your numeric answer, for example, profit is $10,000.

- Multiple entry, where you give several numeric answers.

- True/false questions, where you state whether a statement is true or false.

- Matching pairs of text, for example, matching a technical term with the correct definition.

- Other types could be matching text with graphs and labelling graphs/diagrams.

In every chapter of this Study Text we have introduced these types of questions, but obviously we have had to label answers A, B, C etc rather than using click boxes. For convenience we have retained quite a few questions where an initial scenario leads to a number of sub-questions. There will be questions of this type in the Objective Test Examination but they will rarely have more than three sub-questions.

Guidance re CIMA on-screen calculator

As part of the CIMA Objective Test software, candidates are now provided with a calculator. This calculator is on-screen and is available for the duration of the assessment. The calculator is available in each of the Objective Test Examinations and is accessed by clicking the calculator button in the top left hand corner of the screen at any time during the assessment.

All candidates must complete a 15-minute tutorial before the assessment begins and will have the opportunity to familiarise themselves with the calculator and practise using it.

Candidates may practise using the calculator by downloading and installing the practice exam at http://www.vue.com/athena/. The calculator can be accessed from the fourth sample question (of 12).

Please note that the practice exam and tutorial provided by Pearson VUE at http://www.vue.com/athena/ is not specific to CIMA and includes the full range of question types the Pearson VUE software supports, some of which CIMA does not currently use.

Fundamentals of Objective Tests

The Objective Tests are 90-minute assessments comprising 60 compulsory questions, with one or more parts. There will be no choice and all questions should be attempted.

Structure of subjects and learning outcomes

Each subject within the syllabus is divided into a number of broad syllabus topics. The topics contain one or more lead learning outcomes, related component learning outcomes and indicative knowledge content.

A learning outcome has two main purposes:

(a) To define the skill or ability that a well prepared candidate should be able to exhibit in the examination.

(b) To demonstrate the approach likely to be taken in examination questions.

The learning outcomes are part of a hierarchy of learning objectives. The verbs used at the beginning of each learning outcome relate to a specific learning objective, e.g.

Calculate the break-even point, profit target, margin of safety and profit/volume ratio for a single product or service.

The verb '**calculate**' indicates a level three learning objective. The following tables list the verbs that appear in the syllabus learning outcomes and examination questions.

CIMA VERB HIERARCHY

CIMA place great importance on the definition of verbs in structuring Objective Test Examinations. It is therefore crucial that you understand the verbs in order to appreciate the depth and breadth of a topic and the level of skill required. The Objective Tests will focus on levels one, two and three of the CIMA hierarchy of verbs. However they will also test levels four and five, especially at the management and strategic levels. You can therefore expect to be tested on knowledge, comprehension, application, analysis and evaluation in these examinations.

Level 1: KNOWLEDGE

What you are expected to know.

VERBS USED	DEFINITION
List	Make a list of.
State	Express, fully or clearly, the details of/facts of.
Define	Give the exact meaning of.

For example you could be asked to make a list of the advantages of a particular information system by selecting all options that apply from a given set of possibilities. Or you could be required to define relationship marketing by selecting the most appropriate option from a list.

Level 2: COMPREHENSION

What you are expected to understand.

VERBS USED	DEFINITION
Describe	Communicate the key features of.
Distinguish	Highlight the differences between.
Explain	Make clear or intelligible/state the meaning or purpose of.
Identify	Recognise, establish or select after consideration.
Illustrate	Use an example to describe or explain something.

For example you may be asked to distinguish between different aspects of the global business environment by dragging external factors and dropping into a PEST analysis.

Level 3: APPLICATION

How you are expected to apply your knowledge.

VERBS USED	DEFINITION
Apply	Put to practical use.
Calculate	Ascertain or reckon mathematically.
Demonstrate	Prove with certainty or exhibit by practical means.
Prepare	Make or get ready for use.
Reconcile	Make or prove consistent/compatible.
Solve	Find an answer to.
Tabulate	Arrange in a table.

For example you may need to calculate the projected revenue or costs for a given set of circumstances.

Level 4: ANALYSIS

How you are expected to analyse the detail of what you have learned.

VERBS USED	DEFINITION
Analyse	Examine in detail the structure of.
Categorise	Place into a defined class or division.
Compare/ contrast	Show the similarities and/or differences between.
Construct	Build up or compile.
Discuss	Examine in detail by argument.
Interpret	Translate into intelligible or familiar terms.
Prioritise	Place in order of priority or sequence for action.
Produce	Create or bring into existence.

For example you may be required to interpret an inventory ratio by selecting the most appropriate statement for a given set of circumstances and data.

Level 5: EVALUATION

How you are expected to use your learning to evaluate, make decisions or recommendations.

VERBS USED	DEFINITION
Advise	Counsel, inform or notify.
Evaluate	Appraise or assess the value of.
Recommend	Propose a course of action.

For example you may be asked to recommend and select an appropriate course of action based on a short scenario.

PRESENT VALUE TABLE

Present value of 1.00 unit of currency, that is $(1+r)^{-n}$ where r = interest rate; n = number of periods until payment or receipt.

Periods (n)	Interest rates (r)									
	1%	2%	3%	4%	5%	6%	7%	8%	9%	10%
1	0.990	0.980	0.971	0.962	0.952	0.943	0.935	0.926	0.917	0.909
2	0.980	0.961	0.943	0.925	0.907	0.890	0.873	0.857	0.842	0.826
3	0.971	0.942	0.915	0.889	0.864	0.840	0.816	0.794	0.772	0.751
4	0.961	0.924	0.888	0.855	0.823	0.792	0.763	0.735	0.708	0.683
5	0.951	0.906	0.863	0.822	0.784	0.747	0.713	0.681	0.650	0.621
6	0.942	0.888	0.837	0.790	0.746	0.705	0.666	0.630	0.596	0.564
7	0.933	0.871	0.813	0.760	0.711	0.665	0.623	0.583	0.547	0.513
8	0.923	0.853	0.789	0.731	0.677	0.627	0.582	0.540	0.502	0.467
9	0.914	0.837	0.766	0.703	0.645	0.592	0.544	0.500	0.460	0.424
10	0.905	0.820	0.744	0.676	0.614	0.558	0.508	0.463	0.422	0.386
11	0.896	0.804	0.722	0.650	0.585	0.527	0.475	0.429	0.388	0.350
12	0.887	0.788	0.701	0.625	0.557	0.497	0.444	0.397	0.356	0.319
13	0.879	0.773	0.681	0.601	0.530	0.469	0.415	0.368	0.326	0.290
14	0.870	0.758	0.661	0.577	0.505	0.442	0.388	0.340	0.299	0.263
15	0.861	0.743	0.642	0.555	0.481	0.417	0.362	0.315	0.275	0.239
16	0.853	0.728	0.623	0.534	0.458	0.394	0.339	0.292	0.252	0.218
17	0.844	0.714	0.605	0.513	0.436	0.371	0.317	0.270	0.231	0.198
18	0.836	0.700	0.587	0.494	0.416	0.350	0.296	0.250	0.212	0.180
19	0.828	0.686	0.570	0.475	0.396	0.331	0.277	0.232	0.194	0.164
20	0.820	0.673	0.554	0.456	0.377	0.312	0.258	0.215	0.178	0.149

Periods (n)	Interest rates (r)									
	11%	12%	13%	14%	15%	16%	17%	18%	19%	20%
1	0.901	0.893	0.885	0.877	0.870	0.862	0.855	0.847	0.840	0.833
2	0.812	0.797	0.783	0.769	0.756	0.743	0.731	0.718	0.706	0.694
3	0.731	0.712	0.693	0.675	0.658	0.641	0.624	0.609	0.593	0.579
4	0.659	0.636	0.613	0.592	0.572	0.552	0.534	0.516	0.499	0.482
5	0.593	0.567	0.543	0.519	0.497	0.476	0.456	0.437	0.419	0.402
6	0.535	0.507	0.480	0.456	0.432	0.410	0.390	0.370	0.352	0.335
7	0.482	0.452	0.425	0.400	0.376	0.354	0.333	0.314	0.296	0.279
8	0.434	0.404	0.376	0.351	0.327	0.305	0.285	0.266	0.249	0.233
9	0.391	0.361	0.333	0.308	0.284	0.263	0.243	0.225	0.209	0.194
10	0.352	0.322	0.295	0.270	0.247	0.227	0.208	0.191	0.176	0.162
11	0.317	0.287	0.261	0.237	0.215	0.195	0.178	0.162	0.148	0.135
12	0.286	0.257	0.231	0.208	0.187	0.168	0.152	0.137	0.124	0.112
13	0.258	0.229	0.204	0.182	0.163	0.145	0.130	0.116	0.104	0.093
14	0.232	0.205	0.181	0.160	0.141	0.125	0.111	0.099	0.088	0.078
15	0.209	0.183	0.160	0.140	0.123	0.108	0.095	0.084	0.079	0.065
16	0.188	0.163	0.141	0.123	0.107	0.093	0.081	0.071	0.062	0.054
17	0.170	0.146	0.125	0.108	0.093	0.080	0.069	0.060	0.052	0.045
18	0.153	0.130	0.111	0.095	0.081	0.069	0.059	0.051	0.044	0.038
19	0.138	0.116	0.098	0.083	0.070	0.060	0.051	0.043	0.037	0.031
20	0.124	0.104	0.087	0.073	0.061	0.051	0.043	0.037	0.031	0.026

Please check the CIMA website for the latest version of the maths tables and formulae sheets in advance of sitting your live assessment.

Cumulative present value of 1.00 unit of currency per annum, Receivable or Payable at the end of each year for n years $\frac{1-(1+r)^{-n}}{r}$

Periods	Interest rates (r)									
(n)	1%	2%	3%	4%	5%	6%	7%	8%	9%	10%
1	0.990	0.980	0.971	0.962	0.952	0.943	0.935	0.926	0.917	0.909
2	1.970	1.942	1.913	1.886	1.859	1.833	1.808	1.783	1.759	1.736
3	2.941	2.884	2.829	2.775	2.723	2.673	2.624	2.577	2.531	2.487
4	3.902	3.808	3.717	3.630	3.546	3.465	3.387	3.312	3.240	3.170
5	4.853	4.713	4.580	4.452	4.329	4.212	4.100	3.993	3.890	3.791
6	5.795	5.601	5.417	5.242	5.076	4.917	4.767	4.623	4.486	4.355
7	6.728	6.472	6.230	6.002	5.786	5.582	5.389	5.206	5.033	4.868
8	7.652	7.325	7.020	6.733	6.463	6.210	5.971	5.747	5.535	5.335
9	8.566	8.162	7.786	7.435	7.108	6.802	6.515	6.247	5.995	5.759
10	9.471	8.983	8.530	8.111	7.722	7.360	7.024	6.710	6.418	6.145
11	10.368	9.787	9.253	8.760	8.306	7.887	7.499	7.139	6.805	6.495
12	11.255	10.575	9.954	9.385	8.863	8.384	7.943	7.536	7.161	6.814
13	12.134	11.348	10.635	9.986	9.394	8.853	8.358	7.904	7.487	7.103
14	13.004	12.106	11.296	10.563	9.899	9.295	8.745	8.244	7.786	7.367
15	13.865	12.849	11.938	11.118	10.380	9.712	9.108	8.559	8.061	7.606
16	14.718	13.578	12.561	11.652	10.838	10.106	9.447	8.851	8.313	7.824
17	15.562	14.292	13.166	12.166	11.274	10.477	9.763	9.122	8.544	8.022
18	16.398	14.992	13.754	12.659	11.690	10.828	10.059	9.372	8.756	8.201
19	17.226	15.679	14.324	13.134	12.085	11.158	10.336	9.604	8.950	8.365
20	18.046	16.351	14.878	13.590	12.462	11.470	10.594	9.818	9.129	8.514

Periods	Interest rates (r)									
(n)	11%	12%	13%	14%	15%	16%	17%	18%	19%	20%
1	0.901	0.893	0.885	0.877	0.870	0.862	0.855	0.847	0.840	0.833
2	1.713	1.690	1.668	1.647	1.626	1.605	1.585	1.566	1.547	1.528
3	2.444	2.402	2.361	2.322	2.283	2.246	2.210	2.174	2.140	2.106
4	3.102	3.037	2.974	2.914	2.855	2.798	2.743	2.690	2.639	2.589
5	3.696	3.605	3.517	3.433	3.352	3.274	3.199	3.127	3.058	2.991
6	4.231	4.111	3.998	3.889	3.784	3.685	3.589	3.498	3.410	3.326
7	4.712	4.564	4.423	4.288	4.160	4.039	3.922	3.812	3.706	3.605
8	5.146	4.968	4.799	4.639	4.487	4.344	4.207	4.078	3.954	3.837
9	5.537	5.328	5.132	4.946	4.772	4.607	4.451	4.303	4.163	4.031
10	5.889	5.650	5.426	5.216	5.019	4.833	4.659	4.494	4.339	4.192
11	6.207	5.938	5.687	5.453	5.234	5.029	4.836	4.656	4.486	4.327
12	6.492	6.194	5.918	5.660	5.421	5.197	4.988	4.793	4.611	4.439
13	6.750	6.424	6.122	5.842	5.583	5.342	5.118	4.910	4.715	4.533
14	6.982	6.628	6.302	6.002	5.724	5.468	5.229	5.008	4.802	4.611
15	7.191	6.811	6.462	6.142	5.847	5.575	5.324	5.092	4.876	4.675
16	7.379	6.974	6.604	6.265	5.954	5.668	5.405	5.162	4.938	4.730
17	7.549	7.120	6.729	6.373	6.047	5.749	5.475	5.222	4.990	4.775
18	7.702	7.250	6.840	6.467	6.128	5.818	5.534	5.273	5.033	4.812
19	7.839	7.366	6.938	6.550	6.198	5.877	5.584	5.316	5.070	4.843
20	7.963	7.469	7.025	6.623	6.259	5.929	5.628	5.353	5.101	4.870

MATHS TABLES AND FORMULAE

Present value table

Present value of $1, that is $(1 + r)^{-n}$ where r = interest rate; n = number of periods until payment or receipt.

Periods (n)	Interest rates (r)									
	1%	2%	3%	4%	5%	6%	7%	8%	9%	10%
1	0.990	0.980	0.971	0.962	0.952	0.943	0.935	0.926	0.917	0.909
2	0.980	0.961	0.943	0.925	0.907	0.890	0.873	0.857	0.842	0.826
3	0.971	0.942	0.915	0.889	0.864	0.840	0.816	0.794	0.772	0.751
4	0.961	0.924	0.888	0.855	0.823	0.792	0.763	0.735	0.708	0.683
5	0.951	0.906	0.863	0.822	0.784	0.747	0.713	0.681	0.650	0.621
6	0.942	0.888	0.837	0.790	0.746	0.705	0.666	0.630	0.596	0.564
7	0.933	0.871	0.813	0.760	0.711	0.665	0.623	0.583	0.547	0.513
8	0.923	0.853	0.789	0.731	0.677	0.627	0.582	0.540	0.502	0.467
9	0.914	0.837	0.766	0.703	0.645	0.592	0.544	0.500	0.460	0.424
10	0.905	0.820	0.744	0.676	0.614	0.558	0.508	0.463	0.422	0.386
11	0.896	0.804	0.722	0.650	0.585	0.527	0.475	0.429	0.388	0.350
12	0.887	0.788	0.701	0.625	0.557	0.497	0.444	0.397	0.356	0.319
13	0.879	0.773	0.681	0.601	0.530	0.469	0.415	0.368	0.326	0.290
14	0.870	0.758	0.661	0.577	0.505	0.442	0.388	0.340	0.299	0.263
15	0.861	0.743	0.642	0.555	0.481	0.417	0.362	0.315	0.275	0.239
16	0.853	0.728	0.623	0.534	0.458	0.394	0.339	0.292	0.252	0.218
17	0.844	0.714	0.605	0.513	0.436	0.371	0.317	0.270	0.231	0.198
18	0.836	0.700	0.587	0.494	0.416	0.350	0.296	0.250	0.212	0.180
19	0.828	0.686	0.570	0.475	0.396	0.331	0.277	0.232	0.194	0.164
20	0.820	0.673	0.554	0.456	0.377	0.312	0.258	0.215	0.178	0.149

Periods (n)	Interest rates (r)									
	11%	12%	13%	14%	15%	16%	17%	18%	19%	20%
1	0.901	0.893	0.885	0.877	0.870	0.862	0.855	0.847	0.840	0.833
2	0.812	0.797	0.783	0.769	0.756	0.743	0.731	0.718	0.706	0.694
3	0.731	0.712	0.693	0.675	0.658	0.641	0.624	0.609	0.593	0.579
4	0.659	0.636	0.613	0.592	0.572	0.552	0.534	0.516	0.499	0.482
5	0.593	0.567	0.543	0.519	0.497	0.476	0.456	0.437	0.419	0.402
6	0.535	0.507	0.480	0.456	0.432	0.410	0.390	0.370	0.352	0.335
7	0.482	0.452	0.425	0.400	0.376	0.354	0.333	0.314	0.296	0.279
8	0.434	0.404	0.376	0.351	0.327	0.305	0.285	0.266	0.249	0.233
9	0.391	0.361	0.333	0.308	0.284	0.263	0.243	0.225	0.209	0.194
10	0.352	0.322	0.295	0.270	0.247	0.227	0.208	0.191	0.176	0.162
11	0.317	0.287	0.261	0.237	0.215	0.195	0.178	0.162	0.148	0.135
12	0.286	0.257	0.231	0.208	0.187	0.168	0.152	0.137	0.124	0.112
13	0.258	0.229	0.204	0.182	0.163	0.145	0.130	0.116	0.104	0.093
14	0.232	0.205	0.181	0.160	0.141	0.125	0.111	0.099	0.088	0.078
15	0.209	0.183	0.160	0.140	0.123	0.108	0.095	0.084	0.079	0.065
16	0.188	0.163	0.141	0.123	0.107	0.093	0.081	0.071	0.062	0.054
17	0.170	0.146	0.125	0.108	0.093	0.080	0.069	0.060	0.052	0.045
18	0.153	0.130	0.111	0.095	0.081	0.069	0.059	0.051	0.044	0.038
19	0.138	0.116	0.098	0.083	0.070	0.060	0.051	0.043	0.037	0.031
20	0.124	0.104	0.087	0.073	0.061	0.051	0.043	0.037	0.031	0.026

Cumulative present value of $1 per annum,

Receivable or Payable at the end of each year for n years $\dfrac{1-(1+r)^{-n}}{r}$

Periods (n)	Interest rates (r)									
	1%	2%	3%	4%	5%	6%	7%	8%	9%	10%
1	0.990	0.980	0.971	0.962	0.952	0.943	0.935	0.926	0.917	0.909
2	1.970	1.942	1.913	1.886	1.859	1.833	1.808	1.783	1.759	1.736
3	2.941	2.884	2.829	2.775	2.723	2.673	2.624	2.577	2.531	2.487
4	3.902	3.808	3.717	3.630	3.546	3.465	3.387	3.312	3.240	3.170
5	4.853	4.713	4.580	4.452	4.329	4.212	4.100	3.993	3.890	3.791
6	5.795	5.601	5.417	5.242	5.076	4.917	4.767	4.623	4.486	4.355
7	6.728	6.472	6.230	6.002	5.786	5.582	5.389	5.206	5.033	4.868
8	7.652	7.325	7.020	6.733	6.463	6.210	5.971	5.747	5.535	5.335
9	8.566	8.162	7.786	7.435	7.108	6.802	6.515	6.247	5.995	5.759
10	9.471	8.983	8.530	8.111	7.722	7.360	7.024	6.710	6.418	6.145
11	10.368	9.787	9.253	8.760	8.306	7.887	7.499	7.139	6.805	6.495
12	11.255	10.575	9.954	9.385	8.863	8.384	7.943	7.536	7.161	6.814
13	12.134	11.348	10.635	9.986	9.394	8.853	8.358	7.904	7.487	7.103
14	13.004	12.106	11.296	10.563	9.899	9.295	8.745	8.244	7.786	7.367
15	13.865	12.849	11.938	11.118	10.380	9.712	9.108	8.559	8.061	7.606
16	14.718	13.578	12.561	11.652	10.838	10.106	9.447	8.851	8.313	7.824
17	15.562	14.292	13.166	12.166	11.274	10.477	9.763	9.122	8.544	8.022
18	16.398	14.992	13.754	12.659	11.690	10.828	10.059	9.372	8.756	8.201
19	17.226	15.679	14.324	13.134	12.085	11.158	10.336	9.604	8.950	8.365
20	18.046	16.351	14.878	13.590	12.462	11.470	10.594	9.818	9.129	8.514

Periods (n)	Interest rates (r)									
	11%	12%	13%	14%	15%	16%	17%	18%	19%	20%
1	0.901	0.893	0.885	0.877	0.870	0.862	0.855	0.847	0.840	0.833
2	1.713	1.690	1.668	1.647	1.626	1.605	1.585	1.566	1.547	1.528
3	2.444	2.402	2.361	2.322	2.283	2.246	2.210	2.174	2.140	2.106
4	3.102	3.037	2.974	2.914	2.855	2.798	2.743	2.690	2.639	2.589
5	3.696	3.605	3.517	3.433	3.352	3.274	3.199	3.127	3.058	2.991
6	4.231	4.111	3.998	3.889	3.784	3.685	3.589	3.498	3.410	3.326
7	4.712	4.564	4.423	4.288	4.160	4.039	3.922	3.812	3.706	3.605
8	5.146	4.968	4.799	4.639	4.487	4.344	4.207	4.078	3.954	3.837
9	5.537	5.328	5.132	4.946	4.772	4.607	4.451	4.303	4.163	4.031
10	5.889	5.650	5.426	5.216	5.019	4.833	4.659	4.494	4.339	4.192
11	6.207	5.938	5.687	5.453	5.234	5.029	4.836	4.656	4.486	4.327
12	6.492	6.194	5.918	5.660	5.421	5.197	4.988	7.793	4.611	4.439
13	6.750	6.424	6.122	5.842	5.583	5.342	5.118	4.910	4.715	4.533
14	6.982	6.628	6.302	6.002	5.724	5.468	5.229	5.008	4.802	4.611
15	7.191	6.811	6.462	6.142	5.847	5.575	5.324	5.092	4.876	4.675
16	7.379	6.974	6.604	6.265	5.954	5.668	5.405	5.162	4.938	4.730
17	7.549	7.120	6.729	6.373	6.047	5.749	5.475	5.222	4.990	4.775
18	7.702	7.250	6.840	6.467	6.128	5.818	5.534	5.273	5.033	4.812
19	7.839	7.366	6.938	6.550	6.198	5.877	5.584	5.316	5.070	4.843
20	7.963	7.469	7.025	6.623	6.259	5.929	5.628	5.353	5.101	4.870

FORMULAE

Annuity

Present value of an annuity of $1 per annum receivable or payable for *n* years, commencing in one year, discounted at *r*% per annum:

$$PV = \frac{1}{r}\left[1 - \frac{1}{[1+r]^n}\right]$$

Perpetuity

Present value of $1 per annum receivable or payable in perpetuity, commencing in one year, discounted at *r*% per annum:

$$PV = \frac{1}{r}$$

Growing Perpetuity

Present value of $1 per annum, receivable or payable, commencing in one year, growing in perpetuity at a constant rate of *g*% per annum, discounted at *r*% per annum:

$$PV = \frac{1}{r-g}$$

F2
ADVANCED FINANCIAL REPORTING

Syllabus overview

F2 builds on the competencies gained from F1. It covers how to effectively source the long-term finance required to fund the operations of organisations, particularly their capital investments. It also deepens the coverage of financial reporting to more complex aspects of group accounting and analyses the rules governing the recognition and measurement of various elements of the financial statements. Finally it shows how to analyse financial statements to provide insights about the financial performance and position of the organisation over time and in comparison with others.

Summary of syllabus

Weight	Syllabus topic
15%	**A.** Sources of long-term finance
60%	**B.** Financial reporting
25%	**C.** Analysis of financial performance and position

F2 – A. SOURCES OF LONG-TERM FINANCE (15%)

Learning outcomes
On completion of their studies, students should be able to:

Lead	Component	Indicative syllabus content
1 discuss types and sources of long-term finance for an incorporated entity.	(a) discuss the characteristics of different types of long-term debt and equity finance	• Characteristics of ordinary and preference shares and different types of long-term debt.
	(b) discuss the markets for and methods of raising long-term finance.	• Operation of the stock and bond markets. • Share and bond issues. • Role of advisors.
2 calculate a weighted average cost of capital (WACC) for an incorporated entity.	(a) calculate the cost of equity for an incorporated entity using the dividend valuation model	• Cost of equity using the dividend valuation model, with and without growth in dividends.
	(b) calculate the post-tax cost of debt for an incorporated entity	• Post-tax cost of bank borrowings. • Yield to maturity of bonds and post-tax cost of bonds. • Post-tax cost of convertible bonds up to and including conversion.
	(c) calculate the weighted average cost of capital (WACC) for an incorporated entity.	• WACC and its use.

F2 – B. FINANCIAL REPORTING (60%)

Learning outcomes
On completion of their studies, students should be able to:

Lead	Component	Indicative syllabus content
1 produce consolidated primary financial statements, incorporating accounting transactions and adjustments, in accordance with relevant international accounting standards, in an ethical manner.	(a) produce primary financial statements for a group of entities in accordance with relevant international accounting standards	• Production of: – consolidated statement of comprehensive income – consolidated statement of financial position – consolidated statement of changes in equity – consolidated statement of cash flows including the adoption of both full consolidation and the principles of equity accounting, in accordance with the provisions of IAS 1, IAS 27, IAS 28, IFRS 3, IFRS 10 and IFRS 11.
	(b) discuss the need for and nature of disclosure of interests in other entities	• The need for and nature of disclosure of interests of interests in other entities, in accordance with IFRS 12.
	(c) discuss the provisions of relevant international accounting standards in respect of the recognition and measurement of revenue, leases, financial instruments, provisions, share-based payments and deferred taxation	• The need for and nature of disclosures of contingent assets and liabilities, in accordance with IAS 37. • Recognition and measurement of: – revenue, in accordance with IAS 18 and the provisions of the framework – operating and finance leases, in accordance with IAS 17 – financial instruments, in accordance with IAS 32 and IAS 39 (excluding hedge accounting) – provisions, in accordance with IAS 37 – share-based payments, in accordance with IFRS 2 – provision for deferred taxation, in accordance with IAS 12.
	(d) produce the accounting entries, in accordance with relevant international accounting standards	
	(e) discuss the ethical selection and adoption of relevant accounting policies and accounting estimates.	• Ethics in financial reporting.

Learning outcomes
On completion of their studies, students should be able to:

Lead	Component	Indicative syllabus content
2 demonstrate the impact on the preparation of the consolidated financial statements of certain complex group scenarios.	(a) demonstrate the impact on the group financial statements of: i acquiring additional shareholdings in the period ii disposing of all or part of a shareholding in the period	• Additional acquisition in the period resulting in a simple investment becoming a controlling interest, in accordance with the provisions of IFRS 3. • Calculation of the gain/loss on the disposal of a controlling interest in a subsidiary in the year, in accordance with the provisions of IFRS 3. • Adjustment to parent's equity resulting from acquiring or disposing of shares in a subsidiary, in accordance with the provisions of IFRS 3.
	(b) demonstrate the impact on the group financial statements of consolidating a foreign subsidiary	• Provisions of IAS 21 in respect of consolidating a foreign subsidiary and the calculation of the foreign exchange gains and losses in the period.
	(c) demonstrate the impact on the group financial statements of acquiring indirect control of a subsidiary.	• Impact of indirect effective holdings on the preparation of group financial statements.
3 discuss the need for and nature of disclosure of transactions between related parties.	(a) discuss the need for and nature of disclosure of transactions between related parties	• The need for and nature of disclosure of related party transactions, in accordance with IAS 2.
4 produce the disclosures for earnings per share.	(a) produce the disclosures for earnings per share.	• Calculate basic and diluted earnings per share, in accordance with IAS 33.

F2 – C. ANALYSIS OF FINANCIAL PERFORMANCE AND POSITION (25%)

Learning outcomes
On completion of their studies, students should be able to:

Lead	Component	Indicative syllabus content
1 evaluate the financial performance, financial position and financial adaptability of an incorporated entity.	(a) calculate ratios relevant for the assessment of an entity's profitability, financial performance, financial position and financial adaptability	• Ratios for profitability, performance, efficiency, activity, liquidity and gearing.
	(b) evaluate the financial performance, financial position and financial adaptability of an entity based on the information contained in the financial statements provided	• Interpretation of the primary financial statements and any additional information provided.
	(c) advise on action that could be taken to improve an entity's financial performance and financial position.	• Action that could be realistically taken by the entity's management to improve financial performance and strengthen financial position, taking into account ethical considerations and internal and external constraints.
2 discuss the limitations of ratio analysis.	(a) discuss the limitations of ratio analysis based on financial statements that can be caused by internal and external factors.	• Inter-segment comparisons. • International comparisons.

Long term finance

Chapter learning objectives

A1. Discuss types and sources of long-term finance for an incorporated entity.

(a) Discuss the characteristics of different types of long-term debt and equity finance.

- Characteristics of ordinary and preference shares and different types of long-term debt.

(b) Discuss the markets for and methods of raising long-term finance.

- Operation of the stock and bond markets.

- Share and bond issues.

- Role of advisors.

1 Session content

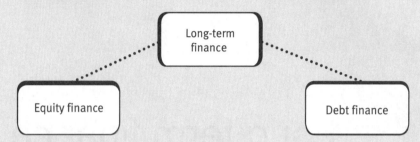

2 Introduction

Sources of long term finance

If a company has a large cash surplus, it may be able to afford to undertake new investment projects without having to resort to external sources of finance.

However, if external funds are required, the company might raise finance from the following sources:

(1) The capital markets:
 - new share issues, for example by companies acquiring a stock market listing for the first time
 - rights issues
 - issues of marketable debt.

 A company must be quoted/listed on a recognised stock exchange in order to be able to raise finance from the capital markets.

(2) Bank borrowings – long-term loans or short-term loans, including bank facilities such as revolving credit facilities (RCFs) and money market lines.

(3) Government and similar sources.

In general, finance can be raised from Equity or Debt sources.

3 Equity finance

Equity is another name for shares or ownership rights in a business.

Important terminology

Share – a fixed identifiable unit of capital in an entity which normally has a fixed nominal value, which may be quite different from its market value. (CIMA Official Terminology, 2005)

Shareholders receive returns from their investment in shares in the form of dividends, and also capital growth in the share price.

Ordinary shares

Ordinary shares pay dividends at the discretion of the entity's directors. The ordinary shareholders of a company are the owners of the company and they have the right to attend meetings and vote on any important matters.

On a winding-up of a company, the ordinary shareholders are subordinate to all other finance providers (i.e. they receive their money last, if there is any left after all other finance providers have been paid).

Preference shares

Preference shares are shares that pay a fixed dividend, which is paid in preference to (before) ordinary share dividends, hence the name.

Also, on a winding-up of a company, the preference shareholders are subordinate to all the debt holders and creditors, but receive their payout before ordinary shareholders.

More details on preference shares

Comparison of preference shares with debt and with ordinary shares

Preference shares pay a fixed proportion of the share's nominal value each year as a dividend. This is why they are often considered to behave in a way which is more similar to debt finance (fixed annual returns) rather than ordinary shares (variable dividend at the discretion of the directors).

However, unlike interest on debt finance, preference share dividends are paid out of post-tax profits, so there is no tax benefit to a company of paying preference share dividends.

Also, there are certain circumstances (e.g. where a company has insufficient distributable profits) when the company will be given permission to not pay its preference share dividends in a year. This is not the case with debt interest, which is an obligation every year, whether or not the company can afford to make the payment.

The lack of tax relief on dividends mentioned above explains why preference shares are relatively unattractive to companies compared with bank borrowings and other forms of fixed rate security such as bonds.

However, they do have some appeal to risk-averse investors looking for a relatively reliable income stream.

Different types of preference shares

There are four types of preference shares:

- cumulative preference shares, for which dividends must be rolled forward if the company is unable to pay the dividend i.e. if a dividend is not paid in year 1, that dividend has to be paid in year 2 along with the 'normal' dividend for year 2.

- non-cumulative preference shares, for which missed dividends do not have to be paid later. There is no roll forward of dividends.

- participating preference shares, which give the holder fixed dividends plus extra earnings based on certain conditions (in a similar way to ordinary shares).

- convertible preference shares, which can be exchanged for a specified number of ordinary shares on some given future date.

Also, note that some preference shares are redeemable, meaning that holders will be repaid their capital (usually at par) a pre-determined future date.

Example of convertible preference shares

Convertible preference shares are fixed-income securities that the investor can choose to turn into a certain number of ordinary shares after a predetermined time span or on a specific date.

The fixed-income component offers a steady income stream and some protection of the investor's capital. However, the option to convert these securities into ordinary shares gives the investor the opportunity to gain from a rise in the share price.

Convertibles are particularly attractive to those investors who want to participate in the rise of hot growth companies while being insulated from a drop in price should the ordinary share price growth not live up to expectations.

If a company were to issue some 5% $10 nominal value preference shares, convertible to ordinary shares in five years' time, the investor would receive a fixed amount of $0.50 each year for the first five years.

In five years' time though, the investor would have the choice to keep the preference shares or convert to a number of ordinary shares. The conversion ratio would have been set when the preference shares were first issued. For example it could be 3, i.e. each preference share could be converted into 3 ordinary shares.

In this example, the investor would be keen to convert if the ordinary shares on the conversion date were worth more than ($10/3 =) $3.33.

For example, if the ordinary share price growth has been impressive and the shares are actually worth $4.50 each on the conversion date, the investor could trade a single preference share (value $10) for 3 ordinary shares worth $13.50 in total.

The shares in a listed, or quoted, company will be traded on a capital market.

Capital markets

Capital markets (or stock markets) must fulfil both primary and secondary functions.

Primary function:

The primary function of a stock market is to enable companies to raise new finance (either equity or debt). Through the stock market, a company can communicate with a large pool of potential investors, so it is much easier for a company to raise finance in this way, rather than contacting investors individually.

Note that in the UK, a company must be a plc before it is allowed to raise finance from the public on the stock market.

Secondary function:

The secondary function of a stock market is to enable investors to sell their investments to other investors. A listed company's shares are therefore more marketable than an unlisted company's, which means that they tend to be more attractive to investors.

Listed v private companies

Private vs public companies

A limited company may be 'private' or 'public'. A private limited company's disclosure requirements are lighter, but for this reason its shares may not be offered to the general public (and therefore cannot be traded on a public stock exchange). This is the major distinguishing feature between a private limited company and a public limited company. Most companies, particularly small companies, are private.

Private limited company (Ltd in UK terminology)

A private company limited by shares, usually called a private limited company, has shareholders with limited liability and its shares may not be offered to the general public, unlike those of a public limited company (see details below).

'Limited by shares' means that the company has shareholders, and that the liability of the shareholders to creditors of the company is limited to the capital originally invested, i.e. the nominal value of the shares and any premium paid in return for the issue of the shares by the company. A shareholder's personal assets are thereby protected in the event of the company's insolvency, but money invested in the company will be lost.

The company will have "Ltd" after its name to indicate its status as a private company.

Public limited company (plc in UK terminology)

A public limited company is a limited liability company that may sell shares to the public. It can be either an unlisted company, or a listed company on the stock exchange. The company will have "Plc" after its name to indicate its status as a public limited company.

A stock exchange listing

When an entity obtains a listing (or quotation) for its shares on a stock exchange this is referred to as a flotation or an Initial Public Offering (IPO).

Advantages of a listing

- Once listed, the market will provide a more accurate valuation of the entity than had been previously possible.

- Creates a mechanism for buying and selling shares in the future at will.

- Raise profile of entity, which may have an impact on revenues, credibility with suppliers and long-term providers of finance.

- Raise capital for future investment.

- Makes employee share schemes more accessible.

Disadvantages of a listing

- Costly for a small entity (flotation, underwriting costs, etc.)

- Making enough shares available to allow a market, and hence loss of at least some control of the original owners.

- Reporting requirements are more onerous.

- Stock exchange rules for obtaining a quotation can be stringent.

UK capital markets

There are two important capital markets in the UK:

- the full Stock Exchange – a market for larger companies. Entry costs are high and scrutiny is very high for companies listed on the 'full list', but the profile of a Stock Exchange listed company's shares is very high, so the shares are extremely marketable.

- the Alternative Investment Market (AIM) – a market for smaller companies, with lower associated costs and less stringent entry criteria.

The operation of stock exchanges

Prices of shares on the stock exchange are determined by the forces of supply and demand in the market. For example, if a company performs well, its shares become attractive to investors. This creates demand which drives up the price of the shares.

Conversely, investors who hold shares in an underperforming company will try to sell those shares, creating supply in the market. This drives down the price of the shares.

The role of advisors in a share issue

Investment banks usually take the lead role in share issues and will advise on:

- the appointment of other specialists (e.g. lawyers)
- stock exchange requirements
- forms of any new capital to be made available
- the number of shares to be issued and the issue price
- arrangements for underwriting
- publishing the offer.

Stockbrokers provide advice on the various methods of obtaining a listing. They may work with investment banks on identifying institutional investors, but usually they are involved with smaller issues and placings.

Institutional investors have little direct involvement other than as investors, agreeing to buy a certain number of shares. They may also be used by the entity and its advisors to provide an indication of the likely take up and acceptable offer price for the shares. Once the shares are in issue institutional investors have a major influence on the evaluation and the market for the shares. Pension funds are examples of institutional investors.

4 Rights issues

A rights issue is where new shares are offered for sale to existing shareholders, in proportion to the size of their shareholding.

The right to buy new shares ahead of outside investors is known as the 'pre-emption rights' of shareholders. Note that the purpose of pre-emption rights is to ensure that shareholders have an opportunity to prevent their stake being diluted by new issues. Pre-emption rights are protected by law, and can only be waived with the consent of shareholders.

Rights issues are cheaper to organise than a public share issue.

An issue price must be set which is:

- low enough to secure acceptance of shareholders, but
- not too low, so as to avoid excessive dilution of the earnings per share.

Rights issues – further detail

Definition

A rights issue may be defined as:

- Raising of new capital by giving existing shareholders the right to subscribe to new shares in proportion to their current holdings. These shares are usually issued at a discount to market price. (CIMA, Official Terminology, 2005)

Explanation

In a rights issue, the entity sets out to raise additional funds from its existing shareholders.

It does this by giving them the opportunity to purchase additional shares. These shares are normally offered at a price lower than the current share price quoted. The entity cannot offer an unlimited supply at this lower price, otherwise the market price would fall to this value. Accordingly the offer they make to the existing shareholders is limited. For example they may offer one new share for every four held.

Selection of an issue price

In theory, there is no upper limit to an issue price but in practice it would never be set higher than the prevailing market price (MPS) of the shares, otherwise shareholders will not be prepared to buy as they could have purchased more shares at the existing market price anyway. Indeed, the issue price is normally set at a discount on MPS. This discount is usually in the region of 20%. In theory, there is no lower limit to an issue price but in practice it can never be lower than the nominal value of the shares. Subject to these practical limitations, any price may be selected within these values. However, as the issue price selected is reduced, the quantity of shares that has to be issued to raise a required sum will be increased.

Selection of an issue quantity

It is normal for the issue price to be selected first and then the quantity of shares to be issued. The effect of the additional shares on earnings per share, dividend per share and dividend cover should be considered (these ratios will be covered later). The selected additional issue quantity will then be related to the existing share quantity for the issue terms to be calculated. The proportion is normally stated in its simplest form, for example, 1 for 4, meaning that shareholders may subscribe to purchase one new share for every four they currently hold.

Market price after issue

- After the announcement of a rights issue there is a tendency for share prices to fall.

- The temporary fall is due to uncertainty about:
  - consequences of the issue
  - future profits
  - future dividends.

- After the actual issue the market price will normally fall again because:
  - there are more shares in issue (adverse affect on earnings per share), and
  - new shares were issued at market price discount.

'Cum rights'

When a rights issue is announced, all existing shareholders have the right to subscribe for new shares, and so there are rights ('cum rights') attached to the shares, and the shares are traded 'cum rights'.

'Ex rights'

On the first day of dealings in the newly issued shares, the rights no longer exist and the old shares are now traded 'ex rights' (without rights attached).

Theoretical prices/values

Theoretical 'ex rights' price is the theoretical price that the class of shares will trade at on the first trading day after issue. It is calculated as follows:

$$\frac{(N \times \text{cum rights price}) + \text{Issue price}}{N+1}$$

N = number of shares in issue before the rights issue.

Illustration 1 – Rights issue

Lauchlan plc has 2m $1 ordinary shares in issue, with a current market value of $5 per share. It offers a 1 for 4 rights issue at $4 per share.

TERP

The cum rights price = $5

Issue price = $4

N = 4

Therefore, TERP = [(4 × $5) + $4]/5 = $4.80

Test your understanding 1 (OTQ style)

Plover Co has 1 million $1 ordinary shares quoted at $4.50. It is considering a 1 for 5 rights issue at $4.20 per share.

Required:

Calculate the theoretical ex rights share price.

Implications of a rights issue

(a) From the viewpoint of the shareholders:

- they have the option of buying shares at preferential price
- they have the option of withdrawing cash by selling their rights
- they are able to maintain their existing relative voting position (by exercising the rights).

(b) From the viewpoint of the company:

- it is simple and cheap to implement
- it is usually successful ('fully subscribed')
- it often provides favourable publicity.

5 Debt finance

This is the loan of funds to a business without conferring ownership rights. The key features of debt financing arising from this 'arm's length relationship' are:

- Interest is paid out of pre-tax profits as an expense of the business.
- It carries a risk of default if interest and principal payments are not met.

Security – charges

The lender of funds will normally require some form of security against which the funds are advanced. This means that, in the event of default, the lender will be able to take assets in exchange of the amounts owing. There are two types of 'charge' or security that may be offered/required:

(1) **Fixed charge** – The debt is secured against a specific asset, normally land or buildings. This form of security is preferred because, in the event of liquidation, it puts the lender at the 'front of the queue' of creditors.

(2) **Floating charge** – The debt is secured against underlying assets that are subject to changes in quantity or value e.g inventory. The floating charge can cover any other assets that are not already subject to fixed charges. This form of security is not as strong; again it confers a measure of security on liquidation as a 'preferred creditor', meaning the lender is higher in the list of creditors than otherwise.

Covenants

A further means of limiting the risk to the lender is to restrict the actions of the directors through the means of covenants. These are specific requirements or limitations laid down as a condition of taking on debt financing. They may include:

(1) **Dividend restrictions** – Limitations on the level of dividends a company is permitted to pay. This is designed to prevent excessive dividend payments which may seriously weaken the company's future cash flows and thereby place the lender at greater risk.

(2) **Financial ratios** – Specified levels below which certain ratios may not fall, e.g. debt to net assets ratio, current ratio.

(3) **Financial reports** – Regular accounts and financial reports to be provided to the lender to monitor progress.

(4) **Issue of further debt** – The amount and type of debt that can be issued may be restricted. Subordinated debt (i.e. debt ranking below the existing unsecured debt) can usually still be issued.

Examples of long term debt finance – terminology

Bank finance

Money market borrowings

The money market consists of financial institutions and dealers in money or credit who wish to either borrow or lend.

The money market is used by participants as a means for borrowing and lending in the short term, from several days to just under a year. This contrasts with the capital market for longer-term funding, for example bonds and equity.

The core of the money market consists of interbank lending – banks borrowing from, and lending to, each other. However, large profit-making entities will also borrow and lend on the money market.

Revolving credit facilities (RCFs)

Under a RCF the borrower may use or withdraw funds up to a pre-approved credit limit. The amount of available credit decreases and increases as funds are borrowed and then repaid.

The borrower makes payments based only on the amount they've actually used or withdrawn, plus interest and the borrower may repay the borrowing over time or in full at any time.

RCFs are very flexible debt financing options, and they enable a company to minimise interest payments because the amount of funds borrowed fluctuates over time and is never more than the company needs.

Often the RCF will be offered by a single bank, or in the case of a large amount of finance required, a syndicate (group) of banks may offer the RCF to reduce the risk to any one lender.

Capital markets

Bonds

A bond is a debt security, in which the issuer owes the holders a debt and, depending on the terms of the bond, is obliged to pay interest (the coupon) and/or to repay the principal at a later date. i.e. a bond is a formal contract to repay borrowed money with interest at fixed intervals.

Thus a bond is like a loan: the issuer is the borrower (debtor), the holder is the lender (creditor) and more commonly referred to as the investor, and the coupon is the interest. Bonds provide the borrower with external funds to satisfy long-term funding requirements.

Bonds and shares are both securities which can be traded in the capital markets, but the major difference between the two is that shareholders have an equity stake in the company (i.e. they are owners), whereas bondholders have a creditor stake in the company (i.e. they are lenders). Another difference is that bonds usually have a defined term, or maturity, after which the bond is redeemed, whereas shares may be outstanding indefinitely.

Commercial paper

Large profit-making entities may issue unsecured short-term loan notes in the capital market, referred to as commercial paper.

These loan notes will generally mature within 9 months, typically between a week and 3 months. The notes can be traded at any time before their maturity date.

Capital markets – further detail

Issuing debt finance (bonds) in the capital markets enables an entity to borrow a large amount of finance from (potentially) a wide range of potential investors.

The bond market can essentially be broken down into three main groups: issuers, underwriters and purchasers.

Issuers

The issuers sell bonds in the capital markets to fund the operations of their organisations. This area of the market is mostly made up of governments, banks and corporations.

The biggest of these issuers is the government, which uses the bond market to help fund a country's operations. Banks are also key issuers in the bond market, and they can range from local banks up to supranational banks such as the European Investment Bank. The final major issuer is corporations, which issue bonds to finance operations.

Underwriters

The underwriting segment of the bond market is traditionally made up of investment banks and other financial institutions that help the issuer to sell the bonds in the market.

In most cases, huge amounts of finance are transacted in one offering. As a result, a lot of work needs to be done to prepare for the offering, such as creating a prospectus and other legal documents. In general, the need for underwriters is greatest for the corporate debt market because there are more risks associated with this type of debt.

The underwriters sometimes place the bonds with specific investors ('bond placement'), or they can attempt to sell the bonds more widely in the market. Alternatively, under a medium term note (MTN) programme, the issuer (via the underwriter) can issue debt securities on a regular and/or continuous basis.

Purchasers

The final players in the bond market are those who buy the bonds. Buyers basically include every group mentioned as well as any other type of investor, including the individual.

Governments play one of the largest roles in the market because they borrow and lend money to other governments and banks. Furthermore, governments often invest in bonds issued by other countries if they have excess reserves of that country's money as a result of trade between countries. For example, Japan is a major holder of U.S. government debt, such as U.S. gilts.

The yield on debt

An investor who purchases a traded debt instrument (e.g. a bond) receives a return, known as a 'yield', in the form of the annual interest (or 'coupon') payments and, if the debt is redeemable, the final redemption payment. This return is also known as the 'yield to maturity' (YTM), or 'redemption yield' on the bond, and it is defined as:

YTM = effective average annual percentage return to the investor, relative to the current market value of the bond.

If the bond is irredeemable, the calculation is very simple. However, it becomes more complex if the bond is redeemable.

Yield on irredeemable debt

For irredeemable debt:

YTM = (annual interest received/current market value of debt) × 100%

The yield calculation is always calculated in units of $100 nominal value of bond.

Example 1

Knife plc, a UK listed company, has some 5% coupon, $100 nominal value, irredeemable bonds in issue, which have a current market value of $95.

Required:

Calculate the yield to maturity for these bonds.

Example 1 answer

YTM = (annual interest/current market value) × 100%

= (5/95) × 100% = 5.26%

Note that the coupon rate is applied to the nominal value to calculate the annual interest, but otherwise, the nominal value is not used in the calculation.

Test your understanding 2 (OTQ style)

Fork plc, a UK listed company, has some 7% coupon, $100 nominal value, irredeemable bonds in issue, which have a current market value of $93.50.

Give your answer to 2 decimal places.

Required:

Calculate the yield to maturity for these bonds.

Yield on redeemable debt

For redeemable debt:

YTM = the internal rate of return (IRR) of the bond price, the annual interest received and the final redemption amount.

This ensures that the yield calculation incorporates a return in the form of the final redemption amount as well as the annual interest amounts.

The internal rate of return (IRR)

Definition

The IRR is the discount rate which gives a zero NPV.

Calculation

It can be estimated by working out the NPV at two different interest rates (L, the lower rate, and H, the higher rate) and then using the following (linear interpolation) formula:

$$L + \left(\frac{NPV_L}{NPV_L - NPV_H}\right)(H - L)$$

This formula does NOT appear in your formula sheet provided in the exam. You will need to know this formula.

Example 2

Knife plc also has some 7% coupon, $100 nominal value bonds in issue, which are redeemable at a 10% premium in 5 years. The current market value of the bonds is $98.

Required:

Calculate the yield to maturity for these bonds.

Example 2 answer

The yield to maturity for these redeemable bonds is found by taking the IRR of the current market value (98 at t_0), the annual interest (7 per annum from t_1 to t_5), and the redemption amount (110 at t_5), as follows:

Time	$	DF 5%	PV	DF 10%	PV
t_0	(98)	1	(98)	1	(98)
$t_1 - t_5$	7	4.329	30.30	3.791	26.54
t_5	110	0.784	86.24	0.621	68.31
			———		———
			18.54		(3.15)

Hence IRR = 5% + [(10% − 5%) × 18.54/(18.54 + 3.15)] = 9.27%

> **Test your understanding 3 (OTQ style)**
>
> Fork plc also has some 4% coupon, $100 nominal value bonds in issue, which are redeemable at a 7% premium in 3 years. The current market value of the bonds is $95.
>
> Give your answer to 2 decimal places.
>
> **Required:**
>
> **Calculate the yield to maturity for these bonds.**

6 Other sources of finance

Retained earnings/existing cash balances

An entity can use its current cash balances to finance new investments.

There is a common misconception that an entity with a large amount of retained earnings in its statement of financial position can fund its new investment projects using these retained earnings. This is not the case.

An entity can only use internal sources of finance to fund new projects if it has enough cash in hand.

The level of retained earnings reflects the amount of profit accumulated over the entity's life. It is not the same as cash.

Sale and leaseback

This means selling good quality fixed assets such as high street buildings and leasing them back over many years (25+). Funds are released without any loss of use of assets.

Any potential capital gain on assets is forgone.

Sale and leaseback is a popular means of funding for retail organisations with substantial high street property e.g. Tesco, Marks and Spencer.

Grants

These are often related to technology, job creation or regional policy. They are of particular importance to small and medium-sized businesses (i.e. unlisted). Their key advantage is that they do not need to be paid back.

Grants can be provided by local governments, national governments, and other larger bodies such as the European Union.

Debt with warrants attached

A warrant is an option to buy shares at a specified point in the future for a specified (exercise) price. Warrants are often issued with a bond as a sweetener to encourage investors to purchase the bonds.

The warrant offers a potential capital gain where the share price may rise above the exercise price.

The holder has the option to buy the share on the exercise date but can also choose to sell the warrant before that date.

Convertible debt

This is similar in effect to attaching a warrant to a debt instrument except that the warrant cannot be detached and traded separately. With convertible debt, the debt itself can be converted into shares at a predetermined price at a date or range of dates in the future.

This has the effect of giving the debt holder a potential capital gain over and above the return from the debt interest. If the value of the shares is greater than that of the debt on the exercise date, then conversion will be made by the investor. If, however, the share value is lower than the debt value, the investor may retain the debt to maturity.

Venture capital

This is finance provided to young, unquoted profit-making entities to help them to expand. It is usually provided in the form of equity finance, but may be a mix of equity and debt.

Venture capitalists generally accept low levels of dividends and expect to make most of their returns as capital gains on exit. A typical exit route is an IPO or flotation, which enables the venture capitalist to sell his stake in the entity on the stock market.

Business angels

Business angels are similar to venture capitalists. Venture capitalists are rarely interested in investing in very small businesses, on the grounds that monitoring progress is uneconomic.

Business angels are wealthy investors who provide equity finance to small businesses.

Government assistance

Governments will often have a number of schemes, aimed at providing assistance to:

- small- and medium-sized profit-making entities
- entities wanting to expand or relocate in particular regions
- promote innovation and technology
- projects that will create new jobs or protect existing ones.

Test your understanding 4 (further OTQs)

(1) _____ preference shares are those for which dividends must be paid in a following year if they are not paid in the current year. _____ preference shares give the holder fixed dividends plus extra earnings based on certain conditions being achieved.

Select the correct words to complete the above sentences, from the following options:

convertible, cumulative, irredeemable, participating, redeemable

(2) Capital markets fulfil two functions, one of which is to enable investors to sell investments to other investors.

Is this the primary function or secondary function? Select the correct answer below.

A   Primary function.

B   Secondary function.

(3) Liam plc has 6m ordinary shares in issue, with a current market price of $5 per share. It offers a rights issue of 1 for every 3 shares held at a price of $4.

Calculate the theoretical ex rights share price. State your answer to the nearest cent (i.e. to two decimal places).

(4) When fixing security, a lender of funds will prefer a f_____ charge.

Select the correct word to complete the above sentence, from the following options:

fixed, floating

(5) Joe plc, a UK listed company, has some 6% coupon, $100 nominal value, irredeemable bonds in issue, which have a current market value of $96.25.

Calculate the yield to maturity for these bonds. State your answer to two decimal places.

(6) Gary plc has some 5% coupon, $100 nominal value bonds in issue, which are redeemable at an 8% premium in 5 years. The current market value of the bonds is $94.

Calculate the yield to maturity for these bonds. State your answer to two decimal places.

7 Chapter summary

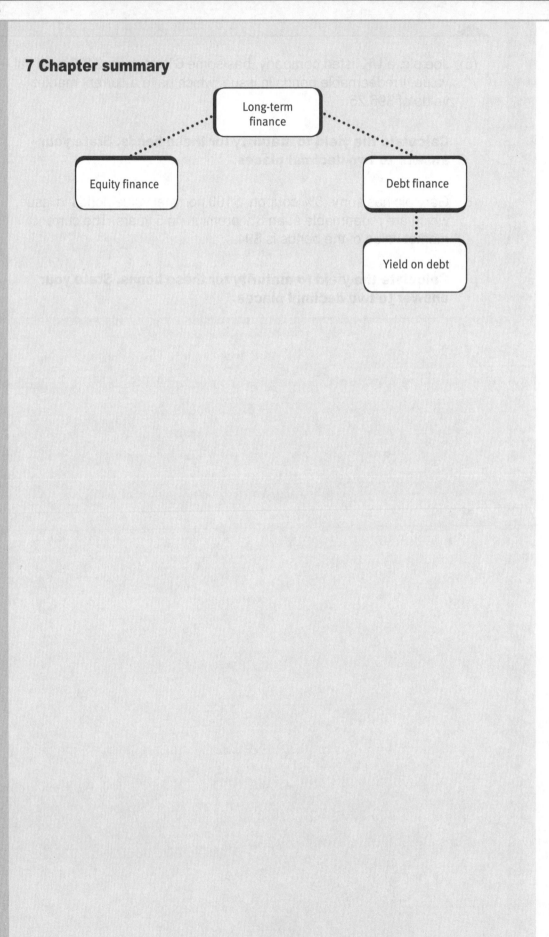

Test your understanding answers

Test your understanding 1 (OTQ style)

(a) The theoretical ex rights price (TERP) is:

$$\frac{(N \times \text{cum rights price}) + \text{Issue price}}{N+1}$$

= [(5 × $4.50) + $4.20]/6 = $4.45

Alternatively, TERP can be calculated by looking at the total value of all the shares as follows:

$$\frac{(1m \times 4.5) + (1/5 \times 1m \times 4.2)}{1m + (1/5 \times 1m)} = \$4.45$$

Test your understanding 2 (OTQ style)

YTM = (annual interest/current market value) × 100%

= (7/93.5) × 100% = 7.49%

Test your understanding 3 (OTQ style)

Year	$	DF 5%	PV	DF 10%	PV
0	(95)	1	(95)	1	(95)
1–3	4	2.723	10.89	2.487	9.95
3	107	0.864	92.45	0.751	80.36
			8.34		(4.69)

Hence IRR = 5% + [(10% − 5%) × 8.34/(8.34 + 4.69)] = 8.20%

Test your understanding 4 (further OTQs)

(1) **Cumulative** preference share are those for which dividends must be paid in a following year if they are not paid in the current year.

Participating preference shares give the holder fixed dividends plus extra earnings based on certain conditions being achieved.

(2) **B Secondary function**

The primary function is to enable companies to raise new finance.

(3) **$4.75**

The theoretical ex rights price (TERP) is:

$$\frac{(N \times \text{cum rights price}) + \text{Issue price}}{N+1}$$

= [(3 × $5) + $4]/4 = $4.75

(4) When fixing security, a lender of funds will prefer a **fixed** charge.

Note: a floating charge secures the debt against the underlying assets that are subject to changes in quantity and value whereas a fixed charge is against a specific asset. Therefore a fixed charge is preferable as, in the event of a liquidation, the lender would have a right to the specific asset secured. The fixed charge holder would be paid earlier than a floating charge holder.

(5) **6.23%**

YTM = (annual interest/current market value) × 100%

= (6/96.25) × 100% = 6.23%

(6) **8.0%**

Year	$	DF 5%	PV	DF 10%	PV
0	(94)	1	(94)	1	(94)
1–5	5	4.329	21.65	3.791	18.96
5	108	0.784	84.67	0.621	67.07
			————		————
			12.32		(7.97)

Hence IRR = 5% + [(10% − 5%) × 12.32/(12.32 + 7.97)] = 8.04%

Cost of capital

Chapter learning objectives

A2. Calculate a weighted average cost of capital (WACC) for an incorporated entity.

(a) Calculate the cost of equity for an incorporated entity using the dividend valuation model.
  - Cost of equity using the dividend valuation model, with and without growth in dividends.

(b) Calculate the post-tax cost of debt for an incorporated entity.
  - Post-tax cost of bank borrowings.
  - Yield to maturity of bonds and post-tax cost of bonds.
  - Post-tax cost of convertible bonds up to and including conversion.

(c) Calculate the weighted average cost of capital (WACC) for an incorporated entity.
  - WACC and its use.

1 Session content

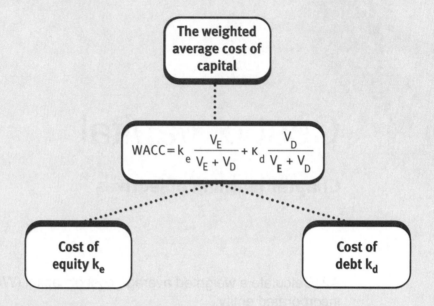

The weighted average cost of capital

$$WACC = k_e \frac{V_E}{V_E + V_D} + K_d \frac{V_D}{V_E + V_D}$$

Cost of equity k_e

Cost of debt k_d

2 Introduction

The weighted average cost of capital (WACC) measures the average cost of an entity's finance. Entities often use the WACC as a discount rate in net present value (NPV) calculations.

The WACC is derived by first estimating the cost of each source of finance separately (e.g. ordinary shares, debt, preference shares) and then taking a weighted average of these individual costs, using the following formula:

$$k_o = k_e \left[\frac{V_E}{V_E + V_D} \right] + k_d \left[\frac{V_D}{V_E + V_D} \right]$$

k_o = WACC

3 The cost of equity – ke

The cost of equity is the rate of return that ordinary shareholders expect to receive on their investment. The main method of computing ke is the dividend valuation model (DVM).

The dividend valuation model (DVM)

The DVM states that the current share price is determined by the future dividends, discounted at the investors' required rate of return.

$$P_0 = \frac{d}{k_e}$$

where k_e = cost of equity

d = is the constant dividend

P_0 = the ex div market price of the share

This is a variant of the formula for a PV of a perpetuity.

We can re-arrange the formula to get the one below:

The dividend valuation model with constant dividends

$$k_e = \frac{d}{P_0}$$

DVM – further detail

The DVM is a method of calculating cost of equity.

This model makes the assumption that the market price of a share is related to the future dividend income stream from that share, in such a way that the market price is assumed to be the present value of that future dividend income stream.

This is known as the fundamental theory of share valuation.

Cum div and ex div share prices

The ex dividend ('ex div') value of a share is the value just after a dividend has been paid. Occasionally in questions, you may be given a share price just before the payment of a dividend (a 'cum div' price). In this case, the value of the upcoming dividend should be deducted from the cum div price to give the ex div price.

For example, if a dividend of 20 cents is due to be paid on a share which has a cum div value of $3.45, the ex div share price to be entered into the DVM formula is $3.45 – $0.20 = $3.25.

Example 1

The ordinary shares of Jones plc are quoted at $4 per share. A dividend of 30 cents is about to be paid. There is expected to be no growth in dividends.

Required:

Calculate the cost of equity.

Example 1 answer

$$k_e = \frac{30}{400 - 30} = 8.1\%$$

Test your understanding 1 (OTQ style)

The ordinary shares of Smith plc are quoted at $12 per share. A dividend of 75 cents per share is about to be paid. There is expected to be no growth in dividends.

Required:

Calculate the cost of equity. Give your answer to 1 decimal place.

Introducing growth

The dividend valuation model with constant growth

$$k_e = \frac{d_1}{P_0} + g \quad \text{or} \quad k_e = \frac{d_0(1+g)}{P_0} + g$$

where g = a constant rate of growth in dividends

d_1 = dividend to be paid in one year's time

d_0 = current dividend

Example 2

The ordinary shares of Jones plc are quoted at $4 per share. A dividend of 30 cents is about to be paid. The expected growth rate of dividend is 5%.

Required:

Calculate the cost of equity.

Example 2 answer

$$k_e = \frac{30 \times 1.05}{400 - 30} + 0.05 = 13.5\%$$

Test your understanding 2 (OTQ style)

The ordinary shares of Smith plc are quoted at $12 per share. A dividend of 75 cents per share is about to be paid. The expected growth rate in the dividend is 8%.

Required:

Calculate the cost of equity. Give your answer to 1 decimal place.

The cost of preference shares

Preference shares usually pay a constant level of dividend, which is quoted as a percentage of nominal value. Hence, the cost of preference shares (k_p) can be calculated using a formula very similar to the one covered earlier for k_e in a no growth situation. The formula is:

$$k_p = \frac{d}{P_0}$$

d = is the constant dividend

P_0 = the ex div market price of the share

k_p = the cost of preference shares

4 The cost of debt – kd

The cost of debt is the rate of return that debt providers require on the funds that they provide.

The value of debt is assumed to be the present value of its future cash flows.

Features

(1) Debt is tax deductible and hence interest payments are made net of tax.

(2) Debt is always quoted in $100 nominal units or blocks.

(3) Interest paid on the debt is stated as a percentage of nominal value. This is known as the coupon rate. It is not the same as the cost of debt. The amount of interest payable on the debt is fixed. The interest is calculated as the coupon rate multiplied by the nominal value of the debt.

(4) Debt is normally redeemable at par (nominal value) or at a premium or discount.

(5) Interest can be either fixed or floating (variable) on borrowings, but bonds normally pay fixed rate interest.

k_d for bank borrowings

The cost of debt for bank borrowings is simply $k_d = r(1-T)$

where: r = annual interest rate in percentage terms

   T = corporate tax rate

k_d for irredeemable, or undated, bonds

It is highly unusual for bonds to be irredeemable but, if it were, the cost of debt could be calculated as follows:

$$k_d = \frac{i(1-T)}{P_0}$$

where i = interest paid each year (per $100 of bond)

   T = marginal rate of tax

   P_0 = ex interest market price of the bonds, normally quoted per 100 unit nominal

Note that this formula can also be applied to redeemable bonds where the redemption value is equal to the current market price or as an approximation for long-dated debt.

Note, for bonds trading at par, P_0 is the nominal value and so this formula can be simplified to $k_d = r(1-T)$, where r is the interest rate, expressed in percentage terms.

Example 3

The 10% long-dated bonds of an entity are quoted at $130 ex int. Corporation tax is payable at 30%.

Required:

Calculate the net of tax cost of debt.

Example 3 answer

$$k_d = \frac{10(1 - 0.30)}{130} = 5.4\%$$

Test your understanding 3 (OTQ style)

The 8% long-dated bonds of an entity are quoted at $127 ex int. Corporation tax is payable at 25%.

Required:

Calculate the net of tax cost of debt. Give your answer to 1 decimal place.

k_d for redeemable bonds

The k_d for redeemable bonds is given by the IRR of the relevant cash flows.

The relevant cash flows would be (assuming that there is no one year delay in the tax saving):

Year	Cash flow	
0	Market value of the bond (or nominal value if being issued or is trading at par)	(P_0)
1 to n	Annual interest payments net of tax	$i(1 - T)$
n	Redemption value of the bond	RV

There are four steps to ensuring an accurate computation:

(1) Identify the cash flows. Note that the interest payments should be included net of tax when calculating the cost of debt for bonds from the viewpoint of the issuer.

(2) Estimate the IRR.

(3) Calculate two NPVs (preferably one –ve and one +ve).

(4) Calculate the IRR.

Example 4

An entity has some 10% bonds quoted at $95.00 ex int redeemable at par in five years' time. Corporation tax is paid at 31%.

Required:

Calculate the entity's cost of debt.

Example 4 answer

Cash flows

Year 0	$95.00
Year 1 – 5	$10 (1 – 0.31) = $6.90
Year 5	$100.00

Discounting

Year	Cash flow	Disc. fact. @ 6%	Present value	Disc. fact. @ 10%	Present value
0	(95.00)	1	(95.00)	1	(95.00)
1 – 5	6.90	4.212	29.06	3.791	26.16
5	100	0.747	74.70	0.621	62.10
Total			+8.76		–6.74

$$IRR = 6\% + (10\% - 6\%) \times \frac{8.76}{(8.76 + 6.74)} = 8.26\%$$

Test your understanding 4 (OTQ style)

An entity has some 8% bonds quoted at $92.00 ex int redeemable at par in three years' time. Corporation tax is paid at 27%.

Required:

Calculate the entity's cost of debt. Give your answer to 2 decimal places.

The cost of convertible bonds

Convertible bonds offer the investor a choice of cash or shares on the redemption date.

In practice, particularly if the value of the cash and shares option is very similar, some investors will choose cash for liquidity reasons, whereas other investors may choose shares, hoping for large dividend returns in the future.

In order to calculate the cost of convertible bonds, we make a simplifying assumption that all investors will make the same decision.

Illustration

Consider a $100 bond which is redeemable at par in 5 years, or convertible into 10 shares at that time. The current share price is $8.60 and historically, dividends (and hence share prices) have grown at 5% per annum.

To decide which option is likely to be chosen by investors, we compare:

- the value of the cash option, that is $100 (redemption at par)

- the value of the conversion option, i.e. $10 \times (\$8.60 \times 1.05^5)$ = $109.76

Hence, it is assumed that all investors will choose the conversion option, and the cost of the convertible debt is calculated in a similar way to the cost of redeemable debt, i.e. it is the IRR of :

Year	Cash flow	$
0	Market value of the loan	(P_0)
1 to n	Annual net interest payments	$i(1 - T)$
n	**The higher of the cash and the conversion option**	C

5 Weighted Average Cost of Capital (WACC)

The weighted average cost of capital (WACC) is the average cost of the entity's finance (equity, bonds, bank loans, and preference shares) weighted according to the proportion each element bears to the total pool of funds.

In the analysis so far carried out, each source of finance has been examined in isolation. However, the practical business situation is that there is a continuous raising of funds from various sources. These funds are used, partly in existing operations and partly to finance new projects. There is not normally any separation between funds from different sources and their application to specific projects.

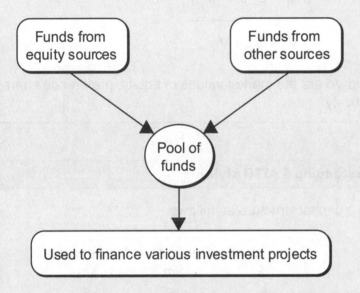

In order to provide a measure for evaluating these projects, the cost of the pool of funds is required. This is variously referred to as the combined or weighted average cost of capital (WACC).

The general approach is to calculate the cost of each source of finance, then to weight these according to their importance in the financing mix.

Procedure for calculating the WACC

Step 1 Calculate weights for each source of capital.

Step 2 Estimate the cost of each source of capital.

Step 3 Multiply the proportion of the total of each source of capital by the cost of that source of capital.

Step 4 Sum the results of step 3 to give the weighted average cost of capital.

Formula – given in the assessment

$$k_o = k_e \left[\frac{V_E}{V_E + V_D} \right] + k_d \left[\frac{V_D}{V_E + V_D} \right]$$

Alternative WACC formula

Using market values for a firm with equity, debt and preference shares in its capital structure, the WACC would be:

$$k_0 = \frac{k_e V_e + k_P V_P + k_d V_d}{V_e + V_P + V_d}$$

where Ve, Vp and Vd are the market values of equity, preference shares and debt respectively.

Test your understanding 5 (OTQ style)

Rebmatt Co has a capital structure as follows.

	Cost of capital %	Book value $m	Market value $m
Bank loans	6	5	5
Bonds	10	8	5
Ordinary shares	15	18	30

Required:

Calculate Rebmatt's WACC, using market values as weights. Give your answer to 2 decimal places.

Test your understanding 6 (integration question)

The following is an extract from the statement of financial position of Gate Co at 30 September 20X4:

	$
Ordinary shares of 25 cents each	250,000
Reserves	350,000
7% preference shares of $1 each	250,000
15% long-dated bonds	150,000
Total long-term funds	1,000,000

The ordinary shares are currently quoted at $1.25 each, the bonds trading at $85 per $100 nominal and the preference shares at 65 cents each. The ordinary dividend of 10 cents has just been paid, and the expected growth rate in the dividend is 10%. Corporation tax is at the rate of 30%.

Required:

Calculate the weighted average cost of capital for Gate Co. Give your answer to 1 decimal place.

Problems with the computation of WACC

Which sources of finance to include

The above examples have concentrated on the cost of long-term finance. Firms also raise finance from short-term sources, e.g. overdrafts, short-term loans, trade credit etc. It is possible to calculate a cost for short-term finance and we need to decide whether it should be included in our calculations. The usual argument is that the weighted average cost of capital is a tool for appraising long-term investments and as these should only be financed by long-term funds then the costs of short-term funds should be excluded. However, if it is clear that short-term finance is being used to fund long-term projects, then it should be included.

Loans without market values

Bank loans do not have market values in the same way as bonds. All we can do in this case is to take the book value of loans as an approximation of market value.

Cost of capital for small entities

There are important factors which are relevant to the cost of capital of small entities:

- If the entity is unquoted, then obtaining the cost of finance is much more difficult.

- The lack of liquidity offered by the entity's securities, plus the smaller size of the entity, tend to make finance more expensive.

---

6 When can WACC be used as a discount rate?

The WACC is often used as a discount rate when using net present value or internal rate of return calculations. However, this is only appropriate if the following conditions are met:

(1) The capital structure is constant. If the capital structure changes, the weightings in the WACC will also change.

(2) The new investment does not carry a different business risk profile to the existing entity's operations.

(3) The new investment is marginal to the entity. If we are only looking at a small investment then we would not expect any of k_e, k_d or the WACC to change materially. If the investment is substantial it will usually cause these values to change.

Test your understanding 7 (further OTQs)

(1) KM plc has 500,000 $1 par value shares in issue that are trading at $1.35. It has recently paid a dividend of $60,000. Dividends are expected to grow by 5% per annum.

The cost of equity is:

A   8.9%

B   9.3%

C   14.3%

D   15.2%

(2) CG has in issue 6% irredeemable debentures currently quoted at $92 per $100 nominal value. CG pays corporate income tax at a rate of 20%.

Calculate the post-tax cost of debt. Give your answer as a percentage to one decimal place.

(3) RP's cost of equity is 12% and the yield on its debt is 7%. Its debt to equity ratio is 3:2 based on book value and 5:3 based on market value. The corporate income tax rate is 25%.

Calculate the weighted average cost of capital (WACC). Give your answer as a percentage to one decimal place.

7 Chapter summary

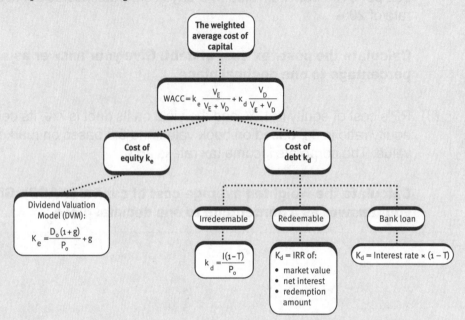

Test your understanding answers

Test your understanding 1 (OTQ style)

$$k_e = \frac{0.75}{12 - 0.75} = 6.7\%$$

Test your understanding 2 (OTQ style)

$$k_e = \frac{0.75 \times 1.08}{12 - 0.75} + 0.08 = 15.2\%$$

Test your understanding 3 (OTQ style)

$$k_d = \frac{8(1 - 0.25)}{127} = 4.7\%$$

Test your understanding 4 (OTQ style)

Cash flows

Year 0	$92.00
Year 1 – 3	$8 (1 – 0.27) = $5.84
Year 3	$100.00

Discounting

Year	Cash flow	Disc. fact. @ 5%	Present value	Disc. fact. @ 12%	Present value
0	(92.00)	1	(92.00)	1	(92.00)
1 – 3	5.84	2.723	15.90	2.402	14.03
3	100	0.864	86.40	0.712	71.20
Total			+10.30		–6.77

$$IRR = 5\% + (12\% - 5\%) \times \frac{10.30}{(10.30 + 6.77)} = 9.22\%$$

Test your understanding 5 (OTQ style)

The calculation is carried out as follows:

	Market value		Cost of capital	Weighted cost
Source	$m	Proportions	%	%
Bank loans	5	0.125	× 6 =	0.75
Bonds	5	0.125	× 10 =	1.25
Ordinary shares	30	0.75	× 15 =	11.25
	——	——		——
	40	1.00		13.25
	——	——		——

WACC = 13.25%

Test your understanding 6 (integration question)

Solution:

Market values of the securities:

Equity (Ve) = 1,000,000 × $1.25 = $1,250,000

Preference (Vp) = 250,000 × $0.65 = $162,500

Bonds (Vd) = 150,000 × 85% = $127,500

So total value = 1,250,000 + 162,500 + 127,500 = $1,540,000

Cost of equity (ke) =

$$\frac{10 \times 1.1}{125} + 0.10 \qquad = \quad 18.8\%$$

Cost of preference shares (kp) =

$$\frac{7}{65} \qquad = \qquad 10.8\%$$

Cost of bonds kd = i(1 − T)/Po

$$\frac{15(1 - 0.3)}{85} \qquad = \quad 12.4\%$$

Weighted average cost of capital

	Market value		Cost of capital	Weighted cost
Source	$000	Proportions	%	%
Equity	1,250	0.812	× 18.8 =	15.3
Preference shares	162.5	0.106	× 10.8 =	1.1
Bonds	127.5	0.082	× 12.4 =	1.0
	1,540	1.00		17.4

WACC = 17.4%

Test your understanding 7 (further OTQs)

(1) **C   cost of equity = 14.3%**

$$k_e = \frac{12 \times 1.05}{135} + 0.05 = 14.3\%$$

Dividend per share = $60,000/500k = $0.12

Dividend has already been paid so don't deduct it from market price of share (price is already ex div)

(2) **Post-tax cost of debt = 5.2%**

$(6 \times 0.8)/92 = 5.2\%$

(3) **WACC = 7.8%**

WACC = $(7 \times 0.75 \times 5/8) + (12 \times 3/8) = 3.3 + 4.5 = 7.8\%$

Financial instruments

Chapter learning objectives

B1. Produce consolidated primary financial statements, incorporating accounting transactions and adjustments, in accordance with relevant international accounting standards, in an ethical manner.

(c) Discuss the provisions of relevant international accounting standards in respect of the recognition and measurement of financial instruments, in accordance with IAS 32 and IAS 39 (excluding hedge accounting).

(d) Produce the accounting entries, in accordance with relevant international accounting standards.

1 Session content

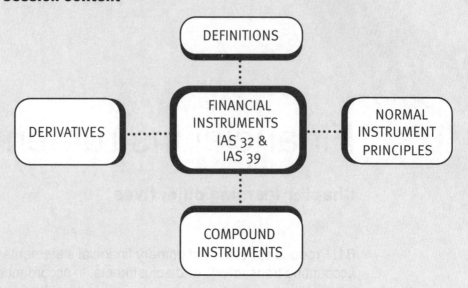

2 Introduction

Definitions

A **financial instrument** is any contract that gives rise to a financial asset of one entity and a financial liability or equity instrument of another entity.

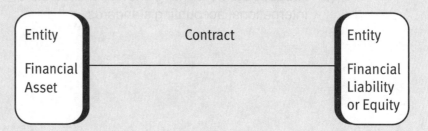

A **financial asset** is any asset that is:

- cash

- an equity instrument of another entity

- a contractual right to receive cash or another financial asset from another entity

- a contractual right to exchange financial instruments with another entity under conditions that are potentially favourable

Examples of financial assets are:

- Investments in ordinary shares of another entity

- Investments in debentures/loan stock/loan notes/bonds i.e. lending money to another entity

A **financial liability** is any liability that is a contractual obligation:

- to deliver cash or another financial asset to another entity

- to exchange financial instruments with another entity under conditions that are potentially unfavourable

Examples of financial liabilities are:

- Issue of debentures/loan stock/loan notes/bonds i.e. borrowing money from another entity

 An **equity instrument** is any contract that evidences a residual interest in the assets of an entity after deducting all of its liabilities.

An example of an equity instrument is:

- Issue of ordinary shares

Accounting standards

There are four accounting standards that deal with financial instruments:

- IAS 32 **Financial instruments: presentation**
- IAS 39 **Financial instruments: recognition and measurement**
- IFRS 7 **Financial instruments: disclosures**
- IFRS 9 **Financial instruments**

IAS 32 deals with the classification of financial instruments and their presentation in financial statements.

IAS 39 deals with how financial instruments are measured and when they should be recognised in financial statements.

IFRS 7 deals with the disclosure of financial instruments in financial statements. This standard is not examinable in the F2 syllabus.

IFRS 9 will eventually supersede IAS 39. It is currently a work in progress, it is effective for annual periods beginning on or after 1 January 2018 (early adoption is possible) therefore it is not examinable.

3 Classification of financial instruments in the issuing entity

IAS 32 **Financial instruments: presentation** provides the rules on classifying financial instruments as liabilities or equity. These are detailed below.

Presentation of liabilities and equity

The issuer of a financial instrument must classify it as a financial liability or equity instrument on initial recognition according to its substance.

Financial liabilities

The instrument will be classified as a liability if the issuer has a contractual **obligation**:

- to deliver cash (or another financial asset) to the holder
- to exchange financial instruments on potentially unfavourable terms.

Equity instruments

A financial instrument is only an equity instrument if there is no such contractual obligation.

Illustration 1 – Preference shares

The above definitions ensure that substance over form is reflected and any obligations are correctly presented as liabilities.

Consider redeemable preference shares. Legally they are called shares however if we consider their characteristics we can see that they are a form of debt finance. The entity receives an inflow of cash upon their issue, it then makes annual payments based on a percentage of the nominal value of the 'shares' and, at a specified point in the future, the cash is repaid.

Even if the preference shares are not redeemable, they are still typically considered to be liabilities if they are 'cumulative'. This means that there is a contractual obligation to pay the preference dividends in a future period if they cannot be paid out in the current year.

Interest, dividends, losses and gains

- The accounting treatment of interest, dividends, losses and gains relating to a financial instrument follows the treatment of the instrument itself.

- For example, dividends paid in respect of preference shares classified as a liability will be charged as a finance expense through profit or loss.

- Dividends paid on shares classified as equity will be reported in the statement of changes in equity.

Offsetting a financial asset and a financial liability

IAS 32 states that a financial asset and a financial liability may only be offset in very limited circumstances. The net amount may only be reported when the entity:

- has a legally enforceable right to set off the amounts

- intends either to settle on a net basis, or to realise the asset and settle the liability simultaneously.

4 Recognition and measurement of financial instruments

IAS 39 **Financial instruments: recognition and measurement** provides guidance on when financial instruments should be recognised in the financial statements and how they should be measured.

Initial recognition of financial instruments

An entity should recognise a financial asset or a financial liability in its statement of financial position when, and only when, it becomes a party to the contractual provisions of the instrument.

Initial measurement of financial instruments

A financial asset or liability should be initially recognised at its **fair value**. Except in the case of assets or liabilities at fair value through profit or loss (see next section), directly attributable transaction costs are added to an asset and deducted from a liability.

Subsequent measurement of financial instruments

Equity instruments are not re-measured after initial recognition.

Subsequent measurement of other financial instruments depends on how that particular financial instrument is classified.

IAS 39 deals separately with **four types of financial asset** and **two types of financial liability**.

Financial liabilities are dealt with first below.

5 Financial liabilities

NB. An entity will raise finance by ISSUING bonds/loan stock/debentures. This creates a financial liability.

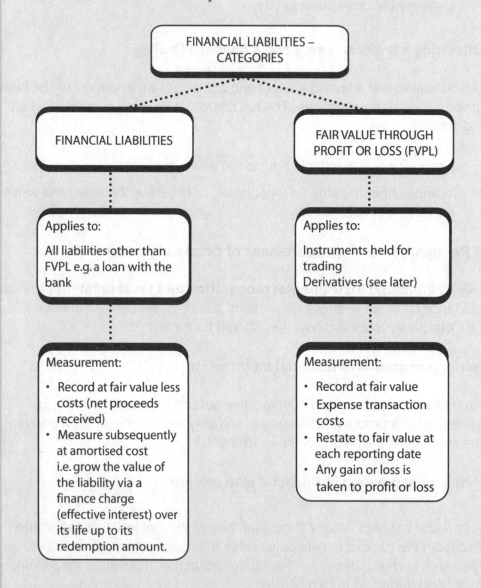

Amortised cost

- One common form of financial instrument for many entities will be loans payable. These will normally be measured at amortised cost. The amortised cost of a liability equals: initial cost plus interest less repayments.

- The interest will be charged on the outstanding balance at the effective rate. This is the internal rate of return of the instrument.

The simplest way to prepare a working for amortised cost is to use the following table.

Year	Opening balance	Effective interest % (P/L)	Coupon paid %	Closing balance (SFP)
	$	$	$	$
1	X	X	(X)	X
2	X	X	(X)	X
3	X	X	(X)	X

The opening balance in year 1 is the net proceeds (i.e. after deduction of any discounts and issue costs):

- Dr Cash
- Cr Liability

Effective interest is calculated on the opening balance each period and is charged to the statement of profit or loss (P/L):

- Dr Finance costs (P/L)
- Cr Liability

The coupon paid is the coupon percentage multiplied by the face/nominal value of the debt:

- Dr Liability
- Cr Cash

The closing balance is the figure for the statement of financial position (SFP) at the reporting date.

Example 1 – amortised cost

A company issues 5% loan notes at their nominal value of $20,000. The loan notes are repayable at par after 4 years.

When the loan notes are issued:

Dr	Bank	$20,000
Cr	Loan notes	$20,000

Financial statement extracts over 4 year term

Note: Because the loan is repayable at par i.e. face (nominal) value of $20,000, the coupon rate is equal to the effective rate.

Statement of profit or loss (P/L)

Year	1	2	3	4
	$	$	$	$
Finance costs (W1)	(1,000)	(1,000)	(1,000)	(1,000)

Statement of financial position (SFP)

Year	1	2	3	4
	$	$	$	$
Non-current liabilities	20,000	20,000		
Current liabilities			20,000	0

(W1) Amortised cost table

Year	Opening balance	Effective interest 5% (P/L)	Coupon paid 5%	Closing balance (SFP)
	$	$	$	$
1	20,000	1,000	(1,000)	20,000
2	20,000	1,000	(1,000)	20,000
3	20,000	1,000	(1,000)	20,000
4	20,000	1,000	(1,000)	
			(20,000)*	0

* The loan notes are repaid at par i.e. $20,000 at the end of year 4.

Test your understanding 1 (integration question)

A company issues 0% loan notes at their nominal value of $40,000. The loan notes are repayable at a premium of $11,800 after 3 years. The effective rate of interest is 9%.

Required:

(a) What amount will be recorded as a financial liability when the loan notes are issued?

(b) What amounts will be shown in the statement of profit or loss and statement of financial position for years 1–3?

Test your understanding 2 (integration question)

A company issues 5% redeemable preference shares at their nominal value of $10,000. The preference shares are repayable at a premium of $1,760 after 5 years. The effective rate of interest is 8%.

Required:

Explain how the instrument should be classified in accordance with IAS 32 *Financial instruments: Presentation*.

What amounts will be shown in the statement of profit or loss and statement of financial position for years 1–5?

Test your understanding 3 (integration question)

Fratton issues $360,000 of redeemable 2% debentures at a discount of 14% on 1 January 20X5. Issue costs were $5,265. The debenture will be redeemed on 31 December 20X7 at par. Interest is paid annually in arrears and the effective interest rate is 8%.

Required:

Show the effect of the transaction on the statement of financial position and statement of profit or loss for the three year term of the debenture.

Test your understanding 4 (OTQ style)

A company issues 4% loan notes with a nominal value of $20,000.

The loan notes are issued at a discount of 2.5% and $534 of issue costs are incurred.

The loan notes will be repayable at a premium of 10% after 5 years. The effective rate of interest is 7%.

Required:

The initial measurement of the loan notes is:

A **$18,966**

B **$19,466**

C **$19,500**

D **$20,034**

Test your understanding 5 (OTQ style)

An entity issues 3% bonds with a nominal value of $150,000. The bonds are issued at a discount of 10% and issue costs of $11,450 are incurred.

The bonds will be repayable at a premium of $10,000 after 4 years. The effective rate of interest is 10%.

The initial recognition of the bonds was correctly recorded by the entity at $123,550. However the entity has not re-measured the bonds and has instead expensed the interest paid to the statement of profit or loss.

Required:

Calculate the carrying value of the bonds that should be presented in the statement of financial position at the end of year 1.

Test your understanding 6 (case style)

The directors of XYZ want to avoid increasing the gearing of the entity. They plan to issue 5 million 6% cumulative redeemable $1 preference shares.

Required:

Explain how the preference shares would be classified in accordance with IAS 32 *Financial instruments: Presentation* and the impact that this issue will have on the gearing of XYZ.

6 Presentation of compound instruments

- A **compound instrument** is a financial instrument that has characteristics of both equity and liabilities.

- Convertible bonds are compound instruments (they are currently debt but can be converted into equity shares).

- As we've already seen in earlier chapters, the bondholder has the prospect of acquiring cheap shares in an entity, because the terms of conversion should be generous. Even if the bondholder wants cash rather than the shares, they will be likely to accept the conversion and then sell the shares at market price to make a profit.

- In exchange though, the bondholders normally have to accept a below-market rate of interest, and will have to wait some time before they get the shares that form a large part of their return. There is also the risk that the entity's shares will under-perform, making the conversion unattractive.

- IAS 32 requires compound financial instruments be split into their component parts:
    - a financial liability (the debt) – measured as the present value of the future cashflows, including redemption, using a discount rate that equates to the interest rate on similar instruments without conversion rights
    - an equity instrument (the option to convert into shares) – calculated as the balancing figure.

- These must be shown separately in the financial statements.

- Subsequently, the liability component is measured at amortised cost and the equity component remains unchanged.

- Any transaction costs would be pro-rated between equity and liability component based on their values.

Example 2 – compound instrument

On 1 January 20X1 Daniels issued a $50m three year convertible bond at par.

- There were no issue costs.

- The coupon rate is 10%, payable annually in arrears on 31 December.

- The bond is redeemable at par on 1 January 20X4.

- Bondholders may opt for conversion. The terms of conversion are two 25 cent shares for every $1 owed to each bondholder on 1 January 20X4.

- Bonds issued by similar companies without any conversion rights currently bear interest at 15%.

- Assume that all bondholders opt for conversion in full.

Accounting treatment

On initial recognition, the method of splitting the bond between equity and liabilities is as follows.

- Calculate the present value of the debt component by discounting the cash flows at the market rate of interest for an instrument similar in all respects, except that it does not have conversion rights.

- Deduct the present value of the debt from the proceeds of the issue. The difference is the equity component.

(1) Splitting the proceeds

The cash payments on the bond should be discounted to their present value using the interest rate for a bond without the conversion rights i.e. 15%.

Date		Cash flow	Discount factor @ 15%	Present value
		$000		$000
20X1–X3	Interest	5,000	2.283	11,415
01/01/X4	Redemption	50,000	0.658	32,900
Present value = the liability component				44,315
Equity (balancing figure)				5,685
Net proceeds of issue				50,000

The journal entry required to record the issue is:

Dr Bank	$50m
Cr Financial Liability	$44.315m
Cr Equity (bal fig) – other reserves	$5.685m

(2) Subsequent remeasurement of liability component

	Opening balance	Effective interest rate 15%	Payments	Closing balance
	$000	$000	$000	$000
20X1	44,315	6,647	(5,000)	45,962
20X2	45,962	6,894	(5,000)	47,856
20X3	47,856	7,144*	(5,000)	50,000

* Note that the effective interest in 20X3 is rounded (due to the discount factors having only been applied to 3 decimal places) to ensure that the closing balance equals the redemption amount of $50 million.

Note: The equity component is not remeasured after initial recognition.

(3) The conversion of the bond

The carrying amounts at 1 January 20X4 are:

	$000
Equity – other reserves	5,685
Liability – bond	50,000
	55,685

The conversion terms are two 25c shares for every $1, so $50m × 2 = 100m shares, which have a nominal value of $25m. The remaining $30.685 million should be classified as the share premium, also within equity. There is no remaining liability, because conversion has extinguished it.

The journal entry on conversion would be:

Dr	Liability	$50m
Dr	Equity – other reserves	$5.685m
Cr	Share capital	$25m
Cr	Share premium	$30.685m

Test your understanding 7 (integration question)

An entity issues 2% convertible bonds at their nominal value of $36,000 on 1 January 20X1.

The bonds are convertible at any time up to maturity into 120 ordinary shares for each $100 of bond. Alternatively the bonds will be redeemed at par after 3 years. Similar non-convertible bonds would carry an interest rate of 9%.

The entity is preparing its financial statements for the year ended 31 December 20X1. They are not sure how to record the convertible bonds and therefore have credited the £36,000 cash received to non-current liabilities and have recognised the interest paid in the year as a finance cost.

Required:

(a) Prepare the journal entry that should have been applied to correctly record the initial recognition of the convertible bonds on 1 January 20X1.

(b) Prepare extracts from the statement of profit or loss and statement of financial position for the year ended 31 December 20X1.

(c) What are the journal entries required to correct the entity's accounting records in the year ended 31 December 20X1?

Test your understanding 8 (OTQ style)

A company issues 4% convertible bonds at their nominal value of $5 million on 1 January 20X3.

Each bond is convertible at any time up to maturity into 2 ordinary shares for every $1 bond. Alternatively the bonds will be redeemed at par after 3 years.

The market rate applicable to non-convertible bonds is 6%.

Required:

Complete the following journal entry required to record the initial recognition of the convertible bonds on 1 January 20X3. Give your figures to the nearest $000:

	$000
Dr Bank	5,000
Cr Financial Liability	
Cr Equity	

Test your understanding 9 (OTQ style)

A company issues 100,000 5% convertible bonds with a nominal value of $100 each on 1 January 20X0.

Each bond is convertible at any time up to maturity into 120 ordinary shares for every $100 bond. Alternatively the bonds will be redeemed at par after five years.

The market rate of interest for a similar five year term bond with no conversion option is 7%.

Upon initial recognition, the liability component of the bond was correctly calculated and recognised as $9,180,000 and the equity component was $820,000.

Required:

Calculate the carrying value of the liability component that would be shown in the statement of financial position at 31 December 20X0. Give your answer to the nearest $.

The directors of QWE are considering different forms of finance to fund an acquisition. They have been advised to raise finance via an issue of convertible bonds however they are not sure what impact this would have on the financial statements.

They are looking to issue 3% convertible bonds with a nominal value of $20 million and a four year term. They are particularly keen to keep their finance costs as low as possible in the statement of profit or loss and therefore are attracted to this form of finance because of the low interest rate of 3%.

They have been told that the market rate of interest for similar bonds with a five year term but no conversion option is 8%.

Required:

Explain how this convertible instrument would be initially recorded in the financial statements of QWE in accordance with IAS 32 Financial Instruments: Presentation and subsequently measured in accordance with IAS 39 Financial Instruments: Recognition and Measurement in the financial statements.

Note: there is no need to perform any calculations.

7 Financial assets

To summarise some rules stated earlier:

- Financial assets and liabilities are initially recognised at fair value (which is typically cash paid/received).

- Except in the case of assets or liabilities at fair value through profit or loss, directly attributable transaction costs are added to an asset and deducted from a liability.

- Subsequent measurement of financial instruments depends on how the instruments have been classified.

NB. If an entity ACQUIRES bonds/debentures/loan stock/shares, it has purchased a financial asset.

IAS 39 deals separately with **four types of financial asset** as follows:

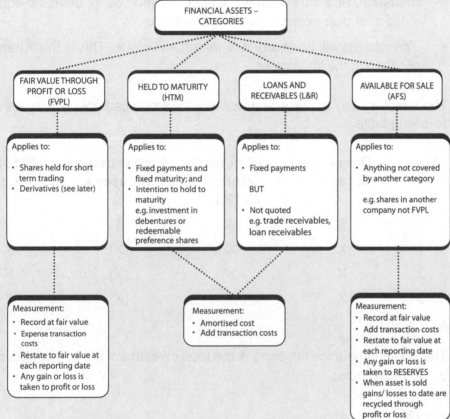

A financial asset could be classified in one or more categories. For example, an investment in the loan stock of another entity could be classified as:

- FVPL – if the loan was to be traded
- HTM – if the loan was quoted and there was an ability and intention to hold to maturity
- L&R – if the loan was unquoted.

Similarly an investment in another entity's ordinary shares could be classified as:

- FVPL – if the shares are held for trading
- AFS – otherwise.

Amortised cost

- Assets classified as loans and receivables or held to maturity will be measured at amortised cost. The amortised cost of an asset equals: initial cost plus interest less cash received.

- The interest will be charged at the effective rate. This is the internal rate of return of the instrument.

The simplest way to prepare a working for amortised cost is to use the following table.

Year	Opening balance	Effective interest % (P/L)	Cash received (coupon) %	Closing balance (SFP)
	$	$	$	$
1	X	X	(X)	X
2	X	X	(X)	X
3	X	X	(X)	X

The opening balance in year 1 is the total investment (cash invested plus transaction costs):

- Dr Asset

- Cr Cash

Effective interest is calculated on the opening balance and is credited to the statement of profit or loss (P/L) as finance income:

- Dr Asset

- Cr Finance income (P/L)

The coupon received is the coupon percentage multiplied by the face value of the instrument:

- Dr Cash

- Cr Asset

The closing balance is the figure for the statement of financial position (SFP) at the reporting date.

Test your understanding 11 (integration question)

Ashes has the following financial assets:

(1) Investments held for trading purposes.

(2) Interest-bearing debt instruments that will be redeemed in five years; Ashes fully intends to hold them until redemption.

(3) A trade receivable.

(4) Derivatives held for speculation purposes.

(5) Equity shares that Ashes has no intention of selling.

Required:

How should Ashes classify its financial assets?

Test your understanding 12 (integration question)

A company invests $5,000 in 10% debentures. The debentures will be repaid at a premium at the end of their term and A intends to hold the debentures until this time. The effective rate of interest is 12%.

Required:

Prepare extracts from the statement of profit or loss and statement of financial position for years 1 and 2 of the instrument's term.

Test your understanding 13 (integration question)

A company invested in 10,000 shares of a listed company in November 20X7 at a cost of $4.20 per share. Transaction costs relating to the investment were $1,300. At 31 December 20X7 the shares have a market value of $4.90. The shares are held for trading purposes.

Required:

(a) Prepare extracts from the statement of profit or loss for the year ended 31 December 20X7 and a statement of financial position as at that date.

(b) Explain how the treatment would differ if there was no plan to sell the shares.

Test your understanding 14 (OTQ style)

MNB acquired 100,000 shares in AB on 25 October 20X0 for $3 per share. The investment resulted in MNB holding 5% of the equity shares of AB. The related transaction costs were $12,000. AB's shares were trading at $3.40 on 31 December 20X0. The investment has been classified as held for trading.

Required:

The journal entry required to record the change in fair value of the investment in shares at 31 December 20X0 is:

A   **Dr Investment $28,000   Cr Profit or loss $28,000**

B   **Dr Investment $28,000   Cr Other comprehensive income $28,000**

C   **Dr Investment $40,000   Cr Profit or loss $40,000**

D   **Dr Investment $40,000   Cr Other comprehensive income $40,000**

Test your understanding 15 (case style)

MNB acquired an investment in a debt instrument on 1 January 20X0 at its par value of $3 million. Transaction costs relating to the acquisition were $200,000. The investment earns a fixed annual return of 6%, which is received in arrears. The principal amount will be repaid to MNB in 4 years' time at a premium of $400,000. The investment has been correctly classified as held to maturity. The investment has an effective interest rate of approximately 7.05%.

MNB has recently employed a new financial controller, Joe, and the finance director has asked you to explain to Joe how the above investment should be accounted for in the financial statements. The finance director is keen for Joe to perform the amortisation calculations, so that she can check that he is doing it correctly. She therefore just wants you to provide an explanation to help him understand how to apply the accounting treatment required in accordance with IAS 39 Financial Instruments: Recognition and Measurement.

Required:

Prepare a briefing note to Joe, explaining how to account for the above investment in the financial statements of MNB.

8 Impairment of financial assets

Impairments apply only to assets categorised as held to maturity or loans and receivables i.e. those that are measured at amortised cost.

Other financial assets are already recorded at fair value and any impairment would have been taken into account when measuring the fair value.

Impairment rules per IAS 39 are as follows:

- Assess at each reporting date whether there is any evidence of impairment, i.e. whether an event has occurred that has a negative impact on the estimated future cash flows of the financial asset.

- If there is evidence, a detailed impairment review must be undertaken.

- The impairment loss (if not given in the question) is the difference between the carrying amount and the present value of the cash flows estimated to arise from the asset, discounted at the asset's original effective interest rate.

- Impairment losses are recognised through the statement of profit or loss.

Example 3 – Impairment of financial asset

On 1 January 20X6, Eve makes a four year loan of $10,000 to Fern. The coupon and effective rate on the loan is 6%. Interest is received at the end of each year.

At the end of December 20X8 it becomes clear that Fern is in financial difficulties. This is the necessary objective evidence of impairment.

It is estimated that the future remaining cash flows from the loan will be only $6,000 instead of $10,600 (the $10,000 principal plus interest for the fourth year of $600).

Accounting treatment

The carrying amount of the principal prior to the impairment will be $10,000 (as the coupon and effective rate are the same).

On 31 December 20X8, the carrying amount should be restated to the present value of the estimated cash flows of $6,000, discounted at the original effective interest rate of 6% for one year.

Present value = $6,000 × 1/1.06 = $5,660

The result is an impairment loss of $4,340 (10,000 – 5,660)

The impairment loss is recognised as an expense in the statement of profit or loss.

The asset will then continue to be accounted for using amortised cost, based on the revised carrying amount of the loan. In the last year, interest income of $340 (6% × 5,660) will be recognised in profit or loss.

The movement on the loan in the final year will be:

Opening balance ($)	Effective interest 6%	Cash received	Closing balance ($)
5,660	340	(6,000)	0

9 Derecognition of financial assets

An entity should derecognise a financial asset when:

- the contractual rights to the cash flows from the financial asset expire; or
- it transfers substantially all the risks and rewards of ownership of the financial asset.

Upon derecognition, any difference between proceeds and carrying value is recognised through profit or loss.

If the asset was classified as available for sale, any gains or losses accumulated within other components of equity are reclassified and included in profit or loss at the date of disposal.

Example 4 – AFS disposal

An entity acquires a financial asset for $970, its fair value, on 1 January 20X1. The entity's reporting date is 31 December and the fair value of the asset at 31 December 20X1 was $1,100.

The entity disposes of the asset on 31 October 20X2 for proceeds of $1,050.

Accounting entries

Initial recognition:

Dr   AFS asset $970

Cr   Bank $970

Being the purchase of the financial asset at fair value.

At reporting date:

Dr   AFS asset $130

Cr   AFS reserve (other equity) $130

Being the re-measurement to the fair value of $1,100 at the reporting date (1,100 – 970 = 130)

At date of disposal:

Dr   Bank $1,050

Cr AFS asset $1,100

Dr Profit or loss $50

Being derecognition of financial asset

and

Dr AFS reserve (other equity) $130

Cr Profit or loss $130

Being the reclassification of AFS gains previously held in equity.

At the date of disposal, the total gain recognised within profit or loss is $80 (130 reclassified less 50 loss on derecognition).

Test your understanding 16 (integration question)

JL acquired an investment in another entity on 1 March 20X2 and classifies the investment as available for sale. The purchase cost was $10,000 and there were transaction costs associated with the transaction of $500.

JL's reporting date is 31 August and the fair value of the investment at 31 August 20X2 was $12,000.

JL sold the investment on 31 October 20X2 for $14,000.

Required:

Prepare the journal entries that would be required at the date of disposal.

Factoring of receivables

In a factoring arrangement, an entity transfers some or all of its receivables (a category of financial assets) to another entity (the factor) in return for a cash advance. The factor then assumes responsibility for collecting the amounts outstanding from the customers.

The legal title to the receivables has transferred to the factor.

The factor pays a cash advance to the entity in return for legal title, e.g. 80% of the carrying value of the receivable.

Accounting treatment

In accordance with IAS 39, the entity should only derecognise the receivables if it has transferred substantially all the risks and rewards of ownership.

Factors to consider are:

- Does the factor have right of recourse (i.e. can the factor recover the cash advanced in the event of the customer not settling the amount outstanding)?

- Can the factor only recover a fixed amount (and if so, does this reflect the majority of the receivables value or not)?

- Who bears the risk of slow payment?

Example 5 – factoring

The following relates to AB for the year ended 31 October 20X5.

AB supplies all its customers on credit terms. On 1 November 20X4 it entered into a factoring agreement with CD with the following terms:

- AB receives 90% of the carrying value of the receivables on the date of transfer to CD

- AB has the right to future sums, the amount will be based on when and whether the receivables pay. The faster they pay, the more AB will receive.

- CD has the right of recourse for any additional losses up to a maximum of $200,000.

AB transfers receivables with a carrying value of $15 million to CD at the reporting date, 31 October 20X5.

Required:

(a) **Explain how the above arrangement would be accounted for in the books of AB.**

(b) **Explain how this would change if there was no limit on the amount of recourse.**

Solution

(a) AB has transferred substantially all risks and rewards as it will receive a minimum of $13,300,000 (90% × $15m less $200,000 recourse). Therefore the receivables should be derecognised. A separate liability will be recognised for the potential repayment of $200,000.

Dr Bank (90% × $15,000,000)	$13,500,000
Cr Receivables	$15,000,000
Cr Liability	$200,000
Dr Profit or loss	$1,700,000

The charge to the profit or loss represents the cost of $1,500,000 receivables that have not been advanced and the potential cost of $200,000 repayable to the factor.

If AB receives additional sums in the future, it will:

Dr   Bank

Dr   Liability

Cr   Profit or loss

(b)   If the factor has full recourse then AB will not have transferred the risks and rewards since it still faces the risk of non-payment entirely. Therefore, the receivables will not be derecognised and the sum advanced represents a loan secured on the receivables.

Dr   Bank (90% × $15,000,000) $13,500,000

Cr   Liability $13,500,000

The loan and receivable balance would then be derecognised when the customer pays the factor, with any difference being expensed through profit or loss.

Test your understanding 17 (case style)

You have just joined ABC as an accountant and you have been asked to review the accounting treatment that your predecessor (Stan) has so far reflected in the draft financial statements for the year ended 30 September 20X7 in respect of a factoring arrangement. Details of the arrangement are provided below.

ABC has an outstanding receivables balance with a major customer amounting to $12 million and entered into the factoring arrangement with FinanceCo on 1 September 20X7. The terms of the arrangement are:

*   FinanceCo advances 80% of the gross receivable to ABC immediately.

*   The balance will be paid (less the charges below) when the debt is collected in full. Any amount of the debt outstanding after four months will be transferred back to ABC at its full book value, with ABC having to return the funds advanced by the factor.

*   FinanceCo will charge 1% per month of the net amount owing from ABC at the beginning of each month. FinanceCo had not collected any of the factored receivable by the reporting date of 30 September 20X7.

Stan debited the cash from FinanceCo to ABC's bank account and derecognised the receivable. He charged the difference as an administrative expense.

Required:

Prepare a brief memo to the Finance Director explaining how the factoring arrangement should have been accounted for in the draft financial statements and showing the journal entries required to correct the accounting treatment put through by Stan.

10 Derivative financial instruments

Definition of derivatives

A derivative is a financial instrument that **derives its value from the value of an underlying asset, price, rate or index**.

- Underlying items include equities, bonds, commodities, interest rates, exchange rates and stock market and other indices.

- Derivative financial instruments include futures, options, forward contracts, interest rate and currency swaps.

Characteristics of a derivative

A derivative has all of the following characteristics:

- Its value changes in response to changes in the underlying item.

- It requires little or no initial investment.

- It is settled at a future date.

The risks associated with derivatives

- Derivatives were originally designed to hedge against fluctuations in agricultural commodity prices on the Chicago Stock Exchange. A speculator would pay a small amount (say $100) now for the contractual obligation to buy a thousand units of wheat in three months' time for $10,000. If in three months time one thousand units of wheat costs $11,000, then the speculator would make a profit of $900 (11,000 – 100 – 10,000). This would be a 900% return on the original investment over 3 months, which is one of the attractions of derivatives to speculators. But if the price had dropped to $9,000, then the trader would have made a loss of $1,100 (100 + 1,000) despite the initial investment only having been $100.

- This shows that losses on derivatives can be far greater than the historical cost carrying amount of the related asset. Therefore, shareholders need to be given additional information about derivatives in order to assess the entity's exposure to loss.

- In most cases, entering into a derivative is at a low or no cost. Therefore it is important that derivatives are recognised and disclosed in the financial statements as they have very little initial outlay but can expose the entity to significant gains and losses.

Recognition and measurement

All derivatives are categorised as fair value through the profit or loss (FVPL).

On initial recognition they are recorded at fair value which is usually nil as the derivative gains value as the underlying item's price moves.

At each reporting date, the derivative is restated to fair value and recorded as a financial asset or financial liability on the statement of financial position. Any gains/losses are taken to the statement of profit or loss.

Types of derivative

- **Forward** – the obligation to buy or sell a defined amount of a specific underlying asset, at a specified price at a specified future date.

- **Forward rate agreements** – a contract to fix the interest charge on a floating rate loan.

- **Futures contracts** – the obligation to buy or sell a standard quantity of a specific underlying item at a specified future date.

- **Swaps** – an agreement to exchange periodic payments at specified intervals over a specified time period.

- **Options** – the right, but not the obligation, to buy or sell a specific underlying asset on or before a specified future date.

Types of derivatives – further detail

Forward contracts

The holder of a forward contract is obliged to buy or sell a defined amount of a specific underlying asset, at a specified price at a specified future date. For example, a forward contract for foreign currency might require £100,000 to be exchanged for $150,000 in three months' time. Both parties to the contract have both a financial asset and a financial liability. For example, one party has the right to receive $150,000 and the obligation to pay £100,000.

Forward currency contracts may be used to minimise the risk on amounts receivable or payable in foreign currencies.

Example

On 1 January 20X9 a dollar based company buys goods from an overseas company. This results in a liability for €8 million which must be settled on 31 March 20X9. The exchange rate on 1 January is €8 = $1. The company takes out a forward exchange contract to buy €8 million for $1 million on 31 March 20X9. This is at the exchange rate ruling at 1 January (i.e. €8 = $1).

At 31 March the exchange rate is actually €8.5 = $1. If the company had not taken out the forward exchange contract it would have made an exchange gain of $58,824 (1,000,000 – 941,176). By taking out the forward exchange contract it has given up the chance to make this gain, but has also protected itself against the possibility of making a loss. In other words, it has used the forward exchange contract to eliminate exchange rate risk.

Forward rate agreements

Forward rate agreements can be used to fix the interest charge on a floating rate loan. For example, a company has a $1m dollar floating rate loan, and the current rate of interest is 7%. The rates are reset to the market rate every six months, and the company cannot afford to pay more than 9% interest. The company enters into a six month forward rate agreement (with, say, a bank) at 9% on $1m. If the market rates go up to 10%, then the bank will pay them $5,000 (1% of $1m for 6 months) which in effect reduces their finance cost to 9%. If the rates only go up to 8% then the company pays the bank $5,000.

Futures contracts

Futures contracts oblige the holder to buy or sell a standard quantity of a specific underlying item at a specified future date. Futures contracts are very similar to forward contracts. The difference is that futures contracts have standard terms and are traded on a financial exchange, whereas forward contracts are tailor made and are not traded on a financial exchange.

Swaps

Two parties agree to exchange periodic payments at specified intervals over a specified time period. For example, in an interest rate swap, the parties may agree to exchange fixed and floating rate interest payments calculated by reference to a notional principal amount. This enables companies to keep a balance between their fixed and floating rate interest payments without having to change the underlying loans.

Options

These give the holder the right, but not the obligation, to buy or sell a specific underlying asset on or before a specified future date.

Example 6 – derivative financial instrument

Entity A enters into a call option on 1 June 20X5, to purchase 10,000 shares in another entity on 1 November 20X5 at a price of $10 per share. The cost of each option is $1. A has a year end of 30 September.

By 30 September the fair value of each option has increased to $1.30. A exercises the option on 1 November and the shares are classified as at fair value through profit or loss. The share price at this date is $12.

Accounting treatment

On 1 June 20X5 the cost of the option is recognised:

Debit	Call option (10,000 × $1)	$10,000
Credit	Cash	$10,000

On 30 September the increase in fair value is recorded:

Debit	Call option (10,000 × ($1.30 – 1))	$3,000
Credit	Profit or loss – gain on option	$3,000

On 1 November the option is exercised, the shares recognised and the call option derecognised. As the shares are financial assets at fair value through profit or loss, they are recognised at $120,000 (10,000 × the current market price of $12).

Debit Investment in shares at fair value	$120,000
Credit Cash (10,000 × $10)	$100,000
Credit Call option (10,000 + 3,000 carrying amount)	$13,000
Credit Profit or loss – further gain (bal fig)	$7,000

The total gain recognised is $10,000 which equates to $1 per share, being the difference between the share price of $12 and the price paid of $11 ($1 for the option and $10 upon exercise). As $3,000 has already been recognised in the year ended 30 September 20X5, the remaining $7,000 is recognised upon exercise.

Test your understanding 18 (integration question)

B entered into a forward contract on 30 November 20X1 to buy platinum for $435m on 31 March 20X2. The contract was entered into on 30 November 20X1 at nil cost.

B does not plan to take delivery of the platinum but to settle the contract net in cash, i.e. B hopes to generate a profit from short term price fluctuations.

The year end is 31 December 20X1 and the price of platinum has moved so that making the equivalent purchase on 31 December 20X1 would require B to spend $455m.

On 31 March 20X2, the value of the underlying item has changed such that the equivalent purchase of platinum would now cost $442m.

Required:

Prepare journal entries to record the above transaction.

Test your understanding 19 (integration question)

On 1 March 20X1, ABC decided to enter into a forward foreign exchange contract to buy 5 million florins for $1 million on 31 January 20X3. ABC's reporting date is 30 June.

Relevant exchange rates were as follows:

1 March 20X1	$1 = 5 florins
30 June 20X1	$1 = 4.7 florins
30 June 20X2	$1 = 4.2 florins

Required:

(a) Prepare relevant extracts from ABC's statement of comprehensive income and statement of financial position to reflect the forward foreign exchange contract at 30 June 20X2, with comparatives.

(b) At 31 January 20X3, the settlement date, the exchange rate is $1 = 4.5 florins. What gain or loss would be recorded in the statement of profit or loss in the year ended 30 June 20X3?

Test your understanding 20 (OTQ style)

AB entered into a forward contract on 31 January 20X1 to purchase B$1 million at a contracted rate of A$1:B$0.75 on 31 May 20X1. The contract cost was $nil. AB prepares its financial statements to 31 March each year.

At 31 March 20X1 an equivalent contract for the purchase of B$1 million could be acquired at a rate of A$1:B$0.80.

Required:

Which one of the following states the correct impact of the forward contract on profit or loss in the year ended 31 March 20X1:

A   **A$ 83,333 gain**

B   **A$ 83,333 loss**

C   **A$ 1,250,000 loss**

D   **A$ 1,333,333 gain**

Test your understanding 21 (further OTQs)

(1) A financial instrument is any contract that gives rise to a financial _____ of one entity and a financial _____ or _____ instrument of another entity.

Select the correct words to complete the above sentence, from the following options:

asset, bond, equity, liability, obligation, share

(2) PT issued 1 million 4% cumulative redeemable $1 preference shares on 1 January 20X1.

Which of the following statements are TRUE in respect of the above financial instrument. Select all that apply.

A   At the date of issue, PT would credit equity share capital with $1 million.

B   If the preference shares were issued at a discount, the effective rate of interest would be lower than 4%.

C   The dividends of $40,000 paid each year would be recognised in the statement of changes in equity.

D   The preference shares would be remeasured each year at amortised cost using the effective interest rate.

(3) SQ issued a $2 million 5% convertible bonds on 1 January 20X1 at par value. The bond is redeemable at par after 5 years or can be converted into equity shares on the basis of 2 shares for every $1 of bond.

The prevailing market rate at 1 January 20X1 for similar bonds without conversion rights was 10% per annum.

Calculate the carrying value of the liability element of the bonds at 31 December 20X1 (to the nearest $).

(4) BD entered into a forward contract on 31 August 20X1 to purchase B$3 million at a contracted rate of A$1: B$1.5. on 30 November 20X1. The contract cost was $nil. At 31 October 20X1, BD's financial year end, an equivalent contract for the purchase of B$3 million could be acquired at a rate of A$1: B$1.7.

Complete the following journal entry to record the financial instrument in the financial statements of BD for the year ended 31 October 20X1 (state the amount to the nearest A$).

Dr

Cr

Note: In the assessment, you would choose the headings for the Dr and Cr from a selection of choices.

(5) KM made an investment in a debt instrument on 1 June 20X0 at its nominal value of $2 million. The instrument carries a fixed coupon interest rate of 6% and the instrument will be redeemed at a premium on 31 May 20X4. KM intends to hold this investment until its redemption date.

How should this instrument be classified in the financial statements of KM?

A   Financial liability

B   Fair value through profit or loss financial asset

C   Held to maturity financial asset

D   Available for sale financial asset

(6) CG acquired 20,000 equity shares in FM on 1 November 20X1 for $5 per share. The related transaction costs were $2,500. The investment was classified as available for sale. At 31 December 20X2, CG's reporting date, FM's shares were trading at $6.25.

How would the gain on the investment be measured and recorded in CG's statement of profit or loss and other comprehensive income for the year ended 31 December 20X2?

A   Gain of $22,500 recorded in profit or loss

B   Gain of $22,500 recorded in other comprehensive income

C   Gain of $25,000 recorded in profit or loss

D   Gain of $25,000 recorded in other comprehensive income

(7) AF acquired an investment on 1 January 20X1 for its fair value of $12,000. Transaction costs of $350 were also incurred. The investment was classified as available for sale and was subsequently remeasured to its fair value of $13,500 on 31 December 20X1, the entity's reporting date.

AF disposed of the investment on 1 April 20X2 for its fair value of $12,800.

Calculate the total gain or loss recognised in the statement of profit or loss upon disposal of the investment.

11 Chapter summary

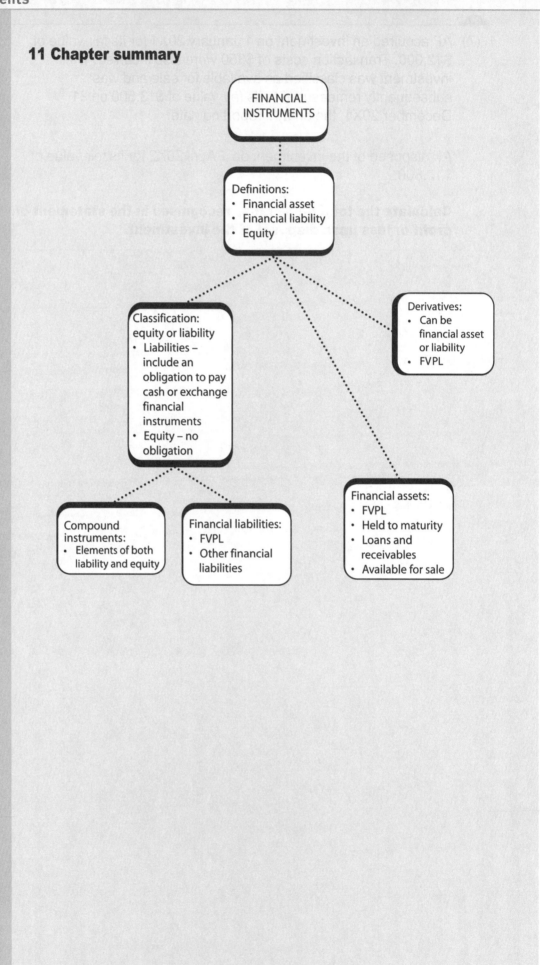

Test your understanding answers

Test your understanding 1 (integration question)

(a) When the loan notes are issued:

    Dr Bank $40,000
    Cr Loan notes $40,000

(b) Financial statement extracts

Statement of profit or loss (P/L)

Year	1	2	3
	$	$	$
Finance costs (W1)	(3,600)	(3,924)	(4,276)

Statement of financial position (SFP)

Year	1	2	3
	$	$	$
Non-current liabilities	43,600		
Current liabilities		47,524	0

(W1) Amortised cost table

Year	Opening balance	Effective interest 9% (P/L)	Coupon paid 0%	Closing balance (SFP)
	$	$	$	$
1	40,000	3,600	–	43,600
2	43,600	3,924	–	47,524
3	47,524	4,276	–	
			(51,800)	0

The loan notes are repaid at par i.e. $40,000, plus a premium of $11,800 at the end of year 3.

Test your understanding 2 (integration question)

The redeemable nature of the preference shares means that there will be an outflow of economic resources at the redemption date and therefore the instrument meets the definition of a financial liability and should be classified as such.

Statement of profit or loss (P/L)

Year	1	2	3	4	5
	$	$	$	$	$
Finance costs (W1)	(800)	(824)	(850)	(878)	(908)

Statement of financial position (SFP)

Year	1	2	3	4	5
	$	$	$	$	$
Non-current liabilities	10,300	10,624	10,974		
Current liabilities				11,352	0

(W1) Amortised cost table

Year	Opening balance	Effective Interest 8% (P/L)	Coupon paid 5%	Closing balance (SFP)
	$	$	$	$
1	10,000	800	(500)	10,300
2	10,300	824	(500)	10,624
3	10,624	850	(500)	10,974
4	10,974	878	(500)	11,352
5	11,352	908	(500)	
			(11,760)	0

Note: Effective interest rate is multiplied by opening balance.

Note: Coupon rate is multiplied by face value of debt i.e. $10,000.

Test your understanding 3 (integration question)

Amortised cost table

Year	Opening balance	Effective interest 8% (P/L)	Coupon paid 2%	Closing balance (SFP)
	$	$	$	$
1	(W1) 304,335	24,347	(7,200)	321,482
2	321,482	25,718	(7,200)	340,000
3	340,000	27,200	(7,200)	
			(360,000)	0
		77,265		

Note: Effective interest rate is multiplied by opening balance.

Note: Coupon rate is multiplied by face value of debt.

Tutorial note

The total finance cost will be as follows:

		$
Redemption value	At par	360,000
Payments	2% × 360,000 × 3 years	21,600
		381,600
Net proceeds (W1)		(304,335)
Total finance cost		77,265

The total finance cost will be allocated at a constant rate based upon carrying value over the life of the instrument. This is performed by applying the 8% effective interest rate.

(W1) Net proceeds = opening balance

	$
Nominal value	360,000
Discount 14%	(50,400)
Issue costs	(5,265)
	304,335

Test your understanding 4 (OTQ style)

The correct answer is A = $18,966

Working

	$
Nominal value	20,000
Discount 2.5%	(500)
	————
Cash received	19,500
Issue costs	(534)
	————
	18,966
	————

Test your understanding 5 (OTQ style)

Carrying value of bonds at the end of year 1 = $131,405

Amortised cost working

Year	Opening balance ($)	Effective interest 10% (P/L)	Coupon paid 3%	Closing balance (SFP) ($)
1	123,550	12,355	(4,500)	131,405

Note: Effective interest rate is multiplied by opening balance.

Note: Coupon rate is multiplied by face value of debt.

Test your understanding 6 (case style)

In substance, the preference shares are a debt instrument. IAS 32 requires that any instrument that contains an obligation to transfer economic benefit be classified as a liability.

The cumulative nature of the returns on the preference shares means that the outflow of benefit is inevitable. The shares are also redeemable so there will be a further outflow at the redemption date.

The preference shares should be classified as a financial liability and would increase the gearing of the entity.

Test your understanding 7 (integration question)

(a) Journal entry to initially recognise convertible bonds:

Dr Bank	$36,000
Cr Financial Liability	$29,614
Cr Equity (bal fig)	$6,386

Year	Cash flow (W) ($)	Discount factor 9%	Present value ($)
20X1–X3	720	2.531	1,822
20X3	36,000	0.772	27,792
			————
			29,614
			————

(W) Cash flow = 2% × 36,000 = $720

(b) **Statement of profit or loss year ended 31 December 20X1**

	$
Finance costs (W1)	(2,665)

Statement of financial position at 31 December 20X1

	$
Equity	
Equity option	6,386
Non-current liabilities (W1)	31,559

(W1) Amortised cost table

Year	Opening balance ($)	Effective interest 9% (P/L)	Coupon paid 2%	Closing balance (SFP) ($)
20X1	29,614	2,665	(720)	31,559

Note: Effective interest rate is multiplied by opening balance.

Note: Coupon rate is multiplied by face value of debt.

(c) Journal entries required

Dr Non-current liabilities		$6,386
Cr Equity reserve		$6,386

being the correct treatment of the initial recognition, after splitting the liability and equity component

Dr Finance costs (2,665 – 720)		$1,945
Cr Non-current liabilities		$1,945

being the adjustment to finance costs to reflect the effective rate applied to the liability component

---

Test your understanding 8 (OTQ style)

Journal entry to record initial recognition of convertible bonds:

	$000
Dr Bank	5,000
Cr Financial Liability	**4,735**
Cr Equity (bal fig)	**265**

Year	Cash flow (W) ($)	Discount factor 6%	Present value ($)
1–3	200,000	2.673	534,600
3	5,000,000	0.840	4,200,000
			4,734,600

(W) Cash flow = 4% × 5,000,000 = $200,000

Test your understanding 9 (OTQ style)

Carrying value of liability component at 31 December 20X0 = $9,322,600

Year	Opening balance ($)	Effective interest 7% (P/L)	Coupon paid	Closing balance (SFP) ($)
1	9,180,000	642,600	(500,000)	9,322,600

Note: Effective interest rate is multiplied by opening balance.

Note: Coupon rate is multiplied by face value of debt (5% × 10m).

Test your understanding 10 (case style)

A convertible bond is an example of a compound instrument, which is considered part liability and part equity. IAS 32 requires that each part is measured separately on initial recognition. The liability element is measured by estimating the present value of the future cash flows from the instrument (interest and potential redemption) using a discount rate equivalent to the market rate of interest for a similar instrument with no conversion terms, i.e. 8% for the bonds that are being considered. The result of this calculation would be credited to non-current liabilities and the remainder would be credited to equity. (The liability value would be lower than the total cash raised by the issue.)

Once recognised, the equity component is not remeasured, however the liability element will be subsequently remeasured at amortised cost using the effective interest rate which in this case will be 8%, the discount rate used to initially value the liability. Therefore the finance cost in the statement of profit or loss will be based on 8% rather than the 3% 'coupon rate'.

The benefit of the 3% coupon is that QWE will only pay interest to the bondholders each year of 3% of the nominal value of the bond and therefore the cash outflow will be lower than that required for a similar liability with no conversion option.

The conversion option makes up for the low annual cash return to the investor as the debt can be converted into equity.

In summary, there would be a liability and equity component that would be reflected in the statement of financial position and an 8% finance cost on the liability element would be reflected in profit or loss.

Test your understanding 11 (integration question)

Financial asset	Classification
1. Investments held for trading purposes	Financial assets at fair value through profit or loss
2. Interest-bearing debt instruments that will be redeemed in five years and held to redemption	Held-to-maturity investments
3. A trade receivable	Loans and receivables
4. Derivatives held for speculation purposes	Financial assets at fair value through profit or loss
5. Equity shares that Ashes has no intention of selling	Available-for-sale financial assets (because they do not fit under any other heading)

Test your understanding 12 (integration question)

Statement of profit or loss (P/L)

Year	1	2
	$	$
Finance income	600	612

Statement of financial position (SFP)

Year	1	2
	$	$
Non-current assets		
Financial assets	5,100	5,212

(W1) Amortised cost table

Year	Opening balance ($)	Effective interest 12% (P/L)	Coupon received 10%	Closing balance (SFP) ($)
1	5,000	600	(500)	5,100
2	5,100	612	(500)	5,212

Note: Effective interest rate is multiplied by opening balance.

Note: Coupon rate is multiplied by face value of the investment.

Test your understanding 13 (integration question)

(a) The financial assets are classified as fair value through profit or loss as the shares are held for trading purposes.

Statement of profit or loss

	$
Gain on financial assets (10,000 × (4.90 – 4.20))	7,000
Finance cost	(1,300)

Statement of financial position

Current assets	$
Investments (10,000 × 4.90)	49,000

(b) The financial asset would instead be classified as available for sale. The transaction costs would be added to the financial asset upon initial recognition rather than being expensed, therefore the initial asset would be recognised at an amount of $43,300.

The asset would be recognised as non-current on the statement of financial position and the subsequent gain of $5,700 (49,000–43,300) would be taken to reserves and shown as other comprehensive income in the statement of comprehensive income. It would be presented as an item that may be reclassified subsequently to profit or loss.

Test your understanding 14 (OTQ style)

The correct journal entry is C:

Dr   Investment $40,000

Cr   Profit or loss $40,000

The investment is held for trading and therefore should be classified as fair value through profit or loss. The transaction costs of $12,000 are therefore expensed and the initial recognition of the investment would be $300,000. The fair value at the year end is $3.40 × 100,000 = $340,000 and therefore the gain to reflect in profit or loss is $40,000.

Test your understanding 15 (case style)

Briefing note to Joe

The investment has been classified as held to maturity. It should be initially recognised at fair value and any transaction costs associated with the investment should be added to the initial recognition of the asset. This is the correct treatment for all categories of financial asset except fair value through profit or loss.

The investment has been acquired at par value which suggests that this is the fair value at the date of acquisition. The transaction costs were $200,000 and therefore the investment will be initially recognised at an amount of $3.2 million.

Subsequent measurement of held to maturity investments is then required using the amortised cost method. This means that the asset is increased to reflect income at the effective rate of interest of 7.05% and reduced by the amount of cash received in the period, which is 6% × nominal value of $3 million.

The cash receipt does not affect profit, the accounting entry is:

Dr Cash

Cr Investment

The effective rate of interest applied to the opening carrying value of the investment however gives rise to finance income which would be reflected in the statement of profit or loss. The accounting entry for this is:

Dr Investment

Cr Profit or loss

Please can you prepare the journal entries for the current year and then send them to either myself or the Finance Director for review.

Test your understanding 16 (integration question)

At date of disposal:

Dr   Bank $14,000

Cr   AFS asset $12,000

Cr   Profit or loss $2,000

Being derecognition of financial asset

and

Dr AFS reserve (other equity) $1,500

Cr Profit or loss $1,500

Being the reclassification of AFS gains previously held in equity (12,000 − (10,000 + 500)).

Test your understanding 17 (case style)

Memo re factoring arrangement

The factored receivable balance should only be derecognised if substantially all of the risks and rewards of ownership have transferred to FinanceCo, the factor.

The terms of the arrangement stipulate that ABC will have to pay back the amounts advanced by FinanceCo if the customer fails to settle the debt within four months and therefore ABC has retained risk of irrecoverable debts. It is also exposed to slow moving risk, as it is required to pay interest on the amounts that remain outstanding on a monthly basis.

Therefore, ABC should continue to recognise the receivables balance and should recognise the cash advance as a short term liability. It is effectively a short term loan, secured on the receivables balance, with a monthly interest rate of 1%.

The journal entry required to correct Stan's accounting treatment is:

Dr	Receivables	$12,000,000
Cr	Liability (80% × $12m)	$9,600,000
Cr	Administrative expenses	$2,400,000
Dr	Finance costs (1% × $9.6m)	$96,000
Cr	Liability	$96,000

Test your understanding 18 (integration question)

On 30 November 20X1 (contract date):

Derivative has no value.

On 31 December 20X1 (reporting date):

Dr	Derivative (financial asset)	$20m
Cr	P/L (gain)	$20m

On 31 March 20X2 (settlement):

Dr	P/L (loss)	$13m
Cr	Derivative (financial asset)	$13m

To record the further change in fair value

Dr	Bank	$7m
Cr	Derivative (to derecognise)	$7m

To record the settlement of the contract

Test your understanding 19 (integration question)

(a) Extracts from financial statements

Statement of profit or loss for year ended 30 June 20X2

	20X2	20X1
	$	$
Gain on derivative (W2)	126,646	63,830

Statement of financial position at 30 June 20X2

	20X2	20X1
	$	$
Derivative asset (W1)	190,476	63,830

Workings

(W1) Value of derivative

	$
Value of forward contract at 1 March 20X1 (FI 5m/5) – $1m	Nil
Value of forward contract at 30 June 20X1 (FI 5m/4.7) – $1m	63,830
Value of forward contract at 30 June 20X2 (FI 5m/4.2) – $1m	190,476

(W2) Gain

	$
Gain for year ended 30 June 20X1	63,830
Gain for year ended 30 June 20X2 (190,476 – 63,830)	126,646

(b) **Gain or loss in year ended 30 June 20X3**

Value of forward contract at 31 January 20X3 (FI 5m/4.5) – $1m	$111,111
Therefore loss would be recognised (190,476 – 111,111)	$79,365

Test your understanding 20 (OTQ style)

The correct answer is B = A$83,333 loss

The value of the derivative will be the difference between the value of the contract when settled compared with the cost of B$1 million being purchased at the year-end rate.

Cost of B$1 million at the contracted rate of B$0.75 = 1m/0.75 = A$1,333,333

Cost of B$1 million at the year end rate of B$0.80 = 1m/0.8 = A$1,250,000

Therefore , the derivative results in a liability at the year-end date of A$83,333 (1,333,333 – 1,250,000) as the contract has unfavourable terms when compared to the year end rate. The loss on the derivative would be charged to the statement of profit or loss in the year to 31 March 20X1.

Note: the journal entry to record the derivative would be

Dr	P/L (loss)	A$83,333
Cr	Derivative liability	A$83,333

Test your understanding 21 (further OTQs)

(1) A financial instrument is any contract that gives rise to a financial **asset** of one entity and a financial **liability** or **equity** instrument of another entity.

(2) **D is the only correct statement.**

A is incorrect as the preference shares should be recognised as a liability, not equity.

B is incorrect. A discount on issue would be an additional cost and therefore would increase the effective rate of interest rather than decrease it.

C is incorrect. The dividends paid would be expensed through profit or loss as a finance cost rather than being shown as a dividend paid in the statement of changes in equity.

(3) **The carrying value of the liability element of the bonds at 31 December 20X1 is $1,683,210.**

Year(s)	Cash flow (W) ($)	Discount factor 10%	Present value ($)
1–5	100,000	3.791	379,100
5	2,000,000	0.621	1,242,000
			1,621,100

(W) Cash flow = 5% × 2 million = $100,000

(W1) **Amortised cost table**

Year	Opening balance ($)	Effective interest 10% (P/L)	Coupon paid 5%	Closing balance (SFP) ($)
20X1	1,621,100	162,110	(100,000)	1,683,210

(4) **Dr P/L – loss on derivative   A$235,294**

Cr   Derivative liability   A$235,294

Cost of B$3 million at the contracted rate of B$1.5 = 3m/1.5 = A$2m

Cost of B$3 million at the year end rate of B$1.7 = 3m/1.7 = A$1,764,706

The contracted rate has unfavourable terms compared to the year end rate and therefore the derivative results in a liability.

(5) **C is the correct answer.**

A is not correct as KM made an investment, therefore it is a financial asset rather than liability.

B is not correct as KM is not holding the investment for trading purposes.

D is not correct as the financial instrument meets the definition of another category – held to maturity.

(6) **B is the correct answer.**

A and C are not correct as gains on available for sale investments are recognised through other comprehensive income.

D is not correct as the transaction costs are added to the asset at initial recognition and therefore the gain is ($6.25 × 20,000) – (($5 × 20,000) + $2,500) = $22,500.

(7) **Total effect on profit at disposal = $450**

Loss on derecognition of investment (12,800 – 13,500)	(700)
Gain reclassified from AFS reserve (13,500 – (12,000 + 350))	1,150
	_____
	450
	_____

You can also calculate the gain by comparing the value at original recognition with the proceeds on disposal = 12,800 – 12,350 = 450.

Share-based payments

Chapter learning objectives

B1. Produce consolidated primary financial statements, incorporating accounting transactions and adjustments, in accordance with relevant international accounting standards, in an ethical manner.

(c) Discuss the provisions of relevant international accounting standards in respect of the recognition and measurement of share-based payments, in accordance with IFRS 2.

(d) Produce the accounting entries, in accordance with relevant international accounting standards.

1 Session content

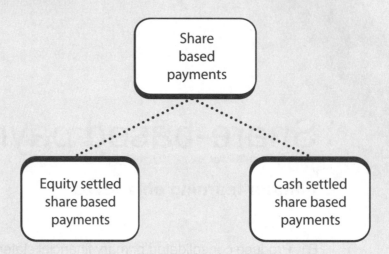

2 Introduction

Share-based payment has become increasingly common. Part of the remuneration of directors is often in the form of shares or options. Employees may also be granted share options.

Many new 'e-businesses' do not expect to be profitable in their early years, so try to attract quality staff by offering them share options rather than high cash salaries.

Share-based payment also occurs when an entity buys goods or services from other parties (such as employees or suppliers), and settles the amounts payable by issuing shares or share options to them.

The problem

If a company pays remuneration in cash, an expense is recognised in profit or loss. If a company 'pays' for employee services in shares or share options, there is no cash outflow and under traditional accounting, no expense would be recognised.

However, when a company issues shares/options to employees, a transaction has occurred; the employees have provided a valuable service to the entity, in exchange for the shares/options. It is illogical not to recognise this transaction in the financial statements.

IFRS 2 **Share-based payment** was issued to deal with this accounting anomaly. IFRS 2 requires that all share-based payment transactions must be recognised in the financial statements.

Types of transaction

IFRS 2 applies to all types of share-based payment transaction. There are two main types:

- in an **equity-settled share-based payment transaction**, the entity rewards staff (or other parties) with equity instruments (e.g. shares or share options)

- in a **cash-settled share-based payment transaction**, the entity rewards staff (or other parties) with amounts of cash measured by reference to the entity's share price. Cash settled share-based payments are also known as share appreciation rights (SAR's).

The most common type of share-based payment transaction is where share options are granted to employees or directors as part of their remuneration.

The basic principles

When an entity receives employee services or goods as a result of a share-based payment transaction, it recognises either an expense or an asset.

- If the goods or services are received in exchange for equity (e.g. for share options), the entity recognises an increase in equity.
    - The double entry is:
        - Dr Expense/Asset
        - Cr Equity (normally a special reserve).

- If the goods or services are received or acquired in a cash-settled share-based payment transaction, the entity recognises a liability.
    - The double entry is:
        - Dr Expense/Asset
        - Cr Liability.

3 Equity-settled share-based payments

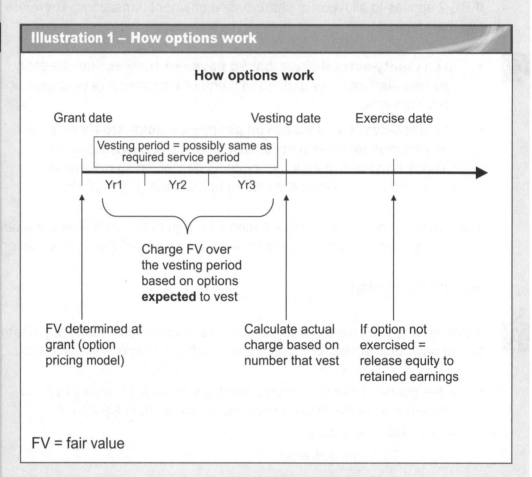

Illustration 1 – How options work

Measurement

The basic principle is that all transactions are measured at fair value at the grant date i.e. the date at which the entity and another party agree to the arrangement.

For equity-settled transactions the fair value is typically the option price at the grant date (rather than the fair value of the goods or services received).

If the options vest immediately i.e. employees are entitled to the shares immediately, it is presumed that the entity has received the benefit of the services and the full amount is recognised on the grant date.

If the options do not vest immediately, as is usually the case, the company should spread the cost of the options over the vesting period, the period during which the specific vesting conditions are satisfied e.g. length of service with the company.

To record the cost on an annual basis:

Dr P/L

Cr Equity (other reserves)

The amount is: total number of options issued and *expected* to vest multiplied by the fair value of an option at grant date, spread over the vesting period.

Example 1 – equity settled scheme

On 1 January 20X1 an entity grants 100 share options to each of its 500 employees. Each grant is conditional upon the employee working for the entity until 31 December 20X3. At the grant date the fair value of each share option is $15.

During 20X1, 20 employees leave and the entity estimates that a total of 20% of the 500 employees will leave during the three- year period.

During 20X2, a further 20 employees leave and the entity now estimates that only a total of 15% of its 500 employees will leave during the three-year period.

During 20X3, a further 10 employees leave.

Accounting treatment

The entity recognises the remuneration expense as the employees' services are received over the three year vesting period. The amount recognised is based on the fair value of the share options granted at the grant date (1 January 20X1).

Assuming that no employees left, the total expense would be $750,000 (100 × 500 × 15) and the expense charged to profit or loss for each of the three years would be $250,000 (750,000/3).

In practice, the entity estimates the number of options expected to vest by estimating the number of employees likely to leave. This estimate is revised at each year end. The expense recognised for the year is based on this re-estimate. On the vesting date (31 December 20X3), it recognises an amount based on the number of options that actually vest.

A total of 50 employees left during the three year period and therefore 45,000 options ((500 – 50) × 100) vested.

The amount recognised as an expense for each of the three years is calculated as follows:

	Cumulative expense at year-end	Expense for the year (change in cumulative)
	$	$
20X1 100 × (500 × 80%) × 15 × 1/3	200,000	200,000
20X2 100 × (500 × 85%) × 15 × 2/3	425,000	225,000
20X3 45,000 × 15	675,000	250,000

Journals to record the equity settled share-based payment will be Dr P/L Cr Equity. The journals each year will be posted using the figures from the "Expense for the year" column.

The financial statements will include the following amounts:

Statement of profit or loss	20X1	20X2	20X3
	$	$	$
Staff costs	200,000	225,000	250,000

Statement of financial position	20X1	20X2	20X3
	$	$	$
Included with equity	200,000	425,000	675,000

Test your understanding 1 (integration question)

On the 1 January 20X5, 400 staff receive 100 share options each. They must work for the company for the next three years and the options become exercisable on 31 December 20X7. The fair value at the time of granting is $20 per option.

In the year ending 31 December 20X5, 10 staff leave and it is thought that during the three year vesting period, the total amount leaving will be 15%.

In 20X6, a further 15 leave but the estimate of total leaving is now reduced to 10%. In the final year 12 staff leave.

Required:

Calculate the expense to be charged in the statement of profit or loss and the balance on the equity reserve that would be shown at the reporting date for each of the three years ended 31 December 20X5, 20X6 and 20X7.

Test your understanding 2 (OTQ style)

Asif has set up an employee option scheme to motivate its sales team of ten key sales people. Each sales person was offered 1 million options, conditional upon the employee remaining with the entity during the vesting period of 5 years. The fair value of each option at the grant date was 20c.

An expense of $320,000 was recognised in year one (this can be assumed to be correct and reflects the expectation at the end of year one that two sales people would leave before the end of the vesting period).

At the end of year two, Asif expects nine of the ten sales people to remain with the entity for the rest of the vesting period.

Required:

Complete the following journal entry to record the expense of the share option scheme in Asif's financial statements in year 2.

Dr Staff costs $

Cr _____ * $

* Select heading from: Cash; Equity; Liability

4 Cash-settled share-based payments

An example of a cash-settled share-based payment transaction is the payment of a bonus to an employee based on the entity's share price. They are also known as share appreciation rights (SAR's).

The basic principle is that the entity measures the goods or services acquired and the liability incurred at the **fair value of the liability**.

A liability is recorded as the bonus creates an obligation on behalf of the employer.

As time progresses, the employer will have a better idea of the actual amount required to pay out as a result of the bonus. Therefore, the liability needs to be remeasured to reflect these values at the end of each period.

- Until the liability is settled, the entity remeasures the fair value of the liability at each reporting date and then at the date of settlement. Notice that this is different from accounting for equity share-based payments, where the fair value is fixed at the grant date.

- Changes in fair value are recognised in profit or loss for the period.

- Where services are received, these are recognised over the period that the employees render the services. (This is the same principle as for equity-settled transactions).

- The expense recognised in each accounting period has a double entry to a provision/liability account.
    - Dr P/L
    - Cr Liability

- On the vesting date, the amount of the liability should equal the cash to be paid.

Example 2 – cash settled scheme

On 1 January 20X1 an entity grants 100 cash share appreciation rights (SAR) to each of its 300 employees, on condition that they continue to work for the entity until 31 December 20X3.

During 20X1 20 employees leave. The entity estimates that a further 40 will leave during 20X2 and 20X3.

During 20X2 10 employees leave. The entity estimates that a further 20 will leave during 20X3.

During 20X3 10 employees leave.

The fair values of one SAR at each year end are shown below.

	Fair value
	$
20X1	10.00
20X2	12.00
20X3	15.00

Accounting treatment

Year	Liability at year-end	Expense for year
	$000	$000
20X1 ((300 – 20 – 40) × 100 × $10 × 1/3)	80	80
20X2 ((300 – 20 – 10 – 20) × 100 × $12 × 2/3)	200	120
20X3 ((300 – 20 – 10 – 10) × 100 × $15)	390	190

The fair value of the liability is remeasured at each reporting date to reflect changes in the estimate of the number of rights expected to vest and changes in the fair value of each right.

Test your understanding 3 (integration question)

On 1 January 20X1 Kindly sets up a cash based payment to each of its 100 employees, on condition that they continue to work for the entity until 31 December 20X3. Each employee has been allocated 100 shares and will receive a payment in cash if the share price exceeds $10 on 31 December 20X3, of the amount by which it exceeds $10.

During 20X1, 5 employees leave. The entity estimates that a further 12 will leave during 20X2 and 20X3.

During 20X2, 10 employees leave. The entity estimates that a further 15 will leave during 20X3.

During 20X3, 18 employees leave.

The fair value per right at the reporting date for each year are shown below.

	$
20X1	1.00
20X2	2.00
20X3	4.00

Required:

Calculate the expense that would be recognised in the statement of profit or loss and the liability that would be recognised in the statement of financial position at the reporting date in each of the three years ended 31 December 20X1, 20X2 and 20X3. Give answers to the nearest $.

Test your understanding 4 (OTQ style)

G grants 100 share appreciation rights (SARs) to its 500 employees on 1 January 20X7 on the condition that the employees stay with the entity for the next two years. The SARs must be exercised at the start of 20X9.

During 20X7, 15 staff leave. As at 31 December 20X7, a further 20 are expected to leave in 20X8.

The fair value of the SARs was $10 at the grant date and $12 at 31 December 20X7.

Required:

Complete the following journal entry to record the expense of the share appreciation rights scheme in the financial statements for the year ended 31 December 20X7.

Dr Staff costs $

Cr _____ * $

* Select heading from: Cash; Equity; Liability

Test your understanding 5 (case style)

The directors of LM would like to avoid increasing staff costs in the statement of profit or loss and are considering offering employees a share based payment scheme in lieu of awarding pay rises. Any such scheme would vest after three years.

The directors are unsure about how such a scheme would be recorded in the financial statements and would like to know if there is a significant difference in accounting treatment depending on whether they choose a share option scheme or share appreciation rights scheme.

Required:

Prepare a briefing note to the directors of LM explaining how the financial statements would be affected by the introduction of both types of share based payment scheme and whether it will satisfy their objective of avoiding an increase in staff costs.

Test your understanding 6 (further OTQs)

(1) JKL granted share options to its 300 employees on 1 January 20X9. Each employee will receive 1,000 share options provided they continue to work for JKL for 3 years from the grant date. The fair value of each option at the grant date was $1.22.

The actual and expected staff movement over the 3 years to 31 December 20Y1 is provided below:

In 20X9 25 employees left and another 40 were expected to leave over the next two years.

In 20Y0 a further 15 employees left and another 20 were expected to leave the following year.

Calculate the charge to JKL's statement of profit or loss for the year ended 31 December 20Y0 in respect of the share options.

(2) EAU granted 1,000 share appreciation rights (SARs) to its 300 employees on 1 January 20X9. To be eligible, employees must remain employed for 3 years from the date of issue and the rights must be exercised in January 20Y2, with settlement due in cash.

By 31 December 20Y0, 60 staff had left in total and a further 10 were expected to leave in the following year.

The fair value of each SAR was $7 at 1 January 20X9, $8 at 31 December 20X9 and $12 at 31 December 20Y0.

An expense of $621,333 was recognised in the year ended 31 December 20X9 in respect of the scheme.

Prepare the accounting entry to record the expense associated with the SARs for the year to 31 December 20Y0 in accordance with IFRS 2 Share-based Payments.

Dr

Cr

5 Chapter summary

```
                          IFRS 2
                            ┊
                            ┊
                    Share based
                    payments
                    • What it is
                    • Types of
                      transactions
                    • Basic principles
              ┊                        ┊
         ┊                                   ┊

  Equity settled share          Cash settled share
  based payments                based payments
  • Measurement                 • Measurement
    – at grant date               – remeasure each
  • Allocating the                  year-end
    expense to                  • Allocating the
    reporting periods             expense to reporting
  Dr P&L                          periods
  Cr Equity                     Dr P&L
                                Cr Liability
```

Test your understanding answers

Test your understanding 1 (integration question)

	20X5	20X6	20X7
Share options	40,000	40,000	40,000
Expected to vest	85%	90%	(3,700)*
	34,000	36,000	36,300
Fair value at grant date	$20	$20	$20
Total cost	$680,000	$720,000	$726,000
Proportion of vesting period passed	1/3	2/3	3/3
Balance on equity reserve	$226,667	$480,000	$726,000
Cost charged to statement of p/l (= equity c/f – equity b/f)	$226,667	$253,333	$246,000

* of the 400 staff 37 have left by the end of the 3 year period. Each staff member had the right to exercise 100 share options, which would have amounted to 3,700 in total. This leaves 36,300 remaining legitimate options.

Test your understanding 2 (OTQ style)

The journal entry in year 2 is:

Dr Staff costs $400,000

Cr Equity $400,000

At the end of year two the amount recognised in equity should be $720,000 (1m × 9 × 20c × 2/5).

At the end of year one the amount recognised in equity was $320,000.

Therefore the charge to the statement of profit or loss for year two is $400,000 (720,000 – 320,000).

Test your understanding 3 (integration question)

Year	Liability at reporting date	Expense for year
	$	$
20X1 ((100–5–12) × 100 × $1 × 1/3)	2,767	2,767
20X2 ((100–5–10–15) × 100 × $2 × 2/3)	9,333	6,566
20X3 ((100–5–10–18) × 100 × $4)	26,800	17,467

Test your understanding 4 (OTQ style)

Journal entry for year ended 31 December 20X7 is:

Dr Staff costs $279,000

Cr Liability $279,000

(500 – 15 – 20) × 100 × $12 × 1/2 = $279,000

Test your understanding 5 (case style)

Briefing note to directors of LM

Share based payments are governed by IFRS 2. The main aim of this accounting standard is to ensure that entities recognise a suitable expense in the statement of profit or loss for any share-based payment scheme they enter into.

The employers are incurring the share-based payments to pay a 3rd party for goods or services acquired, or an employee for their services during employment. The entity should ensure a cost is matched against any benefits they receive. Therefore adopting either a share option scheme or a share appreciation rights scheme will result in an increase in staff costs over the proposed three year period of the scheme.

For both types of scheme, the expense to be recognised is based on the entity's expectation of how many options/rights will vest at the end of the scheme period. The expense is then recognised over this three year period. Expectations are likely to change in each period, depending on staff turnover, and therefore the expense will not necessarily be the same each year.

There are two distinct differences between a share option scheme and a share appreciation rights scheme: one in how the scheme is reflected in the statement of financial position and the second in how it is measured.

Share option scheme

This is an example of an 'equity-settled' share-based payment, where the employees will exercise options to acquire shares at the end of the vesting period and therefore the entity will be required to issue equity instruments. The expense of this type of scheme is based on the fair value of the options at the date they are granted. The accounting entry to record the expense each year is:

Dr Staff costs

Cr Equity reserve

Share appreciation rights (SARs) scheme

A SARs scheme is an example of a 'cash-settled' share-based payment, where the entity will be required to pay cash to the employees at the end of the vesting period. As the entity has an obligation to pay cash at a later date this results in the requirement to recognise a liability and the journal entry each year is:

Dr Staff costs

Cr Liability

As the share price changes, so does the obligation of the entity, and therefore changes in the fair value of the rights should be reflected in the expense each year.

Summary

In conclusion, both schemes would result in an increase in staff costs over the next three years. The amount of the expense would be based on the fair value of the options at the grant date in a share option scheme. However, with a SARs scheme the fair value is re-measured at each reporting date and the change in fair value is therefore also recognised in the staff costs.

Test your understanding 6 (further OTQs)

(1) **The statement of profit or loss charge is $99,633**

20X9:

$(300 - 25 - 40) \times 1,000 \times \$1.22 = \$286,700$ over 3 years = $95,567 charge for 20X9

20Y0:

$(300 - 25 - 15 - 20) \times 1,000 \times \$1.22 = \$292,800 \times 2/3$ years = $195,200 recognisable to date

Less amount recognised in 20X9 = $195,200 − $95,567 = $99,633 charge for 20Y0

(2) **Dr P/L staff costs $1,218,667**

    Cr Liability $1,218,667

20Y0:

Eligible employees $(300 - 60 - 10) = 230$

Equivalent cost of SARs = 230 employees × 1,000 rights × FV $12 = $2,760,000

Cumulative amount to be recognised as a liability = $2,760,000 × 2/3 years = $1,840,000

Less amount previously recognised = $1,840,000 − $621,333 = $1,218,667

Earnings per share

Chapter learning objectives

B4. Produce the disclosures for earnings per share.

(a) Calculate basic and diluted earnings per share, in accordance with IAS 33.

1 Session content

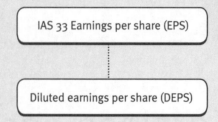

2 Earnings per share

Earnings per share (EPS) is widely regarded as the most important indicator of a company's performance.

It is also used in the calculation of the price-earnings ratio, a ratio closely monitored by analysts for listed companies. The price earnings ratio is equal to market price per share divided by earnings per share and gives an indicator of the level of confidence in the company by the market.

Consequently, EPS is the topic of its own accounting standard, IAS 33, which details rules on its calculation and presentation to ensure consistent treatment and comparability between companies.

Basic EPS

The basic EPS calculation is:

$$EPS = \frac{Earnings}{Number\ of\ shares}$$

This is expressed as dollars or cents per share (cents if the amount is less than $1).

- Earnings: Net profit attributable to ordinary equity shareholders of the parent entity, i.e. group profit after tax less profit attributable to non-controlling interests and irredeemable preference share dividends.

- Number of shares: Weighted average number of ordinary shares on a time weighted basis.

Issue of shares at full market price

An issue at full market price brings additional resources to the entity, but the impact on earnings is only from the date of issue. Therefore the number of shares are time apportioned.

Example 1 – Issue of shares at market price

A has earnings of $300,000 during the year ended 31 December 20X6. On 1 January 20X6 A had share capital of 100,000 $1 shares. On 1 March 20X6 a further 60,000 shares were issued at $3.25 per share.

Calculation of basic EPS for year ended 31 December 20X6

$$\text{EPS} = \frac{\text{Earnings}}{\text{Number of shares}}$$

$$\text{EPS} = \frac{\$300,000}{(100,000 \times 2/12) + (160,000 \times 10/12)}$$

$$\text{EPS} = \frac{\$300,000}{150,000}$$

EPS = $2 per share

Test your understanding 1 (integration question)

A company issued 200,000 shares at market price ($3.00) on 1 July 20X8. There was no issue of shares in the year ended 31 December 20X7.

Relevant information

	20X8	20X7
Profit attributable to the ordinary shareholders for the year ending 31 December	$550,000	$460,000
Number of ordinary shares in issue at 31 December	1,000,000	800,000

Required:

Calculate the EPS for the years ended 31 December 20X7 and 20X8.

Test your understanding 2 (OTQ style)

Gerard's earnings for the year ended 31 December 20X4 are $2,208,000. On 1 January 20X4, the issued share capital of Gerard was 8,280,000 ordinary shares of $1 each. The company issued 3,312,000 shares at full market value on 30 June 20X4.

Required:

Calculate the EPS for Gerard for the year ended 31 December 20X4.

Bonus issue

A bonus issue:

- does not provide additional resources to the issuer.
- means that the shareholder owns the same proportion of the business before and after the issue.

In the calculation of EPS:

- the bonus shares are deemed to have always been in issue and therefore are reflected for the full period.
- the comparative figures are also restated to include the bonus shares.

The EPS calculation becomes:

$$EPS = \frac{\text{Earnings}}{\text{No. of shares before bonus} \times \text{bonus fraction}}$$

$$\text{Bonus fraction} = \frac{\text{No. of shares after bonus issue}}{\text{No. of shares before bonus issue}}$$

E.g. Company B holds 100,000 shares and makes a 1 for 10 bonus issue. 100,000/10 = 10,000 new shares issued.

$$\text{Bonus fraction} = \frac{110,000}{100,000} = \frac{11}{10}$$

- to adjust the comparative figures, multiply the previous year's basic EPS by the inverse of the bonus fraction, i.e. 100,000/110,000 or 10/11.

Example 2 – Bonus issue

A company makes a bonus issue of one new share for every five existing shares held on 1 July 20X8.

	20X8	20X7
Profit attributable to the ordinary shareholders for the year ending 31 December	$550,000	$460,000
Number of ordinary shares in issue at 31 December	1,200,000	1,000,000

Basic EPS for year ended 31 December 20X8 (with comparative)

Calculation of EPS in 20X8 accounts.

$$20X8 \quad \frac{\$550,000}{1,200,000} \quad = 45.8c$$

$$20X7 \quad \frac{\$460,000}{1,200,000} \quad = 38.3c$$

In the example above, the computation for the comparative has been reworked in full. However, if last year's EPS is given then calculate the comparative EPS by multiplying this by the bonus fraction inverted.

Last year's EPS = 46c ($460,000/1m)

The bonus fraction is:

$$\frac{1,200,000}{1,000,000} \quad \text{or} \quad \frac{6}{5}$$

Therefore, the comparative restated is

46c × 5/6 = 38.3c

Test your understanding 3 (integration question)

At 1 April 20X2, Dorabella had 7 million $1 ordinary shares in issue. It made a bonus issue of one share for every seven held on 31 August 20X2. Its earnings for the year were $1,150,000.

Dorabella's EPS for the year ended 31 March 20X2 was 10.7c.

Required:

Calculate the EPS for the year ending 31 March 20X3, together with the comparative EPS for 20X2 that would be presented in the 20X3 accounts.

Test your understanding 4 (OTQ style)

At 1 May 20X3 Rose had 900 million $1 ordinary shares in issue. It made a bonus issue of one share for every 9 held on 1 September 20X3. It's profit before tax for the year was $800m and the income tax expense for the year was $250m.

Required:

Calculate the basic EPS for the year ended 30 April 20X4. Give your answer in cents.

Test your understanding 5 (OTQ style)

At 1 May 20X3 Rose had 900 million $1 ordinary shares in issue. It made a bonus issue of one share for every 9 held on 1 September 20X3. Rose's EPS for the year ended 30 April 20X3 was 40.0c.

Required:

Calculate the comparative EPS that would be presented in the financial statements for the year ended 30 April 20X4.

Rights issue

Rights issues:

- contribute additional resources; and
- are normally priced below full market price.

Therefore, they combine the characteristics of issues at full market price and bonus issues.

Determining the weighted average capital, therefore, involves two steps as follows:

(1) adjust for the bonus element in the rights issue, by multiplying capital in issue before the rights issue by the following fraction:

$$\frac{\text{Actual cum rights price (CRP)}}{\text{Theoretical ex rights price (TERP)}}$$

- The cum rights price will be given to you in the exam question. It is the share price on the last trading day before the rights issue, i.e. the price of a share 'including' the rights.

- The theoretical ex-rights price is the theoretical share price after the rights issue has occurred. This must be calculated.

(2) calculate the weighted average capital in the issue on a time apportioned basis.

Illustration 1 – Theoretical ex rights price

The theoretical ex rights price was introduced in the chapter on Long term finance. Here's a reminder of how to calculate it.

C makes a 1 for 4 rights issue at $1.90 per share.

The cum rights price of C's shares is $2.00.

Calculation of the TERP

	Number of shares	×	Price	=	Value
Before rights	4	×	2.00	=	8.00
Rights issue	1	×	1.90	=	1.90
	___				___
After rights		×	?		

We are looking for the theoretical ex rights price (TERP), i.e. the price of a share after the rights issue, denoted by a question mark above.

Simply calculate the total value after the issue and divide it by the total number of shares after the issue.

	Number of shares	×	Price	=	Value
Before rights	4	×	2.00	=	8.00
Rights issue	1	×	1.90	=	1.90
After rights	5	×	?		9.90

TERP = 9.90/5 = 1.98

The fraction to therefore apply (to the shares before the rights issue) to adjust for the bonus element is:

CRP/TERP = 2/1.98

Example 3 – Rights issue

A company issued one new share for every two existing shares held by way of rights at $1.50 per share on 1 July 20X8. Pre-issue market price was $3.00 per share.

Relevant information

	20X8	20X7
Profit attributable to the ordinary shareholders for the year ending 31 December	$550,000	$460,000
Number of ordinary shares in issue at 31 December	1,200,000	800,000

Calculation of basic EPS for year ended 31 December 20X8, with comparative

20X8

$$\frac{\text{Earnings}}{\text{Weighted average number of shares (W1)}} = \frac{\$550,000}{1,080,000} = 50.9 \text{ cents}$$

20X7

The prior year EPS must be adjusted to reflect the bonus element in the rights issue.

$$EPS = 57.5c\ (W3) \times \frac{\$2.50\ (W2)}{\$3.00} = 47.9\ \text{cents}$$

NB: To restate the EPS for the previous year simply multiply EPS by the inverse of the rights issue bonus fraction.

(W1) 20X8 Weighted average number of shares

The number of shares before the rights issue must be adjusted for the bonus element in the rights issue using the theoretical ex rights price.

6/12 × 800,000 × 3.00/2.50 (W2)	480,000
6/12 × 1,200,000	600,000
	1,080,000

(W2) Theoretical ex rights price

	2 shares	@ $3.00	$6.00
	1 share	@ $1.50	$1.50
	3 shares		$7.50
Theoretical ex rights price	= $7.50/3		$2.50

(W3)

20X7 EPS	=	$460,000
		800,000
	=	57.5 cents

Test your understanding 6 (integration question)

On 31 December 20X1, the issued share capital of a company consisted of 4,000,000 ordinary shares of 25c each. On 1 July 20X2 the company made a rights issue in the proportion of 1 for 4 at 50c per share when the shares were quoted at $1.15. The profit after tax for the year ended 31 December 20X2 was $425,000. The reported earnings per share for the year ended 31 December 20X1 was 8c.

Required:

Calculate the basic EPS for the year ended 31 December 20X2, together with the comparative for 20X1 that would be presented in the 20X2 financial statements.

Test your understanding 7 (OTQ style)

At 1 May 20X3 Rose had 900 million $1 ordinary shares in issue. Its earnings for the year ended 30 April 20X4 was $550m.

On 1 July 20X3, a rights issue took place of 1 share for every 4 held at $2. The market price of each share immediately before the rights issue was $2.50.

Required:

Complete the formula below to provide the bonus fraction that would be applied to the pre-issue number of shares in the calculation of the weighted average number of shares of Rose for the year ended 30 April 20X4.

$$\frac{\$}{\$}$$

Test your understanding 8 (OTQ style)

At 1 January 20X3 Lily had 400 million $1 ordinary shares in issue. On 1 August 20X3, a rights issue took place of 1 share for every 5 held at $2.75. The market price of each share immediately before the rights issue was $3.25.

The theoretical ex rights price of the rights issue is $3.17.

Required:

Calculate the weighted average number of shares that would be used in the basic earnings per share calculation for the year ended 31 December 20X3. Give your answer in millions to one decimal place.

Test your understanding 9 (OTQ style)

At 1 May 20X3 Rose had 900 million $1 ordinary shares in issue. Its earnings for the year ended 30 April 20X4 was $550m and its EPS for the previous year, ended 30 April 20X3, was 40.0c.

On 1 July 20X3, a rights issue took place of 1 share for every 4 held at $2. The market price of each share immediately before the rights issue was $2.50.

Required:

Calculate the comparative basic EPS that would be reflected in the financial statements for the year ended 30 April 20X4. Give your answers in cents to 1 decimal place.

Test your understanding 10 (case style)

XYZ has made a couple of share issues over the past few years. The directors have been reviewing the calculation of the basic earnings per share and have noticed that the calculation of the weighted average number of shares is not consistent each year. The first share issue was a bonus issue to existing shareholders. The second was an issue at full market price.

Required:

Prepare a brief note to the directors explaining why a bonus issue and issue at full market price are treated differently in the calculation of basic earnings per share.

3 Diluted earnings per share (DEPS)

Introduction

Equity share capital may change in the future owing to circumstances which exist now. The provision of a diluted EPS figure attempts to alert shareholders to the potential impact of these changes on the EPS figure.

Examples of dilutive factors are:

- the conversion terms for convertible bonds (or convertible preference shares)
- the exercise price for options (or subscription price for warrants).

When the potential ordinary shares are issued the total number of shares in issue will increase and this can have a dilutive effect on EPS i.e. it may fall. It will fall where the increase in shares outweighs any increase in profits, e.g. from a reduction in finance costs once debt has been converted.

Basic principles of calculation

To deal with potential ordinary shares, adjust basic earnings and number of shares assuming convertibles, options, etc. had converted to equity shares on the first day of the accounting period, or on the date of issue, if later.

DEPS is calculated as follows:

$$\frac{\text{Earnings} + \text{notional extra earnings}}{\text{Number of shares} + \text{notional extra shares}}$$

Importance of DEPS
The basic EPS figure could be misleading to users if at some future time the number of shares in issue will increase without a proportionate increase in resources. For example, if an entity has issued bonds convertible at a later date into ordinary shares, on conversion the number of ordinary shares will rise, no fresh capital will enter the entity and earnings will therefore only rise by the savings made by no longer having to pay the post-tax amount of interest on the bonds. Often the earnings increase is proportionately less than the increase in the shares in issue. This effect is referred to as 'dilution' and the shares to be issued are called 'dilutive potential ordinary shares'.

IAS 33 therefore requires an entity to disclose the DEPS, as well as the basic EPS, calculated using current earnings but assuming that the worst possible future dilution has already happened. Existing shareholders can look at the DEPS to see the effect on current profitability of commitments already entered into to issue ordinary shares in the future.

For the purpose of calculating DEPS, the number of ordinary shares should be the weighted average number of ordinary shares calculated as for basic EPS, plus the weighted average number of ordinary shares which would be issued on the conversion of all the dilutive potential ordinary shares into ordinary shares. Dilutive potential ordinary shares are deemed to have been converted into ordinary shares at the beginning of the period or, if later, the date of the issue of the potential ordinary shares.

Convertible debt

The principles of convertible bonds and convertible preference shares are similar and will be dealt with together.

If the convertible bonds/preference shares had been converted:

- the interest/dividend would be saved therefore earnings would be higher
- the number of shares would increase.

Note: Interest on bonds is tax deductible however preference dividends do not attract tax relief. Therefore, the interest adjustment should only be reflected net of tax in the case of bonds.

Note: If there is an option to convert the debt into a variable number of ordinary shares depending on when conversion takes place, the maximum possible number of additional shares is used in the calculation.

Example 4 – Convertible debt

A company has the following balances:

- $500,000 in 10% cumulative irredeemable preference shares of $1
- $1,000,000 in ordinary shares of 25c = 4,000,000 shares.

Income taxes are 30%.

On 1 April 20X1, the company issued convertible bonds for cash. Assuming the conversion was fully subscribed there would be an increase of 1,550,000 ordinary shares in issue.

The liability element of the bonds is $1,250,000 and the effective interest rate is 8%, resulting in an annual gross interest charge of $100,000.

Trading results for the years ended 31 December were as follows:

	20X2	20X1
	$	$
Profit before interest and tax	1,100,000	991,818
Interest on convertible bonds	(100,000)	(75,000)
Profit before tax	1,000,000	916,818
Income tax	(300,000)	(275,045)
Profit after tax	700,000	641,773

Calculation of basic and diluted EPS for years ended 31 December 20X1 and 20X2.

	20X2	20X1
Basic EPS	$	$
Profit after tax	700,000	641,773
Less: Preference dividend (10% × $500,000)	(50,000)	(50,000)
Earnings	650,000	591,773
EPS based on 4,000,000 shares	16.25c	14.8c

DEPS

Earnings as above	650,000	591,773
Notional extra earnings:		
Interest on the convertible bonds (only 9 months in 20X1)	100,000	75,000
Less: Income tax on interest at 30%	(30,000)	(22,500)
Adjusted earnings	720,000	644,273
EPS based on 5,550,000 shares	13.0c	11.6c

Convertible preference shares are dealt with on the same basis, except that often they do not qualify for tax relief so there is no tax saving foregone to be adjusted for.

Test your understanding 11 (OTQ style)

A company had 8.28 million shares in issue at the start of the year and made no new issue of shares during the year ended 31 December 20X4, but on that date it had in issue convertible loan stock 20X6-20X9.

Assuming the conversion was fully subscribed there would be an increase of 2,070,000 ordinary shares in issue. The liability element of the loan stock is $2,300,000 and the effective interest rate is 10%. Assume a tax rate of 30%.

The earnings for the year were $2,208,000 giving rise to a basic earnings per share of 26.7 cents.

Required:

Calculate the fully diluted EPS for the year ended 31 December 20X4.

Options and warrants to subscribe for shares

An option or warrant gives the holder the right to buy shares at some time in the future at a predetermined price.

The cash received by the entity when the option is exercised will be less than the market price of the shares, as the option will only be exercised if the exercise price is lower than the market price. The increase in resources does not match the increase there would be in resources if the issue of shares were at market value. The options will therefore have a dilutive effect on EPS.

The total number of shares issued on the exercise of the **option** or **warrant** is split into two:

- the number of shares that would have been issued if the cash received had been used to buy shares at fair value (using the average price of the shares during the period);

- the remainder, which are treated like a **bonus issue** (i.e. as having been issued for no consideration).

The number of shares issued for no consideration is added to the weighted average number of shares when calculating the DEPS.

These 'free' shares are equal to:

$$\text{No. of options} \quad \times \quad \frac{FV - EP}{FV}$$

FV = fair value of the share price

EP = exercise price of the shares

Example 5 – Options

On 1 January 20X7, a company has 4 million ordinary shares in issue and issues options over another million shares. The profit after tax for the year attributable to ordinary shareholders is $500,000.

During the year to 31 December 20X7 the average fair value of one ordinary share was $3 and the exercise price for the shares under option was $2.

Calculation of basic EPS and DEPS for the year ended 31 December 20X7.

$$\text{Basic EPS} = \frac{\$500,000}{4,000,000} = 12.5c$$

Options

	$
Earnings	500,000
Number of shares	
Basic	4,000,000
Options (W1)	333,333
	4,333,333

$$\text{The DEPS is therefore} \quad \frac{\$500,000}{4,333,333} = 11.5c$$

(W1) Number of free shares issued

$$\text{Free shares} = \text{No. of options} \times \frac{FV - EP}{FV}$$

$$\text{Free shares} = 1,000,000 \times \frac{3.00 - 2.00}{3.00} = 333,333$$

Test your understanding 12 (OTQ style)

A company had 8.28 million shares in issue at the start of the year and made no issue of shares during the year ended 31 December 20X4, but on that date there were outstanding options to purchase 920,000 ordinary $1 shares at $1.70 per share. The average fair value of ordinary shares was $1.80. Earnings for the year ended 31 December 20X4 were $2,208,000 giving rise to a basic EPS of 26.7c.

Required:

Calculate the fully DEPS for the year ended 31 December 20X4.

Test your understanding 13 (OTQ style)

On 1 January 20X1 Pillbox, a listed entity, had 10 million $1 ordinary shares in issue. The earnings for the year ended 31 December 20X1 were $5,950,000. Pillbox made no new issue of shares during the year. The basic earnings per share was therefore 59.5 cents.

Pillbox is subject to income tax at a rate of 30%.

On 1 January 20X1 Pillbox issued convertible bonds. Assuming the conversion was fully subscribed there would be an increase of 2,340,000 ordinary shares in issue. The liability element of the bonds is $2,600,000 and the effective interest rate is 10%.

Required:

Calculate the diluted EPS for the year ended 31 December 20X1.

Test your understanding 14 (OTQ style)

On 1 January 20X1 Pillbox, a listed entity, had 10 million $1 ordinary shares in issue. The earnings for the year ended 31 December 20X1 were $5,950,000 and Pillbox made no new issue of shares during the year. The basic earnings per share for the year was therefore 59.5c.

Throughout the year ended 31 December 20X1 there were outstanding options to purchase 74,000 ordinary $1 shares at $2.50 per share. The average fair value of one ordinary $1 share was $4.

Required:

Calculate the diluted EPS for the year ended 31 December 20X1.

Test your understanding 15 (further OTQs)

Questions (1) to (3) below are all based on the following scenario:

On 1 January 20X9 CSA, a listed entity, had 3,000,000 $1 ordinary shares in issue. On 1 May 20X9, CSA made a bonus issue of 1 for 3.

On 1 September 20X9, CSA issued 2,000,000 $1 ordinary shares for $3.20 each. The profit before tax of CSA for the year ended 31 December 20X9 was $1,040,000. The income tax expense for the year was $270,000.

The basic earnings per share for the year ended 31 December 20X8 was 15.4 cents.

On 1 November 20X9 CSA issued convertible loan stock. Assuming the conversion was fully subscribed there would be an increase of 2,400,000 ordinary shares in issue. The liability element of the loan stock is $4,000,000 and the effective interest rate is 7%.

CSA is subject to income tax at a rate of 30%.

Required:

(1) Calculate the basic earnings per share to be reported in the financial statements of CSA for the year ended 31 December 20X9 in accordance with the requirements of IAS 33 Earnings Per Share.

(2) Calculate the comparative EPS that would be presented alongside the basic EPS in the financial statements for the year ended 31 December 20X9 in accordance with the requirements of IAS 33 Earnings Per Share.

(3) Calculate the diluted earnings per share for the year ended 31 December 20X9, in accordance with the requirements of IAS 33 Earnings Per Share.

The following scenario relates to question 4 only.

On 1 July 20X2 SJL, a listed entity, had 6 million $1 ordinary shares in issue. On 1 March 20X3, SJL made a rights issue of 1 for every 3 shares held at a price of $4. The market price for the shares on the last day of quotation cum rights was $5 per share. SJL's earnings for the year ended 30 June 20X3 were $4.5 million.

(4) Calculate the basic earnings per share to be reported in the financial statements of SJL for the year ended 30 June 20X3, in accordance with the requirements of IAS 33 Earnings Per Share.

The following scenario relates to question 5 only.

The ordinary shareholders of DPR held options to purchase 200,000 $1 ordinary shares at $4.25 per share. The average fair value of one $1 ordinary share in the period in question was $5.15.

(5) What number of shares should be added to the denominator of the diluted EPS calculation to reflect the free shares that exist within the options (to the nearest whole number of shares)?

4 Chapter summary

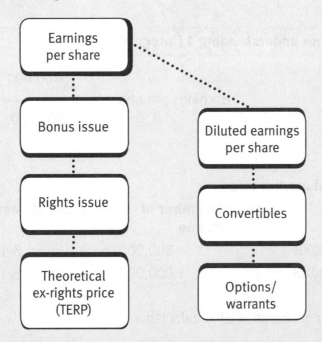

Test your understanding answers

Test your understanding 1 (integration question)

20X7   Earnings per share = $\dfrac{\$460,000}{800,000}$ = 57.5c

Issue at market price

Date	Actual number of shares	Fraction of year	Total
1 Jan 20X8	800,000	6/12	400,000
1 July 20X8	1,000,000	6/12	500,000
Number of shares in EPS calculation			900,000

20X8   Earnings per share = $\dfrac{\$550,000}{900,000}$ = 61.1c

Since the 200,000 shares have only generated additional resources towards the earning of profits for half a year, the number of new shares is adjusted proportionately. Note that the approach is to use the earnings figure for the period without adjustment, but divide by the average number of shares weighted on a time basis.

Test your understanding 2 (OTQ style)

Issue at full market price

Date	Actual number of shares	Fraction of year	Total
1 January 20X4	8,280,000	6/12	4,140,000
30 June 20X4	11,592,000 (W1)	6/12	5,796,000
Number of shares in EPS calculation			9,936,000

(W1) New number of shares

Original number	8,280,000
New issue	3,312,000
New number	11,592,000

The earnings per share for 20X4 would now be calculated as:

$$\frac{\$2,208,000}{9,936,000} = 22.2c$$

Test your understanding 3 (integration question)

The number of shares issued on 31 August 20X2 is 7,000,000 × 1/7 = 1,000,000

The EPS for 20X3 is 1,150,000/8,000,000 × 100 c = 14.4c

The bonus fraction is (7 + 1)/7 = 8/7

20X2 adjusted comparative = 10.7 × 7/8 (bonus fraction inverted) = 9.4c.

Test your understanding 4 (OTQ style)

Basic EPS = 55c

The number of shares after the issue on 1 September 20X3 is 900m × 10/9 = 1,000m

The earnings for the year ended 30 April 20X4 is $800m – $250m = $550m

Therefore, the EPS for the year ended 30 April 20X4 is $550m/1,000m = 55c

Test your understanding 5 (OTQ style)

Comparative EPS = 36.0c

The bonus fraction = 10/9 (1 new share for every 9 held).

The comparative = 40.0 × 9/10 (bonus fraction inverted) = 36.0c.

Test your understanding 6 (integration question)

20X2 EPS

$$\text{EPS} = \frac{\$425,000}{4,754,902 \text{ (W1)}} = 8.9\text{c per share}$$

20X1 EPS

Applying correction factor to calculate adjusted comparative figure of EPS:

$$8\text{c} \times \frac{\text{Theoretical ex rights price}}{\text{Actual cum rights price}} = 8\text{c} \times \frac{1.02 \text{ (W2)}}{1.15} = 7.1\text{c per share}$$

(W1) Current year weighted average number of shares

The number of shares before the rights issue must be adjusted for the bonus element in the rights issue using the theoretical ex rights price.

6/12 × 4,000,000 × 1.15/1.02 (W2)	2,254,902
6/12 × 5,000,000 (*)	2,500,000
	4,754,902

(*) 4m × 5/4 = 5m

(W2) **Theoretical ex rights price**

			$
Prior to rights issue	4 shares	worth 4 × $1.15 =	4.60
Taking up rights	1 share	cost 50c =	0.50
	—		——
	5		5.10
	—		——

i.e. theoretical ex rights price of each share is $5.10 ÷ 5 = $1.02

Test your understanding 7 (OTQ style)

The fraction to apply to the pre-issue number of shares is:

$$\frac{\$2.50}{\$2.40} \text{ (W1)}$$

(W1) **Theoretical ex rights price**

			$
Prior to rights issue	4 shares	worth 4 × $2.50 =	10.00
Taking up rights	1 share	cost $2.00 =	2.00
	—		——
	5		12.00
	—		——

i.e. theoretical ex rights price of each share is $12 ÷ 5 = $2.40

Test your understanding 8 (OTQ style)

Weighted average number of shares = 439.2 million

7/12 × 400m × 3.25/3.17	239.2m
5/12 × 480m (*)	200.0m
	————
	439.2m
	————

(*) 400m × 6/5 = 480m

Test your understanding 9 (OTQ style)

Comparative EPS = 38.4 cents per share

$$40c \times \frac{2.4 \ (W1)}{2.5} = 38.4c \text{ per share}$$

(W1) Theoretical ex rights price

			$
Prior to rights issue	4 shares	worth 4 × $2.50 =	10.00
Taking up rights	1 share	cost $2.00 =	2.00
	—		——
	5		12.00
	—		——

i.e. theoretical ex rights price of each share is $12 ÷ 5 = $2.40

The rights bonus fraction to apply in the weighted average calculation for the current year is 2.50/2.40.

This is inverted and multiplied by the previous year's EPS in order to restate the comparative.

Test your understanding 10 (case style)

Note to directors

You have correctly noticed that the calculation of the weighted average number of shares for the basic earnings per share is different depending on whether a bonus issue or full market price issue has been made. The reason for this difference is explained below.

A bonus issue does not raise any new finance and therefore the profit for the year will have been generated with the same level of resources throughout the year. As the issue results in no additional resources it is treated as if it has always been in existence. For this reason, comparative figures also need to be restated.

The issue at full market price brings additional resources which will impact on profits from the date of issue. Therefore a weighted average number of shares is used to calculate EPS, so that the numerator and denominator are stated on a like for like basis.

Also, please note that the proportions held by shareholders after a bonus issues remain unaffected whilst the proportions of shares held by shareholders after a full market prices share issue may changes (as new investors may acquire the shares).

Please let me know if you have any further queries on the matter.

Test your understanding 11 (OTQ style)

Diluted EPS = 22.9 cents per share

If this loan stock was converted to shares the impact on earnings would be as follows.

	$	$
Basic earnings		2,208,000
Add notional interest saved		
($2,300,000 × 10%)	230,000	
Less tax relief foregone $230,000 × 30%	(69,000)	
		161,000
Revised earnings		2,369,000

Number of shares if loan converted

	$
Basic number of shares	8,280,000
Notional extra shares	2,070,000
Revised number of shares	10,350,000

$$DEPS = \frac{\$2,369,000}{10,350,000} = 22.9c$$

Test your understanding 12 (OTQ style)

	$
Earnings	2,208,000
Number of shares	
Basic	8,280,000
Options (W1)	51,111
	8,331,111

The DEPS is therefore
$$\frac{\$2{,}208{,}000}{8{,}331{,}111} = 26.5c$$

(W1) Number of free shares issued

$$\text{Free shares} = \text{No. of shares under option} \times \frac{FV - EP}{FV}$$

$$\text{Free shares} = 920{,}000 \times \frac{1.80 - 1.70}{1.80} = 51{,}111$$

Tutorial note:

An alternative way of viewing the above calculation (of the free shares) is as follows:

Finance raised via exercise of options would be $1.70 \times 920{,}000 = \$1{,}564{,}000$

To raise this amount of finance via a market price issue would require $1{,}564{,}000/\$1.80 = 868{,}889$ shares

Therefore, the number of free shares awarded in the option scheme $= 920{,}000 - 868{,}889 = 51{,}111$

Test your understanding 13 (OTQ style)

Diluted EPS

Earnings (5.95m + (10% × $2.6m × 70%))	$6,132k
Shares (10m + 2.34m)	12,340k
	————
Diluted EPS	49.7c
	————

Test your understanding 14 (OTQ style)

Diluted EPS

Earnings	$5,950k
Shares (10m + (74k × (4 − 2.50)/4))	10,028k
Diluted EPS	59.3c

Test your understanding 15 (further OTQs)

(1) **Basic earnings per share = 16.5 cents**

Profit after tax ($1,040,000 − $270,000)		$770,000
Weighted average number of shares		
At 1 January 20X9	3,000,000	
Bonus issue	1,000,000	
Full market price issue (2,000,000 × 4/12)	666,667	
		4,666,667
Basic EPS for 20X9 $770,000/4,666,667		16.5 cents

(2) **Comparative EPS (restated) = 11.6 cents**

Last year's EPS 15.4c × 3/4 bonus fraction inverted = 11.6c

(3) **Diluted earnings per share = 11.4 cents**

Reported profit after tax (as in answer (1))	$770,000	
Plus post tax saving of finance costs		
(70% × 7% × $4m × 2/12)	$32,667	
		$802,667
Weighted average number of shares:		
As reported in answer (1)	4,666,667	
Dilution from potential share issue	2,400,000	
		7,066,667
Fully diluted EPS $802,667/7,066,667		11.4 cents

(4) Basic EPS = 65.4 cents

$$EPS = \frac{\$4,500,000}{6,877,193 \ (W1)} = 65.4 \text{ cents}$$

(W1) Current year weighted average number of shares

The number of shares before the rights issue must be adjusted for the bonus element in the rights issue using the theoretical ex rights price.

8/12 × 6m × 5/4.75 (W2)	4,210,526
4/12 × 8m	2,666,667
	6,877,193

(W2) Theoretical ex rights price

			$
Prior to rights issue	3 shares	worth 3 × $5 =	15
Taking up rights	1 share	cost $4 =	4
	4		19

i.e. theoretical ex rights price of each share is $19 ÷ 4 = $4.75

(5) Number of free shares = 34,951

Free shares = 200,000 × (5.15 − 4.25)/5.15 = 34,951

Leases

Chapter learning objectives

B1. Produce consolidated primary financial statements, incorporating accounting transactions and adjustments, in accordance with relevant international accounting standards, in an ethical manner.

(c) Discuss the provisions of relevant international accounting standards in respect of the recognition and measurement of operating and finance leases, in accordance with IAS 17.

(d) Produce the accounting entries, in accordance with relevant international accounting standards.

(e) Discuss the ethical selection and adoption of relevant accounting policies and accounting estimates.

1 Session content

```
                    ┌─────────────┐
                    │   IAS 17    │
                    │   LEASES    │
                    └─────────────┘
```

```
┌──────────────────┐        ┌──────────────────┐
│ OPERATING LEASES │        │  FINANCE LEASES  │
└──────────────────┘        └──────────────────┘
```

```
        ┌──────────────────┐      ┌──────────────────┐
        │  ALLOCATION OF   │      │    ACCOUNTING    │
        │     INTEREST     │      │       AND        │
        └──────────────────┘      │    DISCLOSURE    │
                                  └──────────────────┘
```

```
        ┌──────────────────┐      ┌──────────────────┐
        │    ACTUARIAL     │      │     SUM OF       │
        │                  │      │    THE DIGITS    │
        └──────────────────┘      └──────────────────┘
```

2 Introduction

Definitions

IAS 17 *Leases* defines a lease as an agreement whereby the lessor conveys to the lessee, in return for a payment or series of payments, the right to use an asset for an agreed period of time.

Finance leases and operating leases

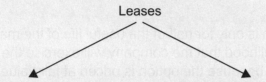

Leases

Finance Lease

'a lease that transfers all the risks and rewards of ownership. Title may or may not be transferred'

Operating lease

'a lease other than a finance lease'

Indications of a finance lease

To determine whether a lease is a finance or operating lease, the substance of the lease agreement should be considered. The following, individually or in combination, would normally lead to the conclusion that a lease is a finance lease:

- Legal title is transferred to the lessee at the end of the lease.

- The lessee has the option to purchase the asset for a price substantially below the fair value of the asset.

- The lease term is for the majority of the asset's useful life.

- The present value of the minimum lease payments amounts to substantially all of the fair value of the asset.

- The leased assets are of such a specialised nature that only the lessee can use them without major modification.

- The lessee bears losses arising from cancelling the lease.

- Lessee has ability to continue the lease for a secondary period at a rate below market rent.

Example 1 – classification of lease

A company has entered into a four-year lease for a machine, with lease rentals of $100,000 payable annually in advance, and with an optional secondary period of three years at rentals of 80%, 60% and 40% of the annual rental in the primary period. It is agreed that these rentals represent a fair commercial rate. The machine has a useful life of eight years and a cash value of $600,000.

Would this lease agreement be a finance lease or an operating lease?

Solution

The contracted lease term is only for half of the useful life of the machine and there is no strong likelihood that the company will exercise the option in four years' time, because the option is priced at fair value, not a discount. Thus the risks and rewards of ownership have not passed to the lessee and this lease should be treated as an operating lease.

3 Operating leases

Under an operating lease the risks and rewards of ownership lie with the lessor, not the lessee. Therefore it can be concluded that the lessee should not record the item being leased as an asset.

Accounting treatment for an operating lease

- Lease payments are charged to the statement of profit or loss on a straight line basis over the term of the lease, unless another systematic basis is more appropriate.

- Any difference between amounts charged and amounts paid will be recognised as prepayments or accruals in the statement of financial position.

Example 2 – operating lease

Zoo Ltd entered into a four year operating lease on 1 January 20X1 for a machine. The initial deposit is $1,000 on 1 January 20X1 followed by four annual payments of $1,000 in arrears on 31 December each year. The annual payments commence on 31 December 20X1.

What is the charge to the statement of profit or loss and what amount would appear on the statement of financial position at the end of the first year of the lease?

Total payments = $5,000 (deposit plus 4 × $1,000 payments)

Statement of profit or loss (extract)

	$
Operating lease expense ($5,000/4)	1,250

Statement of financial position (extract)

	$
Current assets	
Prepayments (paid $2,000 – $1,250 to the P/L)	750

Test your understanding 1 (integration question)

DJT hires a machine under an operating lease for three years with payments to be made as follows:

Year 1	$5,000
Year 2	$10,000
Year 3	$6,000

Prepare extracts from the statement of profit or loss and the statement of financial position for each of the three years.

Test your understanding 2 (OTQ style)

RLP entered into a three year operating lease on 1 May 20X2 for the use of an item of office equipment. It paid a deposit of $750 and will make lease payments of $500 on 30 April 20X3, 20X4 and 20X5.

In the year ended 30 April 20X3, RLP has recorded all payments related to the lease as an expense in the statement of profit or loss.

Calculate the correct expense to be recognised in the statement of profit or loss for the year ended 30 April 20X3.

Test your understanding 3 (OTQ style)

FGH entered into a four year operating lease on 1 April 20X2 for the use of an item of office equipment. It paid a deposit of $600 and will make lease payments of $1,200 on 31 March 20X3, 20X4, 20X5 and 20X6.

In the year ended 31 March 20X3, FGH has recorded all payments related to the lease as an expense in the statement of profit or loss.

Prepare the journal entry required to correct the accounting treatment.

4 Finance leases

Under a finance lease the risk and rewards of ownership lie with the lessee. Therefore, by applying substance over form the lessee should recognise the item being leased as an asset in its statement of financial position.

The outstanding lease rentals create a liability for the lessee, which, when applying substance over form, can be considered a loan.

The meaning of substance over form

In many types of transactions there is a difference between the commercial substance and the legal form:

*   Commercial substance reflects the financial reality of the transaction.

*   Legal form is the legal reality of the transaction.

Financial statements are generally required to reflect commercial substance rather than legal form. We've already seen an example of this in Financial Instruments, where redeemable preference shares are treated as debt rather than equity because of their substance.

Substance over form with a finance lease

When an asset is leased under a finance lease there is a difference between the legal form of that transaction and its commercial substance:

Legal form: the asset remains legally owned by the party leasing it out (the lessor).

Commercial substance: the party making the lease payments (the lessee) has the use of the asset for most or all of its useful life. The lessee has effectively purchased the asset by taking out a loan (the finance lease commitments).

Accounting treatment of the commercial substance of a lease

As the commercial substance of a finance lease is that the lessee is the effective owner of the asset the required accounting treatment is to:

*   record the asset as a non-current asset in the lessee's statement of financial position

*   record a liability in the lessee's statement of financial position for the lease payments payable to the lessor.

Summary of accounting entries

(1) At the **inception** of the lease:

Dr Non-current assets

Cr Finance lease liability

with the lower of:

- the present value of the minimum lease payment

or

- the fair value of the leased asset.

(2) At the **end** of each period of the lease:

Dr Depreciation expense (statement of profit or loss)

Cr Non-current assets

with the depreciation charge for the period.

(3) As each **rental is paid**:

Dr Finance lease liability

Cr Cash

with the rental paid

Dr Finance cost (statement of profit or loss)

Cr Finance lease liability

with the finance charge.

Recording a finance lease

Initial recording

At the start of the lease:

- the fair value or, if lower, the present value of the minimum lease payments (MLPs) should be included as a non-current asset, subject to depreciation
- the same amount (being the obligation to pay rentals) should be included as a loan, i.e. a liability.

In practice, the fair value of the asset or its cash price will often be a sufficiently close approximation to the present value of the MLPs and therefore can be used instead.

Depreciation

The non-current asset should be depreciated over the shorter of:

- the **useful life** of the asset (as in IAS 16)
- the **lease term**.

The lease term is essentially the period over which the lessee has the use of the asset. It includes:

- the primary (non-cancellable) period
- any secondary periods during which the lessee has the option to continue to lease the asset, provided that it is reasonably certain at the outset that this option will be exercised.

Allocation of interest

There are two main methods of allocating the finance cost over the lease period:

- actuarial method
- sum of digits method.

The actuarial method uses the interest rate implicit in the lease (the effective rate) and applies this to the outstanding balance on the liability each period. The liability is effectively being amortised and this treatment is consistent with other financial liabilities that we've seen in the Financial Instruments chapter.

The sum of digits method provides a reasonable approximation to the actuarial method and therefore can be used as an alternative.

Example 3 – allocation of interest

A nightclub hires a revolving dance floor for all its useful life. The dance floor was worth $94,000 on the first day of use, 1 January. The contract tells you that there are four payments of $30,000 to be made on the 31 December of each year and that the implicit rate of interest is 10.538%.

Required:

(a) Calculate the interest allocation on an actuarial basis.

(b) Calculate the interest allocation on a sum of digits basis.

	$
Total payments (4 × $30,000)	120,000
Value of asset	(94,000)
Total interest	26,000

(a) **Actuarial basis**

	Opening	Interest @ 10.538%	Revised total	Payment	Closing
1	94,000	9,906	103,906	(30,000)	73,906
2	73,906	7,788	81,694	(30,000)	51,694
3	51,694	5,447	57,141	(30,000)	27,141
4	27,141	2,859	30,000	(30,000)	–
		26,000			

The implicit rate of interest of 10.538% is used as a method to allocate the finance cost of $26,000 over the life of the lease. In the question payments are made in arrears, hence interest is calculated each year on the opening liability balance.

Note that if lease payments were made in advance each year, the payment would be deducted from the opening liability first and then the interest would be calculated based on the revised liability for the year. This would result in a different implicit interest rate. There would be no finance cost in the final year of the lease as the liability would be extinguished at the start of the period when the final lease payment was made.

(b) Sum of digit basis

n = No. of years borrowing = 4

Sum of the digits = [n × (n+1)]/2

(4 × 5)/2 = 10

					$
Year 1	4/10	×	26,000	=	10,400
Year 2	3/10	×	26,000	=	7,800
Year 3	2/10	×	26,000	=	5,200
Year 4	1/10	×	26,000	=	2,600
					‾‾‾‾‾‾
					26,000

If lease payments were made in advance then, as mentioned above, there would be no finance cost to be allocated to the final year of the lease term.

Therefore, when applying the sum of digits formula, n = lease term minus 1 year (i.e. 3 in the above example).

Test your understanding 4 (integration question)

GBT entered into a four year lease on 1 January 20X0 for a machine with a fair value of $2 million. The lease contract requires the annual payment of $600,000 for four years and the machine has a useful economic life of five years. The interest implicit in the lease is given below.

Required:

(a) Prepare extracts from the statement of profit or loss for the year ended 31 December 20X0 and statement of financial position as at 31 December 20X0, assuming that instalments are paid in:

(1) arrears (implicit rate of interest 7.71%);

(2) advance (implicit rate of interest 13.71%).

(b) Prepare a schedule showing how the interest would be allocated across the lease term if the sum of digits method was used as an alternative (for both payments in advance and arrears).

Prepare all answers to the nearest $000.

Test your understanding 5 (OTQ style)

GTA entered into an agreement to lease an item of plant with a fair value of $1,700,000 on 1 July 20X1. The lease requires the annual payment in arrears of $400,000 for six years and the machine has a useful economic life of seven years. The lease agreement transfers legal title to GTA at the end of the lease agreement. The interest implicit in the lease is 10.84%.

Required:

Complete the following extract from the statement of profit or loss for the year ended 30 June 20X2. Give your answers to the nearest $000.

$000

Statement of profit or loss (extract)
  Depreciation charge
  Finance cost

Test your understanding 6 (OTQ style)

GTA entered into a second agreement to lease a further item of plant, also with a fair value of $1,700,000, on 1 January 20X2. This lease requires the annual payment **in advance** of $400,000 for six years and the machine has a useful economic life of six years. The interest implicit in the lease is 16.32%.

Required:

Calculate the carrying value of the non-current portion of the lease liability at 31 December 20X2. Give your answer to the nearest $000.

Test your understanding 7 (OTQ style)

SLB cannot afford to buy a necessary piece of machinery so it arranges a finance lease. It will lease the machine over the next five years with payments of $1,200,000 on 31 December of each accounting year. The lease contract commences on 1 January 20X0. It is estimated that the machine's fair value is $4,950,000 at this date and the machine has a useful life of five years. Interest is to be allocated on the sum of digits basis.

Required:

Which of the following is the finance cost that would be recognised in SLB's statement of profit or loss in the year ended 31 December 20X0 in respect of the finance lease?

A $210,000

B $350,000

C $420,000

D $1,050,000

Test your understanding 8 (OTQ style)

SLB cannot afford to buy a necessary piece of machinery so it arranges a lease. It will lease the machine over the next five years with payments of $1,200,000 on 1 January of each accounting year. The lease contract commences on 1 January 20X0. It is estimated that the machine's fair value is $4,950,000 at this date and the machine has a useful life of five years. Interest is to be allocated on the sum of digits basis.

Required:

Which three of the following statements are correct in respect of the above lease arrangement?

A   As the lease term equates to the useful life, this would indicate that the arrangement is a finance lease

B   As the total lease payments is in excess of the fair value, this would indicate that the arrangement is a finance lease

C   When calculating the lease liability it is important to deduct the cash payment at the correct point in time as this affects the finance cost calculation

D   The denominator of the sum of digits fraction is (5 × 6)/2 = 15

E   The denominator of the sum of digits fraction is (4 × 5)/2 = 10

5 Inappropriate classification of leases

If an entity inappropriately recognises a finance lease as an operating lease, it will have the following effect on the financial statements:

- Assets will be understated

    Therefore ratios such as return on capital employed and asset turnover will be overstated

- Liabilities will be understated

    Therefore gearing will be understated

This practice is often referred to as 'off balance sheet financing' and is considered to be unethical. Entities should classify leases in accordance with their substance, rather than selecting the classification that enhances their reported performance and position the most.

Effect of incorrect classification

As we have seen in this chapter there is a distinct difference between the accounting treatment of finance leases and operating leases. Therefore an inappropriate classification of a lease can have a significant effect on the statement of financial position of an entity and on the entity's financial ratios.

If we consider a lessee who has a finance lease but is incorrectly treating it as an operating lease, in the statement of financial position there will be no non-current asset recorded which means that the assets that are earning income for the company are effectively understated. Also, no liability will be recognised and therefore the gearing of the entity will be understated.

In the statement of profit or loss there is less effect. The correct treatment under a finance lease would be a depreciation charge based on the fair value of the finance lease asset and the finance cost element of the lease payment. However if the lease is treated as an operating lease then the entire lease payment will be charged to the statement of profit or loss. This will probably mean that the total charge to profit or loss will be similar under both treatments.

6 Sale and leaseback transactions

Introduction

In a sale and leaseback transaction an entity sells one of its assets and immediately leases the asset back.

- This is a common way of raising finance whilst retaining the use of the related assets. The buyer/lessor is normally a bank.

- There are two key questions to ask when assessing the substance of these transactions:
  - Is the new lease a finance lease or an operating lease?
  - If the new lease is an operating lease, was the sale at fair value or not?

- The leaseback is classified in accordance with the usual criteria set out in IAS 17.

Terminology

A sells non-current asset to **B**

(Seller)   (Buyer)

Then

A leases the non-current asset back from **B**

(Lessee)   (Lessor)

Sale and finance leaseback

In accordance with IAS 17, a sale and leaseback arrangement is, in essence, a financing arrangement. The substance of the transaction is that the asset has been used as security for a loan. The accounting treatment required by IAS 17 is as follows:

- The lessee initially defers any gain or loss on disposal of the asset and recognises it over the subsequent lease term.

- The lessee then recognises both a finance lease asset and liability in accordance with normal IAS 17 rules (i.e. as covered earlier in the chapter).

Sale and operating leaseback

A sale and operating leaseback transfers the risks and rewards incidental to ownership of the asset to the buyer/lessor. Therefore it is treated as a disposal and the asset is no longer recognised in the financial statements of the lessee.

However, if the sale is not at fair value then this suggests that it is not a 'straight-forward' sale and the difference between sale proceeds and fair value needs to be considered carefully as follows:

- If sale proceeds are greater than fair value, defer the excess and recognise over the lease term

- If sale proceeds are lower than fair value, consider whether future lease payments are below market price:
    - If yes, defer the difference between proceeds and fair value (a loss) and amortise over lease term

    - If no, recognise total profit or loss on disposal immediately (no deferral)

Summary of sale and leaseback transactions

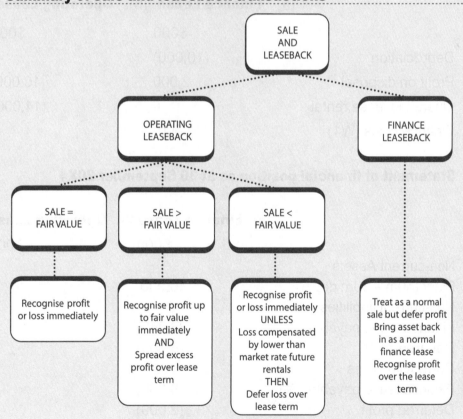

Example 4 – sale and leaseback

A company sells an item of plant on 1 October 20X3 for $50 million, its fair value. The plant had a book value of $40 million at the date of the sale. The company have entered into an agreement to leaseback the plant at a cost of $14 million per annum for the next five years, payable annually in arrears. Depreciation is charged on plant at a rate of 20% per annum on the reducing balance basis. No depreciation has yet been recorded for the current year.

Required:

Prepare extracts from the statement of profit or loss for the year ended 30 September 20X4 and statement of financial position as at 30 September 20X4 assuming:

(a) the lease is a finance lease and interest implicit in the lease is 12% per annum

(b) the lease is an operating lease

Statement of profit or loss for the year ended 30 September 20X4

	(a) Finance Lease	(b) Operating Lease
	$000	$000
Depreciation	(10,000)	–
Profit on disposal	2,000	10,000
Operating lease rental	–	(14,000)
Finance costs (W1)	(6,000)	–

Statement of financial position as at 30 September 20X4

	(a) Finance Lease	(b) Operating Lease
	$000	$000
Non-current Assets		
Plant (50m – 10m dep'n)	40,000	–
Non-current liabilities		
Finance lease payable (W1)	(33,040)	–
Deferred profit	(6,000)	
Current liabilities		
Finance lease payable (W1)	(8,960)	–
Deferred profit	(2,000)	

Working

(W1)

	Opening	Finance cost @ 12%	Cash paid	Closing
Y/e Sep X4	50,000	6,000	(14,000)	42,000
Y/e Sep X5	42,000	5,040	(14,000)	33,040

Current liability = 42,000 – 33,040 = 8,960

Notes to answer – part (a)

- The plant is deemed to be sold for proceeds of $50 million, therefore there is a profit of $10 million over the book value. This profit is deferred over the lease term of 5 years therefore $2 million is recognised each year.

- The plant is brought back onto the statement of financial position at its fair value of $50 million under the finance lease.

- The plant value of $50 million is depreciated over the lease term of 5 years.

- Finance costs are charged to the statement of profit or loss based on the 12% interest rate implicit in the lease i.e. 12% × 50m (see (W1)).

- The total deferred profit at 30 September 20X4 will be $8m ($10m – $2m) of which $2m will be treated as a current liability and $6m as a non-current liability.

Notes to answer – part (b)

- As the plant is sold at its fair value, the full profit of $10 million is recognised immediately and the operating lease rentals are recorded in the statement of profit or loss every year.

Test your understanding 9 (OTQ style)

S enters into a sale and leaseback arrangement which results in an operating leaseback for 5 years from 1 January 20X7. Details at 1 January 20X7 are as follows:

	$m
Carrying amount of non-current asset	6.0
Sale proceeds	8.0
Fair value of non-current asset	7.2

The lease rentals are $4m per year.

Required:

Which three of the following statements is correct in respect of the accounting treatment of the above sale and leaseback arrangement in the financial statements for the year ended 31 December 20X7?

A   As the leaseback is an operating lease, the asset should be derecognised and profit of $2 million recorded in the statement of profit or loss

B   The lease rentals of $4 million should be recognised as an expense in the statement of profit or loss

C   The profit of $2 million should be deferred and recognised over the lease term, therefore only $400,000 of it should be recognised in the current year

D   The asset should continue to be recognised and depreciated for the next five years as S continues to use it and therefore has risks and rewards of ownership

E $800,000 of the profit on disposal should be deferred at the date of sale

F   The total profit to be recognised in the current year in the statement of profit or loss is $1,360,000

Test your understanding 10 (case style)

You work for RP, a manufacturing entity, and have received the following email from the Managing Director:

"The Board has been discussing ways that it can raise some additional finance. We have decided that the best option will be to enter into sale and leaseback arrangements for some of our more significant assets. It will result in a cash inflow to the business whilst allowing us to continue using the assets which are a necessary part of our organisation.

We have discussed one arrangement with the bank already. The bank has agreed to pay us $3.5 million for one of our biggest items of plant and will then lease it back to us for the next 15 years. The carrying value is only $2 million and therefore this arrangement particularly appeals to me as, not only will we receive a significant cash inflow, but it will also immediately boost our current year profit by $1.5 million. We would also not suffer any further depreciation charges, although I appreciate that there would be a rental charge instead.

Another ideal thing about this arrangement is that we would not have to reflect a liability on our statement of financial position. The Board are a little concerned that our gearing level is already high enough.

I would therefore like you to go ahead and make the necessary arrangements."

Required:

Prepare a response to the above email, explaining to the Managing Director the potential consequences of the sale and leaseback arrangement on the financial statements of RP.

7 Lessor accounting

Lessor accounting is the mirror image of the accounting treatment of leases from the lessee's perspective.

Lessor accounting for finance leases

The lessor has passed the risks and rewards of ownership of the leased asset to the lessee.

- Step 1 – Derecognise the asset.
  - The asset is derecognised from the SOFP (at its CV).
  - A finance lease receivable is recognised (at the net investment in the lease).
  - A profit or loss on disposal is recorded in the SOPL.
- Step 2 – No depreciation (risks and rewards held by lessee).
- Step 3 – Record interest income in P/L.
- Step 4 – Record the cash received.

Net Investment of the lease

The finance lease receivable is calculated as the net investment of the lease.

This is calculated as:

- minimum lease payments (MLP) plus any unguaranteed residual value
- discounted as at the interest rate implicit in the lease.

The MLP should already include any guaranteed residual value negotiated within the terms of the lease arrangement.

Test your understanding 11 (OTQ style)

Brendan Ltd leases machinery to Stirling Ltd on 1st January 20X1. The lease is for four years at an annual cost of $2,000 payable annually in arrears. The economic lifetime of the asset is deemed to be 4 years. The normal cash price (and fair value) of the asset is $5,710, the same as its carrying value, and there is no residual value. The present value of the minimum lease payment is $5,710. The implicit rate of interest is 15%.

Required:

What will be the total receivable shown on the SOFP of Brendan Ltd and the impact to the SOPL of Brendan Ltd for the year ended 31st December 20X1?

A Receivable $5710, P/L $856 expense

B Receivable $5710, P/L $856 income

C Receivable $4566, P/L $856 income

D Receivable $4566, P/L $856 expense

Lessor accounting for operating leases

The lessor retains the leased assets risks and rewards.

There is no derecognition of the leased asset by the lessor. Depreciation is charged on the asset by the lessor.

The lessor will account for rental income from the leased asset in the SOPL. Rental income will be spread systematically over the lease term. Typically this is performed on a straight line basis.

Any difference between the income and the cash physically received will be accounted as deferred or accrued income within the SOFP.

Test your understanding12 (OTQ style)

Milner Ltd hires out industrial plant on long-term operating leases. On 1 January 20X1, it entered into a 7 year lease on a mobile driller. The terms of the lease are:

- $175,000 payable on 1 January 20X1

- Six rentals of $70,000 payable on 1 January 20X2 – 20X7

Required:

What will be shown in Milner Ltd's SOFP and SOPL for the year ended 31 December 20X1 in relation to the lease arrangement?

A   SOFP no impact, P/L rental income $175,000

B   SOFP Deferred income $90,000, P/L rental income $85,000

C   SOFP Deferred income $85,000, P/L rental income $90,000

D   SOFP no impact, P/L rental income $70,000

Test your understanding 13 (further OTQs)

Questions (1) to (4) below are based on the following scenario:

Cuthbert Ltd has entered into a finance lease for the use of a machine. The fair value of the machine at the date of inception of the lease is $462,600. Under the terms of the lease five annual instalments of $120,000 are payable at the start of each year. Interest is allocated on an actuarial basis and the rate of interest implicit in the lease is 15%.

(1) **Calculate the finance cost that would be recognised in the statement of profit or loss in the first year of the lease (to the nearest $).**

(2) **Calculate the non-current element of the finance lease liability that would be recognised in Cuthbert Ltd's statement of financial position at the end of year 1 of the lease (to the nearest $).**

(3) **Calculate the total finance cost in the lease (in $).**

(4) **If interest were allocated on a sum of digits basis, what would be the finance cost that would be recognised in Cuthbert's statement of profit or loss in year 2 of the lease (to the nearest $).**

(5) LB entered into an arrangement to sell land and buildings and lease them back on a twenty year finance lease. The sale took place on 1 January 20X5 and LB's reporting date is 31 December. The land and buildings were sold for their fair value of $5 million and had a carrying value of $4.4 million at the date of disposal. LB depreciates its assets on a straight line basis.

Which of the following statements are TRUE in respect of the above sale and leaseback arrangement. Select all that apply.

A LB should charge depreciation of $220,000 for the year in respect of the land and buildings.

B LB should charge depreciation of $250,000 for the year in respect of the land and buildings.

C Profit of $600,000 should be recognised in the year ended 31 December 20X5 in respect of the disposal of the land and buildings.

D The profit on disposal and depreciation are the only two effects of the above arrangement on the statement of profit or loss in the year ended 31 December 20X5.

(6) In _____ lease arrangements the risks and rewards of the asset leased are transferred to the lessee, whereas in _____ lease arrangements they remain with the lessor.

Select the correct words to complete the above sentence, from the following options:

finance, operating

(7) MB entered into a four year operating lease on 1 November 20X5 and was required to pay an initial deposit of $500, plus the first of four annual payments of $250 (payable in advance each year).

Complete the journal entry required to correctly recognise the initial payment of $750 in the financial statements of MB for the year ended 31 October 20X6.

Dr

Dr

Cr

Note: In the assessment, you would choose the headings for the Drs and Crs from a selection of choices.

8 Chapter summary

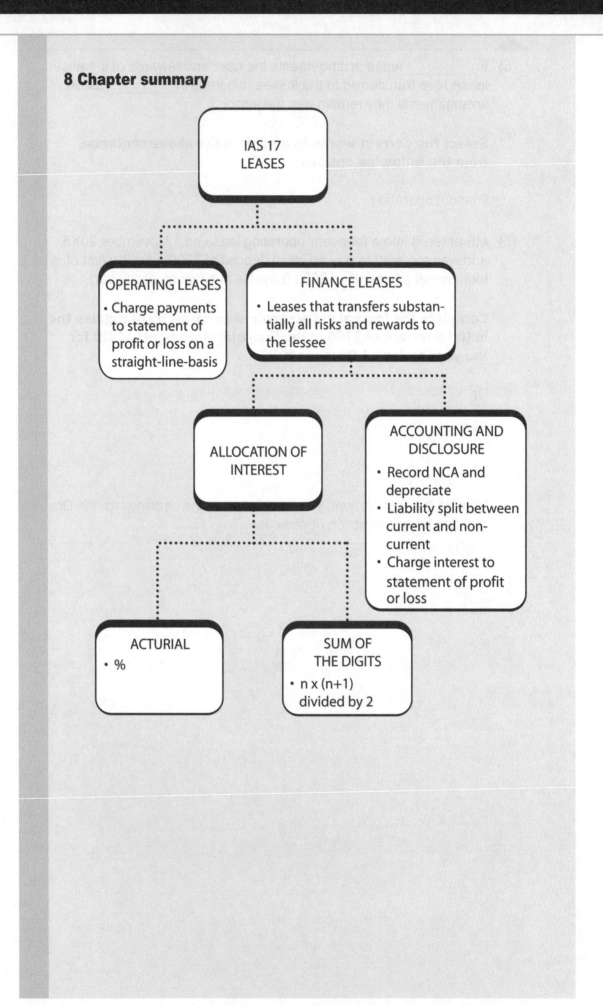

Test your understanding answers

Test your understanding 1 (integration question)

Total lease payments = $5,000 + $10,000 + $6,000 = $21,000.

Length of lease = three years

Annual charge to statement of profit or loss = $21,000/3 = $7,000

Statement of profit or loss (extract)

	1	2	3
Operating lease expense	7,000	7,000	7,000

Statement of financial position (extract)

	1	2	3
Prepayments		1,000	nil
Accruals	2,000		

Workings

By the end of year one, a total of $7,000 has been charged to the statement of profit or loss but only $5,000 has been paid and so an accrued expense is required in the statement of financial position of $2,000.

By the end of year two, a total of $14,000 has been charged to the statement of profit or loss and $15,000 has been paid and so a prepayment is required in the statement of financial position of $1,000.

Test your understanding 2 (OTQ style)

Correct expense for statement of profit or loss in the year ended 30 April 20X3 = $750

Total lease payments = 750 + (3 × 500) = $2,250

Length of lease = three years

Annual charge to statement of profit or loss = $2,250/3 = $750

Test your understanding 3 (OTQ style)

Total lease payments = 600 + (4 × 1,200) = $5,400

Length of lease = four years

Annual charge to statement of profit or loss = $5,400/4 = $1,350

Expense charged to statement of profit or loss in year ended 31 March 20X3 = 600 + 1,200 = $1,800

Therefore, journal entry require to correct accounting treatment is

Dr   Prepayments $450

Cr   Statement of profit or loss $450

Test your understanding 4 (integration question)

(a)

	(1) Arrears	(2) Advance
	$000	$000
Statement of profit or loss (extract)		
Depreciation (2,000/4)	500	500
Finance cost (see workings)	154	192
Statement of financial position (extract)		
Non-current asset (2,000 – 500)	1,500	1,500
Non-current liabilities (see workings)	1,074	992
Current liabilities (see workings)	480	600

Workings

Arrears:

Year	Opening	Interest 7.71%	Total	Payment	Closing
	$000	$000	$000	$000	$000
1	2,000	154	2,154	(600)	*1,554
2	1,554	120	1,674	(600)	**1,074
3	1,074	83	1,157	(600)	557
4	557	43	600	(600)	0

Total liability at the end of year 1 = 1,554*

Non-current liability at the end of year 1 = 1,074 (amount owing at end of year 2)

Current liability at the end of year 1 = 1,554 – 1,074 = 480

Advance:

Year	Opening $000	Payment $000	Revised total $000	Interest 13.71% $000	Closing $000
1	2,000	(600)	1,400	192	*1,592
2	1,592	**(600)	992	136	1,128
3	1,128	(600)	528	72	600
4	600	(600)	0	0	0

Total liability at the end of year 1 = 1,592*

Current liability at the end of year 1 = 600** (amount due to be paid in year 2)

Non-current liability at the end of year 1 = 1,592 – 600 = 992

Tutorial note

Depreciation is calculated on the lower of the lease period or the useful life of the asset. In this scenario the lease period is 4 years and the life of the asset is 5 years. Therefore, depreciate over 4 years.

When it comes to splitting the liability between current and non-current, the non-current liability is the amount outstanding immediately after next year's payments have been made.

(b) **Allocation of interest using sum of digits method**

	Arrears $000	Advance $000
Year 1	160	200
Year 2	120	133
Year 3	80	67
Year 4	40	–
	400	400

Working – total interest

	$000
Total payments (4 × $600,000)	2,400
Value of asset	(2,000)
Total interest	400

Working – for payments in arrears

Sum of digits N = 4 years

n × (n + 1)/2 = (4 × 5)/2 = 10

					$
Year 1	4/10	×	400	=	160
Year 2	3/10	×	400	=	120
Year 3	2/10	×	400	=	80
Year 4	1/10	×	400	=	40

Working – for payments in advance

Sum of digits N = 3 years (lease term minus 1)

n × (n+1)/2 = (3 × 4)/2 = 6

					$
Year 1	3/6	×	400	=	200
Year 2	2/6	×	400	=	133
Year 3	1/6	×	400	=	67

Test your understanding 5 (OTQ style)

	$000
Statement of profit or loss (extract)	
Depreciation (1,700/7)	243
Finance cost (1,700 × 10.84%)	184

Tutorial note re depreciation

Depreciation is typically charged on a leased asset over the lesser of the lease term and the asset's useful life which, in this case, would be 6 years. However, as legal title transfers to GTA at the end of the lease term it is appropriate to depreciate the asset over 7 years (as GTA will still have use of the asset after the lease term finishes).

Test your understanding 6 (OTQ style)

Non-current portion of lease liability at 31 December 20X2 = $1,112,000

Lease working

Year	Opening	Payment	Revised total	Interest 16.32%	Closing
	$000	$000	$000	$000	$000
1	1,700	(400)	1,300	212	1,512
2	1,512	(400)	1,112	181	1,293

Test your understanding 7 (OTQ style)

The correct answer is B

Finance cost in year ended 31 December 20X0 = $350,000

Working:

	$000
Total payments (5 × 1,200)	6,000
Value of asset	(4,950)
Total interest	1,050

Sum of digits = n = 5 years

n × (n + 1)/2 = (5 × 6)/2 = 15

					$000
Year 1	5/15	×	1,050	=	350

Test your understanding 8 (OTQ style)

The correct statements are A, B and E

C is incorrect – the sum of digits fraction is used to calculate the finance cost, it is not based on the carrying value of the liability at a particular point in time. As long as the cash payment is deducted then the closing liability will be correct.

D is incorrect – when payments are made in advance, 'n' in the sum of digits fraction is the lease term minus 1, i.e. 4 rather than 5 in this case.

Test your understanding 9 (OTQ style)

The correct statements are B, E and F

As the sale proceeds exceed the fair value of the non-current asset, the excess profit must be deferred over the lease term.

Profit recognised at date of sale: 7.2 – 6.0 = $1.2m

Profit to be deferred over 5 years:

8.0 – 7.2 = $800,000

$0.8m/5 years = $160,000 should therefore be recognised each year

The total profit recognised in the first year is therefore $1,360,000 = $1.2 million on disposal and $160,000 release of deferred element.

Note, the lease rental of $4 million would also be charged through the statement of profit or loss.

Test your understanding 10 (case style)

Email response to Managing Director

In response to your email regarding the sale and leaseback arrangement that you have provisionally agreed with the bank, I thought I should explain how the arrangement would be accounted for in the financial statements in accordance with IAS 17 Leases.

Importantly, I would need to assess whether the lease arrangement is a finance lease or operating lease. The impact that you have described in your email suggests that you believe that this would be an operating lease arrangement, where the significant risks and rewards of ownership of the plant will have transferred to the bank and we will just be renting it from them.

However, given that the lease term is 15 years, this may indicate that the arrangement is instead a finance lease. One of the key factors that determines whether an arrangement is a finance lease is whether the lease term covers the majority of the useful life of the asset. If it does then there would be a number of consequences as follows:

- The asset should remain on the statement of financial position and would therefore continue to be depreciated.

- The lease would effectively be treated as a loan secured on the plant and therefore a liability of $3.5 million would be recognised upon inception of the arrangement. Interest would then also need to be recognised on this liability which would lead to a further expense in profit or loss over the lease term.

- Any profit made on the sale and leaseback must be deferred and recognised over the lease term. Therefore profit of $100,000 would be recognised each year, rather than the $1.5 million being recognised immediately.

As you can see from the above, the impact in the financial statements may not be the one that you are hoping for. Gearing would increase due to the recognition of the liability and the profit would be recognised over the next 15 years.

If you could send me details of the specific asset that this arrangement is intended for, I will check its remaining useful life and will be able to confirm whether the arrangement will be classified as an operating lease, as you wish, or a finance lease.

Test your understanding 11 (OTQ style)

Answer = **C**

As Brendan Ltd is leasing out the asset to Stirling Ltd, the question is set from the perspective of the lessor.

The lease term is all of the UEL. The PV of MLPs of the lease is equal to the fair value of the asset. This indicates that the risk and rewards transfer to the lessee. The lease is a finance lease.

The asset should be derecognised and a receivable of $5,710 (the net investment in the lease) is recorded at the 1st January 20X1.

To work out the receivable outstanding at 31st December 20X1:

Year	Balance b/f ($)	Interest income @15% ($)	Receipt ($)	Carried forward ($)
1	5,710	856	(2000)	4,566

Therefore, the year end receivable on the SOFP = $4,566.

The SOPL includes rental **income** = $856

Test your understanding12 (OTQ style)

The correct answer is B

Rental income to the SOPL will be determined by spreading the total rental payments (including deposits and incentives) using the straight line basis.

The rental income in 31 December 20X1 is calculated as:

175,000 + (70000 × 6)/7 = 595,000/7 = $85,000

As cash received in 20X1 ($175,000) is higher than the rental income within the SOPL, deferred income of $90,000 ($175,000 – 85,000) will be recognised in the SOFP.

Deferred income = $90,000

Rental income = $85,000

Test your understanding 13 (further OTQs)

(1) **Finance cost = $51,390**

(462,600 – 120,000) × 15% = 51,390

or see below for lease table.

(2) **Non-current lease liability at end of year 1 = $273,990**

Year	Opening	Payment	Total	Interest 15%	Closing
1	462,600	(120,000)	342,600	51,390	393,990
2	393,990	(120,000)	273,990	41,099	315,089
3	315,089	(120,000)	195,089	29,263	224,352
4	224,352	(120,000)	104,352	15,648	120,000
5	120,000	(120,000)	nil	nil	nil

The non-current liability at the end of the year is the amount outstanding immediately after next year's payment.

(3) **Total finance cost = $137,400**

(5 × 120,000) – 462,600 = 137,400

(4) **Sum of digits finance cost in year 2 = $41,220**

n = number of years in lease term minus 1 (as payments in advance) = 4

$[n \times (n + 1)]/2 = (4 \times 5)/2 = 10$

Therefore, year 2 finance cost = $3/10 \times 137,400 = 41,220$

(5) **B is the only correct statement.**

A is incorrect. The asset would be initially recognised upon inception of the finance lease at its fair value of $5 million and therefore the depreciation would be $5m/20 years = $250,000.

C is incorrect. The profit of $600,000 is deferred and recognised over the lease term. Therefore profit of $30,000 (600,000/20 years) would be recognised in the year ended 31 December 20X5.

D is incorrect. As well as profit on disposal and depreciation, there would be a finance cost relating to the finance lease liability.

(6) In **finance** lease arrangements the risks and rewards of the asset leased are transferred to the lessee, whereas in **operating** lease arrangements they remain with the lessor.

(7) **Dr   Prepayments $375**

Dr   Profit or loss $375

Cr   Cash $750

Total payments = $500 + (4 \times 250) = 1,500$

Lease term = 4 years

Therefore, profit or loss expense each year = 1,500/4 = $375

Amount prepaid = 750 – 375 = $375

Revenue and substance

Chapter learning objectives

B1. Produce consolidated primary financial statements, incorporating accounting transactions and adjustments, in accordance with relevant international accounting standards, in an ethical manner.

(c) Discuss the provisions of relevant international accounting standards in respect of the recognition and measurement of revenue, in accordance with IAS 18 and the provisions of the framework.

(d) Produce the accounting entries, in accordance with relevant international accounting standards.

(e) Discuss the ethical selection and adoption of relevant accounting policies and accounting estimates.

1 Session content

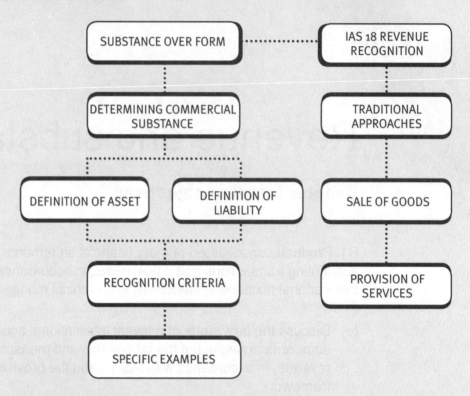

2 Introduction

IAS 18 provides the rules for revenue recognition and generally requires that revenue is recognised in accordance with the substance of the arrangement between entity and customer. The rules of this standard and the general principles of the IASB's Conceptual Framework for Financial Reporting (the Framework) can be used to apply the concept of substance to a range of transactions, where substance is typically different to legal form.

Substance is a key accounting concept in ensuring that the financial statements faithfully represent the underlying transactions and events.

It has already been considered in earlier chapters in the context of:

- Financial instruments – redeemable preference shares are recognised as liabilities

- Leases – finance lease assets are recognised in the lessee's financial statements

3 IAS 18 Revenue

IAS 18 defines revenue as the gross inflow of economic benefits during the period arising in the course of the ordinary activities of an entity.

Revenue does not include:

- Proceeds from sale of non-current assets
- Sales and other similar taxes
- Other amounts collected on behalf of others
  - for example in an agency relationship, agent would only recognise commission

The main issue with revenue is determining when it should be recognised in the financial statements. The basic principles applied are that revenue should only be recognised when both of the following are satisfied:

- it is probable that future economic benefits will flow to the entity
- these benefits can be measured reliably.

IAS 18 deals with the following:

- the sale of goods
- the rendering of services
- interest, royalties and dividends.

Sale of goods

Revenue from the sale of goods should be recognised when all of the following criteria have been met:

- the significant risks and rewards of ownership have transferred to the buyer
- the seller does not retain continuing managerial involvement or control over the goods
- the revenue can be measured reliably
- it is probable that economic benefits will flow to the entity (i.e. that the buyer will pay for the goods)
- the costs to the seller can be measured reliably.

Test your understanding 1 (integration question)

Should revenue from the sale of goods be recognised in the following circumstances?

(a) **Case 1 – sale or return**

Goods are sold by a manufacturer to a retailer, who has the right to return the goods within 28 days if it is unable to sell them.

(b) **Case 2 – sale with delivery included**

Goods have been shipped but have not yet arrived at the customer's premises. The seller is responsible for delivery.

(c) **Case 3 – political change**

Goods have been sold on credit to a customer in a country where there has been a political change, and the incoming government has banned domestic companies from making any payments to other countries.

(d) **Case 4 – payment in advance**

An entity receives $10,000 as an advance payment for the delivery of goods that have not yet been manufactured.

Rendering of services

Revenue from services should be recognised when all of the following criteria have been met:

- the revenue can be measured reliably
- it is probable that economic benefits will flow to the entity (i.e. the buyer will pay for the services)
- the stage of completion of the transaction can be measured reliably
- the costs to the seller can be measured reliably.

The revenue would then be recognised by reference to the stage of completion of the transaction at the reporting date.

Interest, royalties and dividends

Interest, royalties and dividends should be recognised when:

* it is probable that economic benefits will flow to the entity

* the revenue can be measured reliably.

Interest and royalties should be recognised on an accruals basis, i.e. when earned rather than received. Dividends should be recognised when the right to receive them is established.

Measurement of revenue

Revenue should be measured at the fair value of the consideration received or receivable.

* In most cases this will be the amount of cash received or receivable.

* If the effect of the time value for money is material, the revenue should be the discounted present value.

Illustration 1 – discounted present value

A retailer of electrical goods offers two year 0% finance on items offered for sale at $3,000. The market rate of interest on similar finance offers is 7%.

The discount factor for $1 receivable in two year's time with a 7% interest rate is 0.873.

The revenue from sale of goods is the present value of the amount receivable in two year's time, i.e. $2,619 (3,000 × 0.873).

Dr Receivable	$2,619
Cr Revenue	$2,619

The discount on the receivable balance is then unwound over the two year period up to the date of receipt and the interest is recognised as finance income. Therefore, after one year the adjustment would be:

Dr Receivable	$183
Cr Finance income (P/L)	$183

Note that this is in accordance with IAS 39 *Financial Instruments: Recognition and Measurement*. The receivable balance is a financial asset classified as a loan and receivable and is therefore amortised.

Test your understanding 2 (OTQ style)

An entity makes a sale of a computer on 1 March 20X1 for $500,000 plus $50,000 for two years after sales servicing. The goods have been despatched and the full amount has been received from the customer of $550,000.

The reporting date is 31 December 20X1.

Required:

Calculate the amount of revenue that should be recognised in the year ended 31 December 20X1 in respect of the above transaction. State your answer to the nearest $.

Test your understanding 3 (OTQ style)

An entity publishes a magazine and on 1 July 20X2 sold an annual subscription totalling $12,000 payable in advance.

The reporting date is 30 September 20X2.

Required:

Complete the following journal entry to record the above transaction in the financial statements for the year ended 30 September 20X2.

Dr   Cash $12,000

Cr   Revenue $

Cr   _____ (*) $

(*) Choose from the following headings: Accrued income; Deferred income

Test your understanding 4 (OTQ style)

An internet travel agent receives $5,000 on 1 April 20X2 for arranging a holiday to Cyprus. It will pass on 90% of this amount to the holiday company, with payment due on 15 June 20X2. The customer will deal directly with the holiday company in the event of any problems.

The travel agent's financial reporting date is 31 May 20X2.

Required:

Which one of the following statements is correct in respect of the above arrangement in the financial statements for the year ended 31 May 20X2?

A   The travel agent should recognise $5,000 as revenue immediately and should accrue for the $4,500 payment to the holiday company, recognising the expense as a cost of sale

B   The travel agent should recognise $500 as revenue and $4,500 as deferred income.

C   The travel agent should recognise $500 as revenue and $4,500 as a payable.

D   The travel agent should not recognise any revenue. The entire $5,000 should be credited to deferred income.

4 Reporting the substance of transactions

Determining the substance of a transaction

Common features of transactions whose substance is not readily apparent are:

- the legal title to an asset may be separated from the principal benefits and risks associated with the asset

- a transaction may be linked with other transactions which means that the commercial effect of the individual transaction cannot be understood without an understanding of all of the transactions

- options may be included in a transaction where the terms of the option make it highly likely that the option will be exercised.

Identifying assets and liabilities

Key to determining the substance of a transaction is to identify whether assets and liabilities arise subsequent to that transaction by considering:

- who enjoys the benefits of any asset

- who is exposed to the principal risks of any asset.

Assets are defined in the Framework as resources controlled by the entity as a result of past events and from which future economic benefits are expected to flow to the entity.

Liabilities are defined in the Framework as present obligations of the entity arising from past events, the settlement of which is expected to result in an outflow of resources embodying economic benefits from the entity.

Recognition and derecognition of assets and liabilities

Assets and liabilities should be **recognised** in the statement of financial position where:

- it is probable that any future economic benefit associated with the item will flow to or from the entity and

- the item has a cost or value that can be measured with reliability.

When either of these criteria are not met the item should be **derecognised**.

With the case of assets there are two possible outcomes:

- Complete derecognition – when there is a transfer to another party of all the *significant* risks and benefits associated with the asset.

- No derecognition – no *significant* change to benefits and risks.

Off balance sheet financing

One method of off balance sheet financing is to recognise a finance lease as an operating lease – this scenario has already been mentioned in the Leases chapter. It is however not the only method for removing debt from the statement of financial position.

Often the motivation behind transactions that require adjustment for substance over form is the avoidance of liabilities on the statement of financial position. Motivations for keeping financing off the statement of financial position include the following:

(1) *Effect on the gearing (leverage) ratio*. If an entity is able to exclude liabilities from its statement of financial position it can manipulate the gearing ratio to the lowest possible level. High gearing levels tend to have adverse effects on share prices because the share is perceived by the market as riskier.

(2) *Borrowing capacity*. The lower the level of liabilities recorded on the statement of financial position, the greater the capacity for further borrowings.

(3) *Borrowing costs*. An entity with an already high level of borrowings will pay a risk premium for further borrowing in the form of a higher interest rate.

(4) *Management incentives*. Bonuses and performance-related pay may be based upon reported earnings for a period. If an entity is able to benefit from off-balance-sheet financing arrangements, costs may be lower, thus improving earnings.

5 Consignment inventory

Consignment inventory is inventory which:

- is legally owned by one party

- is held by another party, on terms which give the holder the right to sell the inventory in the normal course of business or, at the holder's option, to return it to the legal owner.

This type of arrangement is common in the motor trade.

The manufacturer delivers inventory to the dealer which the dealer can then sell on to a customer.

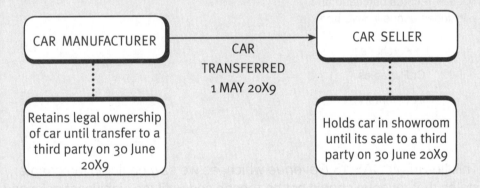

Inventory is legally owned by the manufacturer until:

- Dealer sells inventory onto a third party or

- Dealer's right to return expires and the inventory is still held

However, the inventory is actually held by the dealer.

The accounting issue is to determine which entity should recognise the inventory in the period when it's held by the dealer.

Factors to consider:

- Who bears the risks of the inventory?

- Who has the benefits or rewards of the inventory?

- Who has control over the inventory?

Whoever bears the significant risks of the inventory should recognise it in the statement of financial position.

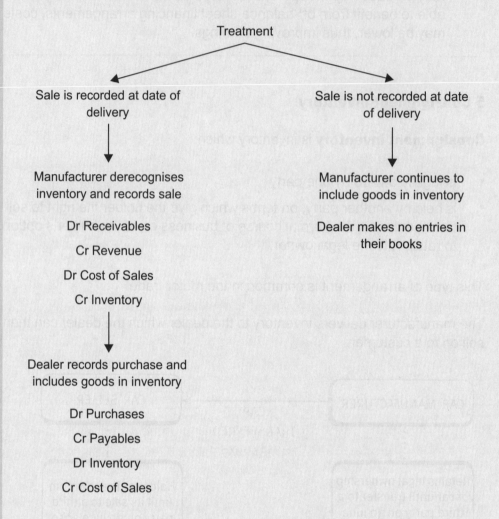

This ties in with IAS 18 *Revenue* which, as we saw earlier in the chapter, states that revenue should not be recognised until the significant risks and rewards of the goods have transferred to the buyer.

Revenue would be recognised at the point that inventory was derecognised, so that income and expense are matched in the same accounting period.

Example 1 – consignment inventory

Carmart, a car dealer, obtains inventory from Zippy, its manufacturer, on a consignment basis. The purchase price is set at delivery. Usually, Carmart pays Zippy for the car the day after Carmart sells to a customer. However, if the car remains unsold after six months then Carmart is obliged to purchase the car. There is no right of return. Further, Carmart is responsible for insurance and maintenance from delivery.

Required:

Describe how Carmart should account for the above scenario.

Solution:

Factors to consider:

- Carmart faces the risk of slow movement and obsolescence as it is obliged to purchase the car and has no right of return.

- Carmart insures and maintains the cars.

- Carmart faces risk of theft.

- Carmart can sell the cars to the public.

In substance there is a sale by Zippy to Carmart on the date of delivery. Zippy derecognises the cars and records the sale. The crs would be classified as the inventory of Carmart and would be held on the SOFP of Carmart if they remained unsold as at the year end.

Test your understanding 5 (case style)

On 1 January 20X6 Gillingham, a manufacturer, entered into an agreement to provide Canterbury, a retailer, with machines for resale.

The terms of the agreement are:

- Canterbury pays the cost of insuring and maintaining the machines.

- Canterbury can also display the machines in its showrooms and use them as demonstration models.

- When a machine is sold to a customer, Canterbury pays Gillingham the factory price at the time the machine was originally delivered.

- All machines remaining unsold six months after their original delivery must be purchased by Canterbury at the factory price at the time of delivery.

- Gillingham can require Canterbury to return the machines at any time within the six-month period.

- Canterbury can return unsold machines to Gillingham at any time during the six-month period, without penalty.

At 31 December 20X6 the agreement is still in force and Canterbury holds several machines which were delivered less than six months earlier.

Required:

Discuss the economic substance of the agreement between Gillingham and Canterbury in respect of the machines, concluding which entity should recognise the machines as inventory for the period that they are held by Canterbury.

6 Sale and repurchase transactions

Sale and repurchase agreements are situations where an asset is sold by one party to another. The terms of the sale provide for the seller to repurchase the asset in certain circumstances at some point in the future.

Sale and repurchase agreements are common in property developments and in maturing inventories such as whisky.

The asset has been 'legally' sold, but there is either a commitment or an option to repurchase the asset at a later date.

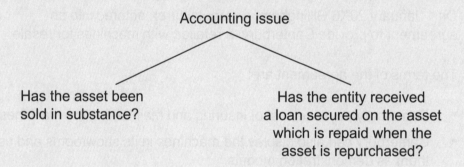

Accounting issue

Has the asset been sold in substance?

Has the entity received a loan secured on the asset which is repaid when the asset is repurchased?

Factors to consider:

- Has the entity transferred the risks and benefits of the asset?

    E.g. can the entity still use the asset? Does the entity bear costs associated with the asset?

- Was the asset "sold" at a price different to market value?
- Is the entity obliged to repurchase the asset?
- If the entity has the option to repurchase the asset are they likely to exercise this option?

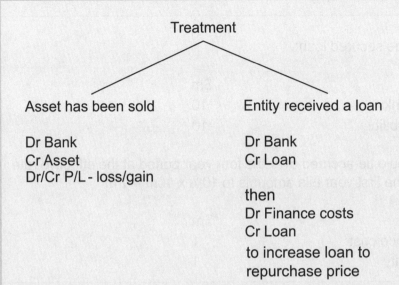

Treatment

Asset has been sold

Dr Bank
Cr Asset
Dr/Cr P/L - loss/gain

Entity received a loan

Dr Bank
Cr Loan

then
Dr Finance costs
Cr Loan

to increase loan to
repurchase price

Example 2 – sale and repurchase

Xavier sells its head office, which cost $10 million, to Yorrick, a bank, for $10 million on 1 January. Xavier has the option to repurchase the property on 31 December, four years later at $14.64 million. Xavier will continue to use the property as normal throughout the period and so is responsible for the maintenance and insurance. The head office was valued at transfer on 1 January at $18 million and is expected to rise in value throughout the four year period. The effective interest rate is 10%.

Required:

Giving reasons, show how Xavier should record the above during the first year following transfer.

Solution:

Factors to consider:

* The option to repurchase is likely to be exercised as the repurchase price is lower than expected value at the repurchase date.

* Xavier continues to insure and maintain the property.

* Xavier will benefit from a rising property price.

* Xavier continues to benefit from use of the property.

Xavier should continue to recognise the head office as an asset in the statement of financial position as the risks and rewards of ownership remain with Xavier. This is a secured loan with effective interest of $4.64 million ($14.64 million – $10 million) over the four year period.

To record the secured loan:

		$m
Dr	Bank	10
Cr	Liability	10

Interest should be accrued over the four year period at the effective rate of 10%. In the first year this amounts to 10% x 10m = 1 m

		$m
Dr	Finance cost	1
Cr	Liability	1

Test your understanding 6 (case style)

On 1 April 20X4 Triangle sold maturing inventory that had a carrying value of $3 million (at cost) to Factorall, a finance house, for $5 million.

Its estimated market value at this date was in excess of $5 million and is expected to be $8.5 million as at 31 March 20X8.

The inventory will not be ready for sale until 31 March 20X8 and will remain on Triangle's premises until this date.

The sale contract includes a clause allowing Triangle to repurchase the inventory at any time up to 31 March 20X8 at a price of $5 million plus interest at 10% per annum compounded from 1 April 20X4.

The proceeds of the sale have been debited to the bank and the sale (and associated profit) have been recognised in Triangle's statement of profit or loss.

Required:

(a) Discuss how the sale of inventory should be accounted for in accordance with the principles of IAS 18 *Revenue* and the IASB's Conceptual Framework for Financial Reporting.

(b) Prepare any accounting adjustments required to Triangle's financial statements for the year ended 31 March 20X5.

Test your understanding 7 (further OTQs)

(1) On 1 April 20X3, LJB sold a freehold property to a finance house for $7 million. The contractual terms require LJB to repurchase the property on 31 March 20X6 for $8.8 million. LJB has the option to repurchase on 31 March 20X4 for $7.6 million, or on 31 March 20X5 for $8.2 million. Prior to disposal, the carrying value of the property was $6 million.

At 31 March 20X4 LJB decided not to take up the option to repurchase.

Which of the following statements are TRUE in respect of LJB's financial statements for the year ended 31 March 20X4? Select all that apply.

A As the option to repurchase has not been exercised, LJB should derecognise the property and record a profit on disposal of $1 million in the statement of profit or loss.

B LJB would recognise the property as part of its non-current assets at 31 March 20X4.

C LJB would recognise a liability of $7 million in its statement of financial position at 31 March 20X4.

D The difference between selling price and repurchase price represents interest on a secured loan.

(2) Revenue is the gross _____ of economic _____ during the period arising in the course of the ordinary activities of an entity.

Revenue should be measured at _____ value.

Select the correct words to complete the above sentence, from the following options:

benefit, fair, inflow, market, receipt, resources

(3) EC signs a contract with a customer to deliver an off the shelf IT system on 1 July 20X2 and to provide support services for a three year period from that date. The total contract price is $600,000 and EC would normally sell equivalent IT systems (without the support service) for $450,000.

Calculate the amount of revenue that should be recognised in EC's statement of profit or loss in respect of the above contract in the year ended 31 December 20X2. (State your answer in $.)

7 Chapter summary

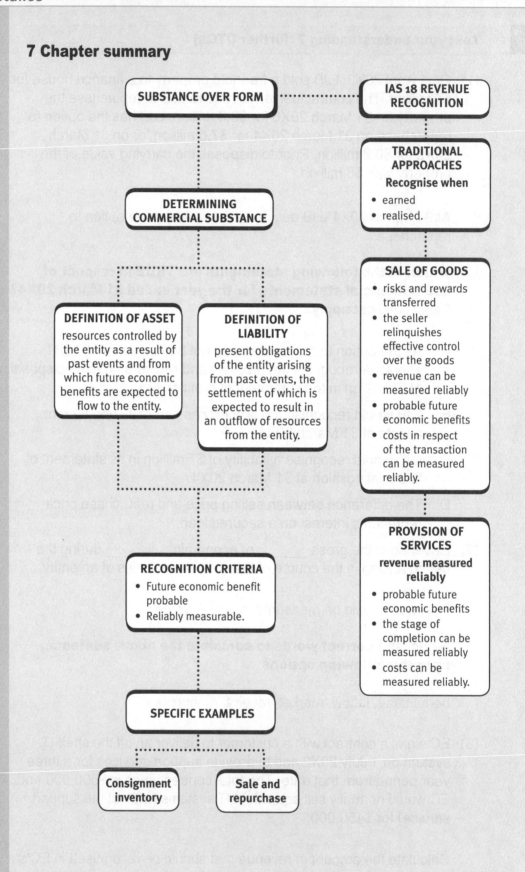

SUBSTANCE OVER FORM .... IAS 18 REVENUE RECOGNITION

TRADITIONAL APPROACHES
Recognise when
- earned
- realised.

DETERMINING COMMERCIAL SUBSTANCE

SALE OF GOODS
- risks and rewards transferred
- the seller relinquishes effective control over the goods
- revenue can be measured reliably
- probable future economic benefits
- costs in respect of the transaction can be measured reliably.

DEFINITION OF ASSET
resources controlled by the entity as a result of past events and from which future economic benefits are expected to flow to the entity.

DEFINITION OF LIABILITY
present obligations of the entity arising from past events, the settlement of which is expected to result in an outflow of resources from the entity.

PROVISION OF SERVICES
revenue measured reliably
- probable future economic benefits
- the stage of completion can be measured reliably
- costs can be measured reliably.

RECOGNITION CRITERIA
- Future economic benefit probable
- Reliably measurable.

SPECIFIC EXAMPLES

Consignment inventory

Sale and repurchase

Test your understanding answers

Test your understanding 1 (integration question)

(a) **Case 1 – sale or return**

Revenue should not be recognised by the manufacturer until either the retailer has sold the goods on or the 28 day return period has completed. The 'significant risks have not yet transferred to the buyer' because the retailer can return the goods.

(The manufacturer would also continue to recognise the goods in inventory. The derecognition of inventory and recognition of revenue should be at the same point in time.)

(b) **Case 2 – sale with delivery included**

Revenue should not be recognised until the customer has accepted the goods. Until that point the risks of ownership still lie with the seller and they still have involvement/control over the goods.

(c) **Case 3 – political change**

Revenue should not be recognised. It is not yet probable that economic benefits will flow to the entity', due to the political issues in the buyer's country.

(d) **Case 4 – payment in advance**

Payment in advance is not revenue. The goods have not yet been manufactured and therefore there has been no transfer of risks and rewards of ownership, or of managerial involvement and control.

The payment in advance should be credited to deferred income and recognised as a liability in the statement of financial position.

Test your understanding 2 (OTQ style)

Revenue for year ended 31 December 20X1 = $520,833

The $500,000 will be recognised as revenue as the goods have been despatched and all criteria has been met for the sale of goods.

The after sales service should be recognised by stage of completion and therefore 10 months of it will be recognised as revenue in the current year.

10/24 × $50,000 = $20,833 for the months March to December.

Tutorial note:

The balance of $29,167 would be shown as deferred income, a liability in the statement of financial position. ($25,000 of this would be considered to be current with the remaining $4,167 non-current.)

Test your understanding 3 (OTQ style)

Dr Cash	$12,000
Cr Revenue	$3,000
Cr Deferred income	$9,000

The entity will recognise 3/12 × $12,000 = $3,000 of the subscription for the months July to September as revenue.

Test your understanding 4 (OTQ style)

The correct statement is C.

The agent will only recognise the commission element of 10% × $5,000 = $500 as revenue. The 90% balance of $4,500 will be shown as a payable balance (due to the holiday company). The $4,500 is not deferred income as it will not be recognised at a later date.

Test your understanding 5 (case style)

The economic substance of the arrangement is determined by analysing which party holds the significant risks and benefits of ownership of the vehicles.

Factors indicating that the risks and benefits of ownership are with Canterbury:

- Canterbury pays the cost of insuring and maintaining the machines, suggesting they are exposed to risk of theft and breakdown.

- Canterbury can display the machines and use them as demonstration vehicles, suggesting they have a certain level of control over the machines held on their premises.

- The price paid by Canterbury is determined at the time of delivery, suggesting that Canterbury will either benefit or suffer from any subsequent sale at a different price.

- Canterbury are required to purchase any machines that they have held for a six month period.

Factors indicating that the risks and benefits of ownership are with Gillingham:

- Gillingham can require Canterbury to return the machines at any time within the six-month period, suggesting that Gillingham still exercise control over the machines

- Canterbury can return unsold machines to Gillingham at any time during the six-month period, without penalty. Therefore they can transfer the significant risk of obsolescence back to Gillingham.

Canterbury does hold some of the risks and rewards of ownership associated with the vehicles however Canterbury can return the vehicles at any time without penalty and, as noted above, this would indicate that the risk of obsolescence is with Gillingham.

As this is seen as the most significant risk, Gillingham should continue to recognise the goods within its inventories.

Test your understanding 6 (case style)

(a) Accounting treatment

There is a clause allowing Triangle to repurchase the inventory, indicating a sale and repurchase agreement. Where there is an option to repurchase, the likelihood of the option being exercised should be assessed.

Triangle can repurchase the inventory at $7,320,500 at 31 March 20X8, i.e.$5 million × 1.1^4 = $7,320,500. Since the market value is expected to be $8.5 million at this time it is likely that Triangle will repurchase the inventory.

Furthermore, since the goods remain on Triangle's premises during the 4 years this would suggest that Triangle are still exposed to the risks of ownership and have managerial involvement/control over the goods. IAS 18 does not allow revenue to be recognised until these have transferred to the buyer.

A final indicator that this is not a straightforward sale is the fact that Triangle have received proceeds of $5 million when the current market value is in excess of this amount. (Note however that this factor alone would not lead to the conclusion that there is not a sale, as Triangle may have chosen to sell the goods at a discount.)

In conclusion, Triangle has not sold the inventory but has simply taken out a loan of $5 million with interest at 10% per annum that is secured on the inventory.

Therefore, Triangle should not have recorded a sale, but instead should have recorded a loan of $5 million with a finance cost of 10% per annum. The goods should remain in inventory at their cost of $3 million.

(b) Accounting adjustments

To correct the entries Triangle recorded in error:

	$m
Dr Revenue (to reverse the sale)	5
Cr Liability	5

Reinstate the closing inventory:

	$m
Dr Closing inventory (SFP)	3
Cr Closing inventory (SP/L)	3

Record the interest for the year at 10% × $5m = $0.5m:

	$m
Dr Finance cost	0.5
Cr Liability	0.5

Test your understanding 7 (further OTQs)

(1) **B and D are correct.**

A is not correct. Although the option to repurchase has not been exercised, there is still a requirement to repurchase at 31 March 20X6 and therefore the risks and rewards of ownership have not transferred to the finance house.

C is not correct. The liability at the year end would be $7.6 million as this is the repurchase price at the reporting date. The extra $0.6 million reflects interest for the year on the liability.

(2) Revenue is the gross **inflow** of economic **benefit** during the period arising in the course of the ordinary activities of an entity.

Revenue should be measured at **fair** value.

(3) **Revenue = $475,000**

Total revenue from support services = 600,000 – 450,000 = 150,000

Annual revenue from support services = 150,000/3 years = 50,000

Revenue to be recognised in current period = 50,000 × 6/12 = 25,000 (for July to Dec)

Therefore, total revenue to be recognised = 450,000 (for IT system) + 25,000 (for service) = $475,000

Provisions, contingent liabilities and contingent assets

Chapter learning objectives

B1. Produce consolidated primary financial statements, incorporating accounting transactions and adjustments, in accordance with relevant international accounting standards, in an ethical manner.

(c) Discuss the provisions of relevant international accounting standards in respect of the recognition and measurement of provisions and the need for and nature of disclosures of contingent assets and liabilities, in accordance with IAS 37.

(d) Produce the accounting entries, in accordance with relevant international accounting standards.

(e) Discuss the ethical selection and adoption of relevant accounting policies and accounting estimates.

1 Session content

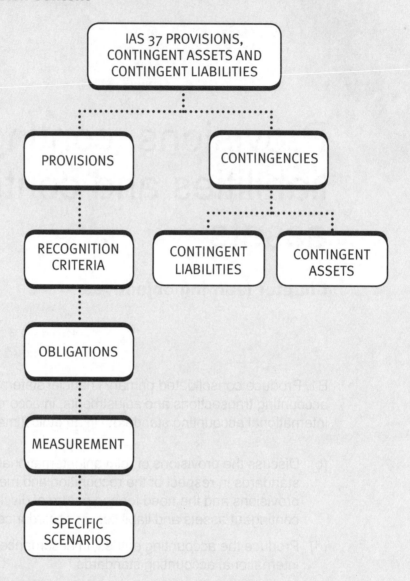

2 Introduction

The problem

Until the issue of IAS 37 *Provisions, Contingent Liabilities and Contingent Assets*, provisions was an accounting area that was open to manipulation.

- Provisions were often recognised as a result of an intention to make expenditure, rather than an obligation to do so.

- Entities would often create provisions to depress profits in good years and then reverse them at a later date when profits needed a boost (a technique known as profit smoothing).

- Several items could be aggregated into one large provision that was then reported as an exceptional item (the 'big bath provision').

- Inadequate disclosure meant that in some cases it was difficult to ascertain the significance of provisions.

As a result, IAS 37 introduced a set of criteria that must be satisfied before a provision can be recognised. The standard also requires comprehensive disclosure of any provisions that have been made so that users can understand the impact that they have had on the financial performance of the reporting entity.

3 Provisions

A **provision** is a liability of uncertain timing or amount.

A **liability** is a present obligation of the entity arising from past events, the settlement of which is expected to result in an outflow from the entity of resources embodying economic benefits.

Recognition of a provision

A provision should be recognised when:

- an entity has a present obligation (legal or constructive) as a result of a past event
- it is probable that an outflow of resources embodying economic benefits will be required to settle the obligation, and
- a reliable estimate can be made of the amount of the obligation.

If any one of these conditions is not met, no provision may be recognised.

Obligations

The obligation can be:

- legal, i.e. arising from
  - a contract
  - legislation
  - other operation of law
- constructive, i.e the entity has created a valid expectation via
  - established pattern of past practice
  - published policy or statement

Example 1 – constructive obligation

A retail store has a policy of refunding purchases by dissatisfied customers, even though it is under no legal obligation to do so. Its policy of making refunds is generally known.

Should a provision be made at the year end?

- The policy is well known and creates a valid expectation.

- There is a constructive obligation.

- It is probable some refunds will be made.

- These can be measured using expected values.

Conclusion: A provision is required.

Probable outflow

The outflow of resources must be considered to be more likely than not.

Where there are a number of similar obligations, probability is assessed across the entire class of obligations rather than individually.

Example 2 – probable outflow

An entity sells goods with a warranty covering customers for the cost of repairs required within the first 12 months after purchase. Past experience suggests that 95% of goods sold will not require a warranty repair.

Should a provision be made for warranty repairs?

If each sale were considered individually, no provision would be made as there is only a 5% probability of the goods being returned for repair.

However, if sales are considered as a whole, there is a high likelihood of 5% being returned for repair. Therefore, a provision should be made for the expected cost of repairs to 5% of the goods sold in the last 12 months.

Reliable estimate

The standard states that situations in which a reliable estimate cannot be made should be rare.

The estimate should be:

- the best estimate of likely outflow
- a prudent estimate
- discounted when time value of money is material

Test your understanding 1 (integration question)

An entity has a policy of only carrying out work to rectify damage caused to the environment when it is required by local law to do so. For several years the entity has been operating an oil rig that causes such damage in a country that did not have legislation in place requiring any rectification.

A new government has now been elected in that country and, at the reporting date, has just brought in legislation requiring rectification of environmental damage. The legislation will have retrospective effect.

Required:

Explain whether a provision should be recognised.

Test your understanding 2 (case style)

You are an accountant working for SZ, a manufacturer that provides warranties to its customers for all sales. Under the terms of the warranty, SZ undertakes to make good manufacturing defects that become apparent within 2 years from the date of sale. Based on past experience, it estimates that 8% of goods will be returned for repair within this 2 year period.

A new Managing Director has recently been appointed and he has asked you to explain to him why there is an expense in the statement of profit or loss relating to warranty claims that have not yet been received.

Required:

Prepare a briefing note for the Managing Director explaining, with reference to the recognition criteria of IAS 37, why an expense is required for future potential warranty repairs.

Test your understanding 3 (case style)

You work as an accountant for PK, a small family business, and the Managing Director has sent you the following email:

"I've recently found out from our health and safety manager that, due to a change in legislation enacted on 30 November 20X0, we are required to fit smoke filters to our factories by 30 June 20X1. I assume this means that we will have to recognise an expense for the fitting of the filters in our financial statements for the year ended 31 December 20X0. We will not be fitting the filters until June 20X1. Please can you drop me a line and confirm whether I'm correct about this.

Many thanks, Bill."

Required:

Prepare an email to the Managing Director explaining whether PK should make a provision for the cost of fitting the smoke filters in its financial statements for the year ended 31 December 20X0.

4 Specific applications

The standard provides additional guidance on how to apply the rules to specific scenarios.

Future operating losses

Provisions cannot be made for future operating losses – as they do not meet the definition of a liability (they are an expectation rather than an obligation).

Onerous contracts

An onerous contract is a contract in which the unavoidable costs of meeting the obligations under the contract exceed the economic benefits expected to be received under it.

A provision is required for the 'least net cost' of exiting the contract, which is the lower of:

- cost of fulfilling the contract
- any compensation/penalties payable for failing to fulfil it

Example 3 – onerous contract

CEG has ten years left to run on the lease of a property that it has recently vacated. The present value of the future rentals at the reporting date is $50,000. The cost of terminating the lease early is $55,000.

How should the above scenario be accounted for?

A provision should be made for $50,000 which is the least net cost of exiting the contract.

To record the provision:

	$000
Dr Expense (profit or loss)	50
Cr Provision	50

When the rental payments are subsequently paid, the provision for the costs of the onerous lease will reduce.

The following entry is posted:

Dr	Provision
Cr	Cash

Restructuring

A restructuring is a programme planned and controlled by management that materially changes the scope of business undertaken or the manner in which that business is conducted.

A provision can only be made if:

* the entity has a detailed formal plan, and
* has raised a valid expectation in those affected that it will carry out the restructuring by
    - starting to implement it, or
    - announcing it

Provision can then only be made for costs that are:

* necessarily entailed by the restructuring, and
* not associated with the ongoing activities of the entity.

Costs specifically not allowed include retraining/relocation of existing staff, marketing and investment in new systems.

Example 4 – restructuring

On 14 June 20X2 a decision is made by the board of directors of KCM to close down a division and a detailed plan is drawn up. At the year end of 30 June 20X2, no announcement has been made in respect of the closure and no steps have been taken to implement the decision. The expected costs of closing the division are $750,000.

Should a provision be made for the expected costs of closing the division?

No – a board decision is not sufficient to require a provision as no obligation exists.

A detailed formal plan must exist, however this alone is not sufficient to create an obligation. The plan must also have been communicated to those affected by it. A constructive obligation will arise at this point in time as management have then created a valid expectation that the plan will proceed and they are unlikely to change their mind.

Test your understanding 4 (case style)

The board of CLH agreed to close down two of its divisions, A and B, at its board meeting on 18 November 20X3. Detailed plans have been formalised for each division's closure and these were approved by the board at this meeting.

The current status of each of the closures is as follows:

Division A

Letters have been sent to customers warning them to seek an alternative source of supply and a redundancy programme was announced to all staff working in the division on 1 December.

The expected costs of closure are $2.5 million and this includes $450,000 for re-deploying staff to other divisions.

Division B

The directors want to deal with the closures one at a time and therefore no announcements have yet been made about the closure of division B. The directors are keen to minimise the effect that the closures will have on staff working in other divisions and have therefore decided to keep this closure quiet for the moment.

The expected costs of closure are $1.5 million. All staff are likely to be made redundant and therefore no re-deployment costs are included in this estimate.

Required:

You have been asked to prepare a memo for the board of directors, briefly explaining the appropriate accounting treatment of the above decisions in the financial statements of CLH for the year ended 31 December 20X3.

Provisions for dismantling/decommissioning costs

When a facility such as an oil well or mine is authorised by the government, the licence normally includes a legal obligation for the entity to decommission the facility at the end of its useful life. IAS 37 requires a provision to be recognised for the decommissioning costs.

The decommissioning costs form part of the cost of the asset and are therefore capitalised and expensed over the life of the asset (as part of the depreciation charge).

The provision is only recorded once damage has been incurred to the land upon which the oil well or mine will be located. The obligation to incur the decommission costs is only created at the point damage/changes to the land occurs.

To record the provision:

Dr Asset (oil well/mine)
Cr Provision

The provision should be based on the present value of the expected decommissioning cost and therefore, in addition, a finance cost will arise each year as the discount is unwound.

To unwind the discount:

Dr   Finance cost (P/L)
Cr   Provision

Example 5 – decommissioning costs

On 1 January 20X1, KJC acquires a mine costing $5 million and, as part of the licence granted by the government for operation of the mine, it will be required to pay decommissioning costs at the end of the mine's useful life of 20 years. The present value of these decommissioning costs is $1 million and the discount rate applied is 10%.

KJC depreciate assets on a straight line basis.

Explain the effect of the above transaction on the financial statements of KJC for the year ended 31 December 20X1.

The total cost to be recognised for the mine is $6 million (the $5 million purchase price plus the $1 million decommissioning cost).

This will then be depreciated over 20 years, resulting in an annual depreciation charge of $300,000 ($6 million/20 years). Note that, by capitalising the decommissioning cost, it's effect on profit is spread over the 20 year life of the mine.

The decommissioning costs are recorded by making a provision. The initial provision is based on the present value of the costs and the provision is increased each year to reflect the unwinding of the discount applied. In the year ended 31 December 20X1 this would create a finance cost of $100,000 (10% × $1 million).

The overall effect on the financial statements for the year ended 31 December 20X1 is:

Statement of profit or loss

	$000
Depreciation ($6 million/20 yrs)	(300)
Finance cost ($1 million × 10%)	(100)

Statement of financial position

	$000
Non-current assets:	
Mine ($6m – $300k)	5,700
Non-current liabilities:	
Provision ($1m + (10% × $1m))	1,100

5 Contingent liabilities and assets

A **contingent liability** is:

- a possible obligation that arises from past events and whose existence will be confirmed only by the occurrence or non-occurrence of one or more uncertain future events not wholly within the control of the entity, or

- a present obligation that arises from past events but is not recognised because:
    - it is not probable that an outflow of resources embodying economic benefits will be required to settle the obligation, or

    - the amount of the obligation cannot be measured with sufficient reliability.

Accounting for a contingent liability

A contingent liability is:

- not recognised

- disclosed in a note, unless the possibility of outflow is remote

A **contingent asset** is a possible asset that arises from past events and whose existence will be confirmed only by the occurrence or non-occurrence of one or more uncertain future events not wholly within the control of the entity.

Accounting for a contingent asset

A contingent asset is:

- not recognised

- disclosed in a note, if an inflow is considered probable.

Disclosures required for contingent liabilities and assets

- Description of nature of contingent liability/asset
- An estimate of its financial effect
- An indication of uncertainties relating to amount or timing of outflow/inflow
- For contingent liabilities, the possibility of any reimbursement

Example 6 – contingent liabilities and assets

Entity A is suing entity B in respect of losses sustained from faulty goods supplied by entity B. Entity A's lawyers are unwilling to state the likelihood of the claim being successful.

Entity B's lawyers have told entity B to expect to have to pay damages but are unable at present to provide a reliable estimate of the amount payable.

How would each entity account for the above scenario?

Entity A has a contingent asset in the form of damages receivable. However, no disclosure would be likely at this point as contingent assets are only disclosed when they are considered probable and entity A's lawyers are unwilling to confirm this.

Entity B has a contingent liability relating to the damages payable. Entity B has a possible liability which would be treated as a contingent liability. Entity B should disclose information about the anticipated payment unless its probability is considered to be remote.

Test your understanding 5 (case style)

BH's directors are unsure how to treat a number of potential transactions in the financial statements for the year ended 31 August 20X5. Details of these transactions are provided below.

Transaction 1

A significant amount of inventory was stolen in July 20X5 and BH has made a claim with its insurance provider to recover the value of the goods. It is hoping to receive $1.5 million from the insurer however it has not yet received confirmation that the claim has been accepted. It is keen however to recognise the $1.5 million to cancel out the effect of the stolen goods on profit for the year.

Transaction 2

A customer is suing BH for production delays caused by the theft of the inventory, as BH was unable to provide replacement goods on a timely basis. BH does not believe that it is responsible for covering the cost of the delay, however BH's lawyers have indicated that there is a possibility, based on precedent, that the customer's claim could be successful.

Transaction 3

BH has placed an order for plant and machinery with a purchase cost of $4 million. The plant and machinery has not been delivered at the year end however BH believes it should recognise a liability for the $4 million as it has signed a contract with the supplier agreeing the price.

Required:

You have been asked to draft a note, to be circulated to the board of directors, explaining how the above transactions should be reflected in the financial statements of BH for the year ended 31 August 20X5. Please note that the majority of the directors do not have a financial background and will not necessarily understand accounting terminology.

Summary

The accounting treatment can be summarised as follows:

Degree of probability of an outflow/inflow of resources	Liability	Asset
Virtually certain	Recognise	Recognise
Probable	Make provision	Disclose by note
Possible	Disclose by note	No disclosure
Remote	No disclosure	No disclosure

Test your understanding 6 (OTQ style qns)

(1) HH has announced the closure of one of its divisions prior to its reporting date and is unsure which costs to include in its provision. The closure is expected to take place on 1 March 20X5 and HH's reporting date is 30 November 20X4.

Which of the costs should be recognised within a provision for closure of the division as at 30 November 20X4? Select all that apply.

A   Redundancy costs

B   Operating loss expected for period from 1 December 20X4 to 1 March 20X5

C   Legal and professional fees relating to closure

D   Staff retraining

(2) KJ operates in the oil industry and causes contamination. It runs its operations in a country in which there is no environmental legislation. KJ has a widely published environmental policy in which it undertakes to clean up all contamination that it causes and it has a record of honouring this policy.

Which one of the following statements is correct?

A   KJ should not make a provision as there is no legislation requiring it to incur costs of cleaning up the contamination.

B   KJ has created a constructive obligation by publishing its environmental policy and therefore a provision is required.

C   KJ should make a provision for the costs of cleaning up the contamination that it is expected to cause.

D   KJ should disclose a contingent liability in case it decides to incur the clean up costs for contamination caused.

(3) **Which one of the following situations would require a provision in the financial statements of FM at its reporting date, 31 October 20X2?**

A   The government introduced new laws on data protection which come into force on 1 January 20X3. FM's directors have agreed that this will require a large number of staff to be retrained and have produced a reliable estimate of the costs of this training.

B   FM have a policy of making refunds to customers for any goods returned within 28 days of sale and has done so for many years. It is under no obligation to make the refunds. It anticipate that 5% of sales made in October 20X2 will be returned by 28 November 20X2.

C   FM has recently purchased an item of machinery and health and safety legislation requires that a major overhaul should be carried out once every 3 years. FM have estimated the cost of the overhaul and are planning to make a provision of 1/3 of the cost to represent the asset's use to date.

D   FM is being sued by a customer for faulty goods supplied. FM's lawyers have estimated that there is a 40% likelihood of the customer's claim being successful and believes that a reliable estimate can be made of the damages that would be payable.

(4) LR have claimed compensation of $30,000 from another entity for breach of copyright. The solicitors of LR have advised that their claim is 80% likely to succeed.

Which one of the following is the correct treatment of the above situation in the financial statements of LR?

A   An asset of $30,000 should be recognised in the financial statements.

B   An asset of $24,000 should be recognised in the financial statements.

C   The claim should be disclosed in a note to the financial statements.

D   The financial statements should not recognise or disclose any information about the claim.

6 Chapter summary

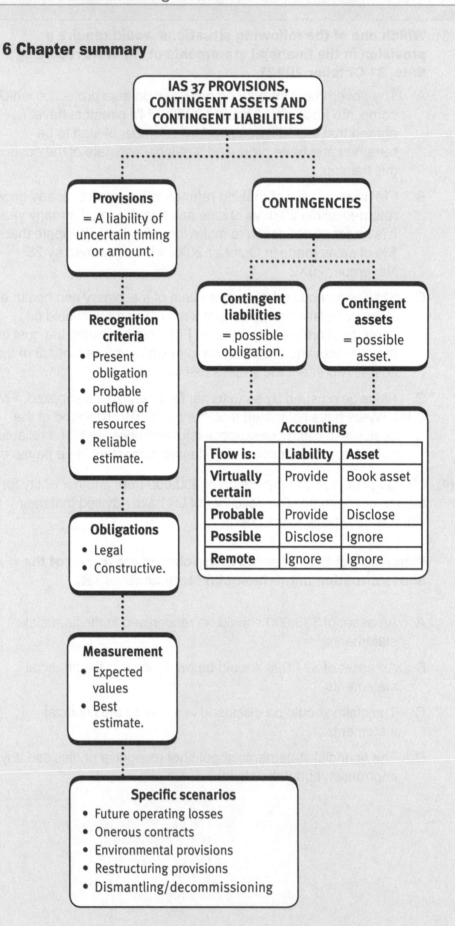

IAS 37 PROVISIONS, CONTINGENT ASSETS AND CONTINGENT LIABILITIES

Provisions
= A liability of uncertain timing or amount.

CONTINGENCIES

Contingent liabilities
= possible obligation.

Contingent assets
= possible asset.

Recognition criteria
- Present obligation
- Probable outflow of resources
- Reliable estimate.

Accounting

Flow is:	Liability	Asset
Virtually certain	Provide	Book asset
Probable	Provide	Disclose
Possible	Disclose	Ignore
Remote	Ignore	Ignore

Obligations
- Legal
- Constructive.

Measurement
- Expected values
- Best estimate.

Specific scenarios
- Future operating losses
- Onerous contracts
- Environmental provisions
- Restructuring provisions
- Dismantling/decommissioning

Test your understanding answers

Test your understanding 1 (integration question)

As the new legislation will have retrospective effect, there is a present obligation arising from the damage already caused by the oil rig and therefore a provision should be made, assuming that a reliable estimate can be made of the costs involved.

Test your understanding 2 (case style)

Briefing note to Managing Director

As requested, please find below an explanation of the reason for the warranty expense in the statement of profit or loss. The accounting standard that is being applied here is IAS 37 Provisions, contingent liabilities and contingent assets. To recognise a provision, the entity will Dr P/L Cr Provision. Before the expense and provision can be recognised, the entity must ensure that IAS 37 is applied properly.

This accounting standard lists three recognition criteria that, if satisfied, result in the recognition of a provision in the financial statements.

Firstly, there must be a present obligation arising from a past event. By offering warranties we have created a contractual obligation to make repairs for any sales made in the past 2 years. The sale itself is the past event giving rise to the obligation.

Secondly, it must be considered probable that there will be an outflow of resources required to satisfy the obligation. The entire class of sales should be considered when assessing the probability and, from our past experience, we consider it probable that 8% of the goods will require repair. The provision is therefore based on this amount.

Finally, a provision can only be made if a reliable estimate can be made of the outflow required. This shouldn't be a problem for warranty repairs as past experience can be used to calculate the average cost of a repair and we have information about the number of goods sold.

As all three of the IAS 37 criteria are satisfied, we are required to make a provision for the expected cost of repairs to 8% of the goods sold in the last 2 years. When the repair costs are then incurred we will deduct the cost from the provision rather than expensing it in the statement of profit or loss (as the expense has already been recognised).

I trust that this explanation is satisfactory however please contact me if you need any further information.

Test your understanding 3 (case style)

Email to Managing Director

Dear Bill,

I can understand why you think there should be an expense recognised, however there is no 'past event giving rise to a present obligation' - the key requirement for a provision to be recognised - and therefore we shouldn't create a provision and recognise an expense for the cost of fitting the filters.

Although the legislation has already been enacted, the requirement to fit the smoke filters does not arise for another six months after the reporting date.

It's also worth noting that, even if there was a requirement to fit the filters by the reporting date and we had not done so, we would still not have to make a provision for the cost of fitting as there is only an obligation to incur the cost when the filters have been installed. However, we would be required to make a provision for any fines or penalties arising from non-compliance with the legislation.

Just let me know if you have any further queries.

Test your understanding 4 (case style)

Memo to Board of Directors of CLH

As requested, please find below an explanation of the appropriate accounting treatment of the two closures planned. The accounting treatment is governed by IAS 37 Provisions, Contingent Liabilities and Contingent Assets – which states that a provision should only be made for closure of a division if there is a formal detailed plan and it has been communicated to those who will be affected by it. It also contains rules on what costs should be provided.

Division A

As notice of the closure has been sent to customers and staff involved, a valid expectation has been created that the closure of the division will go ahead. A constructive obligation therefore exists and provision should be made for the costs of closure. Only the costs necessarily entailed by the closure should be included in the provision. The costs of redeployment are associated with the ongoing activities and should therefore be excluded from the provision.

Assuming that the other closure costs meet the criteria necessary, a provision of $2,050,000 would be made in the financial statements for the year ended 31 December 20X3.

Division B

Although there is a detailed formal plan for this closure, it has not been communicated outside the board of directors and therefore no obligation exists at the year end. Therefore, no provision should be made for the expected costs of closure of division B.

Test your understanding 5 (case style)

Note to Directors

As requested, I've prepared this note to explain how three transactions should be reflected in the financial statements for the year ended 31 August 20X5.

Transaction 1 – $1.5 million potential receipt from insurer re theft of inventory

Unfortunately, we cannot recognise this $1.5 million in the financial statements as we are not certain that we will receive the money.

This is known in accounting terms as a contingent asset and, if we consider it probable (greater than 50% chance) that the claim will be accepted and the amount will be received then we should disclose information about it (the nature of the claim and the likely amount) in a note to the financial statements. If however we only consider it possible rather than probable (i.e. less than 50% chance) then no disclosure should be made at all.

The amount can only be recognised as an asset when its receipt becomes virtually certain. This would be when the insurer confirms that it will pay the money out.

Transaction 2 – customer claim re production delays

The claim by the customer is an example of a contingent liability and should be disclosed in a note to the financial statements unless its likelihood is considered 'remote'.

The delay in providing the goods to the customer gives rise to a potential obligation and the lawyer's opinion suggests that the likelihood is more than remote. We should therefore disclose information about the claim in a note to the financial statements.

If we actually thought that the likelihood was probable (>50% chance) and a reliable estimate could be made of the damages payable then a provision would be required and we would have to recognise the expected damages as an expense in the statement of profit or loss.

The probability is a matter of judgement and this is something that should be discussed further with the lawyers.

Transaction 3 – contract for purchase of plant and machinery

The obligation to pay $4 million does not arise until the plant and machinery has been delivered and accepted by BH. Therefore no liability would be recognised until then.

Test your understanding 6 (OTQ style qns)

(1) **Costs A and C**

B is incorrect as provisions cannot be made for future operating losses.

D is incorrect as staff training relates to the ongoing activities of the business.

(2) **B is the correct statement.**

A is incorrect. Although there is no legal obligation, there is a constructive obligation and therefore a provision is still required.

C is incorrect. A provision would be made only for contamination that had already been caused (as there must be a past event resulting in a present obligation).

D is incorrect. As KJ have created a constructive obligation, it is not considered to be contingent.

(3) **B is the correct answer.**

A is incorrect. There is no obligation at the reporting date.

C is incorrect. There is no present obligation to carry out the overhaul (the entity could choose to sell the asset instead).

D is incorrect. This would be a contingent liability. It fails to meet the recognition criteria for a provision as it is not considered probable (more likely than not).

(4) **C**

An asset cannot be recognised until it is virtually certain (80% would not suggest this). As the success of the claim is considered probable however, disclosure would be made of this contingent asset.

Deferred tax

Chapter learning objectives

B1. Produce consolidated primary financial statements, incorporating accounting transactions and adjustments, in accordance with relevant international accounting standards, in an ethical manner.

(c) Discuss the provisions of relevant international accounting standards in respect of the recognition and measurement of the provision for deferred tax, in accordance with IAS 12.

(d) Produce the accounting entries, in accordance with relevant international accounting standards.

1 Session content

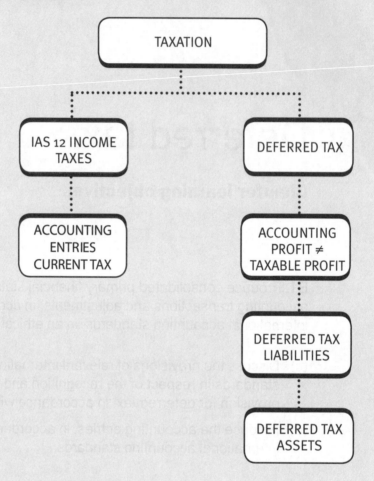

2 IAS 12 Income taxes

IAS 12 covers the general principles of accounting for tax.

The income tax expense in the statement of profit or loss typically consists of three elements:

- current tax expense for the year
- under or over provisions in relation to the tax expense of the previous period
- deferred tax.

The current tax expense, together with under or over provisions, are assessed in F1. A recap can be found in the expandable text below. The F2 syllabus focuses on accounting for deferred tax.

Current tax

Current tax is the estimated amount of tax payable on the taxable profits of the enterprise for the period.

Taxable profits are the profits on which tax is payable, calculated in accordance with the rules of local tax authorities.

At the end of every accounting period, the entity will estimate the amount of tax payable in respect of the period. This estimate is normally recorded as a period end adjustment by making the following double entry:

Dr   Income tax expense (SPL)
Cr   Income tax liability (SFP – current liability)

Under and over provisions

Income tax for the period is accrued in one financial period and then settled in the next. The amount settled often differs from the amount accrued in the previous year's financial statements. The difference between the amount accrued (in the previous year) and the amount settled (in the current year) is recorded in the current year's income tax expense as an under or over provision relating to the prior period.

Amount settled > amount previously recognised => under-provision. This creates an additional tax expense(debit).

Amount settled < amount previously recognised => over-provision. This creates a reduction in tax expense (credit).

Example 1

Simple has estimated its income tax liability for the year ended 31 December 20X4 at $180,000. In the previous year the income tax liability had been estimated as $150,000.

Required:

Calculate the tax charge that will be recognised in the statement of profit or loss for the year ended 31 December 20X4 if the amount that was actually agreed and settled with the tax authorities in respect of 20X3 was:

(a) $165,000

(b) $140,000

State what the income tax liability would be at 31 December 20X4 in each of the above circumstances.

Example 1 answer

(a) **Under provision**

Statement of profit or loss charge:

	$
Current tax expense for year	180,000
Add: under-provision relating to prior year (165,000 – 150,000)	15,000
	———
Income tax expense	195,000
	———

(b) **Over provision**

Statement of profit or loss charge:

	$
Current tax expense for year	180,000
Less: over-provision relating to prior year (150,000 – 140,000)	(10,000)
	———
Income tax expense	170,000
	———

In both situations, the income tax liability at 31 December 20X4 would be $180,000 (reflecting the current year's liability only).

By making an adjustment to the income tax expense to reflect the under/over provision, the remaining balance relating to the previous period has been written off through profit or loss.

3 Deferred tax

Deferred tax is:

- the estimated **future** tax consequences of transactions and events recognised in the financial statements of the **current** and **previous** periods.

Deferred tax does not represent the tax payable to the tax authorities.

Deferred tax is a basis of allocating tax charges to particular accounting periods. It is an application of the accruals concept and aims to eliminate a mismatch between:

- **accounting profit**, the profit before tax figure in the statement of profit or loss, and
- **taxable profit**, the figure on which the tax authorities base their tax calculations.

The differences between accounting profit and taxable profit can be caused by:

- permanent differences (e.g. expenses not allowed for tax purposes)
- temporary differences (e.g. expenses allowed for tax purposes but in a later accounting period)

Only temporary differences are taken into account when calculating deferred tax.

Temporary differences are differences between the carrying amount of an asset or liability in the statement of financial position and its tax base (i.e. the amount attributed to it for tax purposes).

Examples of temporary differences include:

- certain types of income and expenditure that are taxed on a cash, rather than an accruals basis, e.g. certain provisions
- the difference between the depreciation charged on a non-current asset and the actual tax allowances given (see the expandable text below for an example of this scenario)

The accounting problem

One important reason why deferred tax should be recognised is that profit for tax purposes may differ from the profit shown by the financial statements. Such a difference may be caused by permanent or temporary factors. For example, if expenses in the statement of profit or loss are not allowed for tax purposes, a **permanent difference** arises. Nothing can be done about that, and the increased tax charge just has to be accepted.

A **temporary difference** arises when an expense is allowed for both tax and accounting purposes, but the timing of the allowance differs. For example, if relief for capital expenditure is given at a faster rate for tax purposes than the depreciation in the financial statements, the tax charge will be lower in the first years than it would have been based on the accounting profit, but in subsequent years the tax charge will be higher.

It is important to remember that **only temporary differences give rise to deferred tax**.

For example, an item of plant and machinery is purchased by U in 20X0 for $300,000. The asset's estimated useful life is 6 years, following which it will have no residual value. Plant and machinery is depreciated on a straight-line basis.

Tax depreciation for this item is given at 25% on the straight-line basis for the first 4 years.

Let us first calculate the figures that would appear in the financial statements over the six-year life of the asset:

Financial statements	20X0 $000	20X1 $000	20X2 $000	20X3 $000	20X4 $000	20X5 $000
Opening carrying value	300	250	200	150	100	50
Accounting depreciation charge	50	50	50	50	50	50
Closing carrying value	250	200	150	100	50	0

Depreciation is charged at $50,000 per annum ($300,000/6 years).

Now let us look at how this asset would be treated for tax purposes:

Tax computation	20X0 $000	20X1 $000	20X2 $000	20X3 $000	20X4 $000	20X5 $000
Opening carrying value	300	225	150	75	0	0
Tax depreciation	75	75	75	75	–	–
Tax base	225	150	75	0	0	0

We can see from comparing the above two tables that the carrying value of the asset per the accounts differs from the tax base. The annual reduction in the carrying value applied by the entity (that is, accounting depreciation) differs from the reduction applied in the tax computation. By the end of the asset's useful life, the two have caught up, as they both show the asset with a carrying value of 0, but the different treatment over 6 years creates the need for deferred tax.

4 Accounting for deferred tax

Deferred tax is accounted for using a statement of financial position approach as follows:

(1) Establish the temporary difference at the year end = carrying value of net assets less the tax base

(2) Deferred tax balance (for SFP) = temporary difference × tax rate

Note that this could be a liability or asset, depending on whether the future tax consequence would increase or decrease the tax payable.

– It will be a deferred tax liability if the carrying value of net assets is greater than the tax base. This is the situation where there are taxable temporary differences.

– It would be a deferred tax asset if the carrying value of net assets was lower than the tax base. In this situation there would be deductable temporary differences.

(3) Deferred tax expense/credit (for SPL&OCI) = increase/decrease in deferred tax balance in year

The cumulative deferred tax balance in the statement of financial position would be presented as a **non-current** item.

The movement in the deferred tax balance is usually recognised as an adjustment to the income tax expense in the statement of profit or loss. However, if it relates to an item that has been recognised in other comprehensive income then the deferred tax impact should also be recognised in other comprehensive income. This is covered in more detail later in the chapter.

Example 2

Messy Ltd has purchased an asset for $300 and this will be depreciated over three years on a straight line basis.

The tax depreciation will be $140 in year 1, $110 in year 2 and $50 in year 3.

The current tax rate is 30%.

Required:

Prepare the journal entries required to record the deferred tax on the above asset for years 1, 2 and 3.

Example 2 answer

Year	SFP carrying value	Tax base	Temporary difference	Difference × 30%
	$	$	$	$
1	300	300		
	(100)	(140)		
	___	___		
	200	160	40	12
2	(100)	(110)		
	___	___		
	100	50	50	15
3	(100)	(50)		
	___	___		
	0	0	0	0

The difference at 30% represents the total deferred tax liability required in the statement of financial position. The difference is a taxable temporary difference because the accounting depreciation is less than the tax depreciation, i.e. the carrying value in the SFP is greater than the tax base.

The movement in the difference at 30% represents the increase/ (decrease) in the deferred tax liability required for the year. These are the entries to be made to the statement of profit or loss.

Statement of profit or loss	Year 1	Year 2	Year 3
Income tax expense/(credit)	12	3	(15)

Statement of financial position			
Non-current liabilities			
Deferred tax	12	15	0

Journal entries

Year 1

Dr	Income tax expense (SPL)		$12
Cr	Deferred tax liability (SFP)		$12

Year 2

Dr	Income tax expense (SPL)		$3
Cr	Deferred tax liability (SFP)		$3

Year 3

Dr	Deferred tax liability (SFP)		$15
Cr	Income tax expense (SPL)		$15

Test your understanding 1 (integration question)

Aquarius Ltd's draft financial statements for the year ended 31 December 20X9 show a profit before tax of $170,000. At 31 December 20X9 there are cumulative taxable temporary differences of $50,000, i.e. the carrying value of the net assets is higher than the tax base by this amount. Current tax for the year at 30% has been estimated at $33,000.

For the year ended 31 December 20X8 the financial statements had a profit before tax of $145,000. At 31 December 20X8 the cumulative taxable temporary differences were $40,000 and current tax for the year at 30% was $30,000.

Required:

For the years ended 31 December 20X8 and 31 December 20X9:

(a) Prepare the journal entry to record deferred tax for the years ended 31 December 20X8 and 20X9

(b) Prepare extracts from the statement of profit or loss for the year ended 31 December 20X9 and the statement of financial position at 31 December 20X9, both with comparatives, showing how the current and deferred tax would be reflected.

Test your understanding 2 (integration question)

Parker Ltd's statement of financial position includes a number of assets and liabilities that give rise to temporary differences as follows at the current reporting date:

	Carrying value	Tax base
	$000	$000
Property, plant and equipment (1)	26,500	18,000
Held to maturity financial assets (2)	1,020	1,000
Trade receivables (3)	5,700	6,500
Warranty provision (4)	(1,200)	0
Long-term borrowings (2)	(22,200)	(19,500)

(1) Property, plant and equipment is depreciated in the financial statements on a straight line basis over the assets' useful lives. Tax depreciation is 30% on a reducing balance basis.

(2) The held to maturity asset and long-term borrowings are measured using the amortised cost method in the financial statements. Tax is payable/receivable on interest and any redemption premium on a cash received/paid basis and therefore a temporary difference arises.

(3) Trade receivables have a gross receivables balance of $6.5 million however Parker Limited has created a specific allowance against $800,000 which is four months old at the reporting date. Bad debts only become tax deductible after 12 months.

(4) Parker Limited offers one year warranties on its products. Warranty costs are tax deductible when warranty repairs are incurred.

The corporate income tax rate is 25%.

> **Required:**
>
> **Calculate the deferred tax balance on the above assets and liabilities at the reporting date, clearly stating for each item whether the deferred tax balance would be an asset or liability.**

5 Deferred tax on losses

A deferred tax asset is recognised on unutilised losses carried forward (as there will be a future tax benefit when the losses are offset against future profits).

However, the asset can only be recognised to the extent that it is probable that future taxable profits will be available against which the losses can be utilised.

Test your understanding 3 (OTQ style)

Simpson Limited has only been trading for two years and has not yet made a profit. It has losses available for carry forward of $75,000. It expects to make profits of $25,000 per annum for the next two years but is not in a position to estimate profits beyond this.

The current corporate income tax rate is 30%.

Required:

Prepare the journal entry to record the deferred tax arising on the losses.

6 Deferred tax impact in OCI

Any deferred tax charge/credit that relates to an item that has been recognised in other comprehensive income should also be recognised in other comprehensive income.

The most common example of this relates to the revaluation of non-current assets:

- When an asset is revalued upwards, it increases the carrying value of the asset but it does not affect the tax base.

- The cumulative temporary difference therefore increases and this gives rise to an additional deferred tax liability.

- The revaluation surplus is recognised in other comprehensive income.

- Therefore, the movement in the deferred tax liability that relates to the revaluation surplus should also be recognised in other comprehensive income.

Test your understanding 4 (integration question)

On 1 January 20X8 Simone Limited decided to revalue its land for the first time. The land was originally purchased 6 years ago for $65,000 and it was revalued to its current market value of $80,000 on 1 January 20X8.

The difference between the carrying value of Simone's net assets (including the revaluation of land) and the (lower) tax base at 31 December 20X8 was $27,000.

The opening deferred tax liability at 1 January 20X8 was $2,600 and Simone's tax rate was 25%.

Required:

Prepare the journal entry required to record the movement in deferred tax in the year ended 31 December 20X8 in the financial statements of Simone Limited.

7 Deferred tax on share option schemes

Under IFRS 2 *Share-based Payment* an expense relating to a share option scheme is recognised in the statement of profit or loss over the vesting period and this is based on the fair value of the share options at the date they are granted.

For tax purposes however, a deduction is usually given when the options are exercised, i.e. after the end of the vesting period, and this is based on the intrinsic value of the options (the difference between the market price of the shares under option and the exercise price).

There is therefore a temporary difference between the impact of the scheme on profit and the impact in tax and this gives rise to a deferred tax asset (it is a deductible temporary difference giving rise to a future benefit). The deferred tax asset should be calculated using the intrinsic value of the options – as this is the amount on which the tax deduction will be based.

Illustration 1 – deferred tax on share option scheme

EM granted each of its 300 staff 100 options on 1 January 20X5. To exercise the options, the staff must work for the entity for the next three years and the options become exercisable on 31 December 20X7. The fair value at the date of grant is $10 per option and the exercise price is $8.

In the year ending 31 December 20X5, 11 staff leave and it is thought that a further 25 will leave over the remaining two years of the vesting period.

The share price at 31 December 20X5 is $15 and therefore the intrinsic value of each option is $7 (15 – 8). The corporate income tax rate is 20%.

Impact of the above in the financial statements for the year ended 31 December 20X5

Firstly, an expense (staff costs) will be recognised and credited to equity, calculated as follows in accordance with IFRS 2:

(300 – 11 – 25) × 100 × $10 × 1/3 = $88,000

Secondly, a deferred tax asset should be recognised to reflect the future tax benefit that will arise. This is based on the intrinsic value of the options at the reporting date as follows:

Temporary difference = (300 – 11 – 25) × 100 × $7 × 1/3 = $61,600

Note that the above calculation is the tax base, however it is also the temporary difference as the carrying value of the share option scheme is $nil (it does not result in an asset or a liability).

To calculate the deferred tax asset, the temporary difference is multiplied by the tax rate:

Deferred tax asset = 61,600 × 20% = $12,320

The journal entry would be:

Dr   Deferred tax asset $12,320

Cr   SPL – tax expense $12,320

The reduction in the tax expense matches the reduction in profit created by the IFRS 2 expense.

Test your understanding 5 (further OTQs)

(1) Tamsin plc's accounting records show the following:

Income tax payable for the year	$60,000
Opening deferred tax liability	$3,200
Closing deferred tax liability	$2,600

Calculate the income tax expense that would be recognised in Tamsin plc's statement of profit or loss for the year.

(2) On 1 January 20X1 Pegasus plc acquired motor vehicles at a cost of $100,000. The carrying value of the motor vehicles at 31 December 20X2 was $60,000 and the tax base was $56,250. The corporate income tax rate was 30%.

Calculate the deferred tax liability at 31 December 20X2.

(3) A piece of machinery cost $500. Tax depreciation to date has amounted to $220 and depreciation charged in the financial statements to date is $100. The rate of income tax is 30%.

Which three of the following statements are TRUE?

A   The tax base of the asset is $280

B   The tax base of the asset is $400

C   The cumulative temporary difference is $120

D   The cumulative temporary difference is $220

E   The asset gives rise to a deferred tax asset of $36

F   The asset gives rise to a deferred tax liability of $36

G   The asset gives rise to a deferred tax liability of $66

(4) ST has unused tax losses of $150,000 at its reporting date, 31 December 20X3. It estimates that it will make profits of $120,000 over the next five years but cannot be certain of profitability beyond five years' time.

The corporate income tax rate is 25%.

Calculate the deferred tax asset that should be recognised in ST's statement of financial position at 31 December 20X3 in respect of the losses.

(5) In the statement of financial position of XY at 31 March 20X9 there is a warranty provision of $350,000. The balance on the provision at the end of the previous year was $275,000. Warranty costs are deducted for tax purposes on a cash paid basis.

The corporate income tax rate is 20%.

Calculate the charge or credit that would appear in the statement of profit or loss of XY for the year ended 31 March 20X9 in respect of the deferred tax arising on the above warranty provision. State your answer in $ and clearly state whether the amount would be a debit or credit in the statement of profit or loss.

(6) AB made an investment of $250,000 in equity shares in another entity on 1 June 20X3 . It classified the investment as available for sale and the fair value of the investment at 31 October 20X3, the reporting date, was $280,000.

AB will pay tax on the shares when they are sold. The tax base of the shares is therefore $250,000 (their original cost).

The corporate income tax rate is 25%.

Complete the journal entry below to record the deferred tax arising on the available for sale investment in the financial statements of AB for the year ended 31 October 20X3.

Dr

Cr

Note: in the assessment, you would choose the headings for the Dr and Cr from a selection of choices.

(7) EF set up a share option scheme for its employees at the start of the year ended 31 December 20X5. The scheme has a three year vesting period and EF can claim a tax deduction when the options are exercised based on the intrinsic value of the options.

Which one of the following statements is TRUE in respect of the above scheme?

A   There is no deferred tax on the share option schemes as the carrying value and tax base are both $nil

B   A deferred tax charge and liability should be recognised as the share options affect accounting profit now but the tax consequence will arise later

C   The deferred tax calculation should be based on the fair value of the options at the grant date, as this is the value used to calculate the expense within accounting profit

D   A deferred tax asset should be recognised based on the intrinsic value of the options at the reporting date

(8) WS revalued its property, plant and equipment upwards by $100,000 for the first time on 31 December 20X3, its reporting date. Prior to the revaluation, the carrying value of the property, plant and equipment was $850,000 and the tax base was $625,000.

WS's tax rate is 25%. Its deferred tax liability brought forward in respect to the property, plant and equipment was $62,000.

Which three of the following statements are TRUE in respect of deferred tax on the above property, plant and equipment?

A   The deferred tax liability at 31 December 20X3 is $56,250

B   The deferred tax liability at 31 December 20X3 is $81,250

C   There is a deferred tax credit to profit or loss in the year ended 31 December 20X3 of $5,750

D   There is a deferred tax charge to profit or loss in the year ended 31 December 20X3 of $5,750

E   There is a deferred tax charge reflected through other comprehensive income in the year ended 31 December 20X3 of $19,250

F   There is a deferred tax charge reflected through other comprehensive income in the year ended 31 December 20X3 of $25,000

8 Chapter summary

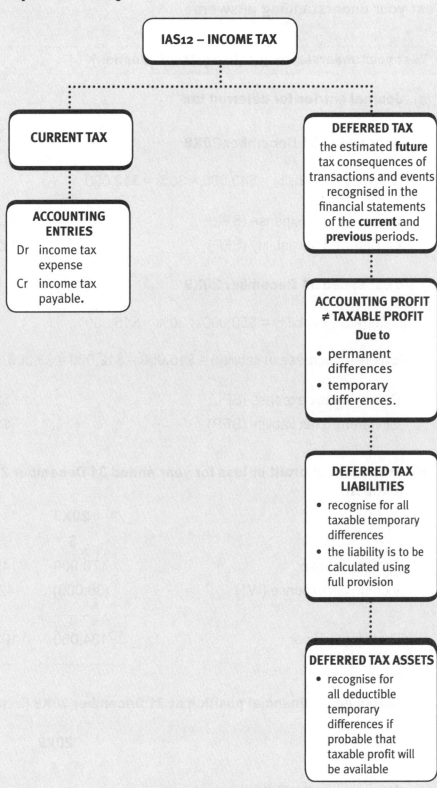

IAS12 – INCOME TAX

CURRENT TAX

ACCOUNTING ENTRIES

Dr income tax expense
Cr income tax payable.

DEFERRED TAX
the estimated **future** tax consequences of transactions and events recognised in the financial statements of the **current** and **previous** periods.

ACCOUNTING PROFIT ≠ TAXABLE PROFIT
Due to
- permanent differences
- temporary differences.

DEFERRED TAX LIABILITIES
- recognise for all taxable temporary differences
- the liability is to be calculated using full provision

DEFERRED TAX ASSETS
- recognise for all deductible temporary differences if probable that taxable profit will be available

Test your understanding answers

Test your understanding 1 (integration question)

(a) Journal entries for deferred tax

Year ended 31 December 20X8

Deferred tax liability = $40,000 × 30% = $12,000

Dr Income tax expense (SPL)		$12,000
Cr Deferred tax liability (SFP)		$12,000

Year ended 31 December 20X9

Deferred tax liability = $50,000 × 30% = $15,000

Expense (increase in liability) = $15,000 − $12,000 = $3,000

Dr Income tax expense (SPL)		$3,000
Cr Deferred tax liability (SFP)		$3,000

(b) Statement of profit or loss for year ended 31 December 20X9 (extract)

	20X9	20X8
	$	$
Profit before tax	170,000	145,000
Income tax expense (W1)	(36,000)	(42,000)
Profit for the year	134,000	103,000

Statement of financial position at 31 December 20X9 (extract)

	20X9	20X8
	$	$
Non-current liabilities:		
Deferred tax liability (from (a))	15,000	12,000
Current liabilities:		
Income tax payable	33,000	30,000

(W1) **Income tax expense**

	31/12/X9	31/12/X8
	$	$
Current tax	33,000	30,000
Deferred tax (from (a))	3,000	12,000
	36,000	42,000

Test your understanding 2 (integration question)

	Temporary difference	Deferred tax balance (25%)	Deferred tax liability /asset
	$000	$000	
Property, plant and equipment	8,500	2,125	liability
Held to maturity financial assets	20	5	liability
Trade receivables	(800)	(200)	asset
Warranty provision	(1,200)	(300)	asset
Long-term borrowings	(2,700)	(675)	asset

Test your understanding 3 (OTQ style)

Dr	Deferred tax asset (SFP)	$15,000
Cr	Statement of profit or loss (SPL)	$15,000

The temporary difference is $75,000 (the value of the losses available for carry forward). However, a deferred tax asset can only be recognised to the extent it is probable that these losses can be utilised and, based on current estimates, the recoverability is only $50,000 (2 × $25,000 profit).

Therefore a deferred tax asset of only $50,000 × 30% = $15,000 can be recognised.

Test your understanding 4 (integration question)

(a) **Journal entry for deferred tax**

Deferred tax liability c/f = $27,000 × 25% = $6,750

of which, amount relating to revaluation surplus on land = ($80,000 − $65,000) × 25% = $3,750

Increase in deferred tax liability to be recorded = $6,750 − $2,600 = $4,150

of which $3,750 should be charged to revaluation reserve and the remainder charged to profit or loss.

Dr Income tax expense (SPL)	$400
Dr Revaluation reserve (SFP)	$3,750
Cr Deferred tax liability (SFP)	$4,150

The impact to revaluation reserve during the year would be noted as part of the movements in other comprehensive income within the SOPLOCI.

Test your understanding 5 (further OTQs)

(1) **Income tax expense = $59,400**

	$
Current tax expense	60,000
Decrease in deferred tax liability (3,200 − 2,600)	(600)
	59,400

(2) **Deferred tax liability at 31 December 20X2 = $1,125**

Temporary difference = 60,000 − 56,250 = 3,750

Deferred tax liability = 30% × 3,750 = 1,125

(3) **A, C and F are true**

The tax base of the asset = $500 – $220 = $280

The cumulative temporary difference = $400 (CV) – $280 = $120

This results in a deferred tax liability of $120 × 30% = $36

(4) **Deferred tax asset = $30,000**

	$
Losses – capped to the extent they are recoverable	120,000
Tax rate	× 25%
	30,000

(5) **Impact in statement of profit or loss = $15,000 credit**

	$
Deferred tax asset at year end (20% × 350,000)	70,000
Deferred tax asset at start of year (20% × 275,000)	55,000
Increase in deferred tax asset	15,000

(6) **Dr AFS reserve $7,500**

Cr Deferred tax liability $7,500

Temporary difference = $280,000 (CV of asset) less $250,000 (tax base) = $30,000

Deferred tax liability = $30,000 × 25%

Gain recorded in AFS reserve, therefore tax effect should also be recorded in AFS reserve. The annual movement in the AFS reserve will be detailed as part of OCI within SOPLOCI.

(7) **D**

The future tax consequence is a deduction, therefore a deferred tax asset should be recognised.

The tax consequence is based on the intrinsic value of the options, therefore the deferred tax asset should reflect this.

(8) **The correct statements are B, C and F**

Deferred tax liability at 31 December 20X3

	$
Carrying value of PPE (850,000 + 100,000)	950,000
Tax base	(625,000)
Temporary difference	325,000
Tax rate	× 25%
	81,250

Deferred tax reflected in OCI

	$
Revaluation surplus	100,000
Tax rate	× 25%
	25,000

Deferred tax impact in profit or loss

	$
Liability at year end	81,250
Less liability at start of year	(62,000)
	———
Total increase in deferred tax liability	19,250
Less: relected in OCI	(25,000)
	———
Credit to SPL	(5,750)
	———

Construction contracts

Chapter learning objectives

B1. Produce consolidated primary financial statements, incorporating accounting transactions and adjustments, in accordance with relevant international accounting standards, in an ethical manner.

(c) Discuss the provisions of relevant international accounting standards in respect of the recognition and measurement of construction contracts, in accordance with IAS 11.

(d) Produce the accounting entries, in accordance with relevant international accounting standards.

1 Session content

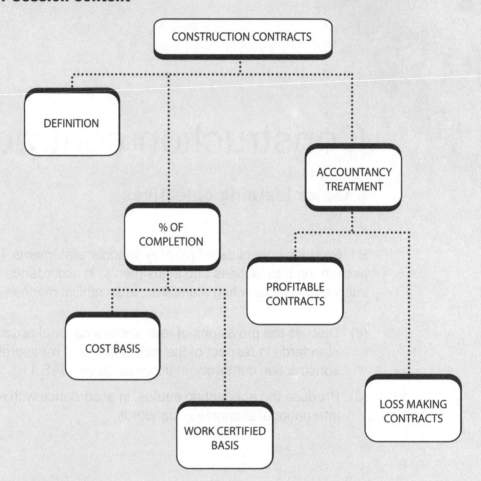

2 Introduction

A construction contract is defined as a contract specifically negotiated for the construction of an asset or a combination of assets that are related. A construction contract is a contract to construct a substantial asset, such as a bridge, a building, a ship or a tunnel.

The nature of a construction contract is such that it will often span more than one accounting period. The accounting issue is therefore when the revenue and costs associated with the contract should be recognised.

There are two alternative views on the situation as follows:

Recognise results on completion	**Recognise results as contract progresses**
Complies with prudence since it will not be certain that the contract is profitable until completion.	Complies with the matching concept as results will match work performed during the accounting period.

Reliable since revenue, costs and profits will be known with certainty on completion.	Less reliable since calculations will involve estimates regarding the future.
Not relevant since reported results will not reflect activities of the entity in the period.	Achieves relevance since reported results will reflect the activities of the entity.
Is likely to cause reported results to be distorted and so incomparable.	Will enable financial statements to be more comparable with other entities.

Therefore, we have a conflict between prudence and the accruals concept. IAS 11 aims to satisfy these requirements by ensuring we match related revenue to related expenditure, whilst maintaining the concept of prudence.

Accounting treatment of construction contracts

IAS 11 states that when the outcome of a construction contract can be estimated reliably, contract revenue and contract costs should be recognised in the statement of profit or loss by reference to the stage of completion of the contract activity at the reporting date.

Consequently:

Revenue	Total contract revenue × % complete
Cost of sales	Total expected contract costs × % complete
Gross profit	Total expected profit × % complete

The stage of completion can be calculated in various ways, e.g. cost basis (internal method), work certified basis (external method).

The cost basis is calculated as follows:

$$\frac{\text{Costs incurred to date}}{\text{Total cost for the contract}} = \text{\% of completion}$$

The work certified basis is calculated as follows:

$$\frac{\text{Work certified to date}}{\text{Total revenue for the contract}} = \text{\% of completion}$$

Work will be certified by an external surveyor who will estimate the value of the uncompleted project.

When the overall outcome (profit or loss) cannot be estimated reliably IAS 11 requires revenue to be recognised equal to costs incurred in period (assuming the revenue will probably be recovered). Therefore, nil profit will be recognised.

Profitable contracts

Workings

- Calculate overall expected profit on the contract.
- Calculate percentage completion of contract as at the reporting date.

Statement of profit or loss

- Revenue for period = (% × total revenue) – revenue previously recognised in prior periods
- Cost of sales = (% × total costs) – costs previously recognised in prior periods
- Gross profit = Revenue – Cost of Sales

Statement of financial position

- Amounts invoiced to customers that remain unpaid at the year end will be held under receivables.
- Separately from receivables, IAS 11 requires the 'gross amount due from/to customers' to be disclosed in the statement of financial position as either an asset or a liability. This represents any contract costs incurred but not yet transferred to cost of sales, i.e. costs that have been spent but that relate to future activity on the contract (work in progress costs) and revenue of work that has been completed but not yet billed to the client.

	$
Costs incurred	X
Recognised profits	X
Recognised losses	(X)
Amounts billed/invoiced/progress billings	(X)
'From'/('To')	X/(X)

- Amounts due from customers = asset (positive figure)
- Amounts due to customers = liability (negative figure)

Contract revenue and costs

Contract revenue

Contract revenue is the amount of revenue the contract has been agreed for, i.e. contract price.

Contract costs

Contract costs consist of costs that directly relate to the contract, i.e. site labour costs, materials, costs of depreciation for equipment used in the contract, costs of hiring/moving equipment for the contract, etc.

Gross amounts due from customers

This represents the total cost incurred plus any recognised profits (in the statement of profit or loss) less amounts invoiced to customers. This amount is shown as an asset because it represents money that has been spent on the project but customers have not yet been invoiced because it relates to a future activity (no work done yet).

Gross amounts due to customers

This represents the total costs incurred plus any recognised profits (in the statement of profit or loss) less amounts invoiced to customers. This amount is shown as a liability because the amounts invoiced to customers exceeds the amount spent on the project so far, therefore strictly this money is owed to customers (although wouldn't actually be repaid).

Accounting treatment

We incur costs on a contract:

Dr   Contract costs
Cr   Bank/payables

We raise an invoice:

Dr   Receivables
Cr   Progress payments

We receive payment from the customer:

Dr   Bank
Cr   Receivables

We record a sales value (based on stage of completion):

Dr   Progress payments
Cr   Revenue

We match related costs (based on stage of completion):

Dr   Cost of sales
Cr   Contract costs

The profit shown in the statement of profit or loss is calculated by looking at the sales account less cost of sales account.

The statement of financial position is calculated by netting off the contract costs and the progress payments accounts.

Example 1 – cost basis contract

Softfloor House Ltd build bars. The project generally takes a number of months to complete. The company has three contracts in progress at the year ended April 20X1.

	A	B	C
	$000	$000	$000
Costs incurred to date	200	90	600
Estimated costs to complete	200	110	100
Contract price	600	300	750
Progress billings	40	70	630

Softfloor calculates the percentage of completion by using the cost basis.

Required:

Calculate the effects of the above contract upon the financial statements.

Example 1 answer

Overall contract profit

	A $000	B $000	C $000
Contract price	600	300	750
Costs incurred to date	(200)	(90)	(600)
Estimated costs to complete	(200)	(110)	(100)
Gross profit	200	100	50

% of completion on cost basis

A 200/400 = 50%
B 90/200 = 45%
C 600/700 = 86% (rounded)

Statement of profit or loss (extract)

	A $000	B $000	C $000
Revenue (% × contract price)	300	135	645
Costs (% × total cost)	(200)	(90)	(600)
Gross profit	100	45	45

Statement of financial position (extract)

	A $000	B $000	C $000
Costs incurred	200	90	600
Profit recognised	100	45	45
Less: progress billings	(40)	(70)	(630)
Amounts due from customers (asset)	260	65	15

Example 2 – work certified basis contract

Hardfloor House Ltd fits out nightclubs. The project generally takes a number of months to complete. The company has three contracts in progress at the year ended April 20X1.

	A	B	C
	$000	$000	$000
Costs incurred to date	320	540	260
Estimated costs to complete	40	90	120
Contract price	416	684	400
Work certified to date	312	456	200
Progress billings	250	350	230

Hardfloor calculates the percentage of completion by using the work certified basis.

Required:

Calculate the effects of the above contract upon the financial statements.

Example 2 answer

Overall contract profit

	A	B	C
	$000	$000	$000
Contract price	416	684	400
Costs incurred to date	(320)	(540)	(260)
Estimated costs to complete	(40)	(90)	(120)
Gross profit	56	54	20

% of completion on work certified basis

A 312/416 =   75%
B 456/684 =   67% (rounded)
C 200/400 =   50%

Statement of profit or loss (extract)

	A	B	C
	$000	$000	$000
Revenue (% × contract price)	312	456	200
Costs (% × total cost)	(270)	(422)	(190)
Gross profit	42	34	10

Statement of financial position (extract)

	A	B	C
	$000	$000	$000
Costs incurred	320	540	260
Profit recognised	42	34	10
Less: progress billings	(250)	(350)	(230)
Amounts due from customers (asset)	112	224	40

Example 3 – contracts spanning number of years

Continuing from example 2, all three contracts were completed in the next financial period with the following cumulative results:

	A	B	C
	$000	$000	$000
Total costs incurred to date	370	640	380
Contract price	416	684	400
Progress billings	410	670	390

Required:

Calculate the effects of the above contracts upon the financial statements in the next financial period.

Example 3 answer

Statement of profit or loss (extract)

	A	B	C
	$000	$000	$000
Revenue (100% × contract price) – amounts recognised	104	228	200
Costs (100% × total cost) – amounts recognised	(100)	(218)	(190)
Gross profit	4	10	10

Statement of financial position (extract)

	A	B	C
	$000	$000	$000
Costs incurred (cumulative)	370	640	380
Profit recognised (cumulative)	46	44	20
Less: progress billings (cumulative)	(410)	(670)	(390)
Amounts due from customers (asset)	6	14	10

Explanatory note

Contract A:

Revenue $416,000 – $312,000 already recognised = $104,000 this year
Cost $370,000 – $270,000 already recognised = $100,000 this year

Overall profit = $416,000 – $370,000 = $46,000

Contract B:

Revenue $684,000 – $456,000 already recognised = $228,000 this year
Cost $640,000 – $422,000 already recognised = $218,000 this year

Overall profit = $44,000 – $34,000 = $10,000

Contract C:

Revenue $400,000 – $200,000 already recognised = $200,000 this year
Cost $380,000 – $190,000 already recognised = $190,000 this year

Overall profit = $20,000 – $10,000 = $10,000

Test your understanding 1 (integration question)

An airport terminal project started in 20X9 and will be completed in 20Y1. The total income of $9 million is anticipated with reasonable certainty at the year-end 31 December 20X9.

The following information is relevant:

	At 31.12.X9	At 31.12.Y0	At 31.12.Y1
	$000	$000	$000
Costs to date	2,800	4,800	7,500
Estimated costs to complete	4,200	2,700	–
Work certified	2,700	6,300	9,000

Required:

Calculate the effects of the above contract upon the statement of profit or loss on the cost basis and work certified basis for all three year ends.

Test your understanding 2 (integration question)

Reeve Ltd has undertaken four long-term contracts in the year. The following information has been obtained at the end of the year in relation to each project:

	A	B	C	D
	$000	$000	$000	$000
Contract price	500	1,000	2,000	3,000
Work certified to date	150	200	500	1,300
Costs incurred to date	200	220	600	700
Estimated costs to complete	200	unknown	1,100	1,100
Amounts billed	140	160	700	1,200

Required:

Prepare extracts from the financial statements for each of the four projects, assuming that % completion is calculated on the work certified basis.

3 Loss making contracts

IAS 11 requires that an expected loss on a construction contract should be recognised immediately.

Revenue will be calculated as before, but the whole loss will then be recorded on the gross profit line and cost of sales will be calculated as a balancing figure.

Example 4 – loss making contract

The following figures relate to a contract:

	$000
Contract price	900
Work certified	495
Costs incurred to date	525
Estimated costs to complete	435
Amounts invoiced to customers	475

Required:

Prepare extracts from the financial statements. The percentage completion should be calculated on the work certified basis.

Example 4 answer

Overall contract

	$000
Contract price	900
Costs to date	(525)
Costs to complete	(435)
Total loss	(60)

% completion on work certified basis

495/900 = 55%

Statement of profit or loss (extract)

	$
Revenue (55% × 900)	495
Cost of sales (balancing figure)	(555)
Gross loss	(60)

As this is a loss making contract, the whole of the loss must be recognised immediately.

Statement of financial position (extract)

Gross amounts due to customers

	$
Costs incurred	525
Losses recognised	(60)
Progress billings	(475)
Amounts due to customers (liability)	(10)

Test your understanding 3 (integration question)

Hindhead builds specialist equipment for use in the building industry. Each piece of equipment takes between one and two years to build and so the entity is required to account for construction contracts.

The entity has four contracts in process at the year end 30 April 20X1:

	A	B	C	D
	$000	$000	$000	$000
Contract price	500	890	420	750
Work certified to date	375	534	280	–
Costs incurred to date	384	700	468	20
Estimated costs to complete	48	115	168	650
Progress billings	360	520	224	–

Required:

Prepare extracts from the financial statements for each of the four projects, assuming that revenues and profits are recognised on the work certified basis.

Test your understanding 4 (integration question)

Details from DV's long-term contract, which commenced on 1 May 20X0, at 30 April 20X1 were:

	$000
Total contract value	3,000
Invoiced to client work done	2,000
Costs to date – attributable to work completed	1,500
Costs to date – inventory purchased but not yet used	250
Estimated costs to complete	400
Progress payments received from client	900

DV uses the percentage of costs incurred to total costs to calculate attributable profit.

Calculate the amount that DV should recognise in its statement of profit or loss for the year ended 30 April 20X1 for revenue, cost of sales and attributable profits on this contract according to IAS 11 Construction Contracts.

Test your understanding 5 (OTQ style qns)

(1) The following information relates to a construction contract:

	$
Contract price	5 million
Work certified to date	2 million
Costs to date	1.8 million
Estimated costs to complete	2.2 million

What is the revenue, cost of sales and gross profit that should be recognised in accordance with IAS 11, assuming that the entity's policy is to calculate attributable profit on the work certified basis?

	Revenue	Cost of sales	Gross profit
A	$2 million	$1.8 million	$200,000
B	$2 million	$1.6 million	$400,000
C	$2 million	$1.55 million	$450,000
D	$2.25 million	$1.8 million	$450,000

(2) The following information relates to a construction contract:

	$
Contract price	300,000
Work certified to date	120,000
Costs to date	100,000
Estimated costs to complete	250,000

What is the revenue, cost of sales and gross profit that should be recognised in accordance with IAS 11, assuming that the entity's policy is to calculate attributable profit on the work certified basis?

	Revenue	Cost of sales	Gross profit
A	$120,000	$170,000	$50,000 loss
B	$120,000	$100,000	$20,000
C	$120,000	$140,000	$20,000 loss
D	$120,000	$70,000	$50,000

(3) An entity has a construction contract in progress. The work certified at the year end is $240,000 and cost of sales has been calculated as $180,000. Costs incurred to date amount to $200,000 and $250,000 has been invoiced to the customer.

Calculate the amount that would be shown in the statement of financial position in respect of the above construction contract.

(4) Complete the following sentence by placing one of the options in each of the spaces.

In scenario (3) above, the balance calculated represents the gross amount due _____ customers and would be recognised as an _____ in the statement of financial position.

Options: from, to, asset, liability

(5) A company is currently accounting for a construction contract. The contract price is $2 million and work certified at the year-end is $1.3 million. Costs incurred to date amount to $1.4 million and it is estimated that a further $1 million will be incurred in completing this project. $1.3 million has been invoiced to the customer.

What is the amount due to/from customers that should be recorded in the statement of financial position in relation to this construction contract? Stage of completion is calculated on a work certified basis.

    A $nil

    B $100,000 liability

    C $300,000 asset

    D $300,000 liability

(6) The following information relates to a construction contract that commenced in the current period:

	$
Contract price	40 million
Percentage complete	45%
Costs to date	16 million
Estimated costs to complete	18 million

Calculate the cost of sales that would be recognised in the statement of profit or loss in respect of the above contract.

(7) The following information relates to a construction contract that commenced in the current period:

	$
Contract price	25 million
Percentage complete	60%
Costs to date	15 million
Estimated costs to complete	15 million

Calculate the cost of sales that would be recognised in the statement of profit or loss in respect of the above contract.

4 Chapter summary

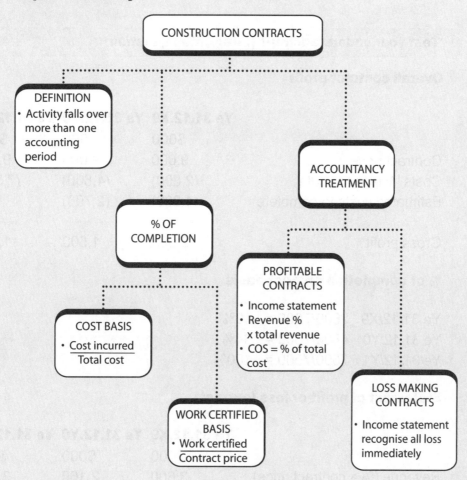

Test your understanding answers

Test your understanding 1 (integration question)

Overall contract profit

	Ye 31.12.X9	Ye 31.12.Y0	Ye 31.12.Y1
	$000	$000	$000
Contract price	9,000	9,000	9,000
Costs incurred to date	(2,800)	(4,800)	(7,500)
Estimated costs to complete	(4,200)	(2,700)	–
Gross profit	2,000	1,500	1,500

% of completion on cost basis

Ye 31/12/X9   2800/7000 =   40%
Ye 31/12/Y0   4800/7500 =   64%
Ye 31/12/Y1   7500/7500 =   100%

Statement of profit or loss (extract)

	Ye 31.12.X9	Ye 31.12.Y0	Ye 31.12.Y1
	$000	$000	$000
Revenue (% × contract price)	3,600	2,160	3,240
Costs (% × total cost)	(2,800)	(2,000)	(2,700)
Gross profit	800	160	540

Workings

	31.12.X9	31.12.Y0	31.12.Y1
% completion	40%	64%	100%
Revenue	40% × 9,000 = 3,600	64% × 9000 – 3,600 = 2,160	9,000 – 3,600 – 2,160 = 3,240
Cost of sales	40% × (2,800 + 4,200) = 2,800	64% × (4,800 + 2,700) – 2,800 = 2,000	100% × 7,500 – 2,800 – 2,000 = 2,700

% of completion on work certified basis

Ye 31/12/X9   2700/9000 =   30%
Ye 31/12/Y0   6300/9000 =   70%
Ye 31/12/Y1   9000/9000 =   100%

Statement of profit or loss (extract)

	Ye 31.12.X9	Ye 31.12.Y0	Ye 31.12.Y1
	$0009	$000	$000
Revenue (% × contract price)	2,700	3,600	2,700
Cost of Sales (% × total cost)	(2,100)	(3,150)	(2,250)
Gross profit	600	450	450

Workings

	31.12.X9	31.12.Y0	31.12.Y1
% completion	30%	70%	100%
Revenue	30% × 9,000 = 2,700	6,300 − 2,700 = 3,600	9,000 − 2,700 − 3,600 = 2,700
Cost of sales	30% × (2,800 + 4,200) = 2,100	70% × (4,800 + 2,700) − 2,100 = 3,150	100% × 7,500 − 2,100 − 3,150 = 2,250

Test your understanding 2 (integration question)

Overall contract profit

	A	B	C	D
	$000	$000	$000	$000
Contract price	500	1,000	2,000	3,000
Costs incurred to date	(200)	(220)	(600)	(700)
Estimated costs to complete	(200)	Unknown	(1,100)	(1,100)
Gross profit	100	?	300	1,200

% of completion on work certified basis

A 150/500 = 30%
B 200/1000 = 20%
C 500/2000 = 25%
D 1300/3000 = 43% (rounded)

Statement of profit or loss (extract)

	A	B	C	D
	$000	$000	$000	$000
Revenue (% × contract price)	150	220	500	1,290
Costs (% × total cost)	(120)	(220)	(425)	(774)
Gross profit	30	nil	75	516

NB: As Project B has an unknown cost to complete it is not possible to reliably estimate the total contract profit. Therefore, costs incurred become cost of sales and the same amount is recognised as revenue so that a nil profit is shown

Contract D's revenue shows as $1,290,000. This is because the rounded percentage of 43% has been applied. Without the rounding the revenue would be $1,300,000 (= work certified).

Statement of financial position (extract)

	A	B	C	D
	$000	$000	$000	$000
Costs incurred	200	220	600	700
Profit recognised	30	–	75	516
Less: progress billings	(140)	(160)	(700)	(1,200)
Amounts due from/(to) customers	90	60	(25)	16

Test your understanding 3 (integration question)

Overall profit/loss on contract

	A	B	C	D
	$000	$000	$000	$000
Contract price	500	890	420	750
Costs to date	(384)	(700)	(468)	(20)
Costs to complete	(48)	(115)	(168)	(650)
Total estimated profit	68	75	(216)	80

% completion on work certified basis

A 375/500 =   75%
B 534/890 =   60%
C 280/420 =   67% (rounded)
D 0/750 =   0%

	A	B	C	D
	$000	$000	$000	$000
Revenue (% × contract price)	375	534	280	20
Cost of Sales (% × total cost)	(324)	(489)	(496)	(20)
Gross profit/loss	51	45	(216)	–

Statement of financial position (extract)

	A	B	C	D
	$000	$000	$000	$000
Costs incurred	384	700	468	20
Profits/losses recognised	51	45	(216)	–
Progress billings	(360)	(520)	(224)	–
Amounts due from customers	75	225	28	20

Project C

A loss has been made on this contract of $216,000 therefore we must recognise the whole of the loss immediately. The revenue will be calculated as normal and the cost of sales becomes the balancing figure.

Project D

Although work has been performed on this project no work has yet been certified, hence we cannot recognise a profit in the statement of profit or loss. However, we cannot ignore that costs have been incurred, hence they become the cost of sales and the revenue becomes the same amount to recognise a nil profit.

Test your understanding 4 (integration question)

The contract makes an overall profit of $850,000 ($3,000,000 – $2,150,000).

Stage of completion = 70% rounded (1,500/2,150)

	$000
Costs to date – attributable to work completed	1,500
Costs to date – inventory purchased but not yet used	250
Estimated costs to complete	400
Total cost	2,150

Statement of profit or loss (extract)	$000
Revenue (3,000 × 70%)	2,100
Cost of sales (2,150 × 70%)	(1,500)
Profit	600

Test your understanding 5 (OTQ style qns)

(1) **B is the correct answer**

	$m
Total revenue	5
Costs to date	(1.8)
Costs to complete	(2.2)
Total profit	1

% completion = 2 million/5 million = 40%

	$m
Revenue (40% × 5)	2
Cost of sales (40% × 4)	(1.6)
Gross profit	0.4

(2) **A is the correct answer**

	$
Total revenue	300,000
Costs to date	(100,000)
Costs to complete	(250,000)
Total loss	(50,000)

	$m
Revenue	120,000
Cost of sales (ß)	(170,000)
Gross loss	(50,000)

(3) **$10,000**

	$
Costs to date	200,000
Recognised profits (240,000 – 180,000)	60,000
Invoiced	(250,000)
	10,000

(4) In scenario (3) above, the balance calculated represents the gross amount due **from** customers and would be recognised as an **asset** in the statement of financial position.

(5) **D $300,000 liability**

Expected outcome:	$m
Total revenue	2
Costs to date	(1.4)
Costs to complete	(1)
Total loss	(0.4)

Statement of financial position (extract)	$m
Costs to date	1.4
Recognised loss	(0.4)
Progress billings	(1.3)
Amount due to customer	(0.3)

(6) Cost of sales = $15.3 million

The overall contract makes a profit of $6 million ($40m – $16m – $18m)

Cost of sales = ($16m + $18m) × 45% = $15.3m

(7) Cost of sales = $20 million

The overall contract makes a loss of $5 million ($25m – $15m – $15m)

The revenue to be recognised will be 60% × total revenue of $25 million = $15 million

Therefore, cost of sales (balancing figure to reflect loss of $5 million) = $20 million

11

Related parties

Chapter learning objectives

B3. Discuss the need for and nature of disclosure of transactions between related parties.

(a) Discuss the need for and nature of disclosure of transactions between related parties, in accordance with IAS 24.

1 Session content

DEFINITION OF A
RELATED PARTY

THE NEED FOR
DISCLOSURE OF
RELATED PARTIES

DISCLOSURE
OF RELATED
PARTIES

2 Introduction

Related party relationships are a normal feature of business.

The existence of a related party relationship and transactions with related parties may affect the profit or loss of an entity. It is therefore important for users to be aware of related parties and any transactions that have occurred in the period.

3 IAS 24 Related Party Disclosures

A **related party** is a person or entity that is related to the entity that is preparing its financial statements (the reporting entity).

A relationship typically exists if control, joint control, common control or significant influence exists between the party and the reporting entity.

Typical related parties are:

- Key management personnel
- Close family members of key management personnel
- Entities that are members of the same group (including parent, subsidiaries, associates and joint ventures).

Note however that the following are normally considered **not** to be related parties:

- two entities simply because they have a director/member of key management personnel in common
- two joint venturers simply because they share joint control of a joint venture
- providers of finance
- key customers and suppliers.

Key management personnel

Key management personnel are those persons having authority and responsibility for planning, directing and controlling the activities of the entity, directly or indirectly, including any director (whether executive or otherwise) of that entity.

Close family members

Close members of the family of a person are those family members who may be expected to influence, or be influenced by, that person in their dealings with the entity.

They would include:

- children
- spouse or domestic partner
- children, and other dependents, of spouse or domestic partner

Related parties – the detail

A person or close member of that person's family is related to a reporting entity if that person:

- has control or joint control over the reporting entity
- has significant influence over the reporting entity
- is a member of the key management personnel of the reporting entity or of a parent of the reporting entity.

An entity is related to a reporting entity if any of the following conditions applies:

- The entity and the reporting entity are members of the same group

- One entity is an associate or joint venture of the other entity

- Both entities are joint ventures of the same third party

- One entity is a joint venture of a third entity and the other entity is an associate of the third entity

- The entity is a post-employment benefit plan for the benefit of employees of either the reporting entity or an entity related to the reporting entity

- The entity is controlled or jointly controlled by a person identified as a related party to the reporting entity

- A person identified as a related party of the reporting entity has significant influence over the entity or is a member of the key management personnel of the entity

Related parties – exclusions from definition

In the context of this standard, the following are not necessarily related parties:

(a) two entities simply because they have a director or other member of key management personnel in common, notwithstanding the above definition of 'related party'

(b) two venturers simply because they share joint control over a joint venture

(c) providers of finance

(d) trade unions

(e) public utilities

(f) government departments and agencies, simply by virtue of their normal dealings with an entity (even though they may affect the freedom of action of an entity or participate in its decision-making process)

(g) a customer, supplier, franchisor, distributor or general agent with whom an entity transacts a significant volume of business, merely by virtue of the resulting economic dependence.

4 Disclosure requirements

A **related party transaction** is a transfer of resources, services or obligations between a reporting entity and a related party, regardless of whether a price is charged.

Where there have been transactions between the entity and a related party, the entity is required to disclose:

- The nature of the related party relationship

- The nature of the transaction

- The amount of the transaction

- Any outstanding balance relating to the transaction

- Any provisions for doubtful debts remaining to the amount of any outstanding balance.

Disclosure requirements

The standard concerns the disclosure of related party transactions in order to make readers of financial statements aware of the position and to ensure that the financial statements show a true and fair view.

If there have been transactions between related parties, an entity shall disclose the nature of the related party relationship as well as information about the transactions and outstanding balances necessary for an understanding of the potential effect of the relationship on the financial statements.

In certain circumstances the existence of a related party should be disclosed, regardless of whether or not there have been any transactions.

Disclosures that related party transactions were made on terms equivalent to those that prevail in arm's length transactions are made only if such terms can be substantiated.

At a minimum, disclosures shall include:

- the amount of the transactions

- the amount of outstanding balances: their terms and conditions, including whether they are secured, and the nature of the consideration to be provided in settlement and details of any guarantees given or received

- provisions for doubtful debts related to the amount of outstanding balances

- the expense recognised during the period in respect of bad or doubtful debts due from related parties.

In addition, IAS 24 requires an entity to disclose key management personnel compensation in total and for each of the following categories:

- short-term employee benefits

- post-employment benefits

- other long-term benefits

- termination benefits

- equity compensation benefits.

Examples of related parties

Examples of related party transactions would be:

- Purchases/sales of goods (even if no price is charged)

- Purchases/sales of property or other assets

- Rendering/receipt of services

- Leasing arrangements

- Management contracts

- Finance arrangements, e.g. loan guarantee.

Example 1

You decide to set up a business in an office block offering training facilities. Your brother is the owner of the building and in order to help you start your business, he agrees to give you your office with no charge for a four year period.

After three successful years of business your student numbers have doubled and you decide to take early retirement and sell your business.

Your business is put up for sale.

Explain what information should be disclosed in the accounts regarding this transaction and why it is important to do this.

Example 1 answer

You must disclose:

- the nature of the related party transaction, i.e. rental of premises
- the related party, i.e. your brother owns the building
- the amount of the transaction, i.e. the fact that you have use of the premises rent free and how much rent you are saving (based on the 'market rate' for the rental of these premises).

This information is important for a prospective buyer of the business because they will need to be aware of these facts when they look at the profits for the business. If you did not disclose this matter, the prospective buyer would think they could make similar profits if they purchased the business. Although the profit figures are correct, they are distorted by the fact that the new owners would incur a rent charge for that building, hence the profits would reduce, assuming all things remain the same.

Test your understanding 1 (case style)

CB is an entity specialising in importing a wide range of non-food items and selling them to retailers. George is CB's founder and chief executive. He owns 40% of CB's equity shares:

- CB's largest customer, XC accounts for 35% of CB's revenue. XC has just completed negotiations with CB for a special 5% discount on all sales.
- During the accounting period, George purchased a property from CB for $500,000. CB had previously declared the property surplus to its requirements and had valued it at $750,000.
- George's son, Arnold is a director in a financial institution, FC. During the accounting period, FC advanced $2 million to CB as an unsecured loan at a favourable rate of interest.

Required:

You are an accountant working for CB and you have been asked by the Financial Director to prepare a briefing note, to be presented at the next Board of Directors meeting, explaining the extent to which the above transactions should be classified and disclosed in CB's financial statements in accordance with IAS 24 *Related Party Disclosures*.

The Finance Director tells you that the Board are not interested in the rules of IAS 24 in general, they just want to know about any disclosure requirements for the specific transactions mentioned above.

He also let you know that George is particularly keen to avoid disclosing his purchase of the property and believes he shouldn't have to as the property is not required by the business anymore. He is happy however for the bank loan to be disclosed as he believes shareholders will be pleased that a favourable rate of interest has been achieved.

Test your understanding 2 (OTQ style qns)

(1) **Which of the following would be regarded as a related party of entity RP?**

Select all that apply.

C, a key customer of RP

P, the direct parent entity of RP

UP, the parent of P and the ultimate parent of the group in which RP is consolidated

Mr D, a director of P

Mrs D, the wife of Mr D, a director of P

O, an entity that is not part of the UP group but of which Mr D is also a director

(2) **Which of the following are not related parties of the reporting entity RP in accordance with IAS 24?**

Select all that apply.

S, who supplies approximately 75% of the goods purchased by RP

V, a joint venture in which RP can exercise joint control

J, the other party that shares joint control of V with RP

MS, a member of key management personnel of RP

MS2, an entity in which MS is also a member of key management personnel

B, the main finance provider of RP

5 Chapter summary

IAS24 Related party disclosures

The need for disclosure of related parties
- Users need to be aware of related party relationships
  - Users need to know which transactions have not been made at arm's length

Disclosure of related parties
- Parent/subsidiary relationships
- Disclosure of transactions and balances
- Key management compensation

Test your understanding answers

Test your understanding 1 (case style)

Briefing note on compliance with IAS 24 Related Party Disclosures

As requested, I've explained the requirements of IAS 24 with respect to each of the transactions identified.

Discount awarded to largest customer

According to IAS 24, a customer with whom an entity transacts a significant volume of business is not a related party merely by virtue of the resulting economic dependence. XC is therefore not a related party and the negotiated discount does not need to be disclosed.

Purchase of property

A party is related to an entity if it has an interest that gives it significant influence over the entity. A party is also related to an entity if he/she is a member of the key management personnel of the entity.

George satisfies both of these definitions. His 40% holding demonstrates the ability of exert significant influence and his chief executive role clearly makes him a member of key management personnel.

Therefore the sale of the property for $500,000 must be disclosed as a related party transaction and its valuation should also be disclosed so that users of the financial statements can understand the impact that the transaction has on the financial statements.

Even if the transaction was at market value, it should still be disclosed. There is no option to avoid disclosure in these circumstances.

Bank loan with favourable interest rate

Providers of finance are not related parties simply because of their normal dealings with the entity. However, if a party is a close member of the family of any individual categorised as a related party, they are also a related party. As Arnold is George's son and George is a related party, Arnold is therefore also a related party. The loan from FC will need to be disclosed along with the details of Arnold and his involvement in the arrangements.

Test your understanding 2 (OTQ style qns)

(1) **The related parties of RP are: P, UP, Mr D and Mrs D**

Key customers (C) and an entity that shares a director in common (O) are specified by IAS 24 as not being related parties.

All of the other parties above are mentioned in the definition of a related party.

(2) **The parties that are not related to RP are: S, J, MS2 and B**

Key suppliers (S), joint venturers who share control of a joint venture (J), an entity that has a member of key management personnel in common (MS2) and providers of finance (B) are specified by IAS 24 as not being related parties.

Joint ventures (V) and a person who has control or significant influence over the entity (MS) are included in the definition of a related party.

Basic group accounts – F1 syllabus

Chapter learning objectives

B1. Produce consolidated primary financial statements, incorporating accounting transactions and adjustments, in accordance with relevant international accounting standards, in an ethical manner.

(a) Produce:
 –   consolidated statement of comprehensive income
 –   consolidated statement of financial position

including the adoption of both full consolidation and the principles of equity accounting, in accordance with the provisions of IAS 1, IAS 27, IAS 28, IFRS 3 and IFRS 10.

1 Session content

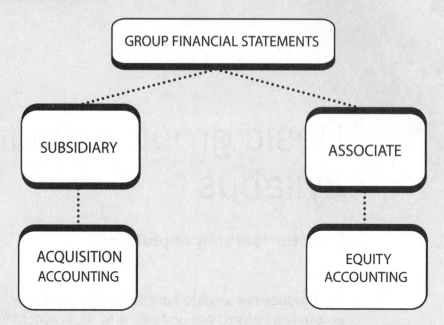

2 Introduction

This chapter covers content that is in the F1 syllabus. If you sat the F1 assessment prior to the 2015 syllabus however a significant proportion of the content of this chapter will be new to you and you should study it carefully before moving onto the next chapter.

If you have studied for F1 under the 2015 syllabus you can either move straight onto the next chapter, or use this chapter first to revise your F1 knowledge. It is essential that you understand the basics of group accounts before attempting the more complex scenarios that will be tested in F2.

3 What is a group?

IFRS 10 – Consolidated financial statements

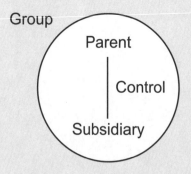

A group will exist where one company (the parent) **controls** another company (the subsidiary).

IFRS 10 *Consolidated Financial* Statements sets out the definition of control and gives guidance on how to identify whether control exists.

In accordance with IFRS 10, an investor controls an investee if and only if the investor has all of the following elements:

- power over the investee (see definition of power below)
- exposure, or rights, to variable returns from its involvement with the investee, and
- the ability to use its power over the investee to affect the amount of the investor's returns.

Power is defined as existing rights that give the current ability to direct the relevant activities, i.e. the activities that significantly affect the investee's returns.

Consolidated financial statements should be prepared when the parent has control over one or more subsidiaries (for examination purposes control is usually established based on ownership of more than 50% of the voting rights). The method of consolidation applied is known as **acquisition accounting**.

> ### Exemption from group accounts
>
> A parent need not present consolidated financial statements if it meets all of the following conditions:
>
> - it is a wholly owned subsidiary or a partially-owned subsidiary and its owners, including those not otherwise entitled to vote, have been informed about, and do not object to, the parent not presenting consolidated financial statements
> - its debt or equity instruments are not traded in a public market
> - it did not file its financial statements with a securities commission or other regulatory organisation for the purpose of issuing any class of instruments in a public market
> - its ultimate parent produces consolidated financial statements available for public use that comply with IFRS.

Acquisition accounting

The following rules are applied:

- The parent and subsidiaries' assets, liabilities, income and expenses are combined in full. This represents the 100% control that the parent has over the subsidiary.

- Goodwill is recognised in accordance with IFRS 3 (revised) *Business Combinations.*

- The share capital of the group is the share capital of the parent only.

- Intra-group balances and transactions are eliminated in full (including profits/losses on intra-group transactions still held in assets such as inventory and non-current assets – the PUP adjustment).

- Uniform accounting policies must be used.

- Non-controlling interests are presented within equity, separately from the equity of the owners of the parent. Profit and total comprehensive income are attributed to the owners of the parent and to the non-controlling interests.

4 Standard consolidation workings

For the consolidated statement of financial position

Note – the workings have been numbered for referencing purposes. In the assessment however you would not have to produce all workings to answer a question.

(W1) Group structure

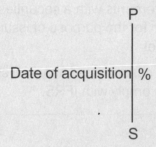

(W2) **Net assets of subsidiary**

	Acquisition Date	Reporting Date
Share capital	X	X
Retained earnings	X	X
Other reserves	X	X
Fair value adjustments	X	X
PUP adjustment (if sub is seller)	–	(X)
	X	X

Difference = post-acquisition reserves

(W3) **Goodwill**

Fair value of P's investment in S	X
Value of NCI at acquisition (using fair value or proportion of net assets method)	X
Less: subsidiary's net assets at acquisition (W2)	(X)
Goodwill at acquisition	X
Impairment	(X)
Goodwill at reporting date	X

(W4) **Non-controlling interest equity**

Value of NCI at acquisition (as in goodwill calculation)	X
NCI% × post-acquisition reserves (W2)	X
NCI% × impairment (W3) (for fair value method only)	(X)
NCI at reporting date	X

(W5) **Consolidated reserves**

	Retained earnings	Other reserves
Parent's reserves	X	X
PUP adjustment (if parent is seller)	(X)	–
Sub: P% × post-acquisition reserves (W2)	X	X
Impairment (P% only for fair value method)	(X)	–
	X	X

5 Non-controlling interest and goodwill

By definition, a subsidiary is an entity that is controlled by another entity – the parent. Control is normally achieved by the parent owning a majority i.e. more than 50% of the equity shares of the subsidiary.

Non-controlling interest (NCI) shareholders own the shares in the subsidiary not owned by the parent entity.

NCI shareholders are considered to be shareholders of the group and thus their ownership interest in the subsidiary is reflected within equity.

When calculating goodwill at acquisition the value of the NCIs is added to the value of the parent's investment in the subsidiary so that the value of the subsidiary as a whole (100%) is compared against all of its net assets.

IFRS 3 *Business Combinations* allows two methods to be used to value the NCI at the date of acquisition:

- Fair value

- Proportion of net assets

IFRS 3 permits groups to choose how to value NCI on an acquisition by acquisition basis. In other words, it is possible for a group to apply the fair value method for some subsidiaries and the proportion of net assets method for other subsidiaries.

Fair value method

The fair value of the non-controlling interest may be calculated using the market value of the subsidiary's shares at the date of acquisition or other valuation techniques if the subsidiary's shares are not traded in an active market. In the assessment, you will be told the fair value of the NCI or will be given the subsidiary's share price in order to be able to calculate it.

Proportion of net assets method

Under this method, the NCI is measured by calculating the share of the fair value of the subsidiary's net assets at acquisition.

Example 1

Sherriff purchased 60% of Nottingham's 3,000 shares on 1 January 20X9. Sherriff paid $5,500 cash for their investment. At 1 January 20X9, the value of Nottingham's net assets was $5,000. Nottingham's share price at this date was $2.25.

Required:

Calculate the goodwill arising on the acquisition of Nottingham, valuing the NCI:

(a) Using the fair value method

(b) Using the proportion of net assets method

Example 1 answer

Goodwill

	Fair value method	Proportion of net assets method
	$	$
Fair value of P's investment	5,500	5,500
Value of NCI at acquisition (W1/ W2)	2,700	2,000
Less: value of S's net assets	(5,000)	(5,000)
Goodwill at acquisition	3,200	2,500

(W1) NCI holding – fair value method

The subsidiary's share price is provided and so this is used to value the NCI's 40% holding in Nottingham.

The NCI owns:

40% × 3,000 shares = 1,200 shares

The fair value of this shareholding is:

1,200 × $2.25 = $2,700

(W2) NCI holding – proportion of net assets method

The NCI's 40% holding is simply valued by taking this proportion of the subsidiary's net assets at acquisition of $5,000.

40% × $5,000 = $2,000

Test your understanding 1 (F1 recap)

Wellington purchased 80% of the equity share capital of Boot for $1,200,000 on 1 April 20X8. Boot's share capital is made up of 200,000 $1 shares and it had retained earnings of $800,000 at the date of acquisition. The fair value of the NCI at 1 April 20X8 was $250,000.

Required:

Calculate the goodwill arising on the acquisition of Boot, valuing the NCI:

(a) Using the fair value method

(b) Using the proportion of net assets method

Test your understanding 2 (F1 recap)

Ruby purchased 75% of the equity share capital of Sapphire for $2,500,000 on 1 April 20X8. Sapphire's share capital is made up of 500,000 $1 shares and it had retained earnings of $1,500,000 at the date of acquisition. The fair value of the NCI at 1 April 20X8 should be calculated by reference to the subsidiary's share price. The market value of a Sapphire share at 1 April 20X8 was $6.

Required:

Calculate the goodwill arising on the acquisition of Sapphire, valuing the NCI:

(a) Using the fair value method

(b) Using the proportion of net assets method

Goodwill and NCI

Prior to a revision to IFRS 3 in 2008, it was only permitted to recognise the NCI using the proportion of net assets method. This method resulted in only the goodwill attributable to the parent shareholders being recognised in the consolidated accounts. Using the information from TYU 1, consider the following alternative calculation of goodwill under this method:

	$000
Fair value of P's investment	1,200
P% × sub's net assets at acquisition (80% × 1,000)	(800)
	———
Goodwill at acquisition	400
	———

In the above calculation, rather than adding in the NCI's share (20%) of the subsidiary's net assets and then subtracting 100% of these net assets, just the parent's share (80%) has been deducted from the fair value of the parent's holding. This achieves the same answer for goodwill but more clearly demonstrates why valuing the NCI at the proportion of net assets is equivalent to only the goodwill attributable to the parent's holding being recognised.

This method was considered inconsistent with the treatment of the other assets of the subsidiary. Since the group controls the assets of the subsidiary, they are fully consolidated in the group accounts, i.e. 100% is added in line by line. Goodwill is an asset of the subsidiary in exactly the same way that property, inventory, etc, are assets of the subsidiary. So if property and inventory are consolidated in full, goodwill should be treated in the same way.

Therefore when IFRS 3 was revised in 2008, the option of valuing the NCI at fair value was introduced. This recognises that the value of the NCI should also reflect the goodwill attributable to their holding. Again, using the information from TYU 1, this can perhaps be more clearly illustrated using the following alternative goodwill calculation under the fair value method:

	$000	$000
Fair value of P's investment	1,200	
P% × sub's net assets at acquisition (80% × 1,000)	(800)	
	———	
Goodwill attributable to P shareholders		400
Fair value of NCI	250	
NCI% × sub's net assets at acquisition (20% × 1,000)	(200)	
	———	
		50
		———
Goodwill at acquisition		450
		———

In this alternative calculation, the subsidiary's net assets have simply been deducted in two separate stages rather than on a single line as has been done in the answer to TYU 1.

These alternative calculations for goodwill will achieve the correct answers, but for assessment purposes it is recommended that you use the format applied in TYU 1. You will only ever have to apply one proforma for the calculation of goodwill and the difference will be how the NCI is valued.

It is worth noting that the fair value of the NCI is not normally proportionate to the fair value of the parent's holding. Again, using TYU 1 to illustrate, the parent's holding of 80% is four times that of the NCI's 20% holding. However, the fair value of the parent's holding of $1,200,000 is more than four times that of the NCI's holding which has a fair value of $250,000. This is because the parent's 80% holding provides control of the subsidiary and so the value of an 80% holding is proportionately more as it includes a premium for obtaining control.

6 Impairment of goodwill

IFRS 3 requires that goodwill is tested at each reporting date for impairment. This means that goodwill is reviewed to ensure that its value is not overstated in the consolidated statement of financial position.

If an impairment loss exists, goodwill is written down and the loss is charged as an expense in the consolidated statement of profit or loss.

This charge against profits will result in a reduction in the equity section of the CSFP. How the impairment loss is charged against equity in the CSFP will depend on the method adopted for valuing the NCI.

Fair value method

As discussed in the expandable text 'Goodwill and NCI', valuing the NCI at fair value is equivalent to recognising goodwill in full, i.e. goodwill attributable to both the parent and NCI shareholders is recognised.

Consequently, any impairment loss is charged to both the parent and NCI shareholders in the equity section of the CSFP in accordance with their percentage holdings.

To record the impairment loss:

- Reduce Goodwill by the full amount of the impairment loss (Cr).
- Reduce NCI equity by the NCI% of the impairment loss (Dr).
- Reduce Consolidated retained earnings by the P% of the impairment loss (Dr).

Proportion of net assets method

As discussed in the expandable text above, valuing the NCI at the proportion of the subsidiary's net assets is equivalent to recognising only the goodwill attributable to the parent shareholders.

Consequently, any impairment loss is only charged to the parent shareholders in the equity section of the CSFP.

To record the impairment loss:

- Reduce Goodwill by the amount of the impairment loss (Cr).
- Reduce Consolidated retained earnings by the amount of the impairment loss (Dr).

Example 2

P acquired 75% of the equity share capital of S on 1 April 20X2, paying $900,000 in cash. At this date, the retained earnings of S were $300,000. Below are the statements of financial position of P and S as at 31 March 20X4:

	P	S
	$000	$000
Non-current assets	1,650	750
Investment in S	900	–
Current assets	450	650
	3,000	1,400
Equity		
Share capital	1,500	500
Retained earnings	900	400
Non current liabilities	100	50
Current liabilities	500	450
	3,000	1,400

It is group policy to value the NCI at fair value at the date of acquisition. The fair value of the NCI in S at 1 April 20X2 was $275,000.

As at 31 March 20X4, goodwill was impaired by $60,000.

Required:

(a) Prepare a consolidated statement of financial position as at 31 March 20X4.

(b) Show how the CSFP would change if the proportion of net assets method were used to value the NCI at acquisition instead.

Example 2 answer

(W1) Group structure

P
|
75% 1 April 20X2, i.e. 2 years since acquisition
|
S

(W2) Net assets of subsidiary

	Acquisition Date	Reporting Date
Share capital	500	500
Retained earnings	300	400
	800	900

100 = post acquisition reserves

These post-acquisition reserves belong to the shareholders of the subsidiary, i.e. 75% to the parent and 25% to the NCI shareholders and are allocated accordingly in the NCI and Consolidated reserves workings (4 and 5 in this example).

(W3) Goodwill

	$000
Fair value of P's investment	900
Fair value of NCI at acquisition	275
Less: sub's net assets at acquisition (W2)	(800)
Goodwill at acquisition	375
Impairment	(60)
Goodwill at reporting date	315

(W4) Non-controlling interest equity

	$000
Value of NCI at acquisition (W3)	275
NCI% × post acquisition reserves (25% × 100 (W2))	25
NCI% × impairment (25% × 60 (W3))	(15)
	285

The NCI is measured at its fair value of $275,000 at the date of acquisition, as given in the question. Since acquisition the subsidiary has made gains of $100,000, as shown in W2. The NCI shareholders are entitled to 25% of these gains. Thus their holding has increased in value by $25,000.

However, because the NCI holding has been valued at acquisition under the fair value method, the NCI shareholders are charged with their 25% share of the $60,000 impairment loss arising on goodwill. This reduces their share of the group's equity to $285,000 at the reporting date.

(W5) Consolidated reserves

	Retained earnings
Parent's reserves	900
Sub (75% × 100 (W2))	75
Impairment (75% × 60 (W3))	(45)
	930

The only reserve in this question is retained earnings. The retained earnings figure in the CSFP represents those belonging to the parent shareholders. This is made up of the parent entity's retained earnings plus their share (75%) of the subsidiary's post acquisition profits less their share of any impairment losses on goodwill. Since the NCI has been valued using the fair value method, the parent shareholders are charged with their 75% share of the impairment loss.

Now that we have completed the workings, the CSFP can be completed. Remember that:

- Parent and subsidiary's assets and liabilities are combined in full.

- Consolidated share capital is parent share capital only.

- The investment in S that is included in P's individual statement of financial position is replaced with goodwill.

- The NCI is part of group equity and should be shown accordingly.

Consolidated statement of financial position as at 31 March 20X4

		$000
Non-current assets	(1,650 + 750)	2,400
Goodwill (W3)		315
Current assets	(450 + 650)	1,100
		3,815
Equity		
Share capital		1,500
Retained earnings (W5)		930
Equity attributable to owners of parent		2,430
Non-controlling interest (W4)		285
Total equity		2,715
Non-current liabilities	(100 + 50)	150
Current liabilities	(500 + 450)	950
		3,815

It is perhaps worth noting that the net assets i.e. assets ($3,815,000) less liabilities ($150,000 + $950,000) of the group at the reporting date are $2,715,000.

This represents the net assets that are under the control of the group.

The net assets are owned by the shareholders of the group and this is reflected within the equity section of the CSFP. A group is owned by two sets of shareholders – the parent shareholders and the NCI shareholders. The parent's share of equity is $2,430,000 whilst the NCI's share is $285,000.

(b) If the proportion of net assets method were used, this would change the goodwill & NCI calculations. Since goodwill is impaired this method would also change retained earnings as the parent shareholders would now suffer the full amount of the impairment loss.

Note: It is being assumed that the question would still state that the impairment loss arising on goodwill is $60,000. (In reality, if goodwill were being measured using the proportion of net assets method, this would result in a different impairment loss compared to that arising under the fair value method.)

W3, W4, W5 and the CSFP would become:

(W3) **Goodwill**

	$000
Fair value of P's investment	900
Value of NCI at proportion of net assets (25% × 800 (W2))	200
Less: sub's net assets at acquisition (W2)	(800)
Goodwill at acquisition	300
Impairment	(60)
Goodwill at reporting date	240

(W4) **Non-controlling interest equity**

	$000
Value of NCI at acquisition (W3)	200
NCI% × post acquisition reserves (25% × 100 (W2))	25
	225

(W5) Consolidated reserves

	Retained earnings
Parent's reserves	900
Sub (75% × 100 (W2))	75
Impairment (W3)	(60)
	915

Consolidated statement of financial position as at 31 March 20X4

		$000
Non-current assets	(1,650 + 750)	2,400
Goodwill (W3)		240
Current assets	(450 + 650)	1,100
		3,740
Equity		
Share capital		1,500
Retained earnings (W5)		915
		2,415
Non-controlling interest (W4)		225
		2,640
Non-current liabilities	(100 + 50)	150
Current liabilities	(500 + 450)	950
		3,740

Tutorial note

There are a variety of workings that can be used to arrive at the final figures for inclusion in the consolidated statement of financial position. The above method combines the calculation of net assets at acquisition with the calculation of post-acquisition reserves within W2. Past solutions often show the calculation of net assets at acquisition as part of the goodwill working and then the calculation of post-acquisition reserves will be separately calculated as part of the retained earnings working. The calculations are effectively the same, but with a slightly different layout.

Test your understanding 3 (F1 recap)

P acquired 80% of the equity share capital of S on 1 April 20X2, paying $2.5m in cash. At this date, the retained earnings of S were $950,000. Below are the statements of financial position of P and S as at 31 March 20X4:

	P	S
	$000	$000
Non-current assets	3,500	2,400
Investment in S	2,500	–
Current assets	1,000	600
	7,000	3,000
Equity		
Share capital	4,000	1,000
Retained earnings	2,150	1,450
Non current liabilities	200	150
Current liabilities	650	400
	7,000	3,000

It is group policy to value the NCI at fair value at the date of acquisition. The fair value of the NCI in S at 1 April 20X2 was $600,000.

An impairment review was carried out at the reporting date and it was determined that goodwill had been impaired by $150,000.

Required:

(a) Prepare a consolidated statement of financial position as at 31 March 20X4.

(b) Show how your answer would differ if the NCI was valued using the proportionate share of net assets.

Test your understanding 4 (F1 recap)

P acquired 75% of the 5 million issued ordinary shares of S on 1 April 20X5, paying $6.5m in cash. At this date, the retained earnings of S were $2.5m.

The retained earnings reported in the financial statements of P and S as at 31 March 20X8 are $10.8 million and $4.5 million respectively.

The group policy is to measure non-controlling interest at fair value at the date of acquisition. The fair value of the non-controlling interest was $2 million on 1 April 20X5.

An impairment review performed on 31 March 20X8 indicated that goodwill on the acquisition of S had been impaired by 20%.

Required:

(1) Calculate the amounts that will appear in the consolidated statement of financial position of the P group as at 31 March 20X8 for:

   (a) Goodwill

   (b) Consolidated retained earnings

   (c) Non-controlling interest.

(2) Re-calculate the above amounts that would appear in the consolidated statement of financial position of the P group as at 31 March 20X8 if group policy was to measure non-controlling interest at the proportion of net assets at the date of acquisition.

7 Consolidated statement of profit or loss and other comprehensive income

The principles of consolidation are continued within the statement of profit or loss and other comprehensive income (CSPLOCI).

A statement of profit or loss and other comprehensive income reflects the income and expenses generated by the net assets shown on the statement of financial position. It incorporates two separate statements: the statement of profit or loss and the statement of other comprehensive income. The full title of the statement is 'Statement of profit or loss and other comprehensive income' however we will use 'Statement of comprehensive income' (SCI) for short.

Since the group controls the net assets of the subsidiary, the income and expenses of the subsidiary should be fully included in the consolidated statement of comprehensive income i.e. add across 100% of the parent plus 100% of the subsidiary.

Standard consolidation workings

Non-controlling interest share of profit/TCI

The share of profit and total comprehensive income that belongs to the NCI is to be calculated as follows:

		$	$
S's profit for the year per S's SPLOCI (time apportioned if mid year acquisition)		X	
Adjustments to S's profit		(X)	
Adjusted profit		X	
NCI share of profits	× NCI%		X
S's OCI per S's SPLOCI (time apportioned if mid year acquisition)		X	
Adjusted TCI		X	
NCI share of total comprehensive income	× NCI%		X

There are various adjustments that may have to be made to the subsidiary's profit when calculating the NCI's share. These will be covered in this chapter.

Consolidation adjustments and the CSOPL

Mid-year acquisitions

If the subsidiary was acquired mid-year then only the post-acquisition results should be consolidated. Unless told otherwise, it is normal to assume that results accrue evenly over the period and therefore the results of the subsidiary should be time apportioned so that only the post-acquisition results are consolidated.

Intra-group investment income

Dividends paid by the subsidiary to the parent should be eliminated upon consolidation from the parent's investment income.

Non-controlling interests

The profit for the year and the total comprehensive income for the year are analysed between the amounts attributable to the owners of the parent and the amounts attributable to the non-controlling interest. This analysis is presented at the bottom of the consolidated SCI and it is common for the NCI figures to be calculated (working shown earlier) with the amounts attributable to the owners of the parent then being computed as a balancing figure.

Goodwill impairment

If the fair value method has been used to value the non-controlling interests at acquisition, the NCI share of profit will be adjusted to reflect their share of any goodwill impairment loss.

Where the proportion of net assets method is used, all of the goodwill impairment is allocated to the parent (as previously discussed) and therefore no adjustment is made to the NCI figure.

Example 3

On 1 July 20X9 Zebedee acquired 75% of the equity shares of Xavier.

The following statements of comprehensive income have been produced by Zebedee and Xavier for the year ended 31 December 20X9.

	Zebedee	Xavier
	$000	$000
Revenue	1,260	520
Cost of sales	(420)	(210)
Gross profit	840	310
Operating expenses	(300)	(150)
Profit from operations	540	160
Investment income	36	–
Profit before tax	576	160
Income tax expense	(130)	(26)
Profit for the year	446	134
Other comprehensive income	100	50
Total comprehensive income	546	184

(1) At 31 December 20X9, goodwill arising on consolidation was reviewed for impairment. An impairment loss of $15,000 had arisen which should be charged to operating expenses. It is group policy to measure NCI at fair value at the date of acquisition.

(2) Zavier paid a dividend of $32,000 on 30 November 20X9.

Required:

Prepare the consolidated statement of comprehensive income for the Zebedee group for the year ended 31 December 20X9.

Example 3 answer

Look out for mid-year acquisitions as the results of the subsidiary may need to be time apportioned. In this scenario, only 6 months of the subsidiary's results should be consolidated as the subsidiary was acquired half way through the year.

Zebedee

Consolidated statement of comprehensive income for the year ended 31 December 20X9

	$000
Revenue (1,260 + (520 × 6/12))	1,520
Cost of sales (420 + (210 × 6/12))	(525)
Gross profit	995
Operating expenses (300 + (150 × 6/12) + 15 impairment)	(390)
Profit from operations	605
Investment income (36 – 24 (W1))	12
Profit before tax	617
Income tax expense (130 + (26 × 6/12))	(143)
Profit for the year	474
Other comprehensive income (100 + (50 × 6/12))	125
Total comprehensive income	599
Profit attributable to:	
Parent shareholders (balancing figure)	461
Non-controlling interests (W2)	13
	474
Total comprehensive income attributable to:	
Parent shareholders (balancing figure)	580
Non-controlling interests (W2)	19
	599

Workings

(W1) Intra-group dividend/investment income

Sub paid $32,000

Parent received (75% × 32,000) $24,000

Always look out for intra-group dividends in CSCI questions. Any dividend paid by the subsidiary will have partly been received by the parent (depending on their percentage holding) and this needs to be eliminated from investment income upon consolidation.

(W2) NCI share of profit and total comprehensive income

		$000	$000
Sub's profit (134 × 6/12)		67	
Impairment expense		(15)	
		⎯⎯	
		52	
NCI share of profits	× 25%		13
Sub's OCI (50 × 6/12)		25	
		⎯⎯	
		77	
NCI share of total comprehensive income	× 25%		19

For each consolidation adjustment, consider whether it affects the non-controlling interest. Here, there is goodwill impairment and, as the NCI is measured at fair value, the NCI's portion of the impairment charge should be allocated against the NCI profit.

By deducting the impairment expense from the subsidiary's profit prior applying the NCI%, the NCI's share of the impairment charge is allocated to the NCI figure.

Test your understanding 5 (F1 recap)

Given below are the statements of comprehensive income for Paris and its subsidiary London for the year ended 31 December 20X5

	Paris	London
	$000	$000
Revenue	3,200	2,560
Cost of sales	(1,200)	(1,080)
Gross profit	2,000	1,480
Operating expenses	(560)	(400)
Profit from operations	1,440	1,080
Investment income	160	–
Profit before tax	1,600	1,080
Income tax expense	(400)	(480)
Profit for the year	1,200	600
Other comprehensive income	300	100
Total comprehensive income	1,500	700

Paris acquired 80% of London's equity shares on 1 October 20X5.

(1) Goodwill was calculated valuing the NCI at fair value at the date of acquisition. At 31 December 20X5, it was determined that goodwill arising on the acquisition had been impaired by $30,000. Impairments are charged to operating expenses.

(2) London paid a dividend of $150,000 on 15 December 20X5.

Required:

Prepare a consolidated statement of comprehensive income for the year ended 31 December 20X5.

8 Mid-year acquisitions

The consolidated statement of financial position (CSFP) reflects the position at the reporting date and therefore figures on the face of the CSFP should never be time apportioned.

However, you may be required to time apportion results in order to calculate the reserves at acquisition (for the net assets working). Depending on the information provided, you will be required to either:

- Subtract the profits for the post acquisition portion of the year from the closing reserves balance, or

- Add the profits for the pre-acquisition portion of the year to the opening reserves balance.

Illustration 1 – Mid-year acquisition

An entity is acquired on 1 March 20X9. Its profits for the year ended 31 December 20X9 are $12,000 and its retained earnings at the reporting date are $55,000.

Retained earnings at acquisition will be $55,000 – (10/12 × $12,000) = $45,000.

9 Intra-group balances

Intra-group balances and transactions must be eliminated in full, as the group is treated as a single entity and therefore cannot trade with or owe money to itself.

- Intra-group balances are eliminated from the consolidated statement of financial position

- Intra-group transactions are eliminated from the consolidated statement of comprehensive income

- Any profit still held within the group's assets from intra-group trading should also be eliminated (the provision for unrealised profit (PUP) adjustment)

Intra-group balances – in transit items

When eliminating intra-group receivables and payables, the account balances may disagree. This is most likely to be due to cash in transit or goods in transit.

Cash in transit

Cash has been sent by one group entity, but has not been received and so is not recorded in the books of the other group entity. The following adjustment will be required:

Cr   Receivables (with the higher amount)

Dr   Bank (with the amount in transit i.e. the difference)

Dr   Payables (with the lower amount)

Goods in transit

Goods have been sent by one entity, but have not been received and so are not recorded in the books of the other group entity. The following adjustment will be required:

Cr   Receivables (with the higher amount)

Dr   Inventory (with the amount in transit i.e. the difference)

Dr   Payables (with the lower amount)

Example 4

Extracts from the statements of financial position of P and its subsidiary S at 31 December 20X8 are as follows:

	P	S
	$000	$000
Current assets		
Inventory	750	140
Receivables	650	95
Cash	400	85
Current liabilities		
Payables	900	200

P acquired 100% of S five years ago.

P and S traded with each other and, at the reporting date, P owed S $25,000. This balance is stated after P had recorded that they had sent a cheque for $5,000 to S shortly before the year-end which S had not received by the reporting date.

Required:

What balances would be shown in P's consolidated statement of financial position at 31 December 20X8 for each category of current asset and current liabilities?

Example 4 answer

Extracts from P's consolidated statement of financial position at 31 December 20X8

		$000
Current assets		
Inventory	(750 + 140)	890
Receivables	(650 + 95 – 30 (W1))	715
Cash	(400 + 85 + 5)	490
Current liabilities		
Payables	(900 + 200 – 25)	1,075

(W1) Intra-group balances

The question states that P owes S $25,000 i.e. a payable. This is to be eliminated by reducing payables.

The question states that there is cash in transit at the reporting date of $5,000. This needs to be recorded by increasing cash.

The intercompany receivable that needs to be eliminated is therefore calculated as a balancing figure:

			$000
Dr	Payables	↓	25
Dr	Cash	↑	5
Cr	Receivables	↓	30

Provision for unrealised profit (PUP) in inventory

P and S may sell goods to each other, resulting in a profit being recorded in the selling entity's financial statements. If these goods are still held by the purchasing entity at the year-end, the goods have not been sold outside of the group. The profit is therefore unrealised from the group's perspective and should be removed.

The adjustment is also required to ensure that inventory is stated at the cost to the group i.e. the cost when the goods were first acquired by the group, not the cost to the purchasing entity after the intra-group transfer.

PUP adjustment = profit on inventory still held in group at year end

In the consolidated statement of financial position, deduct from:

- **Net assets at reporting date column** (in net assets working) **if S sells** the goods or **Consolidated reserves if P sells** the goods – thereby removing the profit from the appropriate entity's retained earnings figure.

- Inventory on the face of the CSFP.

In the consolidated statement of profit or loss:

- Add to cost of sales (to reflect reduction in closing inventory and profit)

- If S is the seller, adjust the NCI to reflect their share of the PUP adjustment

NB. The total intragroup revenue and cost of sales will also be removed from the consolidated SPL as a separate adjustment to the PUP.

The 'PUP' adjustment

Parent sells to subsidiary

P sells goods to S for $400 at cost plus 25%. All goods remain in the inventory of S at the end of the year.

$$\text{Profit made on the sale} \quad \frac{25}{125} \times 400 = 80.$$

Individual financial statements

P records profit	80
S records inventory	400

Group financial statements should show:

Profit	0
Inventory	320

PUP adjustment in Consol SFP

Dr Group retained earnings	↓	80
Cr Group inventory (CSFP)	↓	80

The group profit figure for the parent will be reduced as it is the parent that recorded the profit in this case.

It is important to note that the adjustment takes place in the group accounts only. The individual accounts are correct as they stand and will not be adjusted as a result.

Subsidiary sells to parent

PUP adjustment in Consol SFP

Dr Sub's net assets at reporting date	↓	80
Cr Group inventory (CSFP)	↓	80

The subsidiary's profit will be reduced as it is the subsidiary that recorded the profit in this case. The reduction in the subsidiary's profits needs to be shared between the parent and NCI shareholders in the NCI reserve & consolidated reserves workings. By adjusting for the PUP in the net assets working, this split will automatically be split between the two reserves. S's profits are shared between the parent and the non-controlling interest shareholders.

PUP adjustment in Consol SCI

The PUP adjustment of 80 is always added to cost of sales, regardless of which entity made the profit.

When calculating the split of profit between owners of the parent and NCI, the NCI share of profit would be adjusted for the PUP adjustment if the subsidiary was the seller only.

Cost structures

The cost structure of the intra-group sale may be given to you in one of two ways.

Mark up on cost (Cost plus)

If, for example, goods are sold for $440 and there is a 25% mark up on cost, you need to calculate the profit included within the $440.

	%	$	
Revenue	125	440	
Cost of sales	100		
Gross profit	25	88	= 440 × 25/125

The PUP is $88.

Gross profit margin

The gross profit margin gives the profit as a percentage of revenue. Using the same figures as above but with a gross profit margin of 25%.

	%	$	
Revenue	100	440	
Cost of sales	75		
Gross profit	25	110	= 440 × 25/100

The PUP is $110.

Example 5

The following summarised statements of financial position are provided for P and S as at 30 June 20X8:

	P	S
	$000	$000
Non-current assets	8,000	5,000
Investment in S	7,000	–
Current assets		
Inventory	1,600	850
Receivables	1,350	950
Cash and cash equivalents	850	400
	18,800	7,200

Equity		
Share capital $1	10,000	4,000
Share premium	2,000	500
Retained earnings	5,050	1,400
Current liabilities		
Payables	1,750	1,300
	18,800	7,200

P acquired 90% of S two years ago for $7,000,000 when the balance on the retained earnings of S was $800,000. It is group policy to value NCI at fair value at acquisition and the fair value of the NCI was $650,000 at this date.

S sells goods to P at a profit margin of 20%. As a result at the reporting date, P's records showed a payable due to S of $50,000. However this disagreed to S's receivables balance of $60,000 due to cash in transit.

At the reporting date, P held $100,000 of goods in inventory that had been purchased from S.

There has been no impairment of goodwill.

Required:

Prepare the consolidated statement of financial position at 30 June 20X8.

Example 5 answer

Consolidated statement of financial position as at 30 June 20X8

		$000
Non-current assets	(8,000 + 5,000)	13,000
Goodwill	(W3)	2,350
Current assets		
Inventory	(1,600 + 850 – 20 (W7))	2,430
Receivables	(1,350 + 950 – 60)	2,240
Cash and cash equivalents	(850 + 400 + 10 (W6))	1,260
		21,280

Equity		
Share capital		10,000
Share premium		2,000
Retained earnings	(W5)	5,572
Non-controlling interests	(W4)	708
		18,280
Current liabilities		
Payables	(1,750 + 1,300 – 50)	3,000
		21,280

Note: The intra-group balances are adjusted for on the face of the consolidated statement of financial position. The PUP adjustment, calculated in W7, should be deducted from the carrying value of inventory at the reporting date.

(W1) Group structure

P

| 90% 2 years since acquisition

S

(W2) Net assets of subsidiary

	Acquisition	Reporting date
	$000	$000
Share capital	4,000	4,000
Share premium	500	500
Retained earnings	800	1,400
PUP (W7)	–	(20)
	5,300	5,880

580
Post acq'n profit

Note: As the subsidiary made the sales on which the profit is unrealised, it is their retained earnings that must be reduced. Therefore the PUP adjustment is reflected at the reporting date in W2 above.

(W3) Goodwill

	$000
Fair value of P's investment	7,000
Value of NCI at acquisition (at fair value)	650
Fair value of sub's net assets at acquisition (W2)	(5,300)
Goodwill at acquisition	2,350
Impairment	–
Goodwill at reporting date	2,350

(W4) Non-controlling interest

	$000
Value of NCI at acquisition (W3)	650
NCI% × post acquisition reserves (10% × 580 (W2))	58
	708

(W5) **Reserves**

	Retained earnings
	$000
Parent's reserves	5,050
Sub (90% × 580 (W2))	522
	–––––
	5,572
	–––––

(W6) **Intra-group balances**

			$000
Dr	Payables	↓	50
Dr	Cash	↑	10
Cr	Receivables	↓	60

(W7) **PUP**

Profit in inventory = 20% × $100,000 = $20,000

Test your understanding 6 (F1 recap)

The following summarised statements of financial position are provided for P and S as at 30 June 20X8:

	P	S
	$000	$000
Non-current assets	14,200	10,200
Investment in S	14,500	–
Current assets		
Inventory	5,750	3,400
Receivables	4,250	2,950
Cash and cash equivalents	2,500	1,450
	–––––	–––––
	41,200	18,000
	–––––	–––––

Equity		
Share capital $1	20,000	5,000
Retained earnings	12,600	7,900
Current liabilities		
Payables	8,600	5,100
	41,200	18,000

P acquired 80% of S three years ago for $14,500,000 when the balance on the retained earnings of S was $5,800,000. It is group policy to value NCI at acquisition at the proportionate share of the net assets.

P sells goods to S. As a result, at the reporting date S's records showed a payable due to P of $550,000. However this disagreed to P's receivables balance of $750,000 due to cash in transit.

During the current year, P had sold $1,500,000 (selling price) of goods to S of which S still held one third in inventory at the year end. The selling price was based on a mark-up of 25%.

An impairment loss of $1,000,000 should be charged against goodwill at the reporting date.

Required:

(a) Prepare the consolidated statement of financial position at 30 June 20X8.

(b) Recalculate the following amounts at 30 June 20X8 to reflect what they would have been if S had sold the goods to P instead.

(a) Consolidated retained earnings

(b) Non-controlling interests

Test your understanding 7 (F1 recap)

Below are the statements of profit or loss for Rome and its subsidiary Madrid for the year ended 30 June 20X9.

	Rome	Madrid
	$000	$000
Revenue	10,350	8,400
Cost of sales	(6,200)	(5,150)
Gross profit	4,150	3,250
Operating expenses	(2,450)	(1,600)
Profit before tax	1,700	1,650
Income tax expense	(550)	(450)
Profit for the year	1,150	1,200

(1) Rome acquired 60% of Madrid's equity shares on 1 July 20X7 paying $6 million. At this date the value of Madrid's net assets was $5 million. It is Rome's group policy to value NCIs at acquisition using the proportion of net assets method. As at 30 June 20X9 it was determined that goodwill on acquisition had been impaired by 20%. No impairment loss had arisen previously.

(2) During the year ended 30 June 20X9, Rome sold $1 million of goods to Madrid at a margin of 30%. Half of these goods remained in the inventory of Madrid at the reporting date.

Required:

(a) Prepare a consolidated statement of profit or loss for the Rome Group for the year ended 30 June 20X9.

(b) Assume now that Madrid had sold the goods to Rome instead (all other details remain the same). Prepare the analysis of profit attributable to parent shareholders and NCI for the year ended 30 June 20X9 in this situation.

Provision for unrealised profit (PUP) in NCA

P and S may sell non-current assets to each other, resulting in a profit being recorded in the selling entity's financial statements. If these non-current assets are still held by the purchasing entity at the year-end, the profit is unrealised from the group's perspective and should be removed.

The profit on disposal should be removed from the seller's books (net assets working (at reporting date) if the sub is the seller, consolidated reserves working if the parent is the seller).

In addition to the profit, there is depreciation to consider.

Prior to the transfer, the asset is depreciated based on the original cost. After the transfer depreciation is calculated on the transfer price, i.e. a higher value. Therefore depreciation is higher after the transfer and this extra cost must be eliminated in the consolidated financial statements, i.e. profits need to be increased.

The extra depreciation that has been charged should be removed from the purchaser's books.

Adjustment required – CSFP:

- Profit on disposal – reduce S's net assets working at reporting date if S sells the asset or reduce consolidated reserves if P sells the asset.

- Extra depreciation – increase consolidated reserves if S sells the asset or increase S's net assets at reporting date if P sells the asset.

- Decrease the non-current asset in the CSFP with the net amount.

Adjustment required – CSCI:

- Deduct profit on disposal

- Add back excess depreciation charged (therefore reduce related expense category)

- In NCI share of profit working:
    - If P is seller, add back excess depreciation charged by S
    - If S is seller, deduct profit on disposal made by S

Example 6

P acquired 80% of the share capital of S some years ago. P's reporting date is 31 August. P transfers an asset on 1 March 20X7 for $75,000 when its carrying value is $60,000. The remaining useful life at the date of sale is 2.5 years. The group depreciation policy is straight line on a monthly basis.

What adjustment is required in the consolidated financial statements of P for the year ended 31 August 20X8?

Example 6 answer

Profit recorded on the sale: $75,000 – $60,000 = $15,000

Extra depreciation: ($75,000 – $60,000) × 1.5/2.5 = $9,000

Adjustment required:

Dr Consol RE/profit	↓ $15,000	
Cr Sub's net assets at reporting date/profit	↑ $9,000	
Cr NCA (CSFP)	↓ $6,000	

In the CSCI, the NCI calculation should include an adjustment to add back the excess depreciation of $9,000 charged by the subsidiary since the date of transfer.

Using the same example as above, but if S had sold the asset to P, the adjustment would be:

Dr Sub's net assets at reporting date/profit	↓ $15,000	
Cr Consol RE/profit	↑ $9,000	
Cr NCA (CSFP)	↓ $6,000	

In the CSCI, the NCI calculation would include an adjustment to reduce the subsidiary's profit by $15,000 to eliminate the profit on disposal of the intra-group transfer.

10 Investments in Associates

An **associate** is an entity over which the investor has **significant influence** and which is neither a subsidiary nor a joint venture of the investor.

Associates – further detail

Significant influence is defined as the power to participate in the financial and operating policy decisions of the investee but not control or joint control of those policies.

A holding of 20% or more of the voting power is presumed to give significant influence unless it can be clearly demonstrated that this is not the case. At the same time a holding of less than 20% is assumed not to give significant influence unless such influence can be clearly demonstrated.

IAS 28 explains that an investor probably has significant influence if:

- It is represented on the board of directors.

- It participates in policy-making processes, including decisions about dividends or other distributions.

- There are material transactions between the investor and investee.

- There is interchange of managerial personnel.

- There is provision of essential technical information.

Associates are accounted for using **equity accounting** in accordance with IAS 28.

They are not consolidated as the parent does not have control.

Consolidated statement of financial position

The CSFP will include a single line within non-current assets called 'Investment in associate' calculated as:

Investment in associate

	$
Cost of investment	X
Add: share of post acquisition reserves	X
Less: impairment losses	(X)
Less: PUP (if A has inventory – see later)	(X)
	X

The share of post acquisition reserves, impairment losses and PUP would also be recorded in Consolidated retained earnings.

Consolidated statement of comprehensive income

The CSCI will include a single line before profit before tax called 'Share of profit of associate' calculated as:

Share of associate's profit for the year	X
Less: impairment loss	(X)
Less: PUP (if A is seller – see later)	(X)
	X

If the associate has other comprehensive income, the investor's share will also be recorded in the other comprehensive income section of CSCI.

IAS 28 Investments in Associates and Joint Ventures

The equity method of accounting is normally used to account for associates and joint ventures in the consolidated financial statements.

Joint ventures are in the F2 syllabus – see the next chapter for details.

The equity method should not be used if:

- the investment is classified as held for sale in accordance with IFRS 5, or

- the parent is exempted from having to prepare consolidated accounts on the grounds that it is itself a wholly, or partially, owned subsidiary of another company (IFRS 10).

Adjustments required

Intercompany transactions & balances

Intercompany transactions between the group (whether with the parent or subsidiary) and the associate are not eliminated within the CSCI or CSFP. This is because the associate is outside of the group. Thus the transactions/balances are with a third party to the group and so may be reported within the group financial statements.

However, unrealised profit on transactions must be eliminated on consolidation.

Provisions for unrealised profit (PUP)

IAS 28 requires unrealised profits on transactions between the group and the associate to be eliminated. Only the investor's share of the profit is removed since the group financial statements only reflect the investor's share of the associate profits in the first place.

The PUP adjustment is calculated as:

$$\text{PUP} = \textbf{P\%} \times \text{unrealised profit in inventory}$$

Parent sells to associate

In the CSFP:

- Reduce Consolidated retained earnings (Dr)
- Reduce Investment in associate (Cr)

In the CSCI:

- Increase Cost of sales

Associate sells to parent

In the CSFP:

- Reduce Consolidated retained earnings (Dr)
- Reduce Inventory (Cr)

In the CSCI:

- Reduce Share of profit of associate

Associate PUP with parent the seller

P owns 40% of the equity shares of A.

P has sold $200,000 of goods to A at a mark up on cost of 25%.

At the reporting date 60% of these items remain in A's inventory.

The intercompany sale of $200,000 is not eliminated in the consolidated financial statements. However a PUP adjustment is calculated as:

Goods in inventory	60% × $200,000 = $120,000
Profit in inventory	25/125 × $120,000 = $24,000
PUP	40% × $24,000 = $9,600

The adjustment will be:

Dr Cost of sales	$9,600
Cr Investment in associate	$9,600

In the CSPLOCI, cost of sales will increase.

In the CSFP, retained earnings will therefore be reduced. The investment in Associate will also be reduced.

The associate is holding the inventory, but the associate's inventory is not consolidated on the inventory line in the CSFP and so it is not appropriate to reduce inventory.

PUP with associate the seller

Using the same information as above but with the associate selling to the parent, the adjustment will now be:

Dr Income from associate	$9,600
Cr Inventory	$9,600

In the CSCI, share of profit of associate will reduce.

In the CSFP, retained earnings will therefore be reduced. Inventory will also be reduced as it is the parent company holding the inventory.

Example 7

Below are the statements of financial position of three entities as at 31 December 20X9.

	Tom $000	James $000	Emily $000
Non-current assets			
Property, plant & equipment	959	980	840
Investments: 630,000 shares in James	805	–	–
168,000 shares in Emily	224	–	–
	1,988	980	840
Current assets			
Inventory	380	640	190
Receivables	190	310	100
Cash and cash equivalents	35	58	46
TOTAL ASSETS	2,593	1,988	1,176
Equity			
Share capital ($1 shares)	1,120	840	560
Retained earnings	1,232	602	448
	2,352	1,442	1,008
Current liabilities			
Trade payables	150	480	136
Taxation	91	66	32
TOTAL EQUITY & LIABILITIES	2,593	1,988	1,176

Additional information:

(1) Tom acquired its shares in James on 1 January 20X9 when James had retained earnings of $160,000. NCIs are to be valued at their fair value at the date of acquisition. The fair value of the NCI holding in James at 1 January 20X9 was $250,000.

(2) Tom acquired its shares in Emily on 1 January 20X9 when Emily had retained earnings of $140,000.

(3) An impairment test at the year end shows that the goodwill for James remains unimpaired but that the investment in Emily is impaired by $2,000.

Required:

Prepare the consolidated statement of financial position for the year ended 31 December 20X9.

Example 7 answer

Consolidated statement of financial position as at 31 December 20X9

	$000
Non-current assets	
Goodwill (W3)	55
Property, plant & equipment (959 + 980)	1,939
Investment in associate (W6)	314.4
	2,308.4
Current assets	
Inventory (380 + 640)	1,020
Receivables (190 + 310)	500
Cash and cash equivalents (35 + 58)	93
TOTAL ASSETS	3,921.4
Equity	
Share capital ($1 shares)	1,120
Retained earnings (W5)	1,653.9
	2,773.9
Non-controlling interest (W4)	360.5
	3,134.4
Current liabilities	
Trade payables (150 + 480)	630
Taxation (91 + 66)	157
TOTAL EQUITY & LIABILITIES	3,921.4

Workings

(W1) Group structure

Tom

630/840   168/560

= 75%   = 30%

1 Jan X9 (1 year)   1 Jan X9 (1 year)

James   Emily

(W2) Net assets of sub

	Acquisition date	Reporting date
	$000	$000
Share capital ($1 shares)	840	840
Retained earnings	160	602
	1,000	1,442

Post acquisition profits = 442

(W3) Goodwill

	$000
Fair value of parent's investment	805
NCI at fair value	250
Fair value of sub's net assets at acquisition (W2)	(1,000)
Goodwill at acquisition/ reporting date	55

(W4) **Non-controlling interests**

	$000
NCI at acquisition at fair value (W3)	250
NCI% of post acquisition reserves (25% × 442 (W2))	110.5
	360.5

(W5) **Group retained earnings**

	$000
P's retained earnings	1,232
S: 75% of post acquisition profits (75% × 442 (W2))	331.5
A: 30% of post-acquisition profits (W6)	92.4
A: impairment (W6)	(2)
	1,653.9

(W6) **Investment in associate**

	$000
Cost of investment	224
P% × post acquisition profits (30% × (448 – 140))	92.4
Less: impairment	(2)
	314.4

In the question, the investment in Emily is included in Tom's SFP at its cost of $224,000. The investment was made at the start of the year.

This becomes the starting point for equity accounting i.e. the starting point for the calculation of investment in associate.

At acquisition the retained earnings of Emily were $140,000 and at the reporting date they are $448,000. Therefore the post acquisition reserves of Emily are $308,000 of which 30% belong to Tom i.e. $92,400. This increases both the value of investment in associate and retained earnings.

At the reporting date, the investment is impaired by $2,000. This is a reduction in the value of the Investment and is an expense and so also reduces retained earnings.

Test your understanding 8 (F1 recap)

P acquired 80% of the 1 million issued $1 ordinary shares of S on 1 October 20X3 for $1.5 million when S's retained earnings were $350,000.

P acquired 30% of the 500,000 issued $1 ordinary shares of A on 1 October 20X7 for $300,000 when A's retained earnings were $360,000.

The retained earnings reported in the financial statements of P, S and A as at 30 September 20X8 were $2 million, $750,000 and $400,000 respectively.

An impairment review performed on 30 September 20X8 indicated that there was no impairment to the goodwill arising on the acquisition of S, however the investment in A was impaired by $5,000.

Required:

Calculate the amounts that would appear in the consolidated statement of financial position for the P group as at 30 September 20X8 for:

(a) Investment in associate

(b) Consolidated retained earnings.

11 Chapter summary

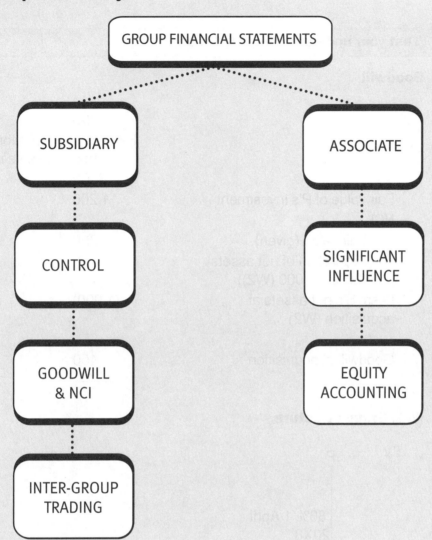

Test your understanding answers

Test your understanding 1 (F1 recap)

Goodwill

	(a) Fair value method $000	(b) Proportion of net assets method $000
Fair value of P's investment	1,200	1,200
NCI		
Fair value (given)	250	
Proportion of net assets (20% × 1,000 (W2))		200
Less: S's net assets at acquisition (W2)	(1,000)	(1,000)
Goodwill at acquisition	450	400

(W1) Group structure

P

| 80% 1 April
20X8

S

(W2) Net assets of subsidiary

	Acquisition $000
Share capital	200
Retained earnings	800
	1,000

Test your understanding 2 (F1 recap)

Goodwill

	(a) Fair value method $000	(b) Proportion of net assets method $000
Fair value of P's investment	2,500	2,500
NCI		
Fair value (25% × 500 × $6)	750	
Proportion of net assets (25% × 2,000 (W2))		500
Less: S's net assets at acquisition (W2)	(2,000)	(2,000)
Goodwill at acquisition	1,250	1,000

(W1) Group structure

P

75% 1 April
20X8

S

(W2) Net assets of subsidiary

	Acquisition $000
Share capital	500
Retained earnings	1,500
	2,000

Test your understanding 3 (F1 recap)

(a) Consolidated statement of financial position at 31 March 20X4

		$000
Non-current assets	(3,500 + 2,400)	5,900
Goodwill (W3)		1,000
Current assets	(1,000 + 600)	1,600
		8,500

Equity		
Share capital		4,000
Retained earnings (W5)		2,430
		6,430
Non-controlling interest (W4)		670
		7,100
Non-current liabilities	(200 + 150)	350
Current liabilities	(650 + 400)	1,050
		8,500

(W1) Group structure

P

80% 1 April 20X2 i.e. 2 years since acquisition

S

(W2) **Net assets of subsidiary**

	Acquisition	Reporting date
	$000	$000
Share capital	1,000	1,000
Retained earnings	950	1,450
	———	———
	1,950	2,450
	———	———

500 post acq'n profit

(W3) **Goodwill**

	$000
Fair value of P's investment	2,500
NCI at fair value at acquisition	600
Less: sub's net assets at acquisition (W2)	(1,950)
	———
Goodwill at acquisition	1,150
Impairment	(150)
	———
Goodwill at reporting date	1,000
	———

(W4) **Non-controlling interest**

	$000
Value of NCI at acquisition (W3)	600
NCI% × post acquisition reserves (20% × 500 (W2))	100
NCI% × impairment (20% × 150 (W3))	(30)
	———
	670
	———

(W5) **Reserves**

	Retained earnings
	$000
Parent's reserves	2,150
Sub (80% × 500 (W2))	400
Impairment (80% × 150 (W3))	(120)
	———
	2,430
	———

(b) Consolidated statement of financial position at 31 March 20X4

		$000
Non-current assets	(3,500 + 2,400)	5,900
Goodwill (W3)		790
Current assets	(1,000 + 600)	1,600
		8,290

Equity		
Share capital		4,000
Retained earnings (W5)		2,400
		6,400
Non-controlling interest (W4)		490
		6,890
Non-current liabilities	(200 + 150)	350
Current liabilities	(650 + 400)	1,050
		8,290

(W1) **Group structure – as for (a)**

(W2) **Net assets of subsidiary – as per W2 in (a)**

(W3) **Goodwill**

	$000
Fair value of P's investment	2,500
Value of NCI at proportion of net assets (20% × 1,950 (W2))	390
Less: sub's net assets at acquisition (W2)	(1,950)
Goodwill at acquisition	940
Impairment	(150)
Goodwill at reporting date	790

(W4) Non-controlling interest

	$000
Value of NCI at acquisition (W3)	390
NCI% × post acquisition reserves (20% × 500 (W2))	100
	——
	490
	——

(W5) Reserves

	Retained earnings
	$000
Parent's reserves	2,150
Sub (80% × 500 (W2))	400
Impairment	(150)
	——
	2,400
	——

Test your understanding 4 (F1 recap)

(a) Goodwill

	(1)	(2)
	Fair value method	Proportion of net assets method
	$000	$000
Fair value of P's investment	6,500	6,500
Value of NCI at acquisition		
– at fair value	2,000	
– at proportion of net assets (25% × 7,500 (W1))		1,875
Less: sub's net assets at acquisition (W1)	(7,500)	(7,500)
	——	——
Goodwill at acquisition	1,000	875
Impairment (20% × goodwill at acquisition)	(200)	(175)
	——	——
Goodwill at reporting date	800	700
	——	——

(b) **Consolidated retained earnings**

	(1)	(2)
	Fair value method	Proportion of net assets method
	$000	$000
Parent's reserves	10,800	10,800
Sub (75% × 2,000 (W1))	1,500	1,500
Impairment loss		
– FV method (75% × 200 (part a))	(150)	
– Proportion of net assets method (part a)		(175)
	———	———
	12,150	12,125
	———	———

(c) **Non-controlling interest**

	(1)	(2)
	Fair value method	Proportion of net assets method
	$000	$000
Value of NCI at acquisition (as in goodwill)	2,000	1,875
NCI% × post acquisition reserves (25% × 2,000 (W1))	500	500
NCI% × impairment (25% × 200 (part a))	(50)	–
	———	———
	2,450	2,375
	———	———

(W1) **Net assets of subsidiary**

	Acquisition	Reporting date
	$000	$000
Share capital	5,000	5,000
Retained earnings	2,500	4,500
	———	———
	7,500	9,500
	———	———

2,000 post acq'n profit

Test your understanding 5 (F1 recap)

Consolidated statement of comprehensive income

	$000
Revenue (3,200 + (2,560 × 3/12))	3,840
Cost of sales (1,200 + (1,080 × 3/12))	(1,470)
	─────
Gross profit	2,370
Operating expenses (560 + (400 × 3/12) + 30 imp)	(690)
	─────
Profit from operations	1,680
Investment income (160 – 120 (W1))	40
	─────
Profit before tax	1,720
Income tax expense (400 + (480 × 3/12))	(520)
	─────
Profit for the year	1,200
Other comprehensive income (300 + (100 × 3/12))	325
	─────
Total comprehensive income	1,525
	─────
Profit attributable to:	
Parent shareholders (balancing figure)	1,176
Non-controlling interests (W2)	24
	─────
	1,200
	─────
Total comprehensive income attributable to:	
Parent shareholders (balancing figure)	1,496
Non-controlling interests (W2)	29
	─────
	1,525
	─────

Workings

(W1) Intercompany dividend

Sub paid $150,000

Parent received (80% × $150,000) = $120,000

(W2) NCI share of profit and total comprehensive income

		$000	$000
Sub's profit (600 × 3/12)		150	
Impairment expense		(30)	
		———	
		120	
NCI share of profit	× 20%		24
Sub's OCI (100 × 3/12)		25	
		———	
		145	
NCI share of TCI	× 20%		29

Test your understanding 6 (F1 recap)

(a) **Consolidated statement of financial position as at 30 June 20X8**

		$000
Non-current assets	(14,200 + 10,200)	24,400
Goodwill	(W3)	4,860
Current assets		
Inventory	(5,750 + 3,400 – 100 (W7))	9,050
Receivables	(4,250 + 2,950 – 750)	6,450
Cash and cash equivalents	(2,500 + 1,450 + 200 (W6))	4,150
		———
		48,910
		———
Equity		
Share capital		20,000
Retained earnings	(W5)	13,180
Non-controlling interests	(W4)	2,580
		———
		35,760
Current liabilities		
Payables	(8,600 + 5,100 – 550)	13,150
		———
		48,910
		———

(W1) **Group structure**

P
|
| 80% 3 years since
| acquisition
|
S

(W2) **Net assets of subsidiary**

	Acquisition	Reporting date
	$000	$000
Share capital	5,000	5,000
Retained earnings	5,800	7,900
	10,800	12,900

2,100
Post acquisition
profit

(W3) **Goodwill**

	$000
Fair value of P's investment	14,500
Value of NCI at acquisition (20% × 10,800 (W2))	2,160
Less: sub's net assets at acquisition (W2)	(10,800)
Goodwill at acquisition	5,860
Impairment	(1,000)
Goodwill at reporting date	4,860

(W4) **Non-controlling interest**

	$000
Value of NCI at acquisition (W3)	2,160
NCI% × post acquisition reserves (20% × 2,100 (W2))	420
	——
	2,580
	——

(W5) **Reserves**

	Retained earnings
	$000
Parent's reserves	12,600
Sub (80% × 2,100 (W2))	1,680
Impairment	(1,000)
PUP (W7)	(100)
	——
	13,180
	——

(W6) **Intra-group balances**

			$000
Dr	Payables	↓	550
Dr	Cash	↑	200
Cr	Receivables	↓	750

(W7) **PUP**

Profit on sale = 25/125 × $1,500,000 = $300,000

Profit in inventory = 1/3 × $300,000 = $100,000

(b) **Revised amounts, S selling to P**

(W2) **Net assets of subsidiary**

The PUP adjustment would be deducted in W2 rather than W5, resulting in post-acquisition profits in the subsidiary of 2,000 (after adjustment).

	Acquisition	Reporting date
	$000	$000
Share capital	5,000	5,000
Retained earnings	5,800	7,900
PUP (W7)		(100)
	10,800	12,800

2,000
Post acquisition
profit

(W4) **Non-controlling interest**

	$000
Value of NCI at acquisition (W3)	2,160
NCI% × post acquisition reserves (20% × 2,000 (W2))	400
	2,560

(W5) **Reserves**

	Retained earnings
	$000
Parent's reserves	12,600
Sub (80% × 2,000 (W2))	1,600
Impairment	(1,000)
	13,200

The overall impact on the reserves of the seller being S rather than P is that the NCI reserve is $20,000 lower and the group reserves (attributable to owners of the parent) is $20,000 higher. This is because 20% of the PUP adjustment has been re-allocated against the NCI.

Test your understanding 7 (F1 recap)

(a) **Consolidated statement of profit or loss**

	$000
Revenue (10,350 + 8,400 – 1,000 (W2))	17,750
Cost of sales (6,200 + 5,150 – 1,000 (W2) + 150 (W2))	(10,500)
Gross profit	7,250
Operating expenses (2,450 + 1,600 + 600 (W1))	(4,650)
Profit before tax	2,600
Income tax expense (550 + 450)	(1,000)
Profit for the year	1,600
Profit attributable to:	
Parent shareholders (balancing figure)	1,120
Non-controlling interests (1,200 × 40%)	480
	1,600

NB. Impairment is not deducted in the NCI working as the NCI has been valued using the proportionate method. The PUP adjustment is also not deducted, as the parent made the profit.

Workings

(W1) Goodwill and impairment

	$000
Fair value of P's investment	6,000
NCI at proportion of net assets (40% × 5,000)	2,000
Fair value of sub's net assets at acquisition	(5,000)
Goodwill at acquisition	3,000
Therefore impairment (20% × 3,000)	600

(W2) Intercompany sales and PUP

Intercompany sales of $1,000,000 to be eliminated by reducing both revenue and cost of sales

PUP adjustment to increase cost of sales:

Goods in inventory = 1/2 × $1,000,000 = $500,000

Profit in inventory = 30% × $500,000 = $150,000

(b) Analysis of profit attributable to parent shareholders and NCI

Profit attributable to:

Parent shareholders (balancing figure)	1,180
Non-controlling interests ((1,200 – 150) × 40%)	420
	———
	1,600
	———

As the subsidiary made the unrealised profit, the PUP adjustment is deducted from the subsidiary's profit prior to applying the NCI%.

Test your understanding 8 (F1 recap)

(a) Investment in associate

	$000
Cost of investment	300
P% × post acquisition profits (30% × (400 – 360))	12
Less: impairment	(5)
	———
	307
	———

(b) Consolidated retained earnings

	$000
P's retained earnings	2,000
S: 80% × (750 – 350)	320
A: 30% × (400 – 360)	12
A: impairment	(5)
	———
	2,327
	———

Basic group accounts – F2 syllabus

Chapter learning objectives

B1. Produce consolidated primary financial statements, incorporating accounting transactions and adjustments, in accordance with relevant international accounting standards, in an ethical manner.

(a) Produce:
- – consolidated statement of comprehensive income
- – consolidated statement of financial position

including the adoption of both full consolidation and the principles of equity accounting, in accordance with the provisions of IAS 1, IAS 27, IAS 28, IFRS 3, IFRS 10 and IFRS 11.

(b) Discuss the need for and nature of disclosure of interests in other entities, in accordance with IFRS 12.

1 Session content

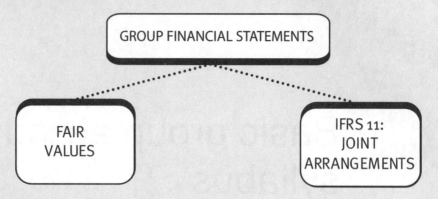

2 Introduction

This chapter principally looks at IFRS 3 *Business Combinations* in more detail and, in particular, the role of fair values in group accounts and the calculation of goodwill.

Towards the end of the chapter there is a quick look at some further group related accounting standards.

3 Goodwill and fair values

The calculation of goodwill is governed by IFRS 3 *Business Combinations*.

Goodwill is a residual amount calculated by comparing, at acquisition, the value of the subsidiary as a whole and the fair value of its identifiable net assets at this time. A residual amount may exist as a result of the subsidiary's:

- Positive reputation
- Loyal customer base
- Staff expertise etc

Goodwill is capitalised as an intangible asset on the consolidated statement of financial position (CSFP). It is subject to an annual impairment review to ensure its value is not overstated on the CSFP.

Goodwill is calculated as:

Fair value of consideration transferred (by parent)		X
Value of NCI at acquisition (at fair value or proportion of net assets)		X
Fair value of sub's net assets at acquisition		(X)
Goodwill at acquisition		X
Impairment		(X)
Goodwill at reporting date		X

> **Negative goodwill**
>
> Occasionally, the consideration paid for the subsidiary may be less than the fair value of the identifiable net assets at acquisition. This may arise when the previous shareholders have been forced to sell the subsidiary and so are selling their holding at a bargain price.
>
> This situation gives rise to 'negative goodwill' at acquisition and represents a credit balance. It is viewed as a gain on a 'bargain purchase' (essentially a discount received) and is credited directly to profits and so the group's retained earnings.

As you can see from the above proforma calculation, the elements of goodwill at acquisition are based on fair values (at the date of acquisition of the subsidiary).

Definition of fair value

Fair value is defined in IFRS 13 *Fair Value Measurement* as 'the price that would be received to sell an asset or paid to transfer a liability in an orderly transaction between market participants at the measurement date'.

We have already seen the two acceptable methods for measuring the non-controlling interest at the acquisition date. The next two sections look at the rules for measuring the fair value of the consideration transferred by the parent upon acquiring the subsidiary; and the fair value of the net assets of the subsidiary at the date of acquisition.

4 Fair value of parent's consideration

The value of the consideration paid by the parent for its holding in the subsidiary can comprise of a number of elements and each must be measured at its fair value at the date of acquisition. The parent should already have reflected this amount in its individual statement of financial position.

The types of consideration that may be included are:

- Cash (FV = amount paid)
- Shares issued by the parent (FV = market price of shares issued)
- Deferred consideration (FV = present value)
- Contingent consideration (FV = probability weighted present value)

Exclusions from consideration

The following should never be recognised as part of consideration paid:

- Legal and professional fees (and other directly attributable costs of acquisition)
- Provisions for future losses in subsidiary acquired

Directly attributable costs of acquisition are expensed to the parent's statement of profit or loss. This is because they are not part of what the parent gives in return for the shareholding in the subsidiary and so do not represent part of the value of that shareholding.

Provisions for future losses or expenses are not part of the value of the parent's holding in the subsidiary. However, they may be provided for in the parent's individual financial statements in accordance with IAS 37 *Provisions, Contingent Liabilities and Contingent Assets* if the recognition criteria are met.

Deferred consideration

This is consideration, normally cash, which will be paid in the future.

It is measured at its present value at acquisition for inclusion within the goodwill calculation, i.e. the future cash flow is discounted.

It is recorded in the parent's individual financial statements by:

Dr Investments

– Cr Deferred consideration liability

Every year after acquisition, the liability will need to be increased to reflect unwinding the discount. The increase in the liability is charged as a finance cost. Therefore, the entry recorded in the parent's individual financial statements is:

Dr Finance cost (and so reduces the parent's retained earnings)

Cr Deferred consideration liability

Contingent consideration

Contingent consideration is consideration that may be paid in the future if certain future events occur or conditions are met. For example, cash may be paid in the future if certain profit targets are met.

Contingent consideration is measured at its fair value at the date of acquisition, to be consistent with how other forms of consideration are measured. This will typically be based on a probability weighted present value.

Adjustments to the value of contingent consideration arising from events after the acquisition date, e.g. a profit target not being met, are normally charged/credited to profits.

Example 1

Malawi has acquired 80% of the shares in Blantyre. The consideration consisted of:

(1) Cash paid $25,460.

(2) Malawi issued 10,000 shares to the shareholders of Blantyre, each with a nominal value of $1 and a market value of $4.

(3) Cash of $20,000 to be paid one year after the date of acquisition.

(4) Cash of $100,000 may be paid one year after the date of acquisition, if Blantyre achieves a certain profit target. It is thought that there is only a 40% chance that this will occur. The fair value of this consideration is to be measured as the present value of the expected value.

(5) Legal fees associated with the acquisition amounted to $15,000.

A discount rate of 10% should be used.

Required:

Calculate the fair value of Malawi's holding in Blantyre to be used in the goodwill calculation.

Example 1 answer

Fair value of parent's consideration

	$
Cash	25,460
Shares (10,000 × $4)	40,000
Deferred consideration ($20,000 × 0.909)	18,180
Contingent consideration ($100,000 × 40% × 0.909)	36,360
Total FV of consideration paid by parent	120,000

The cash payment of $20,000 in one year's time is deferred consideration as it is guaranteed that it will be paid. The future cash flow of $20,000 is discounted back to present value by applying the discount factor as obtained from discount tables (see Formulae & Tables at front of text) using an interest rate of 10% in 1 year's time.

The cash payment of $100,000 in one year's time is contingent consideration as it is dependent on Blantrye achieving a profit target. The question states that the fair value is to be the present value of the expected value. The expected value is 40% × $100,000 = $40,000 as it takes into account the expected probability of the profit target being achieved. This is then discounted to present value by applying the appropriate discount factor using an interest rate of 10% in 1 year's time.

Test your understanding 1 (integration question)

Duck has invested in 60% of Wicket's 10,000 $1 equity shares. Duck paid $5,000 cash consideration and issued 2 shares for every 3 shares acquired. At the date of acquisition the market value of a Duck share was $2.25.

Duck agreed to pay $3,000 cash 2 years after acquisition. A further $1,000 cash will be paid 3 years after acquisition if Wicket achieves a certain profit target. The fair value of this contingent consideration was deemed to be $700.

It is group policy to measure NCI at fair value at the date of acquisition.

The fair value of the NCI at acquisition was $10,000 and the fair value of Wicket's net assets was $15,000.

Legal and professional fees incurred in relation to the acquisition were $2,000.

Assume a discount rate of 10%.

Required:

Calculate the goodwill arising on the acquisition of Wicket.

Test your understanding 2 (OTQ style)

Kane acquired 75% of Aaron's $1 equity shares on 1 January 20X3. Kane paid $1,000,000 at the date of acquisition and agreed to pay a further $2,500,000 2 years after acquisition.

Legal and professional fees of $150,000 were paid in respect of the acquisition.

Assume a discount rate of 8%.

Required:

Calculate the fair value of the consideration that would be recognised in the calculation of goodwill on acquisition of Aaron.

5 Fair value of subsidiary's net assets

At acquisition, the subsidiary's net assets must be measured at fair value for inclusion within the consolidated financial statements.

The group must recognise the identifiable assets acquired and liabilities assumed of the subsidiary.

- An asset or liability may only be recognised if it meets the definition of an asset or liability as at the acquisition date.
  - For example, costs relating to restructuring the subsidiary that will arise after acquisition do not meet the definition of a liability at the date of acquisition.

- An asset is identifiable if it either:
  - is capable of being separated (regardless of whether the subsidiary intends to sell it), or
  - arises from contractual or other legal rights.

Consequently certain intangible assets such as brand names, patents and customer relationships that are not recognised in the subsidiary's individual financial statements may be recognised on consolidation if they are identifiable. These intangibles are no longer internally generated as the Parent has acquired them as part of the acquisition of the subsidiary. They are identifiable and should be included in the consolidated financial statements at their fair value.

- Contingent liabilities of subsidiary are recognised in group accounts upon acquisition.
  - By definition, contingent liabilities are not recognised in the subsidiary's individual financial statements (they are disclosed by note in accordance with IAS 37). On consolidation, however, a contingent liability will be recognised as a liability if its fair value can be measured reliably, i.e. it is recognised even if it is not probable.

Measuring fair value

IFRS 3 provides the following guidance on measuring the fair value of certain assets/liabilities:

Item	Valuation
Property, plant and equipment	Market value. If there is no evidence of market value, depreciated replacement cost should be used
Intangible assets	Market value. If none exists, an amount that reflects what the acquirer would have paid otherwise.
Inventories	(i) Finished goods should be valued at selling prices less the sum of disposal costs and a reasonable profit allowance. (ii) Work in progress should be valued at ultimate selling prices less the sum of completion costs, disposal costs and a reasonable profit allowance. (iii) Raw materials should be valued at current replacement costs.
Receivables, payables and loans	Present value of future cash flows expected to be received or paid. Discounting is unlikely to be necessary for short-term receivables or payables.

Example 2

Brussels acquired 100% of the share capital of Madrid paying consideration of $8 million.

At acquisition, the statement of financial position of Madrid showed equity share capital of $3m and retained earnings of $3.25m. Included in this total is:

- Freehold land with a book value of $400,000 but a market value of $950,000.

- Machinery with a book value of $1.2m. No reliable market value exists for these items. They would cost $1.5m to replace as new. The machinery has an expected life of 10 years and Madrid's machines are 4 years old.

- The fair value of all other assets and liabilities is approximately equal to book value.

Madrid's brand name was internally generated and so is not recognised in their statement of financial position. However, valuation experts have estimated its fair value to be $500,000.

The directors of Brussels intend to close down one of the divisions of Madrid and wish to provide for operating losses up to the date of closure which are forecast as $729,000.

An investment in plant and machinery will be required to bring the remaining production line of Madrid up to date. This will amount to $405,000 in the next 12 months.

Required:

Calculate the goodwill arising on the acquisition of Madrid.

Example 2 answer

The fair value of the subsidiary's net assets is used in the calculation of goodwill. Start by setting up a net assets working and filling in the subsidiary's share capital and retained earnings at acquisition – this gives us the book value of the net assets at acquisition. Note that since the question only requires the calculation of goodwill, only the net assets at acquisition are required.

Net assets of subsidiary

	Acquisition $000
Share capital	3,000
Retained earnings	3,250
Book value of NA at acquisition	6,250

Now consider the adjustments required to adjust the net assets from their book values to their fair values.

Land – this requires an upwards adjustment of $550,000 (fair value of $950,000 less book value of $400,000)

Machinery – the fair value is not given and so needs to be calculated. It will be measured as the depreciated replacement cost. Madrid's machines have an expected life of 10 years and are 4 years old. Therefore, their remaining life is 6 years.

Depreciated replacement cost = 6/10 × $1,500,000 = $900,000

Since their book value is $1.2m and their fair value is $0.9m, a downwards fair value adjustment of $300,000 is required.

Brand – an upwards adjustment of $500,000 is required as its book value is currently zero but its fair value is $500,000. Note that the brand can be recognised on consolidation as the fact that it has a fair value indicates it is separable.

The provision for future operating losses does not represent a liability at acquisition since there is no past event giving rise to an obligation. Similarly, the future investment in machinery does not represent assets that exist at acquisition and so cannot be recognised.

Now process these adjustments to complete the net assets working:

Net assets of subsidiary

	Acquisition $000
Share capital	3,000
Retained earnings	3,250
Fair value adjustments	
Land	550
Machinery	(300)
Brand	500
Fair value of sub's net assets	7,000

Now the goodwill calculation can be completed. Note that there is no NCI as the parent has acquired 100% of the subsidiary.

Goodwill

	$000
Fair value of P's investment	8,000
Fair value of sub's net assets at acquisition (working)	(7,000)
Goodwill on acquisition	1,000

Recording fair value adjustments

The fair value of the subsidiary's net assets at acquisition represents the 'cost' of the net assets to the group at the date of acquisition. Recording fair value adjustments is therefore in accordance with the historical cost concept.

It also ensures an accurate measurement of goodwill. Assuming the fair value of the subsidiary's net assets is higher than their book value, goodwill would be overstated if the fair value adjustments were not recognised.

To record fair value adjustments in the CSFP

- Adjust the net assets working at acquisition and the reporting date as appropriate:
  - The fair value adjustment arises at acquisition so there should always be an adjustment to the net assets at the date of acquisition.
  - The net assets at the reporting date should also be adjusted unless you're told that the assets/liabilities to which the adjustment relates are no longer held by the group.
- Reflect the reporting date adjustment on face of CSFP.

Impact on post-acquisition depreciation

Fair value adjustments often involve adjustments to non-current asset values which will consequently involve an adjustment to depreciation.

Depreciation in the group accounts must be based on the carrying value of the related non-current asset in the group accounts. Therefore if the non-current asset values are adjusted at acquisition then a depreciation adjustment must be made in the post acquisition period.

To record depreciation adjustments in the CSFP:

- Adjust net assets working in reporting date column to reflect the cumulative impact on depreciation of the fair value adjustment.
- Also reflect adjustment on the face of CSFP.
- The extra depreciation will reduce the post acquisition profits of the subsidiary included in consolidated reserves and NCI calculations.

To record depreciation adjustments in the CSCI:

- An adjustment should be made to reflect the impact of the fair value adjustment on the current year's depreciation charge.
- As this depreciation charge relates to the subsidiary's assets, the adjustment should be reflected in the calculation of profit attributable to the NCI.

Example 3

The following summarised statements of financial position are provided for King and Lear as at 31 December 20X7:

	King	Lear
	$000	$000
Non-current assets	1,300	1,200
Investment in Lear	1,900	–
Current assets	200	450
	3,400	1,650
Equity		
Share capital ($1)	2,000	750
Retained earnings	1,250	300
Current liabilities	150	600
	3,400	1,650

King purchased 80% of Lear's equity shares on 1 January 20X5 for $1.9m when Lear's retained earnings were $100,000.

It is group policy to measure the non-controlling interests at fair value at acquisition and the fair value of the non-controlling interests in Lear on 1 January 20X5 was $400,000. At this date Lear's non-current assets had a fair value of $1m and the assets had a remaining useful economic life of 5 years. Their book value at the date of acquisition was $850,000.

As at 31 December 20X7, an impairment loss of $50,000 has arisen on goodwill.

Required:

(a) Prepare the consolidated statement of financial position at 31 December 20X7.

(b) Explain the impact that the fair value adjustment would have on the consolidated statement of comprehensive income for the year ended 31 December 20X7.

Example 3 answer

(a) **Consolidated statement of financial position as at 31 December 20X7**

		$000
Non-current assets	(1,300 + 1,200 + 150 – 90)	2,560
Goodwill	(W3)	1,250
Current assets	(200 + 450)	650
		4,460

Equity		
Share capital		2,000
Retained earnings	(W5)	1,298
Non-controlling interests	(W4)	412
		3,710
Current liabilities	(150 + 600)	750
		4,460

Note: The carrying value of non-current assets is adjusted to reflect the fair value adjustment and subsequent depreciation.

(W1) **Group structure**

(W2) **Net assets of subsidiary**

	Acquisition	Reporting date
	$000	$000
Share capital	750	750
Retained earnings	100	300
Fair value adjustment (1,000 – 850)	150	150
Depreciation adj (150 × 3/5)	–	(90)
	1,000	1,110

110
Post acquisition profit

Note: The fair value adjustment is made at acquisition and then repeated at the reporting date along with any additional depreciation that will have been charged (on the fair value uplift) in the post-acquisition period.

(W3) **Goodwill**

	$000
Fair value of P's investment	1,900
Value of NCI at acquisition (fair value)	400
Fair value of sub's net assets at acquisition (W2)	(1,000)
Goodwill at acquisition	1,300
Impairment	(50)
Goodwill at reporting date	1,250

(W4) **Non-controlling interests**

	$000
Value of NCI at acquisition	400
NCI% × post acquisition reserves (20% × 110 (W2))	22
NCI% × impairment (20% × 50)	(10)
	412

(W5) Consolidated retained earnings

	$000
Parent's reserves	1,250
Sub (80% × 110 (W2))	88
Impairment (80% × 50)	(40)
	1,298

(b) Impact in consolidated statement of comprehensive income

The fair value adjustment of $150,000 results in an additional depreciation charge of $30,000 ($150,000/5) each year in the consolidated financial statements.

This adjustment should be added to the relevant expense category and would also be deducted from the subsidiary's profit when calculating the profit attributable to the NCI.

Test your understanding 3 (integration question)

The following summarised statements of financial position are provided for Romeo and Juliet as at 31 December 20X9:

	Romeo	Juliet
	$000	$000
Non-current assets	3,100	2,000
Investment in Juliet	2,900	–
Current assets	1,250	750
	7,250	2,750
Equity		
Share capital ($1)	4,000	1,000
Retained earnings	2,250	1,250
Current liabilities	1,000	500
	7,250	2,750

Romeo purchased 70% of Juliet's equity shares 1 January 20X8 for $2.9m when Juliet's retained earnings were $800,000.

It is group policy to measure the non-controlling interests at acquisition at their proportionate share of the fair value of the net assets.

At the date of acquisition Juliet's non-current assets had a fair value of $200,000 in excess of their book value and the assets had a remaining useful economic life of 10 years.

As at 31 December 20X9, an impairment loss of $300,000 has arisen on goodwill.

Required:

Prepare the consolidated statement of financial position at 31 December 20X9.

Information for TYUs 4 to 6

BN acquired 75% of the 1 million issued $1 ordinary shares of AB on 1 January 20X0 for $1,850,000 when AB's retained earnings were $885,000.

The carrying value of AB's net assets was considered to be the same as their fair value at the date of acquisition with the exception of AB's property, plant and equipment. The book value of these assets was $945,000 and their market value was $1,100,000. The property, plant and equipment of AB had an estimated useful life of 5 years from the date of acquisition. BN depreciates all assets on a straight line basis.

AB sold goods to BN with a sales value of $400,000 during the year ended 31 December 20X1. All of these goods remain in BN's inventories at the year end. AB makes a 20% gross profit margin on all sales.

The retained earnings reported in the financial statements of BN and AB as at 31 December 20X1 are $4,200,000 and $1,300,000 respectively.

The group policy is to measure non-controlling interest at fair value at the date of acquisition. The fair value of the non-controlling interest was $570,000 on 1 January 20X0.

An impairment review performed on 31 December 20X1 indicated that goodwill on the acquisition of AB had been impaired by 20%. No impairment was recognised in the year ended 31 December 20X0.

Test your understanding 4 (OTQ style)

Calculate the carrying value of goodwill that will appear in the consolidated statement of financial position of the BN group at 31 December 20X1.

Test your understanding 5 (OTQ style)

Calculate the balance on consolidated retained earnings at 31 December 20X1.

Test your understanding 6 (OTQ style)

Which three of the following statements are true in respect of BN's non-controlling interest.

A   The non-controlling is included as a separate part of equity on the face of the consolidated statement of financial position

B   The non-controlling interest is a credit balance and should be presented within non-current liabilities

C   The non-controlling interest should be debited with its share (25%) of the post-acquisition reserves of AB

D   The non-controlling interest is adjusted to reflect its share of the goodwill impairment

E   Upon acquisition of AB, BN will initially credit the NCI with its fair value of $570,000

F   The unrealised profit adjustment results in an increase in the NCI figure

6 NCI in the consolidated statement of comprehensive income

Now that we've covered all of the standard consolidation adjustments, it's worth re-capping on the calculation of the profit and total comprehensive income attributable to the NCI. The following proforma summarises the typical adjustments that would have to be made when calculating NCI in the CSCI.

	$	$
Sub's profit for the year per S's SCI (time apportioned if mid year acquisition)	X	
FV depreciation adjustment	(X)	
PUP (if S is seller)	(X)	
Impairment expense (fair value method only)	(X)	
	—	
Adjusted profit	X	
NCI share of profits × NCI%		X
Sub's other comprehensive income per S's SCI (time apportioned if mid year acquisition)	X	
	—	
Adjusted TCI	X	
NCI share of total comprehensive income × NCI%		X

Test your understanding 7 (integration question)

P acquired 75% of the equity shares of S on 1 December 20X8. Below are their statements of comprehensive income for the year ended 31 March 20X9:

	P $	S $
Revenue	300,000	216,000
Cost of sales and operating expenses	(215,000)	(153,000)
Profit from operations	85,000	63,000
Finance costs	(16,000)	(9,000)
Profit before tax	69,000	54,000
Taxation	(21,600)	(16,200)
Profit for the year	47,400	37,800
Other comprehensive income	25,000	3,000
Total comprehensive income	72,400	40,800

(1) In the post acquisition period P sold $50,000 of goods to S at a margin of 20%. S held $10,000 of these goods in inventory at the year end.

(2) A fair value adjustment of $150,000 was recorded at acquisition to increase the value of S's property, plant & equipment. These assets have a remaining useful economic life of 5 years at acquisition. Depreciation is charged to operating costs.

(3) Goodwill was reviewed for impairment at the year end. It was determined that an impairment loss of $3,000 had arisen which is to be charged to operating expenses. It is group policy to measure NCI at the proportion of net assets at acquisition.

Required:

Prepare the consolidated statement of comprehensive income for the year ended 31 March 20X9.

On 1 July 20X4 Tudor purchased 80% of the shares in Windsor. The summarised draft statement of comprehensive income for each company for the year ended 31 March 20X5 was as follows:

	Tudor	Windsor
	$000	$000
Revenue	60,000	24,000
Cost of sales	(42,000)	(20,000)
Gross profit	18,000	4,000
Operating expenses	(6,000)	(200)
Profit from operations	12,000	3,800
Investment income	75	–
Finance costs	–	(200)
Profit before tax	12,075	3,600
Taxation	(3,000)	(600)
Profit for the year	9,075	3,000
Other comprehensive income	1,500	500
Total comprehensive income	10,575	3,500

(1) The fair values of Windsor's assets at the date of acquisition were mostly equal to their book values with the exception of plant, which was stated in the books at $2 million but had a fair value of $5.2 million. The remaining useful life of the plant in question was four years at the date of acquisition. Depreciation is charged to cost of sales and is time apportioned on a monthly basis.

(2) In the post acquisition period Tudor sold Windsor some goods for $12 million with a margin of 25%. By the year end Windsor had sold $10 million of these goods (at cost to Windsor) to third parties.

(3) Tudor invested $1 million in Windsor's 10% loan notes on 1 July 20X4.

(4) At 31 March 20X5 it was determined that an impairment loss of $100,000 had arisen in respect of goodwill. It is group policy to measure NCI at fair value at acquisition. Impairment losses should be charged to operating expenses.

Required:

Prepare the consolidated statement of comprehensive income for the Tudor Group for the year ended 31 March 20X5.

7 Treatment of investment as available for sale

In the parent's individual financial statements, an investment in a subsidiary is likely to be classified as an available for sale investment, in accordance with IAS 39 Financial instruments: recognition and measurement (see Financial Instruments chapter).

This means that the investment will have been remeasured to fair value since the date of acquisition, with any gains or losses arising being taken to other components of equity.

Upon consolidation, these gains or losses should be reversed back out so that the investment is restated to its fair value at the date of acquisition (for inclusion in the goodwill calculation). The entity will Dr Other components of equity (AFS reserve) Cr Investment in S.

Illustration 1 – Reversal of AFS gains/losses

Root acquired 80% of the share capital of Warner on 1 January 20X2 for $750,000. The investment in Warner was classified as available for sale in the books of Root and is held at fair value. The gains earned to date are included in other components of equity of Root. The fair value of the investment at 31 December 20X4, the reporting date, is $1,150,000.

The amount to be eliminated from Root's SFP upon consolidation is the fair value at the reporting date of $1,150,000.

The amount to be included in the goodwill calculation is the fair value at the date of acquisition, i.e. $750,000.

The gain of $400,000 (1,150,000 – 750,000) that has been recorded in other components of equity since the date of acquisition must be reversed out upon consolidation. Dr Other components of equity 400 Cr Investment 400.

Test your understanding 9 (integration question)

The statements of financial position for ERT and BNM as at 31 December 20X0 are provided below:

	ERT	BNM
ASSETS	**$000**	**$000**
Non-current assets		
Property, plant and equipment	12,000	4,000
Available for sale investment (note 1)	4,000	–
	16,000	4,000
Current assets		
Inventories	2,200	800
Receivables	3,400	900
Cash and cash equivalents	800	300
	6,400	2,000
Total assets	22,400	6,000
EQUITY AND LIABILITIES		
Equity		
Share capital ($1 equity shares)	10,000	1,000
Retained earnings	7,500	4,000
Other reserves	200	–
Total equity	17,700	5,000
Non-current liabilities		
Long term borrowings	2,700	–
Current liabilities	2,000	1,000
Total liabilities	4,700	1,000
Total equity and liabilities	22,400	6,000

Additional information:

(1) ERT acquired a 75% investment in BNM on 1 May 20X0 for $3,800,000. The investment has been classified as available for sale in the books of ERT. The gain on its subsequent measurement as at 31 December 20X0 has been recorded within other reserves in ERT's individual financial statements. At the date of acquisition BNM had retained earnings of $3,200,000.

(2) It is the group policy to value non-controlling interest at fair value at the date of acquisition. The fair value of the non-controlling interest at 1 May 20X0 was $1,600,000.

(3) As at 1 May 20X0 the fair value of the net assets acquired was the same as the book value with the following exceptions:

The fair value of property, plant and equipment was $800,000 higher than the book value. These assets were assessed to have an estimated useful life of 16 years from the date of acquisition. A full year's depreciation is charged in the year of acquisition and none in the year of sale.

The fair value of inventories was estimated to be $200,000 higher than the book value. All of these inventories were sold by 31 December 20X0.

On acquisition ERT identified an intangible asset that BNM developed internally but which met the recognition criteria of IAS 38 *Intangible Assets*. This intangible asset is expected to generate economic benefit from the date of acquisition until 31 December 20X1 and was valued at $150,000 at the date of acquisition.

A contingent liability, which had a fair value of $210,000 at the date of acquisition, had a fair value of $84,000 at 31 December 20X0.

(4) An impairment review was conducted at 31 December 20X1 and it was decided that the goodwill on the acquisition of BNM was impaired by 20%.

(5) ERT sold goods to BNM for $300,000. Half of these goods remained in inventories at 31 December 20X0. ERT makes 20% margin on all sales.

(6) No dividends were paid by either entity in the year ended 31 December 20X0.

Required:

(a) Explain how the fair value adjustments identified above will impact both the calculation of goodwill on the acquisition of BNM and the consolidated financial statements of the ERT group for the year ended 31 December 20X0.

(b) Prepare the consolidated statement of financial position as at 31 December 20X0 for the ERT group.

8 IFRS 11 Joint Arrangements

IFRS 11 *Joint Arrangements* defines two types of arrangement in which there is joint control – a joint venture and a joint operation – and sets out the accounting treatment of each.

A **joint arrangement** is an arrangement of which two or more parties have joint control.

Joint control is the contractually agreed sharing of control of an arrangement, which exists only when decisions about the relevant activities require the unanimous consent of the parties sharing control.

A **joint venture** is a joint arrangement whereby the parties that have joint control of the arrangement have rights to the net assets of the arrangement.

Accounting treatment

Joint ventures are accounted for using the equity method of accounting in accordance with IAS 28 Investments in Associates and Joint Ventures.

Therefore, a joint venture is accounted for in the same way as an associate. See the previous chapter for a recap of the equity method.

Joint operations

A **joint operation** is a joint arrangement whereby the parties that have joint control of the arrangement have rights to the assets, and obligations for the liabilities, relating to the arrangement.

Under IFRS 11, a joint arrangement will either be a joint venture or a joint operation. A joint operation will exist where the arrangement is not structured through a separate vehicle.

A joint operator would account for its share of the assets, liabilities, revenues and expenses relating to its involvement with the joint operation in accordance with the relevant IFRSs

9 Other group related accounting standards

IFRS 12 Disclosure of interests in other entities

IFRS 12 was issued in May 2011 and requires disclosures about an entity's investments in:

- subsidiaries

- joint arrangements (joint operations or joint ventures)

- associates

- unconsolidated 'structured' entities.

The objective of the standard is to enable users of financial statements to understand the risks associated with investments in other entities and to evaluate the effect that they have on the financial statements.

Disclosure requirements include:

- significant judgements and assumptions made in determining whether an investor has control, joint control or significant influence over an investee

- the nature, extent and financial effects of its interests in joint arrangements and associates

- subsidiaries with non-controlling interests, joint arrangements and associates that are individually material

- significant restrictions on the ability of the parent to access and use the assets or settle the liabilities of its subsidiaries

- extended disclosures relating to 'structured entities' (previously known as special purpose entities) such as the terms on which an investor may be required to provide financial support to such an entity.

IAS 27 Separate financial statements

IAS 27 (revised) applies when an entity has interests in subsidiaries, joint ventures or associates and either elects to, or is required to, prepare separate non-consolidated financial statements.

Disclosures required when separate non-consolidated financial statements have been prepared by the parent entity include:

- the fact that exemption from consolidation has been used (usually as an intermediate holding entity) together with details of the ultimate parent who has prepared group financial statements

- in cases other than being an intermediate holding entity, the reason why separate financial statements have been prepared

- a list of names, interests in and principle place of business of each significant subsidiary, joint venture and associate, including details of how they have been accounted for in the separate financial statements.

If the financial statements are not consolidated, they must present interests in other entities in accordance with IAS 32 and IAS 39 (financial instruments).

Test your understanding 10 (case style)

You are an accountant working for a medium-sized entity, DRT, that provides office accommodation and services to a range of businesses. DRT prepares its financial statements in accordance with International Financial Reporting Standards (IFRS).

Until January 20X1, DRT operated a payroll services division providing payroll services for itself and also a number of external customers. On 1 January 20X1 the business of the division and assets with a value of $300,000 were transferred into a separate entity called GHJ, which was set up by DRT.

The sales director of GHJ owns 100% of its equity share capital. A contractual agreement signed by both the sales director of GHJ and a director of DRT states that the operating and financial policies of GHJ will be set by the board of DRT. GHJ has acquired a long-term loan of $1 million with DRT acting as guarantor. Profits and losses of GHJ, after deduction of the sales director's salary, will flow to DRT.

The reporting date of DRT is 31 May 20X1. On 15 June 20X1 you receive the following email from the Managing Director, Marjorie Smith:

"I wonder whether you could clear something up for me. I was discussing the preparation of our financial statements with an acquaintance at the golf club the other day and mentioned that a benefit of having transferred our payroll division to GHJ was not having to recognise the $1 million loan in our statement of financial position. She mentioned however that we may still have to recognise the loan – although she then had to dash off and so didn't have time to go into any further detail.

Could you let me know if she's correct - and if so explain why. After all, the loan agreement is between GHJ and the bank so I don't see why we have to recognise the liability in our financial statements. We specifically gave 100% ownership of GHJ to the sales director in order to avoid having to prepare consolidated financial statements and reflect GHJ as a subsidiary. If we do have to consolidate GHJ then can you let me know the accounting standard that requires this so I can have a look for myself. As you know I am keen to get a better understanding of accounting rules."

Required:

Respond to the Managing Director's email.

Test your understanding 11 (further OTQs)

(1) A joint _____ is where the parties that have joint control of the arrangement have rights to the net assets of the arrangement.

A joint _____ is where the parties that have joint control of the arrangement have rights to the assets, and obligations for the liabilities, relating to the arrangement.

Select the correct words to complete the above sentence, from the following options:

arrangement, control, operation, venture

(2) P owns 75% of S. S sells goods to P for $5,200 with a margin of 20%. 40% of these goods have subsequently been sold on by P to external parties by the reporting date.

Which one of the following adjustments would P make in relation to the above goods when preparing the consolidated statement of financial position?

A   Dr Consolidated retained earnings $520, Cr Inventory $520

B   Dr Consolidated retained earnings $390, Dr NCI $130, Cr Inventory $520

C   Dr Consolidated retained earnings $624, Cr Inventory $624

D   Dr Consolidated retained earnings $468, Dr NCI $156, Cr Inventory $624

(3) Paul acquired a 100% investment in Simon on 1 July 20X2. The consideration consisted of:

- the transfer of 200,000 shares in Paul with a nominal value of $1 each and a market price on the date of acquisition of $4.25 each

- $250,000 cash paid on 1 July 20X2

- $1,000,000 cash, payable on 1 July 20X4 (a discount rate of 8% should be used to value the liability).

Calculate the value of the consideration that Paul should use when calculating goodwill arising on the acquisition of Simon.

(4) K acquired 60% of the ordinary share capital of S on 1 May 20X7 for $140,000. The investment was classified as available for sale with any associated gains or losses recorded within other components of equity in K's individual financial statements. The investment is recorded at its fair value of $162,000 as at 30 November 20X7.

At 30 November 20X7, the other components of equity balance in the individual statements of financial position of K and S was $28,000 and $10,000 respectively.

At the date of acquisition, S did not have any other components of equity in its statement of financial position.

Calculate the other components of equity balance that would appear in the consolidated statement of financial position of the K group as at 30 November 20X7.

The following scenario relates to questions (5) and (6).

Aston acquired 85% of Martin's 250,000 $1 ordinary shares on 1 January 20X4 for $480,000 when the retained earnings of Martin were $90,000. At the date of acquisition, the fair value of Martin's property, plant and equipment was $50,000 higher than its carrying value. It was estimated to have a remaining useful life of ten years at this date.

At 31 December 20X7, the carrying value of property, plant and equipment in the individual statements of financial position of Aston and Martin was $800,000 and $390,000 respectively.

It is group policy to measure NCI at fair value at acquisition and the fair value of the NCI in Martin on 1 January 20X4 was $70,000.

(5)   **Calculate goodwill arising on the acquisition of Martin.**

(6)   **Calculate the carrying value of property, plant and equipment that would appear in the consolidated statement of financial position of the Aston group as at 31 December 20X7.**

(7)   The P group (comprising P and it's subsidiaries) acquired 30% of the equity share capital of A on 1 October 20X6, paying $750,000 in cash. This enabled P to exercise significant influence over the operating and financial policies of A. The balance on A's retained earnings at this date was $1,500,000.

   During the current year, A sold goods to P for $800,000 at a margin of 25%. P still held one quarter of the goods in inventory at 30 September 20X8.

   At 30 September 20X8, an impairment review was carried out and it was determined that the investment in A was impaired by $35,000.

   A's retained earnings at 30 September 20X8 was $2,500,000.

   Calculate the amount that would appear in the consolidated statement of financial position of the P group as at 30 November 20X7 for the investment in A.

(8)   The P group (comprising P and it's subsidiaries) acquired 30% of the equity share capital of A on 1 October 20X6, enabling P to exercise significant influence over the operating and financial policies of A.

   A made a profit for the year ended 30 June 20X7 of $600,000. Profits are deemed to accrue evenly over the year.

   Between 1 October 20X6 and the reporting date, A sold goods to P for $600,000 at a margin of 20%. P still held one quarter of these goods in inventory at 30 June 20X7.

   At 30 June 20X7, an impairment review was carried out and it was determined that the investment in A was impaired by $20,000.

   Calculate the amount that would appear in the consolidated statement of profit or loss of the P group for the year ended 30 June 20X7 in respect of the investment in A.

(9) P acquired 80% of the equity shares of S two years ago. At the date of acquisition, the fair value of S's net assets was the same as the book value with the exception of property, plant and equipment, whose fair value was higher. Property, plant and equipment had an estimated useful life of 5 years from the date of acquisition.

P purchased goods from S during the year and 50% of the items remain in P's inventories at the year end. S earns a 20% mark-up on all sales.

Goodwill impairment arose in the current year. It is group policy to measure NCI at the proportion of net assets.

S paid a dividend of $200,000 two months before the year end.

Which of the following adjustments would be taken into account when calculating the profit attributable to the non-controlling interest in the consolidated statement of profit or loss of the P group for the year ended 31 August 20X6. Select all that apply.

A   Provision for unrealised profit.

B   Depreciation arising from the fair value adjustment.

C   Goodwill impairment.

D   Elimination of intra-group dividends received.

(10) P acquired 75% of the equity share capital of S several years ago when S's retained earnings were $3,250,000. Goodwill arising on the acquisition was $2,000,000 and this was considered to have been impaired by 20% by 30 September 20X7. It is group policy to measure NCI at fair value at the date of acquisition.

P acquired 25% of the equity share capital of V on 1 October 20X6 in a contractual arrangement that will give P joint control over V. V's retained earnings at the date of acquisition were $925,000.

The retained earnings reported in the financial statements of P, S and V as at 30 September 20X7 are $1,570,000, $5,250,000 and $1,165,000 respectively.

Calculate the amount that would appear in the consolidated statement of financial position of the P group as at 30 September 20X7 for consolidated retained earnings.

(11) RW acquired 65% of the equity share capital of SR on 1 April 20X6 for $950,000 when the book value of SR's net assets was $450,000. It is group policy to measure non-controlling interest at fair value at the date of acquisition and the fair value of the NCI in SR at 1 April 20X6 was $350,000.

The only fair value adjustment made was to increase property, plant and equipment by $75,000. The remaining useful life of these assets at acquisition was 5 years.

The net assets reported in the financial statements of SR at 31 March 20X8 are $650,000.

Calculate the amount that would appear in the equity section of the consolidate statement of financial position of the RW group as at 31 March 20X8 for non-controlling interests.

10 Chapter summary

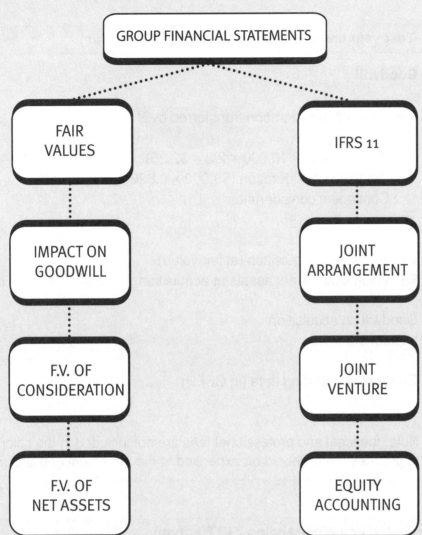

Test your understanding answers

Test your understanding 1 (integration question)

Goodwill

	$
Fair value of consideration transferred by P	
Cash	5,000
Shares (60% × 10,000 × 2/3 × $2.25)	9,000
Deferred consideration ($3,000 × 0.826)	2,478
Contingent consideration	700
	———
	17,178
Value of NCI at acquisition (at fair value)	10,000
Fair value of sub's net assets at acquisition	(15,000)
	———
Goodwill on acquisition	12,178
Impairment	–
	———
Goodwill at reporting date (in CSFP)	12,178
	———

Note: the legal and professional fees are not included in the calculation of goodwill. They should be expensed to the statement of profit or loss.

Test your understanding 2 (OTQ style)

Fair value of consideration = $3,142,500

	$
Cash	1,000,000
Deferred consideration ($2.5 million × 0.857)	2,142,500
	———
	3,142,500
	———

Note: the legal and professional fees are not included in the calculation of goodwill. They should be expensed to the statement of profit or loss.

Test your understanding 3 (integration question)

Consolidated statement of financial position as at 31 December 20X9

		$000
Non-current assets	(3,100 + 2,000 + 200 – 40)	5,260
Goodwill	(W3)	1,200
Current assets	(1,250 + 750)	2,000
		———
		8,460
		———
Equity		
Share capital		4,000
Retained earnings	(W5)	2,237
Non-controlling interests	(W4)	723
		———
		6,960
Current liabilities	(1,000 + 500)	1,500
		———
		8,460
		———

(W1) Group structure

Romeo

70% 1 Jan 20X8 i.e. 2 years since acquisition

Juliet

(W2) **Net assets of subsidiary**

	Acquisition	Reporting date
	$000	$000
Share capital	1,000	1,000
Retained earnings	800	1,250
Fair value adjustment	200	200
Depreciation adj (200 × 2/10)	–	(40)
	2,000	2,410

410
Post acquisition profit

(W3) **Goodwill**

	$000
Fair value of P's investment	2,900
Value of NCI at acquisition (30% × 2,000 (W2))	600
Fair value of sub's net assets at acquisition (W2)	(2,000)
Goodwill at acquisition	1,500
Impairment	(300)
Goodwill at reporting date	1,200

(W4) **Non-controlling interest**

	$000
Value of NCI at acquisition (W3)	600
NCI% × post acquisition reserves (30% × 410 (W2))	123
	723

(W5) Reserves

	Retained earnings
	$000
Parent's reserves	2,250
Sub (70% × 410 (W2))	287
Impairment (W3)	(300)
	———
	2,237
	———

Test your understanding 4 (OTQ style)

Goodwill = $304,000

	$	$
Consideration transferred		1,850,000
Non-controlling interest at fair value		570,000
Net assets at the date of acquisition:		
Carrying value $(1,000,000 + 885,000)	1,885,000	
Fair value increase $(1,100,000 – 945,000)	155,000	
		(2,040,000)
		———
Goodwill on acquisition		380,000
Impairment 20% in 20X1		(76,000)
		———
Goodwill as at 31 December 20X1		304,000
		———

Tutorial note:

The net assets at acquisition has been incorporated into the above calculation. You can alternatively use a net assets table to calculate the amount of $2,040,000 shown above. See the solution to TYU 5 for this alternative working. Note that you would only need the acquisition column for the calculation of goodwill.

Test your understanding 5 (OTQ style)

Consolidated retained earnings

	BN	AB
	$	$
As reported in SFP	4,200,000	1,300,000
Less pre-acquisition retained earnings		(885,000)
Accumulated depreciation on PPE FV adjustment ($155,000 × 2/5 years)		(62,000)
Impairment of goodwill (as in TYU 4 above)		(76,000)
Unrealised profit ($400,000 × 20%)		(80,000)
		197,000
Group share of AB ($197,000 × 75%)	147,750	
	4,347,750	

Tutorial note: The calculation of post-acquisition reserves is shown within the consolidated retained earnings calculation (right-hand column). Notice that the goodwill impairment has also been included. As NCI is valued using the fair value method, the goodwill impairment is included here so that the group share is included in the consolidated retained earnings figure. Alternatively, you can calculate the post-acquisition reserves using a net assets table as follows:

Net assets of subsidiary

	Acquisition	Reporting date
	$000	$000
Share capital	1,000	1,000
Retained earnings	885	1,300
Fair value adjustment (1,100 – 945)	155	155
Depreciation adj (155 × 1/5 × 2 yrs)	–	(62)
PUP adj (400 × 20%)		(80)
Goodwill impairment		(76)
	2,040	2,237

197
Post acquisition reserves

The goodwill impairment has been included in the net assets working so that the group share of it is calculated and included in the consolidated retained earnings. This is a slightly alternative approach to the exercises we've seen so far, where it has been included within consolidated retained earnings on a separate line. The overall result is the same and either method can be used.

Consolidated retained earnings (using net assets table):

	$
Parent's retained earnings	4,200,000
Group share of post acquisition reserves (75% × 197,000 (net asset working))	147,750
	4,347,750

Test your understanding 6 (OTQ style)

The correct statements are A, D and E

B is incorrect, as NCI is part of equity rather than liabilities

C is incorrect, as the NCI would be **credited** with its share of the post-acquisition reserves (not debited)

F is incorrect, as the unrealised profit would result in a **reduction** (not increase) in the NCI

Test your understanding 7 (integration question)

Consolidated statement of comprehensive income for the year ended 31 March 20X9

	$
Revenue (300,000 + (4/12 × 216,000) – 50,000 (W2))	322,000
Cost of sales and operating expenses (215,000 + (4/12 × 153,000) – 50,000 (W2) + 2,000 (W2) + 10,000 (W3) + 3,000 imp)	(231,000)
Profit from operations	91,000
Finance costs (16,000 + (4/12 × 9,000))	(19,000)
Profit before tax	72,000
Taxation (21,600 + (4/12 × 16,200))	(27,000)
Profit for the year	45,000
Other comprehensive income (25,000 + (4/12 × 3,000))	26,000
Total comprehensive income	71,000
Profit attributable to:	
Parent shareholders (balancing figure)	44,350
Non-controlling interests (W4)	650
	45,000
Total comprehensive income attributable to:	
Parent shareholders (balancing figure)	70,100
Non-controlling interests (W4)	900
	71,000

Workings

(W1) Group structure

(W2) Intercompany sales and PUP

Intercompany sales of $50,000 to be eliminated by reducing both revenue and cost of sales

PUP adjustment to increase cost of sales:

Profit in inventory = 20% × $10,000 = $2,000

(W3) Depreciation adjustment

Fair value adjustment = $150,000

Depreciation adjustment = 1/5 × 4/12 × $150,000 = $10,000

(W4) NCI share of profit and total comprehensive income

		$	$
Sub's profit for the year per S's SCI (4/12 × 37,800)		12,600	
Depreciation adjustment (W3)		(10,000)	
		2,600	
NCI share of profits	× 25%		650
Sub's other comprehensive income per S's SCI (4/12 × 3,000)		1,000	
		3,600	
NCI share of total comprehensive income	× 25%		900

Test your understanding 8 (integration question)

Consolidated statement of comprehensive income for the year ended 31 March 20X5

	$000
Revenue (60,000 + (9/12 x 24,000) – 12,000 (W2))	66,000
Cost of sales (42,000 + (9/12 × 20,000) – 12,000 (W2) + 500 (W2) + 600 (W3))	(46,100)
	_____
Gross profit	19,900
Operating expenses (6,000 + (9/12 × 200) + 100 imp)	(6,250)
	_____
Profit from operations	13,650
Investment income (75 – 75 (W4))	–
Finance costs ((9/12 × 200) – 75 (W4))	(75)
	_____
Profit before tax	13,575
Taxation (3,000 + (9/12 × 600))	(3,450)
	_____
Profit for the year	10,125
Other comprehensive income (1,500 + (9/12 × 500))	1,875
	_____
Total comprehensive income	12,000
	_____
Profit attributable to:	
Parent shareholders (balancing figure)	9,815
Non-controlling interests (W5)	310
	_____
	10,125
	_____
Total comprehensive income attributable to:	
Parent shareholders (balancing figure)	11,615
Non-controlling interests (W5)	385
	_____
	12,000
	_____

Workings

(W1) Group structure

(W2) Intercompany sales and PUP

Intercompany sales of $12,000,000 to be eliminated by reducing both revenue and cost of sales

PUP adjustment to increase cost of sales:

Goods in inventory = 12m – 10m = $2,000,000

Profit in inventory = 25% × $2,000,000 = $500,000

(W3) Depreciation adjustment

Fair value adjustment = $5.2m – $2m = $3.2m

Depreciation adjustment = 1/4 × 9/12 × $3.2m = $600,000

(W4) Intercompany interest

Windsor paid interest to Tudor = 10% × $1m × 9/12 = $75,000

(W5) NCI share of profit and total comprehensive income

		$000	$000
Sub's profit for the year per S's SCI (9/12 × 3,000)		2,250	
Depreciation adjustment (W3)		(600)	
Impairment (fair value method)		(100)	
		———	
		1,550	
NCI share of profits	× 20%		310
Sub's other comprehensive income per S's SCI (9/12 × 500)		375	
		———	
		1,925	
NCI share of total comprehensive income	× 20%		385

Test your understanding 9 (integration question)

(a) **Fair value adjustments**

Impact on calculation of goodwill at acquisition:

In this case the calculation of goodwill on the acquisition of BNM should be based on the fair value of the consideration paid plus the fair value of the NCI less the fair value of the net assets acquired. The fair value of the net assets acquired should include any fair value adjustments required to take the book values of individual assets and liabilities up to (or down to) their fair value.

The increase in the values of property, plant and equipment and inventories will increase the value of net assets at acquisition, which in turn will reduce goodwill. The intangible asset will be recognised as an asset at acquisition because it meets the definition of an intangible asset in IAS 38. It will increase the net assets at acquisition and hence reduce goodwill.

The contingent liability is also specifically allowed to be included within the fair value of the net assets at acquisition. However, as a liability this will reduce the fair value of net assets and hence increase goodwill.

Impact on consolidated financial statements for year ending 31 December 20X0:

PPE:

In the consolidated statement of financial position as at 31 December 20X0 the value of PPE will be increased by $800,000 and reduced by the additional depreciation arising for the period. The additional depreciation is calculated as the FV adjustment divided by the estimated remaining life of the assets from the date of acquisition. This additional depreciation will be charged to the consolidated statement of profit or loss each year.

Inventories:

As the inventories have been sold by 31 December 20X0 no adjustment will be required to the inventories balance in the statement of financial position. However, in the consolidated statement of profit or loss an additional charge should be made within cost of sales. This will obviously also impact retained earnings for the group.

Intangible asset:

The intangible asset will be recorded in the consolidated statement of financial position and amortised over its life (which in this case is 20 months). The amortisation charge will go through the consolidated statement of profit or loss and impact group retained earnings.

Contingent liability:

The contingent liability will be recorded as a current liability in the consolidated statement of financial position. In the consolidated statement of profit or loss the reduction in the liability will in effect increase profits.

(b) Consolidated statement of financial position as at 31 December 20X0 for the ERT group

All workings in $000

ASSETS	$000
Non-current assets	
Property, plant and equipment (12,000 + 4,000 + 800 – 50 (W2))	16,750
Goodwill (W3)	208
Intangible asset (150 – 60 (W2))	90
	17,048
Current assets	
Inventories (2,200 + 800 – 30 (W5))	2,970
Receivables (3,400 + 900)	4,300
Cash and cash equivalents (800 + 300)	1,100
	8,370
Total assets	25,418

EQUITY AND LIABILITIES	
Equity	
Share capital ($1 equity shares)	10,000
Retained earnings (W5)	7,893
Non-controlling interest (W4)	1,741
Total equity	19,634
Non-current liabilities	
Long term borrowings	2,700
Current liabilities (2,000 + 1,000 + 84)	3,084
Total liabilities	5,784
Total equity and liabilities	25,418

(W1) Group structure

ERT

75% 1 May X0 i.e.
8 months since
acquisition

BNM

(W2) Net assets of subsidiary

	Acquisition	Reporting date
	$000	$000
Share capital	1,000	1,000
Retained earnings	3,200	4,000
Fair value adjustments:		
Property, plant and equipment	800	800
Depreciation on PPE adj (800 × 1/16)	–	(50)
Inventories	200	–
Intangible asset	150	150
Amortisation on intangible (150 × 8/20)		(60)
Contingent liability	(210)	(84)
	5,140	5,756

616
Post acquisition
reserves

(W3) **Goodwill**

	$000
Consideration paid by ERT	3,800
NCI at fair value	1,600
Fair value of sub's net assets at acquisition (W2)	(5,140)
Goodwill at acquisition	260
Impairment (20%)	(52)
Goodwill at reporting date	208

(W4) **Non-controlling interest**

	$000
NCI at acquisition	1,600
NCI % × post acquisition reserves (25% × 616 (W2))	154
NCI% × impairment (25% × 52 (W3))	(13)
	1,741

(W5) **Group retained earnings**

	$000
Parent's retained earnings	7,500
Sub (75% × 616 (W2))	462
Impairment (75% × 52 (W3))	(39)
PUP (300 × 1/2 × 20%)	(30)
	7,893

(W6) **Other components of equity**

	$000
Parent	200
Reversal of AFS gains on investment in subsidiary (4,000 – 3,800)	(200)
	–
	–
	–

Test your understanding 10 (case style)

Dear Marjorie,

I'm afraid your golf acquaintance is correct. The loan will not appear in the individual statement of financial position of DRT, however we will have to prepare consolidated financial statements reflecting GHJ as a subsidiary and will therefore have to recognise the loan in the consolidated statement of financial position.

Although we do not legally own the equity shares of GHJ, we do have control over the entity – and it is this control that results in GHJ meeting the definition of a subsidiary.

The relevant accounting standard is IFRS 10 *Consolidated Financial Statements*. This standard states that an investor (DRT in this case) controls an investee (GHJ) if it has all of the following:

- power over the investee;

- exposure, or rights, to variable returns from its involvement with the investee; and

- the ability to use its power over the investee to affect the amount of the return.

Power is defined as having the ability to direct the activities of the investee.

You'll notice that it doesn't say anything about owning equity shares, although in most situations control is confirmed by having a majority equity holding.

In our case, it is the contractual agreement that results in the definition being satisfied. We receive all profits or losses of GHJ and therefore have the exposure or rights to its variable returns. We also set the operating and financial policies and therefore have the ability to affect the returns that we receive.

I trust that this explanation is satisfactory, however please let me know if you'd like any further information.

Test your understanding 11 (further OTQs)

(1) A joint **venture** is where the parties that have joint control of the arrangement have rights to the net assets of the arrangement.

A joint **operation** is where the parties that have joint control of the arrangement have rights to the assets, and obligations for the liabilities, relating to the arrangement.

(2) **D** is the correct answer.

PUP adjustment = $5,200 × 20% × 60% = $624 and this is deducted from inventory.

The adjustment is split between NCI and parent shareholders as S, the subsidiary, was the seller.

75% × $624 = $468 is deducted from consolidated retained earnings.

25% × $624 = $156 is deducted from NCI.

(3) **Value of consideration = $1,957,000**

	$000
Shares (200,000 × $4.25)	850
Cash	250
Deferred consideration ($1,000,000 × 0.857)	857
	1,957

(4) **Other components of equity = $12,000**

	$
K's other components of equity	28,000
Reversal of gains on investment in subsidiary (162 – 140)	(22,000)
K's share of S's post-acquisition other components (60% × 10)	6,000
	12,000

(5) Goodwill = $160,000

	$	$
Consideration transferred		480,000
Non-controlling interest at fair value		70,000
Net assets at the date of acquisition:		
Share capital	250,000	
Retained earnings	90,000	
Fair value increase	50,000	
		(390,000)
Goodwill on acquisition		160,000

(6) Property, plant and equipment = $1,220,000

	$
Aston	800,000
Martin	390,000
Fair value increase at acquisition	50,000
Fair value depreciation (50,000 × 4/10)	(20,000)
Goodwill on acquisition	1,220,000

(7) Investment in associate (A) = $1,015,000

	$
Cost of investment	750,000
Share of post-acquisition profits (30% × (2,500–1,500))	300,000
Less: impairment	(35,000)
	1,015,000

The unrealised profit is not deducted from the investment in associate as the inventory is held by the parent at the year end (it would be deducted from group inventory instead).

(8) **Share of associate profit = $106,000**

	$
Profit of A in the post-acquisition period (600,000 × 9/12)	450,000
Unrealised profit (600,000 × 20% × 1/4)	(30,000)
	420,000
P group share	× 30%
	126,000
Less: impairment	(20,000)
	106,000

(9) **Adjustments would be made for A and B.**

C would not be adjusted as NCI is measured using the proportion of net assets and therefore all goodwill impairment should be charged to the parent shareholders.

D is not adjusted as it is eliminated from the parent's investment income and has no impact on the subsidiary's profit.

(10) **Consolidated retained earnings = $2,830,000**

	$000
P's retained earnings	1,570
Share of S's post-acquisition retained earnings (75% × (5,250k – 3,250k))	1,500
Share of goodwill impairment (75% × 20% × 2,000k)	(300)
Share of V's post-acquisition retained earnings (25% × (1,165k – 925k))	60
	2,830

(11) **Non-controlling interest equity = $409,500**

	$
Value of NCI at acquisition	350,000
Share of S's post-acquisition retained earnings (35% × (650k – 450k))	70,000
Share of FV depreciation (35% × 75k × 2/5)	(10,500)
	409,500

You can use a net assets working to calculate the adjusted post-acquisition reserves of the subsidiary and then bring this into your main NCI calculation if you prefer (the depreciation adjustment has been shown separately in the above working).

Net assets of subsidiary

	Acquisition	Reporting date
	$000	$000
Book value	450	650
Fair value adjustments:		
Property, plant and equipment	75	75
Depreciation on PPE adj (75× 2/5)	–	(30)
	525	695

170
Post acquisition reserves

Non-controlling interest

	$
Value of NCI at acquisition	350,000
Share of S's post-acquisition retained earnings (35% × 170k)	59,500
	409,500

14

Complex groups

Chapter learning objectives

B2. Demonstrate the impact on the preparation of the consolidated financial statements of certain complex group scenarios.

(c) Demonstrate the impact on the group financial statements of acquiring indirect control of a subsidiary.

1 Session content

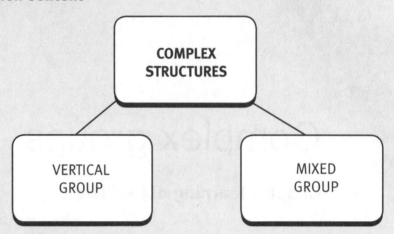

2 Introduction

In this chapter we will start to look at more complex group structures and, in particular, how to deal with the scenario in which the parent invests in a subsidiary that either already has a subsidiary of its own, or subsequently acquires a controlling interest in another entity.

Complex structures can be classified under two headings:

*   Vertical groups
*   Mixed groups.

3 Vertical groups

A vertical group exists when a subsidiary is **indirectly controlled** by the parent. The subsidiary indirectly controlled is often known as a **sub-subsidiary**.

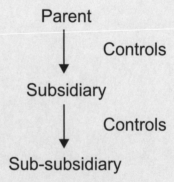

The parent has:

*   direct control of the subsidiary, and
*   indirect control of the sub-subsidiary, via the subsidiary

Therefore, the parent is required to consolidate both the subsidiary and the sub-subsidiary in its group financial statements.

The basic techniques of consolidation are the same as seen previously, with some changes to the goodwill and NCI calculations to reflect the indirect nature of the parent's controlling interest.

4 Establishing the group structure

When establishing the group structure, the following should be carefully considered :

- Control – which entities does the parent control either directly or indirectly?

- Percentages – what are the effective ownership percentages for the consolidation?

- Dates – when did the parent achieve control and so what is the date of acquisition?

Illustration 1 – Effective percentage holding

P

↓   80% of ordinary shares on 31.12.X0

S

↓   80% of ordinary shares on 31.12.X0

Q

Control

P controls S and S controls Q. Therefore P can indirectly control Q. Sub-subsidiaries are treated in almost exactly the same way as ordinary subsidiaries and will need parent ownership % and NCI ownership %.

Effective consolidation percentage

S will be consolidated with P owning 80% and NCI owning 20%.

Q will be consolidated with P owning 80% × 80% = **64%**

and NCI owning **36%**.

Dates

S and Q will both be consolidated from 31 December 20X0.

Illustration 2 – Effective percentage holding

P
↓ 60% of ordinary shares on 31.5.X2
S
↓ 60% of ordinary shares on 31.5.X2
Q

Control

P controls S and S controls Q. Therefore P can indirectly control Q.

Effective consolidation percentage

S will be consolidated with P owning 60% and NCI owning 40%.

Q will be consolidated with P owning 60% × 60% = **36%**

and NCI owning **64%**.

Dates

S and Q will both be consolidated from 31.5.X2.

Illustration 3 – Effective date of control

P
↓ 80% of ordinary shares on 31.1.X2
S
↓ 70% of ordinary shares on 30.4.X1
Q

Control

P controls S and S controls Q. Therefore P can indirectly control Q.

Effective consolidation percentage

S will be consolidated with P owning 80% and NCI owning 20%.

Q will be consolidated with P owning 80% × 70% = **56%**

and NCI owning **44%**.

Dates

Consolidation is based upon the principle of control and Q will be controlled by P when P acquires its holding in S on 31.1.X2 since by this date S already controls Q.

S is consolidated from 31.1.X2.

Q is consolidated from 31.1.X2.

Illustration 4 – Effective date of control

P

↓   60% of ordinary shares on 31.7.X2

S

↓   70% of ordinary shares on 30.9.X2

Q

Control

P controls S and S controls Q. Therefore P can indirectly control Q.

Effective consolidation percentage

S will be consolidated with P owning 60% and NCI owning 40%.

Q will be consolidated with P owning 60% × 70% = **42%**

and NCI owning **58%**.

Dates

P controls S from 31.7.X2 but Q is not controlled by S until 30.9.X2. Therefore P cannot control Q until 30.9.X2.

S is consolidated from 31.7.X2.

Q is consolidated from 30.9.X2.

5 Accounting treatment of sub-subsidiary

Once the effective percentage holding and date of control achieved are established, the sub-subsidiary is consolidated using the same rules as for a direct subsidiary. However, there is one new adjustment required – commonly known as the **indirect holding adjustment** (IHA).

This will affect the calculation of the goodwill and the non-controlling interest reserve (CSFP balance).

Illustration 5

Consider this statement of financial position extract:

	A	B	C
	$000	$000	$000
Investments			
In B	500	–	–
In C	–	400	–

A owns 80% of B. B owns 75% of C.

The sub-subsidiary is controlled by the parent and so is consolidated in the normal way i.e. from the date of acquisition:

• consolidate income, expenses, assets and liabilities fully on a line by line basis

• recognise goodwill

• recognise amounts attributable to owners of the parent and non-controlling interests

However, since the sub-subsidiary is indirectly owned, it will be necessary to record an indirect holding adjustment (IHA). The IHA only effects Goodwill and the NCI reserve in the CSFP.

In a vertical group, the consideration to acquire the sub-subsidiary is paid by the subsidiary and not the parent. The parent will only incur their share of this cost and the NCI in the subsidiary will incur the remainder.

Therefore in the Goodwill calculation, it is necessary to reduce the cost of the investment in the subsidiary's books to the parent's share. The amount of the reduction is the cost that is incurred by the NCI shareholders and so is charged to NCI by reducing the NCI reserve at the date of acquisition.

B had paid $400k to acquire C. A owns 80% of B and the NCI owns 20% of B. Therefore the cost of $400k is incurred (80% × $400k) $320k by A and (20% × $400k) $80k by the NCI.

- $320k is therefore the appropriate cost of the investment for the goodwill calculation.
- $80k will be the cost charged to the NCI shareholders in the NCI reserve.

This would be reflected in the standard workings as follows:

Goodwill of C

	$000
Investment (incurred by B)	400
Less: IHA (20% × 400)	(80)
Investment by A (80% × 400)	320
Value of NCI at acquisition	X
Less fair value of net assets of C at acquisition	(X)
Goodwill at acquisition	X

NCI of B

	$000
Value of B's NCI at acquisition (as in goodwill calculation)	X
Less IHA (as in goodwill calculation)	(80)
NCI% of B's post-acquisition reserves	X
	X

The $80k represents the cost charged to the NCI shareholders and will be charged to the NCI reserve.

Note that the IHA affects C's goodwill but that it should be deducted from B's NCI as it is B's NCI shareholders that have incurred part of the cost of the investment in C.

Example 1 – David, Colin and John

The draft statements of financial position of David, Colin and John at 31 December 20X4 are as follows:

	David	Colin	John
	$000	$000	$000
Investment in subsidiary (at cost)	120	80	–
Other assets	280	180	130
	400	260	130
Share capital ($1 shares)	200	100	50
Retained earnings	100	60	30
Other liabilities	100	100	50
	400	260	130

You ascertain the following:

- David acquired 75,000 $1 shares in Colin on 1 January 20X4 for $120,000 when the retained earnings of Colin amounted to $40,000.

- Colin acquired 40,000 $1 shares in John on 30 June 20X4 for $80,000 when the retained earnings of John amounted to $25,000; they had been $20,000 on the date of David's acquisition of Colin.

- Goodwill has suffered no impairment.

Produce the consolidated statement of financial position of the David group at 31 December 20X4. It is group policy to value the non-controlling interest using the proportion of net assets method.

Example 1 answer

Step 1

Draw a diagram of the group structure noting the dates of acquisition.

David
| 75% acquired 1 January 20X4
Colin
| 80% acquired 30 June 20X4
John

Then work through the steps of control, ownership percentages and dates as this will influence the remaining workings.

Control

David controls Colin and Colin controls John. Therefore David can indirectly control John.

Effective consolidation percentages

Colin will be consolidated with David owning 75% and NCI owning 25%.

John will be consolidated with David owning 75% × 80% = **60%**

and NCI owning **40%**.

Dates of acquisition

Colin is consolidated from 1 January 20X4.

John is consolidated from the date on which David acquired control i.e. 30 June 20X4.

Step 2

Start with the net assets consolidation working as normal.

Care must be taken to use the correct date of acquisition. The relevant date will be that on which David (the parent) acquired control of each entity as above. Therefore, the information given regarding John's reserves at 1 January 20X4 is irrelevant in this context.

(W2) **Net assets of subsidiaries**

	Colin		John	
	At acq'n	At rep date	At acq'n	At rep date
	1.1.X4	**31.12.X4**	**30.6.X4**	**31.12.X4**
	$000	$000	$000	$000
Share capital	100	100	50	50
Reserves	40	60	25	30
	140	160	75	80

Step 3

(W3) **Goodwill**

- Two calculations are required, one for each subsidiary.

- They should always be calculated separately as, if one results in positive goodwill and the other negative, each goodwill figure would be accounted for differently and they should not be netted off.

- For the sub-subsidiary, the goodwill is calculated from the perspective of the ultimate parent company (David) rather than the immediate parent (Colin). Therefore, the cost of John is only David's share of the amount that Colin paid for John, i.e. $80,000 × 75% = $60,000. There is therefore an IHA of $20,000.

- Remember to use the effective share owned by David when deducting the share of net assets.

	Colin	John
	$000	$000
Sub's investment in sub-sub		80
IHA (25% × 80)		(20)
Fair value of P's investment	120	60
NCI holding at proportion of net assets		
(25% × 140 (W2))	35	
(40% × 75 (W2))		30
Fair value of sub's net assets at acquisition (W2)	(140)	(75)
Goodwill on acquisition/at reporting date	15	15

Step 4

(W4) Non-controlling interest

When calculating the NCI reserve relating to Colin, it is necessary to deduct the IHA as calculated in the goodwill working (W3).

This is to maintain double entry principles and to reflect that the NCI is charged with its share of the cost of investment in John. Again, be careful to use the NCI's effective percentage in John from your group structure diagram.

	$000
Colin:	
NCI at acquisition (W3)	35
NCI% × post acquisition reserves (25% × (160 − 140 (W2)))	5
IHA (W3)	(20)
John:	
NCI at acquisition (W3)	30
NCI% × post acquisition reserves (40% × (80 − 75 (W2)))	2
	52

Step 5

(W5) Group retained earnings

	$000
David	100
Colin: 75% × (160 − 140) (W2)	15
John: 60% × (80 − 75) (W2)	3
	118

Note that again, only the parent or effective interest of 60% is taken of the post-acquisition profits in John.

Step 6

Summarised consolidated statement of financial position of the David group at 31 December 20X4

	$000
Goodwill (15 + 15) (Step 3)	30
Other assets (280 + 180 + 130)	590
	620
Equity and liabilities:	
Share capital	200
Retained earnings (Step 5)	118
	318
Non-controlling interest (Step 4)	52
Liabilities (100 + 100 + 50)	250
Total equity and liabilities	620

Test your understanding 1 (integration question)

The following are the statements of financial position at 31 December 20X7 for H group companies:

	H $000	S $000	T $000
Investment in subsidiaries	65	55	
Sundry assets	280	133	100
	345	188	100
Equity share capital ($1 shares)	100	60	50
Retained earnings	45	28	25
Liabilities	200	100	25
	345	188	100

On 1 January 20X1, H acquired 45,000 of the $1 equity shares of S for $65,000 in cash when the retained earnings of S were $10,000.

On the same date, S acquired 30,000 of the $1 equity shares of T for $55,000 in cash. The retained earnings of T at this date were $8,000.

It is group policy to measure NCI at fair value at the date of acquisition. At 1 January 20X1, the fair value of the NCI in S was $20,000 and the fair value of the NCI in T, reflecting H's effective holding, was $50,000.

Required:

Prepare the consolidated statement of financial position of the H group as at 31 December 20X7.

Test your understanding 2 (integration question)

The summarised statements of financial position for three entities as at 31 December 20X6 are provided below.

	Manchester	Leeds	Sheffield
	$000	$000	$000
Property, plant and equipment	44	4	27
Investments (at cost)	41	40	–
Current assets	29	31	43
	114	75	70
Share capital $1	40	10	20
Share premium reserve	4	10	–
Retained earnings	60	15	35
Current liabilities	10	40	15
	114	75	70

Manchester purchased 80% of the ordinary share capital of Leeds for $41,000 on 31 December 20X1 when the balance on the retained earnings of Leeds was $5,000. The balance on the retained earnings of Sheffield at this date was $15,000.

Leeds had purchased 75% of the ordinary share capital of Sheffield for $40,000 on the 31 December 20X0 when the balance on the retained earnings of Sheffield was $11,000.

It is group policy to use the proportionate share of net assets method to value the non-controlling interest.

Leeds supplies Manchester with a component on a regular basis. Leeds also supplies Sheffield with raw materials. Both items are supplied on a mark-up of 25% and at the end of the year, $15,000 remained in Manchester's inventory from $26,250 worth of sales during the year and $5,000 remained in Sheffield's inventory from $8,750 worth of sales during the year.

Required:

Prepare the consolidated statement of financial position for the Manchester group at 31 December 20X6.

Test your understanding 3 (integration question)

The summarised statements of financial position for three entities at 30 April 20X6 are provided below:

	Parsley $000	Coriander $000	Thyme $000
Non-current assets			
Property, plant and equipment	596,330	320,370	489,800
Investments (at cost)	485,000	335,000	–
Current assets	87,320	56,550	54,800
	1,168, 650	711,920	544,600
Equity			
Share capital ($1 shares)	100,000	75,000	50,000
Retained earnings	875,400	525,500	435,750
	975,400	600,500	485,750
Non-current liabilities	150,000	80,000	30,000
Current liabilities	43,250	31,420	28,850
	1,168,650	711,920	544,600

(1) Parsley acquired 80% of the equity shares of Coriander on 1 May 20X3 at a cost of $350 million. At this time, the retained earnings of Coriander were $255 million and the fair value of the non-controlling interest was $80 million.

(2) At 1 May 20X3 it was determined that land in the books of Coriander with a carrying value of $100 million had a fair value of $135 million.

(3) Coriander acquired 70% of the equity shares of Thyme on 1 May 20X4 at a cost of $335 million. At this time, the retained earnings of Thyme were $285 million and the fair value of the non-controlling interest was $175 million.

(4) At 1 May 20X4 it was determined that plant in the books of Thyme had a fair value of $20 million in excess of its carrying value. The plant is being depreciated over its remaining life of 10 years.

(5) During the year ended 30 April 20X6, Parsley sold $35 million of goods to Coriander at a margin of 20%. Coriander still held one-fifth of these goods in inventory at the reporting date.

(6) It is group policy to measure NCI at fair value at the date of acquisition. At 30 April 20X6 it was determined that no impairment had arisen in respect of the goodwill of Coriander but that the goodwill of Thyme had suffered an impairment loss of $8 million.

Required:

Prepare the consolidated statement of financial position for the Parsley Group at 30 April 20X6.

6 Statement of comprehensive income preparation for vertical groups

Treat the sub-subsidiary in exactly the same way as a directly owned subsidiary but remember to use the effective percentages when calculating non-controlling interests' share of profit and total comprehensive income.

Test your understanding 4 (integration question)

Alpha purchased 80% of Bravo's equity share capital of $250 million on 1 January 20X0 when the balance on Bravo's retained earnings was $20 million. The consideration paid was $250 million and the fair value of the NCI at the date of acquisition was $54 million.

Bravo purchased 60% of Charlie's equity share capital of $150 million on 1 January 20X1 when Charlie's retained earnings stood at $30 million. The consideration paid was $200 million and the fair value of the NCI (based on Alpha's effective holding) at the date of acquisition was $150 million.

It is group policy to measure NCI at fair value at the date of acquisition. At 31 December 20X3 an impairment test was carried out and neither goodwill in Bravo or Charlie was considered to be impaired. When a similar test was carried out at 31 December 20X4, the goodwill in Bravo was still considered unimpaired, however goodwill in Charlie was considered to have been impaired by 10% of its original value.

During the year, Bravo paid dividends of $15 million and Charlie paid dividends of $5 million to their shareholders.

The statements of profit or loss for the year ended 31 December 20X4 are as follows:

	Alpha $m	Bravo $m	Charlie $m
Revenue	200	170	160
Cost of sales	(44)	(30)	(32)
Gross profit	156	140	128
Operating expenses	(10)	(7)	(7)
Investment income	16	7	–
Profits before taxation	162	140	121
Income tax	(24)	(15)	(10)
Profit for the year	138	125	111

Required:

Prepare the consolidated statement of profit or loss for the year ended 31 December 20X4.

Note: work in millions to 1 decimal place, i.e. to the nearest $100,000.

7 Mixed groups

A mixed group exists where the parent has a direct holding in the sub-subsidiary as well as the indirect holding via the subsidiary.

$$
\begin{array}{ccc}
 & P \rightarrow & \rightarrow \\
\% & \downarrow & \downarrow \\
 & S & \% \\
\% & \downarrow & \downarrow \\
 & Q \leftarrow & \leftarrow
\end{array}
$$

Accounting for a mixed group is very similar to that of a vertical group. The only slight difference is that, in the calculation of goodwill, there will be two elements to the parent's investment: one direct and one indirect, and only the indirect investment should be adjusted for the IHA.

Illustration 6

$$P \rightarrow \rightarrow$$

1 April 20X2   70%   ↓   ↓

S   30%   1 April 20X2

1 April 20X2   40%   ↓   ↓

Q ← ←

Control

P controls S. Therefore S is a subsidiary.

P controls Q. P is able to direct 40% + 30% = 70% of the voting rights of Q. Therefore Q is a sub-subsidiary.

Effective consolidation percentage

S will be consolidated with P owning 70% and the NCI owning 30%.

Q will be consolidated with P owning 58% and the NCI owning 42%.

P's indirect ownership (70% × 40%)	28%
P's direct ownership	30%
	——
	58%
	——

Dates

The date of acquisition for S and Q is 1 April 20X2.

Example 2

The summarised draft statements of financial position of three entities at 31 December 20X5 are:

	P	S	Q
	$000	$000	$000
Property, plant and equipment	1,500	450	120
Investments (at cost)			
In S	400		
In Q	200	80	
Current assets	250	125	35
	2,350	655	155
Share capital $1	300	150	50
Retained earnings	1,925	420	75
Current liabilities	125	85	30
	2,350	655	155

(1) On 1 January 20X3, P acquired 80% of the equity shares of S and 70% of the equity shares of Q. S's retained earnings at this date were $250,000 and Q's retained earnings were $20,000.

(2) On the same date, 1 January 20X3, S acquired 15% of the equity shares of Q.

(3) It is group policy to measure NCIs using the fair value method. The fair value of S's NCI at the date of acquisition was $70,000 and the fair value of Q's NCI (based on P's effective holding) was $50,000 .

Required:

Prepare the consolidated statement of financial position of the P Group as 31 December 20X5.

Example 2 answer

Step 1 – draw up W1 Group structure

(W1) Group structure

```
                    P  →   →
1 Jan 20X3   80%    ↓           ↓
                    S       70%    1 Jan 20X3
1 Jan 20X3   15%    ↓           ↓
                    Q  ←   ←
```

S will be consolidated as a 80% sub (NCI owning 20%) from 1 Jan 20X3. Q will be consolidated as a 82% sub (NCI owning 18%) from 1 Jan 20X3.

P's direct ownership	70%
P's indirect ownership	
(80% × 15%)	12%
	——
	82%
	——

P achieves control of both S and Q on 1 January 20X3 – and on this date obtains both a direct and indirect holding. Both shareholdings must be taken into account (as above) when calculating goodwill and an IHA will need to be applied to the indirect element.

Step 2 – now complete the workings for S and Q, remembering to bring in the IHA when dealing with Q. Deal with S first as it is the straightforward subsidiary.

(W2) **Net assets – S**

	Acq'n	Reporting date
	$000	$000
Share capital	150	150
Retained earnings	250	420
	400	570

Post acquisition reserves = 170

Net assets – Q

	Acq'n	Reporting date
	$000	$000
Share capital	50	50
Retained earnings	20	75
	70	125

Post acquisition reserves = 55

(W3) Goodwill – S

	$000
Fair value of P's investment	400
NCI holding at fair value	70
Fair value of sub's net assets at acquisition (W2)	(400)
Goodwill at acquisition/reporting date	70

Goodwill – Q

	$000	$000
Fair value of P's investment – Direct		200
Fair value of P's investment – Indirect:		
Sub's cost of investment	80	
Less: IHA (20% × 80)	(16)	
		64
NCI at fair value		50
Fair value of sub's net assets at acquisition (W2)		(70)
Goodwill at acquisition/reporting date		244

(W4) Non-controlling interests – S

	$000
NCI at acquisition (W3)	70
NCI% × post acquisition reserves (20% × 170 (W2))	34
Less IHA (W3)	(16)
	88

Non-controlling interests – Q

	$000
NCI at acquisition (W3)	50
NCI% × post acquisition reserves (18% × 55 (W2))	9.9
	59.9

(W5) Retained earnings

	$000
P's reserves	1,925
Sub: P% × post acquisition reserves	
S: 80% × 170 (W2)	136
Q: 82% × 55 (W2)	45.1
	2,106.1

Step 3 – Finally complete the proforma CSFP. Both S and Q are subsidiaries therefore the assets and liabilities of all three entities are added together on a line by line basis.

Consolidated statement of financial position as at 31 December 20X5

		$000
Property, plant and equipment	(1,500 + 450 + 120)	2,070
Goodwill	(70 + 244) (W3)	314
Current assets	(250 + 125 + 35)	410
		2,794
Equity		
Share capital		300
Retained earnings	(W5)	2,106.1
		2,406.1
Non-controlling interest	(88 + 59.9) (W4)	147.9
		2,554
Current liabilities	(125 + 85 + 30)	240
		2,794

The summarised draft statements of financial position of three entities at 30 September 20X4 are:

	Holdings	Pepper	Salt
	$000	$000	$000
Property, plant and equipment	1,000	700	225
Investments (at cost)			
In Pepper	350		
In Salt	175	50	
Current assets	370	300	75
	1,895	1,050	300
Share capital $1	500	300	100
Retained earnings	1,145	550	150
Current liabilities	250	200	50
	1,895	1,050	300

(1) On 1 October 20X1, Holdings acquired 70% of the equity shares of Pepper and 60% of the equity shares of Salt. Pepper's retained earnings at this date were $100,000 and Salt's retained earnings were $50,000.

(2) On the same date, 1 October 20X1, Pepper acquired 20% of the equity shares of Salt.

(3) It is group policy to measure NCIs using the proportion of fair value of net assets method.

Required:

Prepare the consolidated statement of financial position of the Holdings Group at 30 September 20X4.

The statements of financial position of three entities at 30 June 20X6 are given below:

	A	B	C
	$000	$000	$000
Non-current assets			
Property, plant and equipment	9,300	3,600	4,250
Investments (at cost)	10,000	4,000	–
Current assets			
Inventory	1,750	700	400
Receivables	1,050	550	420
Cash and cash equivalents	1,550	1,010	330
	23,650	9,860	5,400
Equity			
Share capital $1	15,000	7,000	4,000
Retained earnings	4,150	730	870
Non-current liabilities	2,000	750	250
Current liabilities	2,500	1,380	280
	23,650	9,860	5,400

On 1 July 20X5 A acquired two shareholdings. The first was 60% of the equity share capital of B for $6m cash. The retained earnings of B were $500,000 and the fair value of the NCI holding was $3.5m. The second was 10% of the equity share capital of C for $1m cash.

On the same date, B acquired 60% of the equity share capital of C for $4m cash. The retained earnings of C were $570,000 and the fair value of the NCI holding was $2.5m

At 1 July 20X5, property, plant and equipment in the books of B had a fair value of $250,000 in excess of its carrying value. The items had a remaining useful economic life of 5 years at this time.

At 30 June 20X6, B and C held goods in inventory which had been purchased from A for a total of $360,000. A had sold the goods at a 20% mark up.

At 30 June 20X6, goodwill arising on the acquisition of B had been impaired by $250,000. There was no impairment to goodwill arising on the acquisition of C. It is group policy to measure NCIs at fair value at acquisition.

Required:

Prepare the consolidated statement of financial position at 30 June 20X6.

Test your understanding 7 (OTQ style qns)

(1) D has owned 80% of the equity shares of E since 1 January 20X3. E has owned 60% of the equity shares of F since 1 January 20X1. There has been no impairment of goodwill in either E or F.

The balance on F's retained earnings was as follows:

– $12 million on 1 January 20X1

– $24 million on 1 January 20X3

– $30 million on 31 December 20X6, the current reporting date

What amount would be included in the consolidated retained earnings of the D group at 31 December 20X6 in respect of F? (State your answer in $)

(2) Alpha owns shares carrying 70% of the voting rights in Beta and 25% of the voting rights in Gamma. Beta owns shares carrying 30% of the voting rights in Gamma.

Which one of the following statements is correct?

A Gamma is an associate of Alpha because Alpha controls Beta and Gamma is an associate of Beta.

B Gamma is an associate of Alpha because the effective interest of Alpha in Gamma's profits is 25% + (70% × 30%) = 46%.

C Gamma is a subsidiary of Alpha and should be consolidated in the Alpha Group's financial statements.

D The Alpha group consolidated financial statements will reflect NCI of 45% in Gamma.

(3) KT acquired 75% of the 500,000 $1 equity shares of HA on 1 August 20X3 for $850,000. HA had acquired 60% of the 200,000 $1 equity shares of SP on 1 August 20X2 for $550,000.

Which three of the following statements are correct in respect of the goodwill that would be recognised in the consolidated financial statements of the KT Group?

A   Goodwill would relate to HA only. SP is an associate as KT's effective holding is 45%.

B   Goodwill in SP would be recognised on 1 August 20X2.

C   Goodwill in SP would initially be recognised at the same date as the goodwill in HA.

D   An indirect holding adjustment of $137,500 (25% × $550,000) would be reflected in the calculation of goodwill in SP.

E   An indirect holding adjustment of $220,000 (40% × $550,000) would be reflected in the calculation of goodwill in SP.

F   The indirect holding adjustment would be a debit to non-controlling interest.

(4) BT acquired 80% of the equity shares of GT on 1 February 20X4. GT then acquired 60% of the equity shares of ST on 1 February 20X6 for $300,000 when the retained earnings of ST were $175,000.

No fair value adjustments were required to the net assets of either GT or ST on acquisition. It is group policy to measure the NCI at fair value at the date of acquisition. The fair value of the NCI of ST, reflecting BT group's effective holding was $280,000 on 1 February 20X6.

At the reporting date of 31 January 20X9, ST had retained earnings of $325,000.

Calculate the amount that would appear in the equity section of the BT group's consolidated statement of financial position as at 31 January 20X9 in respect of the non-controlling interest in ST. State your answer to the nearest $.

(5) SJP owns 75% of the ordinary share capital of its subsidiary, DJR. The shares were acquired on 1 November 20X5 when DJR's reserves were $152,000. DJR acquired a 65% investment in its subsidiary, CLR, on 1 May 20X5. CLR's reserves were $189,000 on 1 May 20X5 and $202,000 on 1 November 20X5.

Reserves for the three entities at 31 October 20X6, the reporting date of the SJP group, were:

SJP = $266,000

DJR = $178,000

CLR = $214,000

There has been no impairment of goodwill in respect of either investment since acquisition and no intra-group trading.

Calculate the amount that would appear in the SJP group's consolidated statement of financial position as at 31 October 20X6 for consolidated reserves. State your answer in $s.

(6) SW purchased 80% of the equity share capital of DW on 1 July 20X3. DW purchased 70% of the equity share capital of LM on 1 January 20X6.

LM's profit for the year ended 30 June 20X6 was $250,000.

Profits are deemed to accrue evenly over the year.

Calculate the amount that would be included in consolidated profit attributable to the non-controlling interest for the year ended 30 June 20X6 in respect of LM.

8 Chapter summary

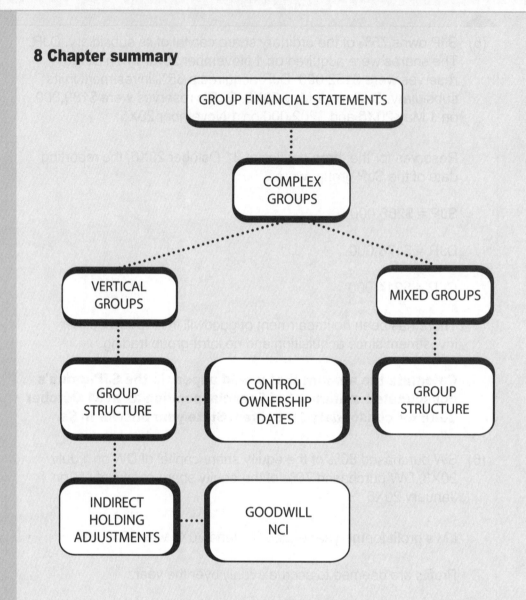

Test your understanding answers

Test your understanding 1 (integration question)

Consolidated statement of financial position as at 31 December 20X7

	$
Goodwill (15,000 + 33,250) (W3)	48,250
Other net assets (280,000 + 133,000 + 100,000)	513,000
	———
	561,250
	———

Capital and reserves

Equity share capital	100,000
Retained earnings (W5)	66,150
NCI (W4)	70,100
Liabilities (200,000 + 100,000 + 25,000)	325,000
	———
	561,250
	———

Workings

(W1) Group structure

H
↓   45/60 = 75% on 1.1.X1
S
↓   30/50 = 60% on 1.1.X1
T

Effective consolidation percentages:

	S	T
Group interest	75%	45% (75% × 60%)
Non controlling interest	25%	55%
	———	———
	100%	100%
	———	———

(W2) **Net assets**

	S		T	
	Acq'n date 1.1.X1	**Rep. date 31.12.X7**	**Acq'n date 1.1.X1**	**Rep. date 31.12.X7**
	$	$	$	$
Share capital	60,000	60,000	50,000	50,000
Retained earnings	10,000	28,000	8,000	25,000
	70,000	88,000	58,000	75,000

(W3) **Goodwill**

	S	T
	$	$
Sub's investment in sub-sub		55,000
IHA (25% × 55,000)		(13,750)
Fair value of P's investment	65,000	41,250
NCI at fair value	20,000	50,000
Fair value of sub's net assets at acquisition (W2)	(70,000)	(58,000)
Goodwill on acquisition	15,000	33,250

(W4) **Non-controlling interest**

	$
S:	
NCI at acquisition (W3)	20,000
NCI% × post acquisition reserves (25% × (88,000 – 70,000) (W2))	4,500
IHA (W3)	(13,750)
T:	
NCI at acquisition (W3)	50,000
NCI% × post acquisition reserves (55% × (75,000 – 58,000) (W2))	9,350
	70,100

(W5) Consolidated retained earnings

	$
Retained earnings of H	45,000
Group share of post-acquisition profits	
S: 75% × (88,000 – 70,000) (W2)	13,500
T 45% × (75,000 – 58,000) (W2)	7,650
	———
	66,150
	———

Test your understanding 2 (integration question)

Consolidated statement of financial position of the Manchester group as at 31 December 20X6

		$000
PPE	(44 + 4 + 27)	75
Goodwill	(21 + 11) (W3)	32
Current assets	(29 + 31 + 43 – 4 PUP (W6))	99
		——
		206
		——
Share capital		40
Share premium		4
Retained earnings	(W5)	76.8
Non-controlling interest	(W4)	20.2
Current liabilities	(10 + 40 + 15)	65
		——
		206
		——

Workings

(W1) Group structure

Manchester

↓ 80% of ordinary shares on 31.12.X1

Leeds

↓ 75% of ordinary shares on 31.12.X0

Sheffield

Control

Manchester controls Leeds and Leeds controls Sheffield. Therefore Manchester can indirectly control Sheffield.

Effective consolidation percentages

	Leeds	**Sheffield**
Parent interest	80%	60% (80% × 75%)
Non controlling interest	20%	40%
	100%	100%

Dates

Leeds is consolidated from 31 December 20X1.

Sheffield is also consolidated on 31 December 20X1 i.e. the date on which Manchester acquired control.

(W2) Net assets – Leeds

	Acq'n (31.12.X1)	**Reporting date**
Share capital	10	10
Share premium	10	10
Retained earnings	5	15
PUP (W6)		(4)
	25	31

Net assets – Sheffield

	Acq'n (31.12.X1)	Reporting date
Share capital	20	20
Retained earnings	15	35
	35	55

(W3) Goodwill

	Leeds $000	Sheffield $000
Sub's investment in sub-sub		40
IHA (20% × 40)		(8)
Fair value of P's investment	41	32
NCI at proportion of net assets		
(20% × 25 (W2))	5	
(40% × 35 (W2))		14
Fair value of sub's net assets at acquisition (W2)	(25)	(35)
Goodwill on acquisition/reporting date	21	11

(W4) Non-controlling interests

	$000
Leeds:	
NCI at acquisition (W3)	5
NCI% × post acquisition reserves (20% × (31 – 25) (W2))	1.2
IHA (W3)	(8)
Sheffield:	
NCI at acquisition (W3)	14
NCI% × post acquisition reserves (40% × (55 – 35) (W2))	8
	20.2

(W5) Retained earnings

Manchester	60
Leeds: 80% × (31 – 25) (W2)	4.8
Sheffield: 60% × (55 – 35) (W2)	12
	——
	76.8
	——

(W6) PUP

Leeds sells to Manchester and Sheffield, therefore adjust (W2) & inventory on CSFP

Amount left in inventories: $(15,000 + 5,000) = $20,000

$$PUP = 20,000 \times {}^{25}/_{125} = 4,000$$

Test your understanding 3 (integration question)

Consolidated statement of financial position as at 30 April 20X6

	$000
Goodwill (W3) (65,000 + 80,000)	145,000
Property, plant and equipment (596,330 + 320,370 + 489,800 + 35,000 (W2) + 20,000 (W2) – 4,000 (W2))	1,457,500
Investments (485,000 + 335,000 – 350,000 (W3) – 335,000 (W3))	135,000
Current assets (87,320 + 56,550 + 54,800 – 1,400 (W6))	197,270
	———————
	1,934,770
	———————

Equity	
Share capital	100,000
Retained earnings (W5)	1,168,100
	1,268,100
Non-controlling interests (W4) (67,100 + 236,050)	303,150
	1,571,250
Non-current liabilities (150,000 + 80,000 + 30,000)	260,000
Current liabilities (43,250 + 31,420 + 28,850)	103,520
	1,934,770

Workings

(W1) Group structure

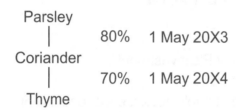

Coriander will be an 80% subsidiary from 1 May 20X3 (3 years) (NCI owning 20%).

Thyme will be a 56% (80% × 70%) subsidiary from 1 May 20X4 (2 years) (NCI owning 44%).

(W2) Net assets – Coriander

	Acq'n	Reporting date
	$000	$000
Share capital	75,000	75,000
Retained earnings	255,000	525,500
Fair value adjustment – land (135m –100m)	35,000	35,000
	365,000	635,500

Post acq'n profits = 270,500

Net assets – Thyme

	Acq'n	Reporting date
	$000	$000
Share capital	50,000	50,000
Retained earnings	285,000	435,750
Fair value adjustment – plant	20,000	20,000
Depreciation adjustment (20,000 × 2/10)		(4,000)
	355,000	501,750

Post acq'n
profits
= 146,750

(W3) **Goodwill – Coriander**

	$000
Fair value of P's investment	350,000
NCI at fair value	80,000
Fair value of sub's net assets at acquisition (W2)	(365,000)
Goodwill at acquisition/reporting date	65,000

Goodwill – Thyme

	$000	$000
Sub's investment in sub-sub	335,000	
IHA (20% × 335,000)	(67,000)	
Fair value of P's investment		268,000
NCI at fair value		175,000
Fair value of sub's net assets at acquisition (W2)		(355,000)
Goodwill at acquisition		88,000
Impairment		(8,000)
Goodwill at reporting date		80,000

(W4) Non-controlling interests – Coriander

	$000
NCI at acquisition (W3)	80,000
NCI% × post acquisition reserves (20% × 270,500 (W2))	54,100
IHA (W3)	(67,000)
	67,100

Non-controlling interests – Thyme

	$000
NCI at acquisition (W3)	175,000
NCI% × post acquisition reserves (44% × 146,750 (W2))	64,570
NCI% × impairment loss (44% × 8,000 (W3))	(3,520)
	236,050

(W5) Retained earnings

	$000
P's reserves	875,400
PUP (W6)	(1,400)
Sub: P% × post acquisition reserves	
Coriander: 80% × 270,500 (W2)	216,400
Thyme: 56% × 146,750 (W2)	82,180
Impairment: P% × impairment loss	
Thyme: 56% × 8,000 (W3)	(4,480)
	1,168,100

(W6) PUP

Goods in inventory = 35,000 × 1/5 = 7,000

Profit in inventory = 7,000 × 20% = 1,400

Consolidated statement of comprehensive income for the year ended 31 December 20X4

	$m
Revenue (200 + 170 + 160)	530
Cost of sales (44 + 30 + 32)	(106)
Gross profit	424
Operating expenses (10 + 7 + 7 + 13 (W3))	(37)
Investment income (16 + 7 − 12 − 3 (W2))	8
Profit before tax	395
Tax (24 + 15 + 10)	(49)
Profit for the year	346
Profit attributable to:	
Parent shareholders (balance)	270.6
NCI shareholders (W4)	75.4
	346

Workings

(W1) Group structure

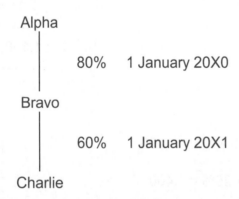

Bravo is consolidated as an 80% subsidiary from 1 January 20X0.

Charlie is consolidated as a 48% (80% × 60%) subsidiary from 1 January 20X1.

(W2) **Intra-group dividends**

Dividends will be paid to shareholders based on their actual shareholdings i.e. the effective shareholding percentages used for consolidation purposes are not relevant.

Bravo to Alpha   80% × 15 = $12m
Charlie to Bravo   60% × 5 = $3m

(W3) **Goodwill impairment – Charlie**

	$m	$m
Parent's investment		
Investment by Bravo	200	
Less IHA (20% × 200)	(40)	
	─────	
Alpha's effective (80% × 200)		160
Fair value of NCI at acquisition		150
Less fair value of net assets at acquisition (150 + 30)		(180)
		─────
		130
Impairment in 20X4		× 10%
		─────
		13
		─────

(W4) **NCI share of profit**

		$m	$m
Bravo:			
Profit for year		125	
Intra-group dividend eliminated (W2)		(3)	
		─────	
		122	
NCI share	× 20%	─────	24.4
Charlie:			
Profit for year		111	
Goodwill impairment (W3)		(13)	
		─────	
		98	
NCI share	× 52%	─────	51.0
			─────
			75.4
			─────

Consolidated statement of financial position as at 30 September 20X4

		$000
Property, plant and equipment	(1,000 + 700 + 225)	1,925
Goodwill	(70 + 99) (W3)	169
Current assets	(370 + 300 + 75)	745
		2,839
Equity		
Share capital		500
Retained earnings	(W5)	1,534
		2,034
Non-controlling interest	(240 + 65) (W4)	305
		2,339
Liabilities	(250 + 200 + 50)	500
		2,839

Workings

(W1) Group structure

$$
\begin{array}{l}
\text{1 Oct 20X1} \quad 70\% \qquad \text{Holdings} \quad \rightarrow \quad \rightarrow \\
\qquad\qquad\qquad\qquad\qquad \downarrow \qquad\qquad\qquad \downarrow \\
\qquad\qquad\qquad\qquad \text{Pepper} \qquad 60\% \quad \text{1 Oct 20X1} \\
\text{1 Oct 20X1} \quad 20\% \qquad \downarrow \qquad\qquad\qquad \downarrow \\
\qquad\qquad\qquad\qquad \text{Salt} \quad \leftarrow \quad \leftarrow
\end{array}
$$

Pepper will be consolidated as a 70% sub (NCI owning 30%) from 1 Oct 20X1.

Salt will be consolidated as a 74% sub (NCI owning 26%) from 1 Oct 20X1.

Holdings' direct ownership	60%
Holdings' indirect ownership	
(70% × 20%)	14%
	——
	74%
	——

(W2) Net assets – Pepper

	Acq'n	Reporting date
	$000	$000
Share capital	300	300
Retained earnings	100	550
	——	——
	400	850
	——	——

Post acq'n profits
= 450

Net assets – Salt

	Acq'n	Reporting date
	$000	$000
Share capital	100	100
Retained earnings	50	150
	——	——
	150	250
	——	——

Post acq'n
profits = 100

(W3) Goodwill – Pepper

	$000
Fair value of P's investment	350
NCI at proportion of net assets (30% × 400 (W2))	120
Fair value of sub's net assets at acquisition (W2)	(400)
Goodwill at acquisition/reporting date	70

Goodwill – Salt

	$000	$000
Fair value of P's investment – Direct		175
Fair value of P's investment – Indirect:		
Sub's investment	50	
Less: IHA (30% × 50)	(15)	
		35
NCI at proportion of net assets (26% × 150 (W2))		39
Fair value of sub's net assets at acquisition (W2)		(150)
Goodwill at acquisition/reporting date		99

(W4) Non-controlling interests – Pepper

	$000
NCI at acquisition (W3)	120
NCI% × post acquisition reserves (30% × 450 (W2))	135
Less IHA (W3)	(15)
	240

Non-controlling interests – Salt

	$000
NCI at acquisition (W3)	39
NCI% × post acquisition reserves (26% × 100 (W2))	26
	65

(W5) **Retained earnings**

	$000
P's reserves	1,145
Sub: P% × post acquisition reserves	
Pepper: 70% × 450 (W2)	315
Salt: 74% × 100 (W2)	74
	———
	1,534
	———

Test your understanding 6 (integration question)

Consolidated statement of financial position as at 30 June 20X6

	$000
Property, plant and equipment	17,350
(9,300 + 3,600 + 4,250 + 250 (W2) − 50 (W2))	
Goodwill (W3) (1,500 + 1,330)	2,830
Investments (10,000 + 4,000 − 6,000 − 4,000 − 1,000)	3,000
Current assets	
Inventory (1,750 + 700 + 400 − 60 (W6))	2,790
Receivables (1,050 + 550 + 420)	2,020
Cash and cash equivalents (1,550 + 1,010 + 330)	2,890
	———
	30,880
	———
Equity	
Share capital	15,000
Retained earnings (W5)	4,186
	———
	19,186
Non-controlling interest (1,872 + 2,662) (W4)	4,534
	———
	23,720
Non-current liabilities (2,000 + 750 + 250)	3,000
Current liabilities (2,500 + 1,380 + 280)	4,160
	———
	30,880
	———

Workings

(W1) Group structure

```
                        A  →   →
1 July 20X5   60%       ↓           ↓
                        B       10%   1 July 20X5
1 July 20X5   60%       ↓           ↓
                        C  ←   ←
```

B will be consolidated as a 60% sub (NCI owning 40%) from 1 July 20X5. C will be consolidated as a 46% sub (NCI owning 54%) from 1 July 20X5.

A's indirect ownership – 60% x 60%	36%
A's direct ownership	10%
	——
	46%
	——

(W2) Net assets – B

	Acq'n	Reporting date
	$000	$000
Share capital	7,000	7,000
Retained earnings	500	730
Fair value adjustment	250	250
Depreciation adjustment (250 × 1/5)		(50)
	——	——
	7,750	7,930
	——	——

Post acq'n
profits
= 180

Net assets – C

	Acq'n	Reporting date
	$000	$000
Share capital	4,000	4,000
Retained earnings	570	870
	———	———
	4,570	4,870
	———	———

Post acq'n profits
= 300

(W3) **Goodwill – B**

	$000
Fair value of P's investment	6,000
NCI at fair value	3,500
Fair value of sub's net assets at acquisition (W2)	(7,750)
	———
Goodwill at acquisition	1,750
Impairment	(250)
	———
Goodwill at reporting date	1,500
	———

Goodwill – C

	$000	$000
P's investment – direct		1,000
Consideration paid by Sub	4,000	
IHA (40% × 4,000)	(1,600)	
	———	
P's investment – indirect		2,400
NCI at fair value		2,500
Fair value of sub's net assets at acquisition (W2)		(4,570)
		———
Goodwill at acquisition/reporting date		1,330
		———

(W4) Non-controlling interests – B

	$000
NCI at acquisition (W3)	3,500
NCI% × post acquisition reserves (40% × 180 (W2))	72
NCI% × impairment loss (40% × 250 (W3))	(100)
IHA (W3)	(1,600)
	1,872

Non-controlling interests – C

	$000
NCI at acquisition (W3)	2,500
NCI% × post acquisition reserves (54% × 300 (W2))	162
	2,662

(W5) Retained earnings

	$000
P's reserves	4,150
PUP (W6)	(60)
Sub: P% × post acquisition reserves	
B: 60% × 180 (W2)	108
C: 46% × 300 (W2)	138
Impairment: P% × impairment loss	
B: 60% × 250 (W3)	(150)
	4,186

(W6) PUP

	$000
Profit in inventory (20/120 × 360)	60

Test your understanding 7 (OTQ style qns)

(1) **Amount in respect of F = $2,880,000**

D's effective holding in F = 80% × 60% = 48%

Date that D achieves control of F is 1 January 20X3 (when it acquires the controlling interest in E).

Therefore, impact of F on consolidated retained earnings is

48% × ($30m – $24m) = $2,880,000

(2) **C is correct.**

A and B are incorrect. Gamma is a subsidiary of the Alpha group as 55% of its voting rights are held within the group (25% directly and 30% indirectly, via Beta).

The effective interest that Alpha has in Gamma is 25% + (70% × 30%) = 46% and this is used to allocate post-acquisition reserves between owners of the parent and the NCI.

The NCI share of post-acquisition reserves would be the remaining 54%, therefore D is also incorrect.

(3) **The correct statements are C, D and F**

A is incorrect. SP is a subsidiary of KT as it indirectly controls it via HA (KT controls HA and HA controls SP).

B is incorrect. KT gains control of SP when it acquires the shares in HA, therefore KT should consolidated SP from 1 August 20X3.

E is incorrect. The indirect holding adjustment reflects the share of the consideration paid for SP that has been incurred by HA's NCI shareholders (i.e. 25%).

(4) **NCI relating to ST = $358,000**

	$
Fair value of NCI at acquisition	280,000
NCI share of post-acquisition reserves in ST	
52% (see below) × (325,000 – 175,000)	78,000
	―――――
	358,000
	―――――

BT's effective holding in ST = 80% × 60% = 48%

Therefore, NCI in ST = 52%

The IHA would be an adjustment to the NCI in GT rather than ST.

(5) **Consolidated reserves = $291,350**

	$
SJP's reserves	266,000
SJP shareholders share of subsidiaries' reserves:	
DJR: 75% × (178,000 – 152,000)	19,500
CLR: 75% × 65% × (214,000 – 202,000)	5,850
	―――――
	291,350
	―――――

(6) **Consolidated profit attributable to LM's NCI = $55,000**

	$
LM post-acquisition profit 6/12 × 250,000	125,000
NCI share (see below)	× 44%
	―――――
	55,000
	―――――

SW's effective holding in LM = 80% × 70% = 56%

Therefore, NCI in LM = 44%

15

Changes in group structure

Chapter learning objectives

B2. Demonstrate the impact on the preparation of the consolidated financial statements of certain complex group scenarios.

(a) Demonstrate the impact on the group financial statements of acquiring additional shareholdings in the period and disposing of all or part of a shareholding in the period.

- Additional acquisition in the period resulting in a simple investment becoming a controlling interest, in accordance with the provisions of IFRS 3.

- Calculation of the gain/loss on the disposal of a controlling interest in a subsidiary in the year, in accordance with the provisions of IFRS 3.

- Adjustment to parent's equity resulting from acquiring or disposing of shares in a subsidiary, in accordance with the provisions of IFRS 3.

1 Session content

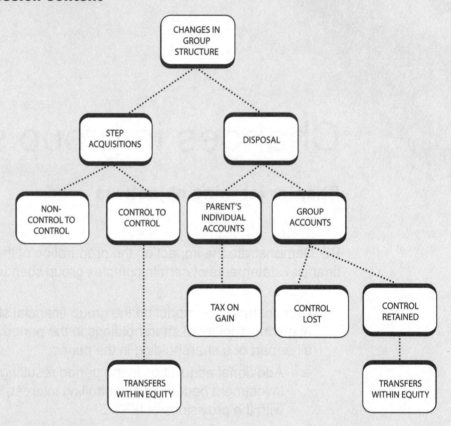

2 Introduction

In this chapter, we will consider how to account for changes in the group structure when the parent acquires further shares in an entity or disposes of some or all of its shareholding in an entity.

The key to dealing with these scenarios is to consider whether the parent has achieved, or lost, a controlling shareholding - if so it will have acquired, or disposed of, a subsidiary.

If the parent's percentage holding changes but there is control both before and after the transaction, then there is no acquisition or disposal of a subsidiary. Instead there is a change in the balance of ownership between the parent shareholders and the non-controlling interests and the transaction only affects group equity.

3 Step acquisitions

A step acquisition occurs when the parent acquires a controlling interest in another entity in stages.

The parent will only start to consolidate the investment from the date it achieves control. It is at this point in time that goodwill and the non-controlling interest in the subsidiary are initially recognised.

There are two possible scenarios that you may come across in your assessment.

(1) **Non-control to control**

E.g. the parent acquires 40% of the equity shares of an entity and then purchases a further 20% to bring the total shareholding up to 60%.

The investment becomes a subsidiary when the additional 20% of the shares are acquired, as this is when control is achieved.

(2) **Control to control**

E.g. the parent acquires 60% of the equity shares of an entity and then purchases a further 15% to bring the total shareholding up to 75%.

The investment is a subsidiary from the date of the first investment, as this is when control was achieved. Upon the second investment the parent increases its ownership of the subsidiary by acquiring more shares from the non-controlling interest.

Each scenario will now be considered in more detail.

4 Non-control to control

The date at which control is achieved is the date of acquisition of the subsidiary. Therefore, from this date the investment will be consolidated using the acquisition method of accounting, i.e.:

- consolidate income, expenses, assets and liabilities on a line by line basis

- recognise goodwill

- recognise non-controlling interests.

At the date when control is achieved:

(1) Remeasure the previously held interest to fair value

(2) Recognise any resulting gain or loss within the statement of profit or loss (and so retained earnings).

The scenario is accounted for as if the previously held interest has been disposed of for fair value (hence the gain / loss) and the fair value then re-invested in acquiring part of the shares in the subsidiary.

This fair value will therefore appear as part of the parent's investment in the calculation of goodwill:

	$
Fair value of previously held interest	X
Fair value of consideration to acquire additional interest	X
Fair value of P's controlling shareholding at acquisition date	X

Example 1

Ayre acquired 10% of the equity shares of Byrne for $18,000 on 1 January 20X6 and classified the investment as available for sale in its financial statements in accordance with IAS 39. At 31 December 20X6, the fair value of the 10% investment in Byrne was $24,000 and this was reflected in Ayre's statement of financial position, resulting in gains of $6,000 being recorded in other components of equity.

On 1 June 20X7, Ayre acquires a further 50% of Byrne's equity shares for $160,000.

At this date the fair value of the original 10% investment was $28,000, the fair value of the net assets of Byrne was $200,000 and the fair value of the non-controlling interest (now that Byrne has become a subsidiary) was $100,000.

It is group policy to measure non-controlling interests at fair value at the date of acquisition.

Required:

Explain how the above transaction would be accounted for on 1 June 20X7, the date that Ayre achieved control of Byrne, and calculate goodwill arising on the acquisition.

Example 1 answer

(W1) Group Structure

Ayre

| 60% (10% + 50%)

Byrne

At the date control is achieved, the original investment is remeasured to fair value (i.e. from $24,000 to $28,000) and a gain is recognised in profit or loss to reflect the deemed disposal of the investment. The gains previously recorded in other components of equity (of $6,000) are recycled to profit as would be the case if the investment had been disposed of (in accordance with IAS 39).

Dr Investment (28,000 – 24,000)	4,000
Dr Other components of equity	6,000
Cr Profit (28,000 FV – 18,000 cost)	10,000

Goodwill calculation

	$
Fair value of P's investment	
Fair value of previously held interest	28,000
Fair value of consideration for additional interest	160,000
	————
	188,000
Fair value of NCI at acquisition	100,000
Fair value of sub's net assets at acquisition	(200,000)
	————
Goodwill at acquisition	88,000
	————

The statements of financial position of two entities, Major and Tom as at 31 December 20X6 are as follows:

	Major	Tom
	$000	$000
Investment	160	
Other assets	350	250
	510	250
Equity share capital	200	100
Reserves	250	122
Liabilities	60	28
	510	250

Major acquired 40% of Tom on 31 December 20X1 for $90,000. At this time the reserves of Tom were $76,000. A further 20% of shares in Tom was acquired by Major on 31 December 20X4 for $70,000. At this date, the fair value of the existing holding in Tom was $105,000 and Tom's reserves were $100,000. The investments are stated at cost in Major's statement of financial position.

The book value of Tom's net assets was deemed to be equal to fair value. It is group policy to measure non-controlling interests at the proportion of net assets at the date of acquisition.

Required:

Prepare the consolidated statement of financial position for the Major group as at 31 December 20X6.

Original holding an associate

IFRS 3 views a step acquisition in which control is achieved as being a disposal of a previously held equity interest which is then replaced with the acquisition of a subsidiary.

In TYU 1 the requirement to produce consolidated financial statements only arises when Major acquires the controlling shareholding in Tom on 31 December 20X4 (as Major has no other investments).

However, if Major had other subsidiaries and therefore was already producing consolidated financial statements, it would have been accounting for Tom as an associate in the period from 31 December 20X1 to 31 December 20X4. Therefore, upon achieving control on 31 December 20X4, the gain that would be recorded in the consolidated statement of profit or loss would be a gain on disposal of an associate.

Let's assume that Major had other subsidiaries that had already been consolidated into its figures provided in TYU 1 (but Tom's results were not included).

The gain on disposal of associate would be calculated as follows:

(W6) **Gain on disposal of associate**

	$	$
Fair value of original 40% investment at 31 December 20X4		105,000
Less: carrying value of associate at disposal		
Cost of investment	90,000	
Share of post acquisition reserves		
40% × (100,000 – 76,000)	9,600	
		(99,600)
Gain on disposal		5,400

As well as recording the gain of $5,400 above, Major's share of the post-acquisition reserves of Tom whilst it was an associate should also be included. This amounts to $9,600 as can be seen in the calculation above and therefore the overall impact of the associate in group retained earnings is $15,000 (the difference between original cost and fair value at 'disposal').

Total impact of Tom (if reflected as an associate) in group retained earnings

	$
Share of post-acquisition reserves to disposal:	
40% × (100,000 – 76,000)	9,600
Gain on deemed disposal of associate	5,400
	15,000

When producing a group retained earnings working it is easier to compare original cost to fair value and not worry about the fact that the original investment was an associate. However, if a consolidated statement of profit or loss were being produced, the gain on disposal that would need to be reflected would be $5,400 and not $15,000.

This is further demonstrated in TYUs 3 and 4 in this chapter.

Test your understanding 2 (integration question)

The statements of financial position of two entities, Heat and Wave as at 30 June 20X5 are as follows:

	Heat	Wave
	$000	$000
Investment	142	–
Other assets	358	225
	500	225
Equity share capital	250	150
Reserves	200	55
Liabilities	50	20
	500	225

Heat acquired 35% of Wave on 1 July 20X3 for $62,000 when the reserves of Wave were $30,000. Heat then acquired a further 40% of Wave's shares on 1 July 20X4 for $80,000 when Wave's reserves were $45,000. On 1 July 20X4 the fair value of the existing holding in Wave was $70,000 and the fair value of the NCI share in Wave was $50,000. The investments are stated at cost in Heat's statement of financial position.

It is group policy to measure NCI at fair value at the date of acquisition.

Required:

Prepare the consolidated statement of financial position for the Heat group as at 30 June 20X5.

5 Control to control

Where the parent already owns a controlling shareholding and subsequently purchases additional shares, they are simply purchasing the shares from the NCI shareholders. This means that the transaction is between the owners of the group, with the parent's share increasing and the NCI's share decreasing.

For example if the parent holds 80% of the shares in a subsidiary and buys 5% more the relationship remains one of a parent and subsidiary. As such, the subsidiary will be consolidated in the group accounts in the normal way but the NCI has decreased from 20% to 15%.

Where there is such a transaction:

- There is no change to the carrying value of goodwill

- The income, expenses, assets and liabilities continue to be consolidated line by line

- If the step acquisition happens mid-year, it will be necessary to time apportion profits when determining the NCI share of profits

- No gain or loss arises as this is a transaction within equity i.e. a transaction between owners

- A difference may arise that will be taken to other components of equity which can be determined using the following proforma.

	$
Transfer from NCI (= reduction in NCI reserve)	X
Cash paid	(X)
Difference to other components of equity	X/(X)

The transfer from NCI will represent the proportionate reduction in the NCI reserve at the date of the step acquisition, which reflects the amount that the parent is effectively purchasing from the NCI.

The following double entry is posted to record the control of the acquisition:

Dr NCI

Cr Cash

Dr/Cr Other components of equity

Example 2

Earl has owned 60% of Grey for many years. At acquisition, the NCI in Grey had a fair value of $100,000 and Grey's net assets had a fair value of $200,000.

On 1 July 20X8, Earl purchased a further 10% of Grey's shares for $30,000. At this time, the net assets of Grey had a carrying value of $225,000.

Required:

Calculate the adjustment required within equity as a result of this transaction.

Example 2 answer

At the date of the step acquisition, the NCI equity interest in Grey was:

	$
NCI at acquisition at fair value	100,000
NCI% × post acquisition reserves (40% × (225,000 – 200,000))	10,000
	110,000

As a result of the step acquisition, the NCI holding is reduced by 10% of 40% i.e. a quarter. Therefore, the difference to equity can be calculated as:

	$
Decrease in NCI (10/40 × 110,000)	27,500
Cash paid	(30,000)
Difference to other components of equity	(2,500)

To explain why the difference to equity is a decrease, it is possible to think of the above as Earl buying net assets valued at $27,500 for $30,000 and thus suffering a "loss" on the transaction. However, this is not strictly a loss as it arises on a transaction between owners.

The amount of $27,500 would be deducted from the carrying value of the NCI reserve.

An alternative way to achieve the answer would be to produce the following journal entry:

	$
Cr Cash	30,000
Dr NCI (10/40 × 110,000)	27,500
Dr Other components of equity – balance	2,500

Test your understanding 3 (OTQ style)

Gordon has owned 80% of Mandy for many years. It has just acquired a further 10% of Mandy's shares for $50,000.

At acquisition the fair value of the NCI in Mandy was $100,000. The net assets of Mandy at acquisition were $300,000 and are $400,000 at the date of acquisition of the additional shares.

It is group policy to value the NCI at fair value at the date of acquisition.

Required:

Calculate the difference that will be taken to other components of equity on the acquisition of the additional shares in Mandy. Clearly state whether this will be a debit or credit entry to the consolidated reserves of Gordon.

Test your understanding 4 (OTQ style)

Gordon has owned 80% of Mandy for many years. It has just acquired a further 15% of Mandy's shares for $95,000.

At acquisition the fair value of the NCI in Mandy was $100,000. The net assets of Mandy at acquisition were $300,000 and are $400,000 at the date of acquisition of the additional shares.

It is group policy to value the NCI at fair value at the date of acquisition.

Required:

Complete the following journal entry that would record the purchase of the additional shares in the consolidated financial statements of the Gordon Group.

Dr   Non-controlling interest $

Cr   Cash $

__(*) Other components of equity $

(*) Select from: Dr; Cr

Test your understanding 5 (integration question)

Statements of financial position as at 31 December 20X2:

	ZX $000	CV $000
Non-current assets		
Property, plant and equipment	20,250	11,000
Investment in CV (held at cost)	11,750	–
	32,000	11,000
Current assets	16,000	5,000
Total assets	48,000	16,000
Equity and liabilities		
Share capital ($1 shares)	5,000	1,000
Retained earnings	28,200	10,200
Total equity	33,200	11,200
Total liabilities	14,800	4,800
Total equity and liabilities	48,000	16,000

Additional information

ZX acquired 60% of the 1 million $1 equity shares of CV on 1 January 20X1 for $8,750,000 when CV's retained earnings were $9,280,000. The group policy is to measure non-controlling interest at the date of acquisition at its proportionate share of the fair value of the net assets.

ZX assessed the goodwill on the acquisition of CV to be impaired by 10% of its initial carrying amount on 31 December 20X1 and charged this in arriving at the consolidated profit for that year.

ZX acquired an additional 20% of CV's equity share capital on 31 December 20X2 for $3,000,000.

Required:

Prepare the consolidated statement of financial position for the ZX Group as at 31 December 20X2.

6 Disposal scenarios

During the year, the parent may sell some or all of its shares in the subsidiary.

There are two possible scenarios:

(1) Control to non-control

The parent may have sold:

- its entire shareholding in subsidiary
- part of its shareholding, leaving a residual holding between 20% and 50%, i.e. an associate
- part of its shareholding, leaving a residual holding of less than 20%, i.e. a financial asset.

In all three of these situations the parent no longer has a controlling interest in the entity and therefore must recognise a disposal of a subsidiary.

(2) Control to control

The parent disposes of part of its shareholding, leaving a controlling interest after the sale. This situation is the reverse of the control to control acquisitions that we considered earlier in the chapter. There is no change in the status of the investment, it should continue to be recognised as a subsidiary.

However the balance of ownership has changed, with the parent selling part of its share to the non-controlling interest. This is reflected within group equity.

The basic principles are summarised below.

	Control lost	Control retained
Consolidated statement of comprehensive income (CSCI) gain or loss	Gain or loss to the group is calculated and included in the group profit for the year.	No gain or loss is recorded.
CSCI consolidation	Subsidiary's income and expenses will be consolidated up to the date of disposal i.e. they will be time apportioned in the case of a mid year disposal.	Subsidiary's income and expenses will be consolidated for the year.
Consolidated statement of financial position (CSFP) consolidation	Subsidiary's assets and liabilities are no longer added across.	Subsidiary's assets and liabilities are still added across at year end.
Goodwill	Goodwill is eliminated.	Goodwill remains the same.
NCI	NCI is eliminated.	NCI is increased to reflect the higher percentage of the subsidiary not owned by the parent entity.

7 Control to non-control

When **control is lost** (i.e. the subsidiary is completely disposed of or becomes an associate or investment), the group:

- Recognises:
    - the consideration received
    - any investment retained in the former subsidiary at fair value at the date of disposal

- Derecognises:
    - the assets and liabilities of the subsidiary at the date of disposal
    - the goodwill in the subsidiary at the date of disposal
    - the non-controlling interest at the date of disposal

- Any difference between these amounts is recognised as an exceptional gain or loss on disposal in the consolidated statement of profit or loss.

Gain/loss on disposal of subsidiary

	$	$
Proceeds		X
Fair value of retained interest		X
		—
		X
Less: carrying value of subsidiary disposed of:		
Net assets of subsidiary at disposal date	X	
Goodwill at disposal date	X	
Less: NCI at disposal date	(X)	
	—	
		(X)
		—
Gain/loss to the group		X
		—

The gain to the group is presented in the consolidated statement of profit or loss after profit from operations.

Disposal in parent's accounts

The gain on disposal in the parent's financial statements is calculated as follows:

	$
Sale proceeds	X
Carrying amount (usually cost) of shares sold	(X)
	—
	X
Tax – at given rate	(X)
	—
Net gain to parent	X
	—

The tax arising as a result of the disposal is always calculated based on the gain in the parent's books. This is because the parent and subsidiary are distinct separate legal entities – the group does not legally exist. Tax can only be calculated in relation to a legal entity.

However, the link to the group accounts is that the tax arising on the gain forms part of the parent's tax charge and so forms part of the group's tax charge. The group's tax charge is simply arrived at by adding together the parent and subsidiary's tax charge, like all other expenses.

Example 3

Rock acquired a 70% investment in Dog for $2,000 two years ago. It is group policy to measure non-controlling interests at fair value at the date of acquisition. The fair value of the non-controlling interest at the date of acquisition was $800 and the fair value of Dog's net assets was $1,900. The goodwill has not been impaired.

Rock has made a disposal of shares in Dog. The net assets of Dog recorded in the consolidated financial statements at the date of disposal were $2,400.

Rock pays tax at 30%.

Required:

(a) Rock has disposed of all of its shares in Dog for sale proceeds of $3,000. Calculate the profit/loss on disposal that would be recorded in:

(1) Rock's individual statement of profit or loss (including the tax charge)

(2) the Rock group's consolidated statement of profit or loss (including the tax charge)

(b) Now assume that Rock disposed of half of its shares in Dog for $1,500 and that the remaining holding had a fair value of $1,300 at the date of disposal.

(1) Calculate the profit/loss on disposal that would be recorded in the consolidated statement of profit or loss (ignoring any tax effect).

(2) Explain how the residual holding would subsequently be accounted for in the consolidated statement of financial position of the Rock group.

Example 3 answer

(a) Disposal of all shares

(1) **Gain in Rock's individual statement of profit or loss**

	$
Sale proceeds	3,000
Cost of shares sold	(2,000)
	————
Gain on disposal	1,000
Tax at 30%	(300)
	————
Impact on profit for the year	700
	————

(2) **Gain in consolidated statement of profit or loss**

	$	$
Sale proceeds		3,000
Less: carrying value of subsidiary at disposal date		
Net assets at disposal	2,400	
Goodwill at disposal (W1)	900	
Less: NCI at disposal (W2)	(950)	
	————	
		(2,350)
		————
		650
Tax on gain as per Rock (part a)		(300)
		————
Impact on consolidated profit for year		350
		————

(W1) **Goodwill**

	$
Fair value of P's investment	2,000
Fair value of NCI at acquisition	800
Fair value of sub's net assets at acquisition	(1,900)
	————
Goodwill at acquisition/ disposal	900
	————

(W2) **NCI at disposal date**

	$
NCI at acquisition	800
NCI% × post acquisition reserves (30% × (2,400 – 1,900))	150
	950

(b) Disposal of half of shares

    (1) **Gain in consolidated statement of profit or loss**

	$	$
Sale proceeds		1,500
Fair value of remaining holding		1,300
Less: carrying value of subsidiary at disposal date		
Net assets at disposal	2,400	
Goodwill at disposal (W1)	900	
Less: NCI at disposal (W2)	(950)	
		(2,350)
		450

    (2) The remaining holding of 35% would indicate that Rock has significant influence over Dog and therefore should be recognised as an associate. The associate is initially recognised at its fair value of $1,300 and is then accounted for using the equity method, with 35% of subsequent movements on reserves being added to the carrying value.

Subsequent treatment of any investment retained

The remaining investment is re-measured to fair value at the date of disposal and the subsequent measurement will then depend on the status of the investment.

Remaining investment an associate

The equity method would be used to subsequently account for this investment. The fair value would become the deemed cost of the associate and the group share of any subsequent movements on reserves would be added to this amount each period.

Remaining investment does not suggest significant influence (i.e. not an associate)

The investment would be recognised in accordance with IAS 39 *Financial Instruments: Recognition and Measurement*. It would subsequently be re-measured to fair value at each reporting date with the gains/losses recognised in:

- profit or loss – if the investment was classified as fair value through profit or loss

- other comprehensive income – if the investment was classified as available for sale

Test your understanding 6 (integration question)

Hague has held a 60% investment in Maude for several years, using the fair value method to value the non-controlling interest. Half of the goodwill has been impaired. The group's year end is 31 December 20X5. A disposal of this investment has been made on 31 October 20X5. Details are:

	$
Cost of investment	6,000
Maude – Fair value of net assets at acquisition	2,000
Maude – Fair value of NCI at acquisition	1,000
Maude – Net assets at disposal	3,000
Maude – Fair value of a 30% investment at disposal	5,000
Maude – Profit for the year ended 31 December 20X5	2,200

Required:

(a) Assuming a full disposal of the holding and proceeds of $10,000, calculate the profit/loss arising:

    (i)   in Hague's individual accounts

    (ii) in the consolidated accounts.

Tax is 25%.

(b) Assuming a disposal of half the holding and proceeds of $5,000:

    (i)   calculate the profit/loss arising in the consolidated accounts

    (ii) explain how the residual holding will be accounted for and calculate the figures for inclusion in Hague's consolidated statement of comprehensive income for the year ended 31 December 20X5 and consolidated statement of financial position at 31 December 20X5.

Ignore any tax impacts.

Test your understanding 7 (integration question)

The statements of profit or loss for the year ended 31 December 20X9 are as follows:

Statements of profit or loss

	Kathmandu	Nepal
	$	$
Revenue	553,000	450,000
Operating costs	(450,000)	(400,000)
Profit from operations	103,000	50,000
Investment income	8,000	–
Profit before tax	111,000	50,000
Tax	(40,000)	(14,000)
Profit for the year	71,000	36,000

Additional information

- On 1 January 20X5 Kathmandu acquired 75% of the shares of Nepal for $100,000 when the fair value of Nepal's net assets was $90,000. At that date, the fair value of the non-controlling interest holding in Nepal was $35,000. It is group policy to measure the NCI at fair value at the date of acquisition.

- The carrying value of the net assets of Nepal included in the consolidated financial statements at 1 January 20X9 was $130,000.

- Nepal paid a dividend of $10,000 on 31 March 20X9.

- Goodwill has not been impaired.

- On 1 July 20X9 Kathmandu sold 40% of the total shares in Nepal for $120,000. The disposal has not been recorded in Kathmandu's statement of profit or loss. The residual holding of 35% has a fair value of $95,000 and leaves the Kathmandu group with significant influence.

Required:

Prepare the consolidated statement of profit or loss of the Kathmandu group for the year ended 31 December 20X9.

8 Control to control disposal

If there is a sale of shares but the parent still retains control then, from the group perspective, there is simply a transaction between owners with the parent's share decreasing and the NCI's share increasing.

For example if the parent holds 80% of the shares in a subsidiary and sells 5%, the relationship remains one of a parent and subsidiary. The subsidiary will continue to be consolidated in the group accounts in the normal way, but the NCI has risen from 20% to 25%.

Where there is such an increase in the non-controlling interest:

- No gain or loss on disposal is calculated
- No adjustment is made to the carrying value of goodwill
- The difference between the proceeds received and change in the non-controlling interest is accounted for in other components of equity as follows:

	$
Cash proceeds received	X
Transfer to NCI (increase in NCI)	(X)
Difference to other components of equity	X/(X)

The transfer to NCI will represent the share of the net assets (always) and goodwill (fair value method only) of the subsidiary at the date of disposal which the parent has effectively sold to the NCI.

The journal entry to record the disposal is:

Dr Cash

Cr NCI

Dr/Cr Other components of equity

Consolidated statement of comprehensive income

- Consolidate the subsidiary's results for the whole year.

- Calculate the non-controlling interest relating to the periods before and after the disposal separately and then add together.

  For example, if the shares are sold on 1 November and year end is 31 December:

  $(10/12 \times \text{profit} \times 20\%) + (2/12 \times \text{profit} \times 25\%)$

Consolidated statement of financial position

- Consolidate as normal, with the increase in non-controlling interest reflected in the NCI reserve

- Take the difference between proceeds and the transfer to the NCI to other components of equity as previously discussed.

Example 5

Until 30 September 20X7, Juno held 90% of Hera. On that date it sold 15% for $100,000. At the date of the sale, the net assets of Hera were $650,000 and the goodwill was $150,000. It is group policy to measure the NCI at fair value at the date of acquisition.

Required:

(a) Demonstrate how the disposal transaction should be accounted for in the Juno Group financial statements.

(b) Demonstrate how this would differ if group policy was to measure NCI at the proportion of net assets instead.

Example 5 answer

(a)

	$
Dr Cash	100,000
Cr Non-controlling interest (15% × (650,000 + 150,000))	120,000
Dr Other components of equity (ß)	20,000

Alternatively:

	$
Cash proceeds received	100,000
Transfer to NCI (15% × (650,000 + 150,000))	(120,000)
Difference to other components of equity	(20,000)

To explain why the difference to equity is a decrease, it is possible to think of the above as Juno selling net assets valued at $120,000 for only $100,000 and thus they have suffered a "loss" on the transaction.

(b)

	$
Dr Cash	100,000
Cr Non-controlling interest (15% × 650,000)	97,500
Cr Other components of equity (ß)	2,500

Alternatively:

	$
Cash proceeds received	100,000
Transfer to NCI (15% × 650,000)	(97,500)
Difference to other components of equity	2,500

Test your understanding 8 (OTQ style)

David has owned 90% of Goliath for many years. It has just sold 25% of Goliath's share capital for $100,000.

It is group policy to measure NCI at fair value at the date of acquisition and the fair value of the NCI in Goliath at this date was $35,000.

Goliath's net assets were $200,000 at acquisition and are $350,000 at the date of disposal.

Goodwill arising on the acquisition of Goliath was $175,000 and there has been no impairment to date.

Required:

Which one of the following statements is true in respect of the disposal of the shares in Goliath.

A A gain on disposal should be recognised in the statement of profit or loss at the date of disposal.

B There will be a credit to other components of equity of $31,250 at the date of disposal.

C The non-controlling interest is credited with $131,250 at the date of disposal.

D The remaining holding is re-measured to fair value at the date of disposal of the shares.

Test your understanding 9 (further OTQs)

(1) Snooker purchased 80% of the shares in Billiards a number of years ago. The consideration paid was $100,000 and the net assets of Billiards had a fair value of $62,500 at the date of acquisition. It is group policy to measure NCI at fair value at acquisition and the fair value of the NCI in Billiards at this date was $22,500. Goodwill has not suffered any impairment since acquisition.

On 1 August 20X9, Snooker disposed of half of its holding in Billiards for $90,000. The remaining holding of 40% is considered to have a fair value of $90,000 on 1 August 20X9 and the carrying value of Billiards' net assets in the consolidated financial statements of Snooker at this date was $110,000.

Calculate the profit or loss on disposal that would be recognised in the Snooker group consolidated statement of profit or loss for the year ended 31 August 20X9 as a result of the sale of shares by Snooker.

(2) Pepsi acquired 80% of Sprite's 200,000 $1 equity share capital on 1 January 20X2 for $300,000 when Sprite's retained earnings were $25,000. It is group policy to measure NCI at acquisition at fair value and the fair value of the NCI in Sprite on 1 January 20X2 was $65,000. The fair value of Sprite's net assets was considered to be equal to book value.

On 31 December 20X4, when the retained earnings of Sprite were $100,000, Pepsi purchased an additional 8% of Sprite's equity shares for $26,000.

Prepare the journal entry required to record the purchase of shares on 31 December 20X4 in the consolidated financial statements of the Pepsi group.

(3) On 1 October 20X3, Howard acquired 14m of the 20m $1 equity shares of Sylvia for $45 million in cash. At the date of acquisition the fair value of Sylvia's net assets was $53 million and the fair value of the NCI was $17.4 million. It is group policy to measure the NCI at fair value at the date of acquisition.

On 30 September 20X5 Howard sold 2m of the shares in Sylvia for $10m, when the carrying value of the net assets of Sylvia in the consolidated financial statements of the Howard group were $63 million. Goodwill has not been impaired.

Calculate the adjustment that should be recorded in group reserves as a result of the sale of shares on 30 September 20X5. (Clearly state whether the adjustment would be a debit or credit and state your answer in $s.)

(4) William acquired 40% of the 100,000 $1 equity shares in Mary on 1 September 20X0 for $150,000. On 1 September 20X5 William acquired a further 30% of the equity shares in Mary for $260,000, when the fair value of the original 40% holding was $285,000.

The reserves of Mary were $325,000 on 1 September 20X0 and $575,000 on 1 September 20X5.

It is group policy to measure the NCI at the proportion of the fair value of the net assets at the date of acquisition. The fair value of Mary's net assets was deemed to equate to book value.

Calculate goodwill arising on the acquisition of the controlling interest in Mary on 1 September 20X5 (state your answer in $).

9 Chapter summary

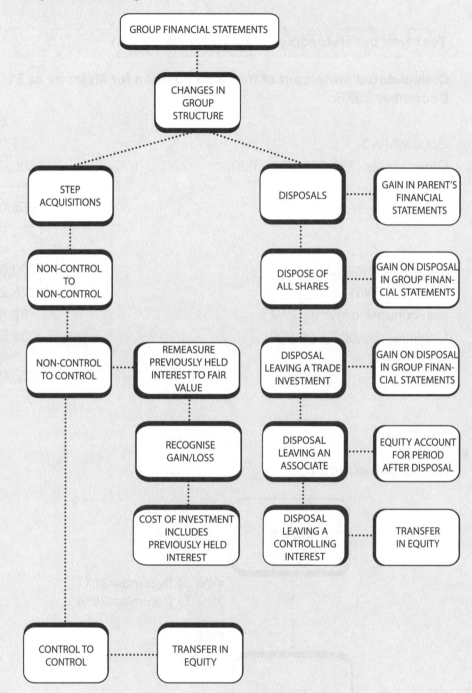

Test your understanding answers

Test your understanding 1 (integration question)

Consolidated statement of financial position for Major as at 31 December 20X6

	$
Goodwill (W3)	55,000
Other assets (350,000 + 250,000)	600,000
	655,000
Equity share capital	200,000
Reserves (W5)	278,200
Non-controlling interest (W4)	88,800
Liabilities (60,000 + 28,000)	88,000
	655,000

Workings

(W1) Group structure

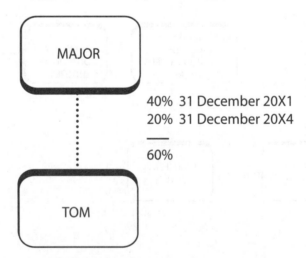

Therefore, Tom becomes a subsidiary of Major from December 20X4.

The investment will need to be remeasured to fair value

Dr Investment (105,000 – 90,000)	15,000
Cr Profit (and therefore credit to W5 retained earnings)	15,000

(W2) Net assets

	At Acquisition 20X4	At Reporting date
	$	$
Share capital	100,000	100,000
Retained reserves	100,000	122,000
	200,000	222,000

Post acquisition profits = $22,000

(W3) Goodwill

	$
Fair value of P's investment	
Fair value of previously held interest	105,000
Fair value of consideration for additional interest	70,000
	175,000
NCI at proportion of net assets (40% × 200,000 (W2))	80,000
Fair value of sub's net assets at acquisition (W2)	(200,000)
Goodwill at acquisition/reporting date	55,000

(W4) Non-controlling interest

	$
NCI at acquisition (W3)	80,000
NCI% × post acquisition reserves (40% × 22,000 (W2))	8,800
	88,800

(W5) Group Reserves

	$
Major	250,000
Gain on re-measurement to fair value of original investment (W1)	15,000
Tom (60% × $22,000 (W2))	13,200
	278,200

Test your understanding 2 (integration question)

Consolidated statement of financial position for Heat Group as at 30 June 20X5

	$
Goodwill (W3)	5,000
Other assets (358,000 + 225,000)	583,000
	———
	588,000
	———
Equity share capital	250,000
Reserves (W5)	215,500
Non-controlling interest (W4)	52,500
Liabilities (50,000 + 20,000)	70,000
	———
	588,000
	———

Workings

(W1) Group structure

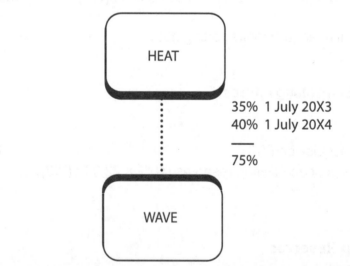

HEAT

35% 1 July 20X3
40% 1 July 20X4
———
75%

WAVE

Therefore, Wave becomes a subsidiary of Heat from 1 July 20X4.

The investment will need to be remeasured to fair value:

Dr Investment (70,000 – 62,000)	8,000
Cr Profit (and therefore to W5 retained earnings)	8,000

(W2) **Net assets**

	At Acquisition 20X4	At Reporting date
	$	$
Share capital	150,000	150,000
Retained earnings	45,000	55,000
	195,000	205,000

Post acquisition profits = $10,000

(W3) **Goodwill**

	$
Fair value of P's investment	
Fair value of previously held interest	70,000
Fair value of consideration for additional interest	80,000
	150,000
NCI at fair value	50,000
Fair value of sub's net assets at acquisition (W2)	(195,000)
Goodwill at acquisition/ reporting date	5,000

(W4) **Non-controlling interest**

	$
NCI at acquisition (W3)	50,000
NCI% × post acquisition reserves (25% × 10,000 (W2))	2,500
	52,500

(W5) **Retained earnings**

	$
Heat	200,000
Gain on re-measurement of investment to fair value (W1)	8,000
Wave (75% × $10,000 (W2))	7,500
	215,500

Test your understanding 3 (OTQ style)

The consolidated other components of equity will increase by $10,000

At the date of the purchase of additional shares, the NCI's share of equity is:

	$
NCI holding at acquisition at fair value	100,000
NCI% x post acquisition reserves (20% × (400,000 – 300,000))	20,000
	120,000

Adjustment to other components of equity

	$
Decrease in NCI (10/20 × $120,000)	60,000
Cash paid	(50,000)
Difference to other components of equity – credit	10,000

The journal to record the control to control acquisition is

Dr NCI 60,000

Cr Cash 50,000

Cr Other components of equity 10,000

Test your understanding 4 (OTQ style)

Journal entry to record purchase of additional shares:

Dr NCI (15/20 × 120,000 (W))	$90,000
Cr Cash	$95,000
Dr Equity – other components (bal fig)	$5,000

Working

At the date of the purchase of additional shares, the NCI's share of equity is:

	$
NCI holding at acquisition at fair value	100,000
NCI% × post acquisition reserves (20% × (400,000 – 300,000))	20,000
	————
	120,000
	————

Test your understanding 5 (integration question)

Consolidated statement of financial position for the ZX Group as at 31 December 20X2

	$000
ASSETS	
Non-current assets	
Property, plant and equipment (20,250 + 11,000)	31,250
Goodwill (W3)	2,324
	————
	33,574
Current assets (16,000 + 5,000)	21,000
	————
Total assets	54,574
	————

EQUITY AND LIABILITIES
Equity attributable to owners of the parent

Share capital ($1 shares)	5,000
Reserves (W5)	27,734
	32,734
Non-controlling interest (W4)	2,240
	34,974
Total equity	34,974
Total liabilities (14,800 + 4,800)	19,600
Total equity and liabilities	54,574

Workings

(W1) Group structure

```
                                                      ZX

                            1.1.X1   60%              |
                        31.12.X2     20%              |
                                   ─────              |
                 At reporting date  80%              |
                                                      CV
```

(W2) Net assets of subsidiary

	Acquisition date	Reporting date
	$000	$000
Share capital	1,000	1,000
Retained earnings	9,280	10,200
	10,280	11,200

920
Post acquisition profits

(W3) **Goodwill**

	$000
Consideration paid by parent	8,750
NCI at proportion of net assets (40% × 10,280 (W2))	4,112
Fair value of net assets at acquisition (W2)	(10,280)
Goodwill at acquisition	2,582
Impairment 10% in 20X1	(258)
Goodwill at 31 December 20X2	2,324

(W4) **Non-controlling interests**

	$000
NCI at acquisition (W3)	4,112
NCI share of post acquisition reserves (40% × 920 (W2))	368
NCI at date of transfer of additional 20% to ZX	4,480
50% (20/40) transferred on 31 December 20X2	(2,240)
NCI at 31 December 20X2	2,240

(W5) **Group reserves**

	$000
ZX's reserves	28,200
CV: 60% × 920 (W2)	552
Impairment (W3)	(258)
Adjustment to parent's equity (W6)	(760)
	27,734

(W6) **Adjustment to parent's equity**

	$000
Consideration paid	(3,000)
Decrease in NCI (W4)	2,240
Difference to parent's equity (debit)	(760)

Test your understanding 6 (integration question)

(a)

   (i)   **Gain in Hague's individual accounts**

	$
Sale proceeds	10,000
Less cost of shares sold	(6,000)
Gain to parent	4,000
Tax at 25%	(1,000)
Post tax gain	3,000

(ii) **Gain in Hague Group accounts**

	$
Sale proceeds	10,000
Fair value of retained interest	–
Less carrying value of subsidiary disposed of:	
Net assets of subsidiary at disposal date	3,000
Goodwill at disposal date (W1)	2,500
Less: NCI at disposal (W2)	(400)
	(5,100)
Gain before tax	4,900
Tax on gain as per parent company – part (a)(i)	1,000

(W1) **Goodwill**

	$
Fair value of P's investment	6,000
NCI at fair value	1,000
Fair value of sub's net assets at acquisition	(2,000)
Goodwill at acquisition	5,000
Impairment (50% × 5,000)	(2,500)
Goodwill at disposal	2,500

(W2) **NCI at disposal date**

	$
NCI at acquisition (W1)	1,000
NCI% × post acquisition reserves (40% × (3,000 – 2,000))	400
NCI% × impairment (40% × 2,500)	(1,000)
	400

(b)

(i) Group profit or loss

		$
Sale proceeds		5,000
Fair value of retained interest		5,000
		10,000
Less carrying value of subsidiary disposed of:		
Net assets of subsidiary at disposal date	3,000	
Goodwill at disposal date (W1)	2,500	
Less: NCI at disposal (W2)	(400)	
		(5,100)
Gain		4,900

(ii) After the date of disposal, the residual holding will be equity accounted, with a single amount in the consolidated statement of profit or loss for the share of the post tax profits for the period after disposal and a single amount in the statement of financial position for the fair value at disposal date of the investment retained plus the share of post-acquisition retained profits.

Investment in associate for CSFP

	$
Cost (investment retained)	5,000
Share of post acquisition profits	110
30% × (2,200 × 2/12)	
	5,110

Share of profit of associate for CSCI

Share of profits for the year	
30% × (2,200 × 2/12)	110

Test your understanding 7 (integration question)

Consolidated statement of profit or loss for the year ended 31 December 20X9

	$
Revenue (553,000 + (6/12 × 450,000))	778,000
Operating costs (450,000 + (6/12 × 400,000))	(650,000)
Profit from operations	128,000
Investment income (8,000 – (75% × 10,000))	500
Gain on disposal (W5)	79,000
Income from associate (W7)	6,300
Profit before tax	213,800
Tax (40,000 + (6/12 × 14,000))	(47,000)
Profit for the year	166,800
Profit attributable to:	
Parent shareholders	162,300
NCI shareholders (W6)	4,500
	166,800

Workings

(W1) Group structure

Kathmandu

	1 Jan 20X5	75%
	1 July 20X9	(40%)
		35%

Nepal

(W2) Nepal net assets

	Acquisition	Disposal 1 July 20X9
	$	$
Net assets b/f		130,000
Profit to disposal (6/12 × 36,000)		18,000
Dividend (paid March)		(10,000)
	90,000	138,000

48,000
Post acquisition reserves

(W3) Goodwill

	$
Fair value of P's investment	100,000
NCI at fair value	35,000
Fair value of sub's net assets at acquisition (W2)	(90,000)
Goodwill at acquisition/ disposal	45,000

(W4) NCI

	$
NCI at acquisition (W3)	35,000
NCI% × post acquisition reserves (25% × 48,000 (W2))	12,000
NCI at disposal	47,000

(W5) Gain on disposal

	$	$
Proceeds		120,000
Fair value of remaining interest		95,000
Net assets at disposal	138,000	
Goodwill at disposal	45,000	
NCI at disposal	(47,000)	
		(136,000)
Gain on disposal		79,000

(W6) NCI share of profits for the year

	$
NCI% × sub's profit for year (25% × 6/12 × 36,000)	4,500

(W7) Income from associate

	$
P% × A's profit for the year (35% × 6/12 × 36,000)	6,300

Test your understanding 8 (OTQ style)

The correct statement is C.

A is incorrect. David retains a controlling interest and therefore no gain or loss on disposal is recorded within profit.

B is incorrect. Other components of equity would be **debited** with $31,250 (not credited).

	$
Cash received	100,000
Increase in NCI (25% × (350,000 + 175,000))	(131,250)
Difference to other components of equity – decrease => debit	(31,250)

D is incorrect. There is no change in the status of the investment and therefore no re-measurement is required.

Test your understanding 9 (further OTQs)

(1) Consolidated profit on disposal = $42,000

	$	$
Sale proceeds		90,000
Fair value of retained interest		90,000
Less carrying value of subsidiary disposed of:		
Net assets of subsidiary at disposal date	110,000	
Goodwill at disposal date (W1)	60,000	
Less: NCI at disposal (W2)	(32,000)	
		(138,000)
Consolidated profit on disposal		42,000

(W1) Goodwill

	$
Fair value of P's investment	100,000
NCI at fair value	22,500
Fair value of sub's net assets at acquisition	(62,500)
Goodwill at acquisition and disposal	60,000

(W2) NCI at disposal date

	$
NCI at acquisition	22,500
NCI% × post acquisition reserves 20% × (110,000 − 62,500)	9,500
	32,000

(2) **Journal entry to record transfer between owners:**

Dr NCI (see below)   **$32,000**

Cr Cash   **$26,000**

Cr Other components   **$6,000**
of equity (bal fig)

Decrease in NCI:

	$
NCI at acquisition at fair value	65,000
NCI% × post acquisition reserves (20% × (100,000 – 25,000))	15,000
	─────
Carrying value of NCI at 31 December 20X4	80,000
	─────
Decrease in NCI (80,000 × 8/20)	32,000
	─────

(3) **Adjustment = $2,760,000 increase**

	$000
Cash received	10,000
Increase in NCI (10% × (63,000 net assets + 9,400 goodwill))	(7,240)
	─────
Difference to other components of equity – credit	2,760
	─────

Dr Cash 10,000

Cr NCI 7,240

Cr Other components of equity 2,760

Goodwill:

	$000
Consideration paid	45,000
Fair value of NCI at acquisition	17,400
Less fair value of net assets at acquisition	(53,000)
	─────
Goodwill at acquisition	9,400
	─────

(4) **Goodwill = $72,500**

	$
Fair value of P's investment	
Fair value of previously held interest	285,000
Fair value of consideration for additional interest	260,000
	545,000
NCI at proportion of net assets (30% × 675,000)	202,500
Fair value of sub's net assets at acquisition (100,000 + 575,000)	(675,000)
	72,500

Consolidated statement of changes in equity

Chapter learning objectives

B1. Produce consolidated primary financial statements, incorporating accounting transactions and adjustments, in accordance with relevant international accounting standards, in an ethical manner.

(a) Produce:
  –   consolidated statement of changes in equity

including the adoption of both full consolidation and the principles of equity accounting, in accordance with the provisions of IAS 1, IAS 27, IAS 28, IFRS 3, IFRS 10 and IFRS 11.

B2. Demonstrate the impact on the preparation of the consolidated financial statements of certain complex group scenarios.

(a) Demonstrate the impact on the group financial statements of:
  (i)   acquiring additional shareholdings in the period
  (ii) disposing of all or part of a shareholding in the period

1 Session content

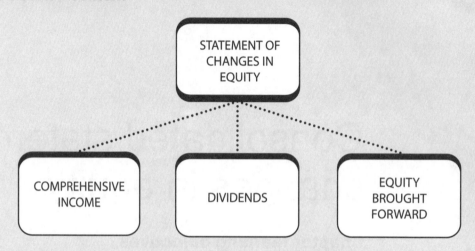

2 Consolidated statement of changes in equity – the basics

The statement of changes in equity explains the movement in the equity section of the statement of financial position from the previous reporting date to the current reporting date.

From a group perspective, the equity of the group belongs partly to the parent shareholders and partly to the NCI shareholders. A consolidated statement of changes in equity (CSOCIE) will therefore be made up of two columns reflecting:

* The changes in equity attributable to parent shareholders, made up of share capital, share premium, retained earnings and any other reserves

* The changes in equity attributable to NCI shareholders

NB. In practice the CSOCIE will have a total column. This is not included in the examples within this chapter.

The basic CSOCIE proforma is as follows:

	Parent shareholders	NCI shareholders
	$000	$000
Equity brought forward (b/f)	X	X
Comprehensive income	X	X
Dividends		
P's dividend	(X)	
NCI% × S's dividend		(X)
Equity carried forward (c/f)	X	X

Equity b/f

Parent shareholders

This is made up of the share capital, share premium, retained earnings and any other reserves as reported in last year's CSFP.

Share capital and share premium is that of the parent company only. The retained earnings and other reserves are consolidated and will need to be calculated using a working (the group reserves working).

Therefore, to calculate consolidated equity attributable to the parent shareholders b/f, the same format can be used as for group reserves but starting with the parent's equity rather than just the parent's reserves. By doing this, the parent's share capital and premium will also be included. Remember, we're calculating the position at the start of the year so only use the subsidiary's post acquisition reserves up to the b/f date.

NCI shareholders

This is the NCI figure that would have been reflected in last year's CSFP and can be calculated using the typical NCI working, but again remember to use only post acquisition reserves up to the b/f date.

Comprehensive income

These figures come from the foot of the consolidated statement of comprehensive income where the comprehensive income of the group is split between the parent and NCI shareholders. You will need to demonstrate your knowledge of this statement to calculate the consolidated figures for inclusion in the CSOCIE.

Dividends

The CSOCIE reflects the dividends which are being paid outside of the group, i.e. the parent company's dividend and the share of the subsidiary's dividend paid to non-controlling interest shareholders.

Note that the share of the subsidiary's dividend that has been paid to the parent company will have been eliminated in the group accounts as it is an intra-group transaction.

Equity c/f

Parent shareholders

Similar to the balances b/f, the equity c/f figures can be calculated using a working similar to group reserves but remembering to include the parent's share capital and share premium balances as well as their retained earnings / other reserves. In other words the working will start with the parent's equity c/f (rather than just its reserves).

When including the subsidiary, post acquisition reserves up to the c/f date (i.e. reporting date) will be used.

NCI shareholders

This is the NCI figure as calculated for a CSFP using the standard NCI reserve working.

Example 1

The following are the statements of changes in equity for Fulham and Putney for the year ended 31 March 20X7:

	Fulham $	Putney $
Equity b/f	132,500	60,000
Comprehensive income	85,500	21,000
Dividends	(10,000)	(6,000)
Equity c/f	208,000	75,000

Fulham acquired 80% of Putney's equity shares on 1 April 20X4 when Putney's net assets had a fair value of $35,000. No fair value adjustments were required at acquisition. It is Fulham's group policy to record NCIs at fair value at acquisition. The NCI holding in Putney had a fair value of $7,500 at the date of acquisition.

Required

Prepare the consolidated statement of changes in equity for the year ended 31 March 20X7.

Example 1 answer

Equity b/f and c/f attributable to the parent shareholders can be calculated using the format of the group reserves working but starting with the parent's equity rather than simply the parent's reserves. This ensures that other elements of equity such as share capital and share premium are also included:

	B/f	C/f (i.e. reporting date)
	$	$
Parent's equity	132,500	208,000
Sub: P% × post acquisition reserves		
(80% × (60,000 – 35,000))	20,000	
(80% × (75,000 – 35,000))		32,000
	152,500	240,000

The post-acquisition reserves is calculated by comparing the net assets at the start/end of the year (depending on whether we're calculating equity b/f or c/f) and their value at the date of acquisition. It is important to remember that net assets equals equity – so the net assets figures at the start and end of the year can be picked up from the individual entity SOCIEs provided in the question.

The NCI share of equity c/f is the figure that would be presented on the face of the consolidated statement of financial position. To calculate the b/f figure produce a similar working but based on opening rather than closing figures where necessary.

	B/f	C/f (i.e. reporting date)
	$	$
NCI at acqn at fair value	7,500	7,500
NCI% × post acquisition reserves		
(20% × (60,000 – 35,000))	5,000	
(20% × (75,000 – 35,000))		8,000
	12,500	15,500

The foot of the consolidated statement of comprehensive income should now be replicated in order to calculate the split of comprehensive income between the parent and NCI shareholders. It is important to remember that the total comprehensive income of the group will be 100% of the parent plus 100% of the subsidiary (subject to time apportionment) plus/minus any consolidation adjustments.

Since the subsidiary has paid a dividend, the intra-group element of this will have been eliminated on consolidation.

	$
P and S comprehensive income (85,500 + 21,000)	106,500
Less elimination of inter-co dividend (80% × 6,000)	(4,800)
	101,700
Total comprehensive income attributable to:	
Parent shareholders (balancing figure)	97,500
Non-controlling interests (20% × 21,000)	4,200
	101,700

Rather than calculating the comprehensive income attributable to P's shareholders as a balancing figure, you can alternatively lay your working out as follows:

	$
P comprehensive income	85,500
Less elimination of inter-co dividend (80% × 6,000)	(4,800)
P share of sub comprehensive income (80% × 21,000)	16,800
	97,500

This method may be slightly quicker. Calculate the NCI share of comprehensive income first, then add the remaining parent share of the subsidiary's comprehensive income to 100% of the parent's comprehensive income.

Note that in this case the NCI's share of comprehensive income is simply NCI% x S's Comprehensive Income because there are no consolidation adjustments that affect the subsidiary's comprehensive income. If such adjustments exist it may be necessary to produce a working - we'll see this shortly in example 2.

Finally, the dividend figures can be calculated on the face of the CSOCIE proforma:

	Parent shareholders $	NCI shareholders $
Equity b/f	152,500	12,500
Comprehensive income	97,500	4,200
Dividends		
P's dividend	(10,000)	
NCI% × S's dividend		(1,200)
Equity c/f	240,000	15,500

Test your understanding 1 (integration question)

The following are the statements of changes in equity for Islington and Southwark for the year ended 31 March 20X7:

	Islington $	Southwark $
Equity b/f	210,000	125,000
Comprehensive income	50,000	35,000
Dividends	(15,000)	(10,000)
Equity c/f	245,000	150,000

Islington acquired 75% of Southwark's equity shares on 1 April 20X4 when Southwark's net assets had a fair value of $80,000. No fair value adjustments were required at acquisition. It is Islington's group policy to record NCIs at fair value at acquisition. The NCI holding in Southwark had a fair value of $25,000 at the date of acquisition.

Required

Prepare the consolidated statement of changes in equity for the year ended 31 March 20X7.

Test your understanding 2 (integration question)

The following are the statements of changes in equity for Pitcher and Straw for the year ended 31 March 20X9:

	Pitcher	Straw
	$	$
Equity b/f	175,000	80,000
Comprehensive income	42,500	15,000
Dividends	(10,000)	(4,000)
Equity c/f	207,500	91,000

Pitcher acquired 80% of Straw's equity shares on 1 April 20X5 when Straw's net assets had a fair value of $55,000. No fair value adjustments were required at acquisition. It is Pitcher's group policy to record NCIs at their proportion of the subsidiary's net assets at acquisition.

Required

Prepare the consolidated statement of changes in equity for the year ended 31 March 20X9.

Example 2 – with consolidation adjustments

The following are the statements of changes in equity for Penguin and Smarties for the year ended 31 March 20X9:

	Penguin	Smarties
	$	$
Equity b/f	275,000	180,000
Comprehensive income	100,000	50,000
Dividends	(20,000)	(10,000)
Equity c/f	355,000	220,000

Penguin acquired 80% of Smarties' equity shares on 1 April 20X7 when Smarties' net assets had a carrying value of $125,000. At this time property had a fair value of $40,000 in excess of its carrying value. The property had a remaining life of 20 years.

At 31 March 20X9, Smarties held inventory which had been purchased from Penguin for $20,000. Penguin had sold these goods at a margin of 25%.

It is Penguin's group policy to record NCIs at their fair value at acquisition. The fair value of the NCI holding in Smarties at 1 April 20X7 was $30,000.

Required

Prepare the consolidated statement of changes in equity for the year ended 31 March 20X9.

Example 2 answer

Consolidated statement of changes in equity for the year ended 31 March 20X9

	Parent shareholders $	NCI shareholders $
Equity b/f (W4/W3)	317,400	40,600
Comprehensive income (W5)	125,400	9,600
Dividends		
P's dividend	(20,000)	
NCI% × S's dividend (20% × 10,000)		(2,000)
Equity c/f (W4/W3)	422,800	48,200

Workings

(W1) Group structure

Penguin

80% | 1 April 20X7
i.e. 2 years since acquisition

Smarties

(W2) Net assets of subsidiary

	Acq	B/f	C/f (i.e. reporting date)
	$	$	$
Net assets = equity	125,000	180,000	220,000
Fair value adjustment	40,000	40,000	40,000
Depreciation adjustment			
(40,000 × 1/20)		(2,000)	
(40,000 × 2/20)			(4,000)
	165,000	218,000	256,000
		Post acquisition reserves = 53,000	Post acquisition reserves = 91,000

(W3) NCI share of equity

	B/f	C/f (i.e. reporting date)
	$	$
NCI at acqn at fair value	30,000	30,000
NCI% × post acquisition reserves		
(20% × 53,000 (W2))	10,600	
(20% × 91,000 (W2))		18,200
	40,600	48,200

(W4) Parent's share of equity

	B/f	C/f (i.e. reporting date)
	$	$
Parent's equity	275,000	355,000
PUP (P is seller) (W7)		(5,000)
Sub: P% × post acquisition reserves		
(80% × 53,000 (W2))	42,400	
(80% × 91,000 (W2))		72,800
	317,400	422,800

(W5) Comprehensive income

There are some consolidation adjustments to deal with. Following the approach adopted when producing a consolidated statement of comprehensive income, firstly consider what the consolidated comprehensive income for the year would be in total, taking into account all of the consolidation adjustments:

	$
P and S comprehensive income (100,000 + 50,000)	150,000
Consolidation adjustments:	
Inter-company dividend (80% × 10,000)	(8,000)
PUP (W7)	(5,000)
FV depreciation (W8)	(2,000)
	135,000

Then, calculate the NCI share of comprehensive income and the parent shareholders' share will be the balancing figure:

Total comprehensive income attributable to:	
Parent shareholders (balancing figure)	125,400
Non-controlling interests (W6)	9,600
	135,000

(W6) NCI share of total comprehensive income

	$	$
Sub's total comprehensive income	50,000	
Depreciation adjustment (W8)	(2,000)	
	_____	
	48,000	
NCI share of total comprehensive income × 20%		9,600

(W7) PUP

Profit in inventory = 25% × $20,000 = $5,000

(W8) Depreciation adjustment

Fair value adjustment = $40,000

Depreciation adjustment = 1/20 × $40,000 = $2,000 per annum

Alternative workings for comprehensive income

An alternative approach to the comprehensive income workings would be to start with a calculation of the subsidiary's adjusted comprehensive income and then split this between parent and NCI share – adding the parent's share to 100% of the parent's adjusted comprehensive income.

It would make sense to calculate the NCI figure first – as this is based on the subsidiary's adjusted comprehensive income only – and then bring in the parent shareholders' figure.

So, workings 5 and 6 above would become:

(W5) NCI share of total comprehensive income

	$
Sub's total comprehensive income	50,000
Depreciation adjustment (W8)	(2,000)
	_____
	48,000
NCI share	× 20%
	_____
	9,600
	_____

(W6) Parent share of total comprehensive income

	$
Parent's comprehensive income	100,000
Less: inter-co dividend (80% × 10,000)	(8,000)
Less: PUP (parent seller)	(5,000)
Parent share of subsid (80% × 48,000)	38,400
	125,400

Care must be taken when dealing with consolidation adjustments. You need to consider carefully whether the adjustment should be made to the subsidiary's or the parent's comprehensive income.

Test your understanding 3 (integration question)

P bought 60% of S on 1 April 20X4 when S's net assets had a book value of $6,000.

The following are the statements of changes in equity for the year ended 31 March 20X7:

	P	S
	$	$
Equity b/f	50,600	22,670
Comprehensive income	6,000	3,500
Dividends	(2,500)	(500)
Equity c/f	54,100	25,670

The following information is available:

(1) On 1 April 20X4 a property in the books of S had a fair value of $24,000 in excess of its carrying value. At this time, the plant had a remaining life of 10 years.

(2) During the year S sold goods to P for $4,400. Of this amount $500 was included in inventory of P at the year end. S earns a 35% margin on its sales.

(3) Goodwill amounting to $800 arose on the acquisition of S. Goodwill was impaired by 10% of the original value in the year ended 31 March 20X6 and a further 10% of the book value in the year ended 31 March 20X7.

(4) It is P's group policy to value NCIs at fair value at acquisition. At 1 April 20X4, the fair value of the NCI holding in S was $2,500.

Required

Prepare the consolidated statement of changes in equity for the P group for the year ended 31 March 20X7.

3 Changes in group structure

Changes in group structure are reflected in the consolidated statement of changes in equity as shown in the proforma below.

The CSOCIE proforma is as follows:

	Parent shareholders	NCI shareholders
	$000	$000
Equity brought forward (b/f)	X	X
Comprehensive income	X	X
Dividends		
P's dividend	(X)	
NCI% × S's dividend		(X)
Acquisition/(disposal) of subsidiary		X/(X)
Transfer between owners	X/(X)	X/(X)
Equity carried forward (c/f)	X	X

Acquisition or disposal of subsidiary

This will affect the NCI column. Upon acquisition of a subsidiary, the NCI is credited initially with either:

- Fair value of the NCI at acquisition
- The NCI proportion of the fair value of the net assets at acquisition

and this credit would be reflected as an increase in the equity attributable to the NCI.

When a subsidiary is disposed of, the NCI at the date of disposal is derecognised and would therefore be reflected as a decrease in the equity attributable to the NCI. The consolidated profit or loss on disposal of the subsidiary would be reflected in the comprehensive income attributable to the equity shareholders of the parent.

Transfer between owners

As we've just seen in the previous chapter, if the parent either acquires more shares in a subsidiary or sells shares but retains control there is an adjustment to both the NCI and the parent's reserves. This therefore needs to be reflected in the statement of changes in equity.

Test your understanding 4 (integration question)

On 1 January 20X5 Thunder acquired 80% of the equity share capital of Lightning when the net assets of Lightning were $65,000. It acquired a further 10% of the equity share capital of Lightning on 30 September 20X6 for $10,000.

The following are the statements of changes in equity for the year ended 31 December 20X6:

	Thunder $	Lightning $
Equity b/f	156,000	80,000
Comprehensive income	24,000	13,800
Dividends	(10,000)	(1,000)
Equity c/f	170,000	92,800

(1) At the date of acquisition, the fair value of Lightning's net assets was deemed to equal their book value.

(2) Thunder's group policy is to record the NCI at fair value at acquisition. The fair value of the NCI holding in Lightning was $23,000 at acquisition.

(3) Both Thunder and Lightning paid their dividends on 30 June 20X6.

Required

Prepare the consolidated statement of changes in equity for the Thunder group for the year ended 31 December 20X6.

Papilla acquired 70% of the equity share capital of Satago three years ago when Satago's net assets were $650,000. Goodwill of $150,000 was recognised on acquisition and there has been no subsequent impairment.

The statements of changes in equity of Papilla and Satago for the year ended 31 March 20X7 are below.

Statements of changes in equity for the year ended 31 March 20X7

	Papilla	Satago
	$000	$000
Equity b/f	1,570	770
Comprehensive income	90	100
Dividends	(50)	(20)
Equity c/f	1,610	850

You are provided with the following additional information:

(1) Papilla's group policy is to value NCI at fair value at the date of acquisition. The NCI in Satago had a fair value of $250,000 when the shares were acquired.

(2) On 1 December 20X6, Papilla disposed of 10% of the equity share capital of Satago for $110,000.

(3) Both Papilla and Satago paid their dividends on 31 January 20X7.

Required

Prepare the consolidated statement of changes in equity for the Papilla group for the year ended 31 March 20X7.

Test your understanding 6 (integration question)

The Bennett group consists of a number subsidiaries, all wholly owned apart from Collins. On 30 June 20X7, Bennett disposed of 50% of the equity shares of Collins for $300,000.

Bennett had originally acquired 80% of the equity shares of Collins on 1 March 20X5 for $250,000 when the book value of Collins' net assets were $180,000. The book value was considered to equal fair value. The fair value of the NCI in Collins at acquisition was $70,000 and it was group policy to measure NCI at fair value at acquisition.

The remaining 30% investment had a fair value of $160,000 on 30 June 20X7.

Goodwill in Collins had not been impaired.

The statements of changes in equity for the year ended 31 December 20X7 for the Bennett group, excluding Collins, and for Collins were as follows:

Statements of changes in equity for the year ended 31 December 20X7

	Bennett group	Collins
	$000	$000
Equity b/f	400	250
Comprehensive income	145	80
Dividends	(50)	(30)
Equity c/f	495	300

All of the dividends were paid on 31 May 20X7.

Required

Prepare the consolidated statement of changes in equity of the Bennett group for the year ended 31 December 20X7.

Test your understanding 7 (OTQ style qns)

(1) WM owns 75% of the equity share capital of MY. The equity attributable to the non-controlling interest at 31 December 20X3 was $650,000. The total comprehensive income of MY for the year ended 31 December 20X4 was $300,000. Dividends were paid by both group entities during the year ended 31 December 20X4. The dividends paid by MY were $60,000.

Calculate the closing balance on equity attributable to the NCI that would be reflected in the consolidated statement of changes in equity at 31 December 20X4.

(2) There are a number of transactions/classes of transactions that you would expect to see on the face of the consolidated statement of changes in equity.

For each of the headings below, identify whether they would appear on the face of the consolidated statement of changes in equity and, if so, which column(s) would they affect (by placing a X in the relevant box).

Equity attributable to:	Parent	NCI
Comprehensive income for year		
Dividends paid to parent shareholders		
Dividends paid to NCI		
Adjustment re purchase of additional shares in a subsidiary		
Disposal of shares in subsidiary resulting in loss of control		
Disposal of shares in subsidiary but retaining control		

(3) HN owned 80% of the equity share capital of AE at 31 March 20X1. HN purchased a further 8% of AE's equity shares on 30 September 20X1 for $300,000.

The HN group has started to prepare its consolidated statement of changes in equity for the year ended 31 March 20X2 but is unsure of how to deal with the purchase of the additional shares.

The comprehensive income attributable to the non-controlling interest (NCI) is $135,000 for the first six months and $81,000 for the second six months of the year.

The draft statement, excluding the purchase of shares is:

Consolidated statement of changes in equity for the year ended 31 March 20X2

Attributable to:	Parent	NCI
	$000	$000
Equity b/f	2,500	450
Comprehensive income	1,250	216
Dividends paid on 1 Jan 20X2	(100)	(25)
Adjustment for additional purchase of AE shares		

Select the correct amounts (from the values provided below) to be included in respect of the additional purchase in the consolidated statement of changes in equity for the HN group for the year ended 31 March 20X2:

(a) **In equity attributable to parent shareholders column**

(b) **In equity attributable to non-controlling interests column**

Values to select from (in $000):

47   (47)   66   (66)   76   (76)   224   (224)   234   (234)   253   (253)

The information below relates to questions (4) and (5).

CR acquired 70% of the equity share capital of TM on 1 January 20X1 when TM's net assets had a book value of $3,125,000. At the date of acquisition, an adjustment of $625,000 was made to increase TM's plant and equipment to fair value. The plant and equipment had a remaining life of 10 years at this time. No other fair value adjustments were considered necessary.

It is group policy to measure the non-controlling interest at fair value at the date of acquisition and the fair value of the non-controlling interest in TM on 1 January 20X1 was $1,500,000.

Goodwill has been tested for impairment and none has arisen since acquisition.

The individual statements of changes in equity of CR and TM for the year ended 31 December 20X4 are:

	CR	TM
	$000	$000
Equity b/f	14,500	6,600
Comprehensive income	2,750	1,500
Dividends paid on 1 Jan 20X2	(200)	(100)
Equity c/f	17,050	8,000

(4) **Calculate the equity attributable to the parent shareholders at 1 January 20X4 (i.e. the brought forward figure in the consolidated statement of changes in equity for the year ended 31 December 20X4).**

(5) **Which one of the following statements is INCORRECT in respect of the consolidated statement of changes in equity for the year ended 31 December 20X4?**

    A   The statement will show the full dividend paid by the parent and the NCI share of the dividend paid by the subsidiary

    B   The closing balance in the parent shareholders' column will agree to the consolidated retained earnings balance in the consolidated statement of financial position

    C   The closing balance in the NCI column will agree to the NCI equity balance in the consolidated statement of financial position

    D   100% of the parent's comprehensive income is reflected in the comprehensive income for the year attributable to the parent shareholders and the subsidiary's comprehensive income is split between parent shareholders and NCI

4 Chapter summary

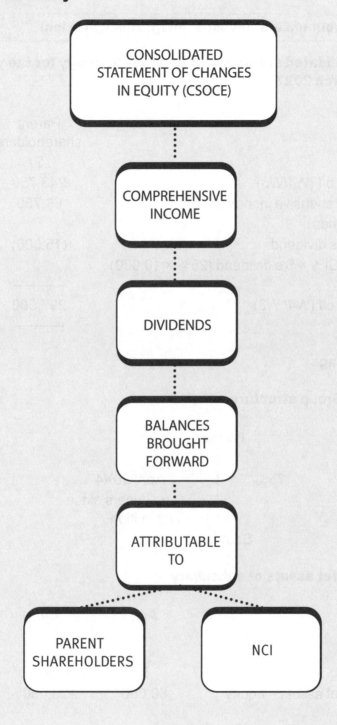

Test your understanding answers

Test your understanding 1 (integration question)

Consolidated statement of changes in equity for the year ended 31 March 20X7

	Parent shareholders $	NCI shareholders $
Equity b/f (W4/W3)	243,750	36,250
Comprehensive income (W5)	68,750	8,750
Dividends		
P's dividend	(15,000)	
NCI% × S's dividend (25% × 10,000)		(2,500)
Equity c/f (W4/ W3)	297,500	42,500

Workings

(W1) Group structure

Islington

75%   1 April 20X4
           i.e. 3 years since
           acquisition

Southwark

(W2) Net assets of subsidiary

	Acq $	B/f $	C/f (i.e. reporting date) $
Net assets = equity	80,000	125,000	150,000
		Post acquisition reserves = 45,000	Post acquisition reserves = 70,000

(W3) **NCI share of equity**

	B/f	C/f (i.e. reporting date)
	$	$
NCI at acqn at fair value	25,000	25,000
NCI% × post acquisition reserves		
(25% × 45,000 (W2))	11,250	
(25% × 70,000 (W2))		17,500
	――――	――――
	36,250	42,500
	――――	――――

(W4) **Parent's share of equity**

	B/f	C/f (i.e. reporting date)
	$	$
Parent's equity	210,000	245,000
Sub: P% × post acquisition reserves		
(75% × 45,000 (W2))	33,750	
(75% × 70,000 (W2))		52,500
	――――	――――
	243,750	297,500
	――――	――――

(W5) **Comprehensive income**

	$
P comprehensive income	50,000
Less elimination of inter-co dividend (75% × 10,000)	(7,500)
P share of sub comprehensive income (75% × 35,000)	26,250
	――――
	68,750
	――――
Non-controlling interests (25% × 35,000)	8,750
	――――

Tutorial note:

The comprehensive income working above can alternatively be set out as follows:

(W5) Comprehensive income

	$
P and S comprehensive income (50,000 + 35,000)	85,000
Less elimination of inter-co dividend (75% × 10,000)	(7,500)
	77,500
Total comprehensive income attributable to:	
Parent shareholders (balancing figure)	68,750
Non-controlling interests (25% × 35,000)	8,750
	77,500

Test your understanding 2 (integration question)

Consolidated statement of changes in equity for the year ended 31 March 20X9

	Parent shareholders	NCI shareholders
	$	$
Equity b/f (W4/W3)	195,000	16,000
Comprehensive income (W5)	51,300	3,000
Dividends		
P's dividend	(10,000)	
NCI% × S's dividend (20% × 4,000)		(800)
Equity c/f (W4/ W3)	236,300	18,200

Workings

(W1) Group structure

(W2) Net assets of subsidiary

	Acq	B/f	C/f (i.e. reporting date)
	$	$	$
Net assets = equity	55,000	80,000	91,000
		Post acquisition reserves = 25,000	Post acquisition reserves = 36,000

(W3) NCI share of equity

	B/f	C/f (i.e. reporting date)
	$	$
NCI at acqn at proportion of net assets (20% × 55,000)	11,000	11,000
NCI% × post acquisition reserves		
(20% × 25,000 (W2))	5,000	
(20% × 36,000 (W2))		7,200
	———	———
	16,000	18,200
	———	———

(W4) Parent's share of equity

	B/f	C/f (i.e. reporting date)
	$	$
Parent's equity	175,000	207,500
Sub: P% × post acquisition reserves		
(80% × 25,000 (W2))	20,000	
(80% × 36,000 (W2))		28,800
	195,000	236,300

(W5) Comprehensive income

	$
P comprehensive income	42,500
Less elimination of inter-co dividend (80% × 4,000)	(3,200)
P share of sub comprehensive income (80% × 15,000)	12,000
	51,300
Non-controlling interests (20% × 15,000)	3,000

Alternative W5 layout

(W5) Comprehensive income

	$
P and S comprehensive income (42,500 + 15,000)	57,500
Less elimination of inter-co dividend (80% × 4,000)	(3,200)
	54,300
Total comprehensive income attributable to:	
Parent shareholders (balancing figure)	51,300
Non-controlling interests (20% × 15,000)	3,000
	54,300

Test your understanding 3 (integration question)

Consolidated statement of changes in equity

	Parent shareholders $	NCI shareholders $
Equity b/f (W7/W8)	57,674	7,216
Comprehensive income (W6)	6,211.8	341.2
Dividends		
P's dividend	(2,500)	
NCI% × S's dividend (40% × 500)		(200)
Equity c/f (W7/W8)	61,385.8	7,357.2

Workings

(W1) Group structure

```
        P
        |
60%  |  1 April 20X4
        |  i.e. 3 years since acquisition
        S
```

(W2) Net assets of subsidiary

	Acq $	B/f $	C/f (i.e. reporting date) $
Net assets = equity	6,000	22,670	25,670
Fair value adjustment	24,000	24,000	24,000
Depreciation adjustment (W3)		(4,800)	(7,200)
PUP (sub is seller) (W4)			(175)
	30,000	41,870	42,295
		Post acquisition reserves = 11,870	Post acquisition reserves = 12,295

(W3) Depreciation adjustment

Fair value adjustment = $24,000

Depreciation adjustment = 1/10 × $24,000 = $2,400 per annum

Therefore, depreciation b/f = 2 × $2,400 = $4,800 and depreciation c/f = 3 × $2,400 = $7,200

(W4) PUP adjustment

Profit in inventory = 35% × $500 = $175

(W5) Goodwill and impairment

	$
Goodwill at acquisition	800
Impairment y/e 31 March 20X6 (10% × 800)	(80)
Goodwill at 31 March 20X6	720
Impairment y/e 31 March 20X7 (10% × 720)	(72)

(W6) Total comprehensive income

NCI share:	$	$
Sub's TCI for the year per S's SCI	3,500	
Depreciation adjustment (W3)	(2,400)	
PUP (sub is seller) (W4)	(175)	
Impairment (fair value method)	(72)	
Sub's adjusted TCI	853	
NCI share × 40%		341.2

Parent shareholders' share:	$
Parent TCI	6,000
Less inter-co dividend received (60% × 500)	(300)
Add share of Sub's adjusted TCI (60% × 853)	511.8
	6,211.8

(W7) Parent's share of equity

	B/f	C/f (i.e. reporting date)
	$	$
Parent's equity	50,600	54,100
Sub: P% × post acquisition reserves		
(60% × 11,870 (W2))	7,122	
(60% × 12,295 (W2))		7,377
Impairment loss: b/f (60% × 80) (W5)	(48)	
c/f (60% × (80 + 72) (W5))		(91.2)
	57,674	61,385.8

(W8) NCI share of equity

	B/f	C/f (i.e. reporting date)
	$	$
NCI at acqn at fair value	2,500	2,500
NCI% × post acquisition reserves		
(40% × 11,870 (W2))	4,748	
(40% × 12,295 (W2))		4,918
NCI% × impairment loss: b/f (40% × 80) (W5)	(32)	
c/f (40% × (80 + 72) (W5))		(60.8)
	7,216	7,357.2

Consolidated statement of changes in equity for the year ended 31 December 20X6

	Parent shareholders $	NCI shareholders $
Equity b/f (W4/W5)	168,000	26,000
Comprehensive income (W3/W2)	34,585	2,415
Dividends		
P's dividend	(10,000)	
NCI% × S's dividend (20% × 1,000)		(200)
Transfer between owners (W6)	3,935	(13,935)
Equity c/f (W8/W9)	196,520	14,280

Workings

(W1) Group structure

Thunder

80%　　1 January 20X5 (2 years ago)

+　　　30 September 20X6 (3 months ago)

10%

90%

Lightning

(W2) NCI share of comprehensive income

			$
Up to 30 September	13,800 × 9/12 × 20%		2,070
From 1 October	13,800 × 3/12 × 10%		345
			2,415

(W3) Parent share of comprehensive income

	$
Parent comprehensive income	24,000
Less inter-co dividend received	(800)
(80% × 1,000)	
Parent share of subsid comp income	11,385
(13,800 – 2,415 (W2))	
	———
	34,585
	———

(W4) Parent's share of equity b/f

	$
Parent's equity b/f	156,000
Sub: P% × post acquisition reserves	
(80% × (80,000 – 65,000))	12,000
	———
	168,000
	———

(W5) NCI share of equity b/f

	$
NCI at acqn at fair value	23,000
NCI% × post acquisition reserves	
(20% × (80,000 – 65,000))	3,000
	———
	26,000
	———

(W6) Transfer between owners

	$
NCI b/f (W5)	26,000
NCI share of comp income to 30 September (W2)	2,070
NCI dividend paid 30 June	(200)
	———
Carrying value of NCI prior to transfer	27,870
Proportion transferred to parent	× 10/20
	———
Decrease in NCI at date of transfer	13,935
Cash paid by parent	(10,000)
	———
Increase in equity attrib. to parent s/hrs	3,935
	———

(W7) Post-acquisition reserves of Lightning

	$
Net assets(= equity) b/f	80,000
Comprehensive income to 30 September (9/12 × 13,800)	10,350
Dividends paid 30 June	(1,000)
	———
Net assets at 30 September	89,350
Less net assets at acquisition	(65,000)
	———
Post-acquisition reserves to 30 September	24,350
	———
Post-acquisition reserves from 1 October to 31 December (3/12 × 13,800)	3,450
	———

(W8) Parent's share of equity c/f

	$
Parent's equity c/f	170,000
Sub: P% × post acquisition reserves (80% × 24,350 (W7))	19,480
Adjustment re purchase of additional 10% (W6)	3,935
(90% × 3,450 (W7))	3,105
	———
	196,520
	———

(W9) NCI share of equity c/f

	$
NCI at acqn at fair value	23,000
NCI% × post acquisition reserves	
(20% × 24,350 (W7))	4,870
Adjustment re purchase of additional 10% (W6)	(13,935)
NCI% × post acquisition reserves after purchase	345
(10% × 3,450 (W7))	
	14,280

Test your understanding 5 (integration question)

Consolidated statement of changes in equity for the year ended 31 March 20X7

	Parent shareholders $000	NCI shareholders $000
Equity b/f (W4/W5)	1,654	286
Comprehensive income (W3/W2)	145	33
Dividends		
P's dividend	(50)	
NCI% × S's dividend (40% × 20)		(8)
Transfer between owners (W6)	11	99
Equity c/f (W8/W9)	1,760	410

Workings

(W1) Group structure

Papilla

70%	3 years ago
− 10%	4 months ago
60%	

Satago

(W2) NCI share of comprehensive income

		$000
Up to 30 November	100 × 8/12 × 30%	20
From 1 December	100 × 4/12 × 40%	13
		33

(W3) Parent share of comprehensive income

		$000
Parent comprehensive income		90
Less inter-co dividend	(60% × 20)	(12)
P share of sub comp income	(100 – 33 (W2))	67
		145

(W4) Parent's share of equity b/f

	$000
Parent's equity b/f	1,570
Sub: P% × post acquisition reserves	
(70% × (770 – 650))	84
	1,654

(W5) NCI share of equity b/f

	$000
NCI at acqn at fair value	250
NCI% × post acquisition reserves	
(30% × (770 – 650))	36
	286

(W6) **Transfer between owners**

	$000
Net assets of Satago b/f	770
Comprehensive income to 30 November (8/12 × 100)	67
Net assets at 1 December 20X6	837
Goodwill	150
Net assets plus goodwill at date of transfer	987
	× 10%
Transferred to NCI	99
Cash received by parent	110
Increase in equity attrib. to parent s/hrs	11

(W7) **Post-acquisition reserves of Satago**

	$000
Net assets(= equity) b/f	770
Comprehensive income to 30 November (8/12 × 100)	67
Net assets at 30 September	837
Less net assets at acquisition	(650)
Post-acquisition reserves to 30 November	187
Post-acquisition reserves from 1 December to 31 March:	
Comprehensive income (4/12 × 100)	33
Dividends paid 31 January	(20)
	13

(W8) Parent's share of equity c/f

	$000
Parent's equity c/f	1,610
Sub: P% × post acquisition reserves	
(70% × 187 (W7))	131
Adjustment re sale of shares (W6)	11
(60% × 13 (W7))	8
	———
	1,760
	———

(W9) NCI share of equity c/f

	$000
NCI at acqn at fair value	250
NCI% × post acquisition reserves	
(30% × 187 (W7))	56
Adjustment re sale of shares (W6)	99
NCI % of post acquisition reserves after sale of shares (40% × 13 (W7))	5
	———
	410
	———

Test your understanding 6 (integration question)

Consolidated statement of changes in equity for the year ended 31 December 20X7

	Parent shareholders	NCI shareholders
	$000	$000
Equity b/f (W4/ W5)	456	84
Comprehensive income (W3/ W2)	311	8
Dividends		
P's dividend	(50)	
NCI% × S's dividend (20% × 30)		(6)
Disposal of subsidiary (W7)		(86)
	———	———
Equity c/f (W8)	717	–
	———	———

Workings

(W1) Group structure

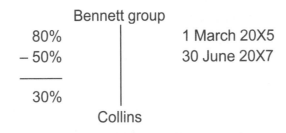

Bennett group

80%   1 March 20X5

– 50%   30 June 20X7

30%

Collins

(W2) NCI share of comprehensive income

		$000
Up to date of disposal	80 × 6/12 × 20%	8

(W3) Parent share of comprehensive income

	$000
Parent comprehensive income	145
Less inter-co divi (80% × 30)	(24)
P share of sub comp income ((80 × 6/12) – 8 (W2))	32
Group profit on disposal of subsidiary (W6)	146
Share of associate profit (80 × 6/12 × 30%)	12
	311

(W4) Parent's share of equity b/f

	$000
Parent's equity b/f	400
Sub: P% × post acquisition reserves	
(80% × (250 – 180))	56
	456

(W5) NCI share of equity b/f

	$000
NCI at acqn at fair value	70
NCI% × post acquisition reserves	
(20% × (250 − 180))	14
	84

(W6) Group profit on disposal of subsidiary

	$000	$000
Sale proceeds		300
Fair value of retained interest		160
Less carrying value of subsidiary disposed of:		
Net assets of subsidiary at disposal date		
(250 + (6/12 × 80) − 30)	260	
Goodwill at disposal date		
(250 + 70 − 180)	140	
Less: NCI at disposal (W7)	(86)	
		(314)
Consolidated profit on disposal		146

(W7) NCI at disposal

	$000
NCI at acqn at fair value	70
NCI% × post acquisition reserves	
(20% × (260 − 180))	16
	86

(W8) Parent's share of equity c/f

	$000
Parent's equity c/f	495
Sub: P% × post acquisition reserves	
(80% × (260 – 180))	64
Profit on disposal of subsidiary (W6)	146
Assoc: (30% × (300 – 260))	12
	———
	717
	———

Test your understanding 7 (OTQ style qns)

(1) **Closing balance on equity attributable to NCI at 31 December 20X4 = $710,000**

	$000
NCI equity b/f at 1 January 20X4	650
Comprehensive income (25% × 300)	75
Dividends paid (25% × 60)	(15)
	———
	710
	———

(2) **Equity attributable to:**

	Parent	NCI
Comprehensive income for year	X	X
Dividends paid to parent shareholders	X	
Dividends paid to NCI		X
Adjustment re purchase of additional shares in a subsidiary	X	X
Disposal of shares in subsidiary resulting in loss of control		X
Disposal of shares in subsidiary but retaining control	X	X

When there has been a change in percentage holdings in a subsidiary, this is reflected as a transfer between owners and there would be an adjustment in both parent and NCI equity.

When a disposal of shares results in a loss of control the subsidiary must be derecognised. The impact in the parent column (gain on disposal) is included within comprehensive income and would not therefore be shown as a separate heading in the consolidated statement of changes in equity. The deduction from NCI would however be reflected.

(3) **Solutions are:**

(a) **In equity attributable to parent shareholders column = $(66,000)**

(b) **In equity attributable to NCI column = $(234,000)**

Transfer between owners

	$000
NCI b/f	450
NCI share of comprehensive income to 30 September	135
	585
Proportion transferred to parent	× 8/20
Decrease in NCI at date of transfer	234
Cash paid by parent	(300)
Decrease in equity attributable to parent shareholders	(66)

(4) **Equity attributable to parent shareholders b/f = $16,801,250**

	$
Parent's equity b/f	14,500,000
Sub: P% × post acquisition reserves b/f	2,301,250
(70% × 3,287,500 (see below))	
	16,801,250

Net assets of subsidiary

	Acq $000	B/f $000
Net assets = equity	3,125	6,600
Fair value adjustment	625	625
Depreciation adjustment (625 × 3/10)		(187.5)
	3,750	7,037.5

Post acquisition reserves = 3,287.5

(5) **The incorrect statement is B.**

The closing balance in the parent shareholders column represents **equity** attributable to the parent shareholders'. This includes consolidated retained earnings but also the parent's share capital, share premium and the parent's share of any other reserves.

Consolidated statement of cash flows

Chapter learning objectives

B1. Produce consolidated primary financial statements, incorporating accounting transactions and adjustments, in accordance with relevant international accounting standards, in an ethical manner.

(a) Produce:
- – consolidated statement of cash flows

including the adoption of both full consolidation and the principles of equity accounting, in accordance with the provisions of IAS 1, IAS 27, IAS 28, IFRS 3, IFRS 10 and IFRS 11.

B2. Demonstrate the impact on the preparation of the consolidated financial statements of certain complex group scenarios.

(a) Demonstrate the impact on the group financial statements of:
- (i) acquiring additional shareholdings in the period
- (ii) disposing of all or part of a shareholding in the period

1 Session content

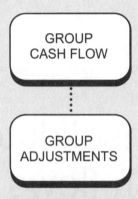

GROUP CASH FLOW

GROUP ADJUSTMENTS

- Acquisition/disposal of subsidiary
- Associates
- Non-controlling interests

2 Objective of statements of cash flows

- IAS 7 **Statement of cash flows** provides guidance on the preparation of a statement of cash flows.

- The objective of a statement of cash flows is to provide information on an entity's changes in cash and cash equivalents during the period.

- The statement of financial position and statement of comprehensive income (SCI) are prepared on an accruals basis and do not show how the business has generated and used cash in the accounting period.

- The SCI may show profits on an accruals basis even if the company is suffering severe cash flow problems.

- Statements of cash flows enable users of the financial statements to assess the **liquidity, solvency** and **financial adaptability** of a business.

Definitions:

- **Cash** consists of cash in hand and deposits repayable upon demand, less overdrafts. This includes cash held in a foreign currency.

- **Cash equivalents** are short-term, highly liquid investments that are readily convertible into known amounts of cash and are subject to an insignificant risk of changes in value.

- **Cash flows** are inflows and outflows of cash and cash equivalents.

3 Classification of cash flows

IAS 7 does not prescribe a specific format for the statement of cash flows, although it requires that cash flows are classified under three headings:

- cash flows from operating activities, defined as the entity's principal revenue earning activities and other activities that do not fall under the next two headings
- cash flows from investing activities, defined as the acquisition and disposal of long-term assets and other investments (excluding cash equivalents)
- cash flows from financing activities, defined as activities that change the size and composition of the entity's equity and borrowings

Classification of cash flows

Cash flows from operating activities

There are two methods of calculating the cash from operations.

- The **direct method** shows operating cash receipts and payments. This includes cash receipts from customers, cash payments to suppliers and cash payments to and on behalf of employees. The Examiner has indicated that the direct method will not be examined and is not considered further within this text.
- The **indirect method** starts with profit before tax and adjusts it for non-cash charges and credits, to reconcile it to the net cash flow from operating activities.

IAS 7 permits either method.

Under the **indirect method** adjustments are needed for a number of items, the most frequently occurring of which are:

- depreciation, amortisation and impairment
- profit or loss on disposal of non current assets
- change in inventory
- change in receivables
- change in payables

Cash flows from investing activities

Cash flows to appear under this heading include:

- cash paid for property, plant and equipment and other non-current assets
- cash received on the sale of property, plant and equipment and other non-current assets
- cash paid for investments in or loans to other entities (excluding movements on loans from financial institutions, which are shown under financing)
- cash received for the sale of investments or the repayment of loans to other entities (again excluding loans from financial institutions).

Cash flows from financing activities

Financing cash flows mainly comprise receipts or repayments of principal from or to external providers of finance.

Financing **cash inflows** include:

- receipts from issuing shares or other equity instruments
- receipts from issuing debentures, loan notes and bonds and from other long-term and short-term borrowings (other than overdrafts, which are normally included in cash and cash equivalents).

Financing **cash outflows** include:

- repayments of amounts borrowed (other than overdrafts)
- the capital element of finance lease rental payments
- payments to reacquire or redeem the entity's shares.

Interest and dividends

There are divergent and strongly held views about how interest and dividends cash flows should be classified. Some regard them as part of operating activities, because they are as much part of the day to day activities as receipts from customers, payments to suppliers and payments to staff. Others regard them as part of financing activities, the heading under which the instruments giving rise to the payments and receipts are classified. Still others believe they are part of investing activities, because this is what the long-term finance raised in this way is used for.

IAS 7 allows interest and dividends, whether received or paid, to be classified under any of the three headings, provided the classification is consistent from period to period.

The practice adopted in this workbook is to classify:

- interest received as a cash flow from investing activities
- interest paid as a cash flow from operating activities
- dividends received as a cash flow from investing activities
- dividends paid as a cash flow from financing activities.

4 Proforma statement of cash flows

Group statement of cash flows

	$	$
Cash flows from operating activities		
Group profit before tax	X	
Adjustments for:		
Finance costs	X	
Investment income	(X)	
Share of associate's profit	(X)	
Depreciation	X	
Amortisation	X	
Impairments	X	
Profit/loss on sale of property, plant and equipment	(X)/X	
	⎯⎯	
	X	
(Increase)/decrease in inventory	(X)/X	
(Increase)/decrease in receivables	(X)/X	
Increase/(decrease) in payables	X/(X)	
	⎯⎯	
Cash generated from operations	X	
Interest paid	(X)	
Tax paid	(X)	
	⎯⎯	
Net cash from operating activities		X
Cash flows from investing activities		
Sale proceeds on disposal of property, plant and equipment	X	
Purchases of property, plant and equipment	(X)	
Investment income received	X	
Dividends received from associate	X	
Acquisition/ sale of subsidiary, net of cash balances	(X)/X	
	⎯⎯	
Net cash used in investing activities		X

Cash flows from financing activities

Loans – issue/repayment	X/(X)
Share issues	X
Dividends paid to NCI	(X)
Dividends paid to parent shareholders	(X)

Net cash used in financing activities	X

Increase / decrease in cash and cash equivalents	X/(X)
Opening cash and cash equivalents	X

Closing cash and cash equivalents	X

5 Single entity statement of cash flows

Single entity statements of cash flows have already been assessed in F1.

In the F2 assessment, questions are more likely to focus on the group aspects of a consolidated statement of cash flows. However, this section contains a few revision exercises to remind you of the method first.

A typical question will ask you to calculate a cash-flow figure/adjustment that would be presented on the statement of cash flows. You may also be tested on which section of the statement a particular figure would appear under and therefore you should have good knowledge of the proforma statement itself (shown above).

A balancing figure approach is typically used to calculate a cash-flow figure/adjustment. By plotting the movements in the statement of financial position balance from the beginning to end of a period the cash-flow/adjustment is derived as the missing figure.

NB: In the exercises in this chapter, workings have been shown using both column format and T account format. It is important that you choose the method that works best for you – the one that helps you get to the right answer!

Test your understanding 1 (F1 revision)

Y's statement of profit or loss for the year shows the following:

	$000
Finance costs	(240)
Tax	(180)

Y's opening and closing statements of financial position show the following:

	Closing	Opening
	$000	$000
Accrued interest	130	80
Income tax payable	120	100
Deferred tax	100	50

Required:

(a) How much were finance costs paid in the year?

(b) How much tax was paid in the year?

Test your understanding 2 (F1 revision)

Z's opening and closing statements of financial position show the following:

	Closing	Opening
	$000	$000
Non-current assets (NBV)	250	100

During the year depreciation of $20,000 was charged and a revaluation surplus of $60,000 was recorded. Assets with a net book value of $15,000 were disposed and non-current assets acquired under finance leases totalled $30,000.

Required:

How much cash was spent on non-current assets in the year?

Test your understanding 3 (F1 revision)

Extracts from X's statements of financial position at the beginning and end of the year are as follows:

	Closing	Opening
	$000	$000
Inventory	150	240
Receivables	275	200
Payables	180	90

At the year end the following exchange differences were recorded upon re-translation of monetary items:

	$000
Receivables	35 Gain
Payables	18 Loss

Required:

Calculate the adjustments required in respect of movements in working capital that should be shown in the operating activities section of the statement of cash flows, clearly reflecting whether the adjustments should be positive or negative.

6 The consolidated statement of cash flows

In a consolidated statement of cash flows, there are further issues that you may be required to deal with:

- Dividends paid to non-controlling interests (financing cash outflow)
- Dividends received from the associate (investing cash inflow)
- Cash flows related to the acquisition or disposal of a subsidiary during the year (cash received/paid net of the sub's cash balance)
- If there has been an acquisition or disposal of a subsidiary during the year, the impact of it will need to be considered when using workings to calculate cash flows.

Dividends paid to non-controlling interests

- When a subsidiary has paid a dividend, only the share paid to the non-controlling interest is reflected in the consolidated financial statements (the share paid to the parent is eliminated as an intra-group transaction).

- The dividends paid to the non-controlling interests should be disclosed separately from the dividends paid to the parent shareholders in the statement of cash flows.

- To calculate the amount paid, reconcile the non-controlling interest in the statement of financial position from the opening to the closing balance.

Example 1

The following information has been extracted from the consolidated financial statements of WG for the years ended 31 December:

	20X7	20X6
	$000	$000
NCI in consolidated SFP	780	690
NCI's total comprehensive income in CSCI	120	230

Required:

What is the dividend paid to non-controlling interests in the year 20X7?

Example 1 answer

Steps:

(1) Set up a working (column or T account style).

(2) Insert the opening and closing balances and the NCI share of comprehensive income for the year.

(3) The balancing figure is the cash paid to the NCI.

Non-controlling interests

	$000
Bal b/f	690
Comprehensive income attributable to the NCI	120
	810
Dividends paid (balance)	(30)
	780
Bal c/f	780

or

Non-controlling interests

	$000		$000
Dividends paid (bal fig)	30	Balance b/f	690
Balance c/f	780	Share of TCI in year	120
	810		810

Watch out for an acquisition or disposal of a subsidiary in the year. This will affect the NCI and will need to be taken account of in the working, showing the NCI that has been acquired or disposed of in the period.

Note that, where the column format is produced, the result is the NCI column from the consolidated statement of changes in equity.

Information for TYUs 4 and 5

Extracts from Group A's consolidated financial statements for the year ended 31 December 20X1 are shown below.

Extract from consolidated statement of financial position as at 31 December:

	20X1	20X0
	$000	$000
Retained earnings	4,325	1,625
Non-controlling interests	580	440

Extract from consolidated statement of comprehensive income for year ended 31 December 20X1:

	$000
Profit attributable to:	
Equity shareholders of the parent	3,200
Non-controlling interest	300
	3,500
Total comprehensive income attributable to:	
Equity shareholders of the parent	3,800
Non-controlling interest	500
	4,300

Test your understanding 4 (OTQ style)

Required:

Using the information above, calculate the dividends paid to the non-controlling interest that would be reflected within cash flows from financing activities in the consolidated statement of cash flows of Group A for the year ended 31 December 20X1.

Test your understanding 5 (OTQ style)

Required:

Using the information above, calculate the dividends paid to the parent shareholders that would be reflected within cash flows from financing activities in the consolidated statement of cash flows of Group A for the year ended 31 December 20X1.

Dividends received from associates

- Associates generate cash flows into the group to the extent that dividends are received out of the profits of the associate.

- Such dividends received from associates should be disclosed separately in the statement of cash flows.

- To calculate the amount received, reconcile the investment in associate in the statement of financial position from the opening to the closing balance.

- The share of profit/loss of the associate is a non-cash item included within profit and therefore will be an adjustment in the operating activities section of the statement of cash flows.

- If other comprehensive income includes any share of OCI of the associate then this should be taken into account when calculating the cash flow, but should not be adjusted for within operating activities as it is not part of profit.

Example 2

The following information has been extracted from the consolidated financial statements of H for the year ended 31 December 20X1:

Consolidated statement of profit or loss and other comprehensive income

	$000
Profit from operations	734
Share of profit of associate	48
Profit before tax	782
Income tax expense	(304)
Profit for the period	478
Other comprehensive income:	
Share of other comprehensive income of associate	12

Group statement of financial position

	20X1	20X0
	$000	$000
Investment in associate	466	456

Required:

Show the figures relevant to the associate to be included in the group statement of cash flows for the year ended 31 December 20X1.

Example 2 answer

When dealing with the dividend from the associate, the process is the same as we have already seen with the non-controlling interest.

Set up a working (column or T-account format) and bring in all the balances that relate to the associate. When you balance the account, the balancing figure will be the cash received from the associate.

(W1) Dividend received from associate

	$000
Bal b/f	456
Share of profit of associate	48
Share of OCI of associate	12
	516
Less Bal c/f	(466)
Dividend received from associate	50

(W1) Dividend received from associate

or

Associate

	$000		$000
		Dividend received	
Balance b/f	456	(bal fig)	50
Profit of associate	48		
OCI of associate	12	Balance c/f	466
	___		___
	516		516
	___		___

Extracts from statement of cash flows for the year ended 31 December 20X1

	$000
Cash flows from operating activities	
Profit before tax	782
Adjustment for:	
Share of profit of associate	(48)
Investing activities	
Dividend received from associate (W1)	50

Test your understanding 6 (OTQ style)

Group B's statement of profit or loss reports 'Share of profit of associate' of $750,000 and the statement of other comprehensive income reports 'Share of other comprehensive income of associate' of $25,000. The opening and closing statements of financial position show:

	Closing	Opening
	$000	$000
Investment in associate	500	200

> **Required:**
>
> Calculate the dividends received from associate that would appear within cash flows from investing activities in the consolidated statements of cash flows of Group B.

Acquisition and disposal of subsidiaries

Standard accounting practice

- If a subsidiary joins or leaves a group during a financial year, the cash flows of the group should include the cash flows of that subsidiary for the same period that the results of the subsidiary are included in the statement of comprehensive income.

- Cash payments to acquire subsidiaries and receipts from disposals of subsidiaries must be reported separately in the statement of cash flows under investing activities.

Acquisitions

- In the statement of cash flows we must record the actual cash flow for the purchase, not the net assets acquired. The cash outflow is net of any cash balances purchased with the subsidiary.

- All assets and liabilities acquired must be included in any workings to calculate the cash movement for an item during the year. If they are not included in deriving the balancing figure, the incorrect cash flow figure will be calculated. This applies to all assets and liabilities acquired and also to the NCI reconciliation (to calculated dividends paid to NCI).

Disposals

- The statement of cash flows will show the cash received from the sale of the subsidiary, net of any cash balances that were transferred out with the sale.

- When calculating the movement between the opening and closing balance of an item, the assets and liabilities that have been disposed of must be taken into account in order to calculate the correct cash figure. As with acquisitions, this applies to all asset and liability reconciliations and also to the NCI reconciliation (to calculated dividends paid to NCI).

Example 3

The extracts of an entity's statement of financial position is shown below:

	20X8	20X7
	$	$
Inventory	74,666	53,019

During the year, a subsidiary was acquired. At the date of acquisition, the subsidiary had an inventory balance of $9,384.

Required:

Calculate the movement on inventory for the statement of cash flows.

Example 3 answer

At the beginning of the year, the inventory balance of $53,019 **does not** include the inventory of the subsidiary.

At the end of the year, the inventory balance of $74,666 **does** include the inventory of the newly acquired subsidiary.

In order to calculate the correct cash movement, the acquired inventory must be excluded as it is dealt with in the cash paid to acquire the subsidiary. The comparison of the opening and closing inventory figures is then calculated on the same basis.

The movement on inventory is: (74,666 – 9,384) – 53,019 = $12,263 increase. This is shown as a negative adjustment in cash flows from operating activities.

Example 4

The same principle applies if there is a disposal in the period.

For example, the year end receivables balance was as follows:

	20X8	20X7
	$	$
Receivables	52,335	48,911

During the year, a subsidiary was disposed of. At the date of disposal the subsidiary had a receivables balance of $6,543.

Required:

Calculate the movement on receivables for the statement of cash flows.

Example 4 answer

At the beginning of the year, the receivables balance of $48,911 **does** include the receivables of the subsidiary.

At the end of the year, the receivables balance of $52,335 **does not** include the receivables of the disposed subsidiary.

In order to calculate the correct cash movement, the receivables of the disposed subsidiary must be excluded.

The movement on receivables is:

52,335 – (48,911 – 6,543) = $9,967 increase, which is shown as a negative adjustment in cash flows from operating activities.

Example 5

The following are excerpts from a group's consolidated financial statements

	Closing balance $000	Opening balance $000
Group statement of financial position extracts		
Receivables	500	400
Loans	300	600

During the accounting period, a subsidiary was sold, and another acquired. Extracts from the individual statements of financial position are as follows:

	Sold $000	Acquired $000
Receivables	60	70
Loans	110	80

Required:

Demonstrate how the above transactions would be reflected in the consolidated statement of cash flows.

Example 5 answer

Consolidated statement of cash flows (extracts)

	$000
Cash flows from operating activities	
Adjustments for:	
Increase in receivables (W1)	(90)
Cash flows from financing activities	
Repayment of loans (W2)	(270)

(W1) Receivables

	$000
Opening balance	400
Disposal of subsidiary	(60)
Acquisition of subsidiary	70
	410
Increase in receivables (= deduction in operating activities)	90
Closing balance	500

(W2) Loans

	$000
Opening balance	600
Disposal of subsidiary	(110)
Acquisition of subsidiary	80
	570
Therefore redemption/cash paid (bal figure)	(270)
Closing balance	300

Test your understanding 7 (OTQ style)

Group P's opening and closing statements of financial position show the following:

	Closing	Opening
	$000	$000
Non-current assets (NBV)	500	150

During the year depreciation of $50,000 was charged. During the year, the group acquired a 75% shareholding in a subsidiary which held non-current assets of $200,000 and disposed of a 60% shareholding in a subsidiary which held non-current assets of $180,000 at the date of disposal.

No other disposals occurred during the year.

Required:

How much cash was spent on non-current assets in the year?

Test your understanding 8 (integration question)

Group R's opening and closing statements of financial position show the following:

	Closing	Opening
	$000	$000
Inventory	100	200
Receivables	300	200
Payables	500	200

During the period the group acquired a subsidiary with the following working capital:

	$000
Inventory	50
Receivables	200
Payables	40

During the period the group disposed of a subsidiary with the following working capital:

	$000
Inventory	25
Receivables	45
Payables	20

Required:

Prepare the extracts required in respect of movements in working capital that should be shown in the operating activities section of the statement of cash flows?

Example 6

Extracts from the consolidated financial statements of the Kelly Group are given below:

Consolidated statements of financial position as at 31 March

	20X5		20X4	
	$000	$000	$000	$000
Non-current assets				
Property, plant and equipment	5,900		4,400	
Goodwill	85		130	
Investment in associate	170		140	
	――――		――――	
		6,155		4,670
Current assets				
Inventories	1,000		930	
Receivables	1,340		1,140	
Cash and cash equivalents	215		140	
	――――		――――	
		2,555		2,210
		――――		――――
		8,710		6,880
		――――		――――
Share capital	2,000		1,500	
Share premium	300		–	
Revaluation reserve	50		–	
Retained earnings	3,400		3,320	
	――――		――――	
		5,750		4,820
Non-controlling interests		75		175
		――――		――――
Equity		5,825		4,995

Non-current liabilities

Interest-bearing borrowings	1,400	1,000
Obligations under finance leases	210	45
Deferred tax	340	305
	1,950	1,350

Current liabilities

Trade payables	885	495
Accrued interest	7	9
Income tax payable	28	21
Obligations under finance leases	15	10
	935	535
	8,710	6,880

Consolidated statement of comprehensive income for the year ended 31 March 20X5

	$000
Revenue	875
Cost of sales	(440)
Gross profit	435
Other operating expenses	(210)
Profit from operations	225
Finance cost	(100)
Gain on sale of subsidiary	30
Share of associate's profit	38
Profit before tax	193
Tax	(48)
Profit for the year	145

Other comprehensive income

Gains on land revaluation	50

Total comprehensive income for the year	195

Profit attributable to:

Equity holders of the parent	120
Non-controlling interests	25
	145

Total comprehensive income attributable to:

Equity holders of the parent	170
Non-controlling interests	25
	195

Notes:

Dividends

Kelly, the parent company, paid a dividend of $40,000 during the year.

Property, plant and equipment

The following transactions took place during the year:

- Land was revalued upwards by $50,000 on 1st April 20X4.

- During the year, depreciation of $80,000 was charged in the income statement.

- Additions include $300,000 acquired under finance leases.

- A property was disposed of during the year for $250,000 cash. Its carrying amount was $295,000 at the date of disposal. The loss on disposal has been included within cost of sales.

Gain on sale of subsidiary

On 1 January 20X5, Kelly disposed of an 80% owned subsidiary for $390,000 in cash. The subsidiary had the following net assets at the date of disposal:

	$000
Property, plant and equipment	635
Inventory	20
Receivables	45
Cash	35
Payables	(130)
Income tax	(5)
Interest-bearing borrowings	(200)
	400

This subsidiary had been acquired on 1 January 20X1 for a cash payment of $220,000 when its net assets had a fair value of $225,000 and the non-controlling interest had a fair value of $50,000.

Goodwill

The Kelly Group uses the fair value method for measuring NCI at the date of acquisition.

Required:

Prepare the consolidated statement of cash flows of the Kelly group for the year ended 31 March 20X5 in the form required by IAS 7 Statement of cash flows.

Example 6 answer

Consolidated statement of cash flows for the year ended 31 March 20X5

	$000	$000
Cash flows from operating activities		
Profit before tax	193	
Adjustments for:		
Share of associate's profit	(38)	
Gain on sale of subsidiary	(30)	
Finance cost	100	
Depreciation	80	
Loss on disposal of property (250 – 295)	45	
Increase in inventory (1,000 – (930 – 20))	(90)	
Increase in receivables		
(1,340 – (1,140 – 45))	(245)	
Increase in payables (885 – (495 – 130))	520	
	————	
	535	
Interest paid (W2)	(102)	
Tax paid (W3)	(1)	
	————	
		432
Cash flows from investing activities		
Sale of property	250	
Purchases of property, plant and equipment (W4)	(2,160)	
Dividends received from associate (W5)	8	
Proceeds from sale of subsidiary, net of cash balances (390 – 35)	355	
	————	
		(1,547)

Cash flows from financing activities

Repayments of finance leases (W6)	(130)
Cash raised from interest-bearing borrowings (W7)	600
Issue of shares (2,000 + 300 – 1,500)	800
Dividends paid to equity shareholders of parent	(40)
Dividends paid to non-controlling interests (W8)	(40)
	1,190
Increase in cash and cash equivalents	75
Opening cash and cash equivalents	140
Closing cash and cash equivalents	215

(W1) Goodwill

	$000
Bal b/f	130
Disposal of subsidiary (see below)	(45)
	85
Impairment (balance)	–
Bal c/f	85

or

Goodwill

	$000		$000
Bal b/f	130	Disposal of sub (below)	45
		Bal c/f	85
	130		130

Goodwill of disposed sub:

	$000
Fair value of P's investment	220
NCI at fair value	50
Fair value of sub's net assets at acquisition	(225)
	____
Goodwill at acquisition/ disposal	45
	____

(W2) Finance costs

	$000
Bal b/f	9
Charge in CSCI	100
Bal c/f	(7)
	____
Cash paid	102
	____

or

Finance costs

	$000		$000
Cash (bal fig)	102	Bal b/f	9
Bal c/f	7	SCI	100
	____		____
	109		109
	____		____

(W3) **Tax payable**

	$000
Bal b/f (21 + 305)	326
Disposal of subsidiary	(5)
CSCI charge	48
	369
Cash paid (balance)	(1)
	368
Bal c/f (28 + 340)	368

or

Tax

		Bal b/f – income tax	21
		Bal b/f – deferred tax	305
Disposal of sub	5		
		SCI – group	48
Tax paid (bal fig)	1		
Bal c/f – income tax	28		
Bal c/f – deferred tax	340		
	374		374

(W4) **Property, plant and equipment**

	$000
Bal b/f	4,400
Revaluation	50
Depreciation	(80)
Finance leases	300
Disposal of property	(295)
Disposal of subsidiary	(635)
	3,740
Cash (balance)	2,160
Bal c/f	5,900

PPE

Bal b/f	4,400		
Revaluation	50	Depreciation	80
Finance leases	300	Disposal – property	295
Cash (bal fig)	2,160	Disposal – sub	635
		Bal c/f	5,900
	6,910		6,910

(W5) Investment in associates

	$000
Bal b/f	140
Share of profit of associate	38
	178
Bal c/f	(170)
Dividend (cash) received	8

or

Investments in associates

Bal b/f	140		
Share of profits of associate	38	Dividend received (bal fig)	8
		Bal c/f	170
	178		178

(W6) Finance leases

	$000
Bal b/f (10 + 45)	55
New leases	300
	355
Repayments (cash) (balance)	(130)
Bal c/f (15 + 210)	225

or

Finance leases

		Bal b/d (10 + 45)	55
		New leases	300
Repayments (bal fig)	130		
Bal c/d (15 + 210)	225		
	_____		_____
	355		355
	_____		_____

(W7) **Interest-bearing borrowings**

	$000
Bal b/f	1,000
Disposal of sub	(200)
	_____
	800
New loans/cash (balance)	600
	_____
Bal c/f	1,400
	_____

or

Interest-bearing borrowings

		Bal b/d	1,000
Disposal of sub	200		
		Cash (bal fig)	600
Bal b/d	1,400		
	_____		_____
	1,600		1,600
	_____		_____

(W8) Non-controlling interests

	$000
Bal b/f	175
Comprehensive income per CSCI	25
Disposal of sub (below)	(85)
	115
Cash paid (balance)	(40)
Bal c/f	75

or

Non-controlling interests

		Bal b/f	175
Disposal of sub (below)	85	Comprehensive income per CSCI	25
Dividends paid (bal fig)	40		
Bal c/f	75		
	200		200

NCI of disposed sub:

	$000
NCI at acquisition at fair value	50
NCI% × post acquisition reserves (20% × (400 – 225))	35
NCI at disposal	85

The group financial statements of Linford are given below:

Consolidated statement of comprehensive income for the year ended 30 September 20X9

	$m
Revenue	600
Cost of sales	(300)
Gross profit	300
Operating expenses	(150)
Finance costs	(44)
Share of associate profit	17
Profit before tax	123
Taxation	(35)
	88
Other comprehensive income:	
Gain on revaluation of PPE	15
	103
Profit attributable to:	
Parent shareholders	78
Non-controlling interests	10
	88
Total comprehensive income attributable to:	
Parent shareholders	91
Non-controlling interests	12
	103

Consolidated statements of financial position as at

	30 Sept 20X9		30 Sept 20X8	
	$m	$m	$m	$m
Non-current assets				
Goodwill	25		19	
Property, plant and equipment	240		280	
Investments in associates	80	345	70	369
Current assets				
Inventory	105		90	
Receivables	120		100	
Cash and cash equivalents	30		75	
		255		265
		600		634
Share capital		100		100
Retained earnings		194		142
Revaluation reserve		103		90
Non controlling interest		72		40
		469		372
Non-current liabilities				
12% loan stock	–		90	
Deferred taxation	30		24	
		30		114
Current liabilities				
Trade payables	65		55	
Taxation	10		8	
Overdraft	26		85	
		101		148
		600		634

Notes to the accounts

(1) Acquisition of subsidiary

During the year ended 30 September 20X9, Linford purchased 80% of the issued equity share capital of Christie for $100m, payable in cash. The net assets of Christie at the date of acquisition were assessed as having fair values as follows:

	$m
PPE	60
Inventory	30
Receivables	25
Bank and cash	10
Trade payables	(15)
Taxation	(5)
	105

It is group policy to measure NCI at the proportionate share of the fair value of net assets at acquisition.

(2) Goodwill

Goodwill suffered an impairment during the year.

(3) Property, plant and equipment

The only disposal in the year was of land with a carrying value of $90m. The profit on disposal of $10m is included within operating expenses. Depreciation of $58m was charged on PPE in the year.

Required:

Prepare the consolidated statement of cash flows for Linford group for the year ended 30 September 20X9.

Test your understanding 10 (further OTQs)

(1) Which three of the following items would be included in the 'cash flows from investing activities' section of the consolidated statement of cash flows?

    A   Acquisition of subsidiary, net of cash acquired

    B   Goodwill on acquisition of subsidiary

    C   Gain on disposal of subsidiary

    D   Investment income received

    E   Dividends received from associate

    F   Share of associate profit

(2) FG's consolidated statement of financial position shows receivables of $6,500,000 at 31 May 20X2 and $5,300,000 at 31 May 20X1. FG acquired 80% of the share capital of AB on 1 January 20X2, when AB had a receivables balance of $2,200,000.

Calculate the adjustment that should be made to profit to reflect the movement in receivables within the operating activities section of the consolidated statement of cash flows of the FG group for the year ended 31 May 20X2. Clearly state whether the amount should be added to or deducted from profit.

(3) SB's consolidated statement of financial position shows an investment in associate of $3,200,000 at 30 November 20X4 and $1,200,000 at 30 November 20X3. SB's share of associate profit for the year ended 30 November 20X4 was $2,300,000 and its share of associate other comprehensive income was $150,000.

There were no acquisitions or disposals of associates in the year ended 30 November 20X4.

Which of the following is the amount that would be shown as dividends received from associate in the investing activities section of the consolidated statement of cash flows of the SB group for the year ended 30 November 20X4?

    A $300,000

    B $450,000

    C $2,000,000

    D $4,450,000

(4) Which one of the following statements is INCORRECT in respect of the preparation of the consolidated statement of cash flows?

A   Dividends from associate are a cash inflow within investing activities

B   Dividends to non-controlling interest are a cash inflow within financing activities.

C   A gain on disposal of subsidiary should be deducted from profit in the cash flow from operating activities section as it is a non-cash item included within profit.

D   Goodwill impairment should be added back to profit in the cash flow from operating activities section as it is a non-cash item included within profit.

(5) The carrying value of property, plant and equipment (PPE) in XY's consolidated statement of financial position was $8,900,000 at 31 March 20X2 and $9,500,000 at 31 March 20X1. There were no disposals or revaluation of PPE in the year. Depreciation of $1,000,000 was charged to profit in the year ended 31 March 20X2. XY disposed of 20% of its shares in ABC on 31 October 20X1 but retained a controlling interest. The PPE in ABC at the date of disposal was $1,100,000.

Calculate the cash outflow from purchase of PPE that would be shown in the investing activities section of the consolidated statement of cash flows of the XY group for the year ended 31 March 20X2.

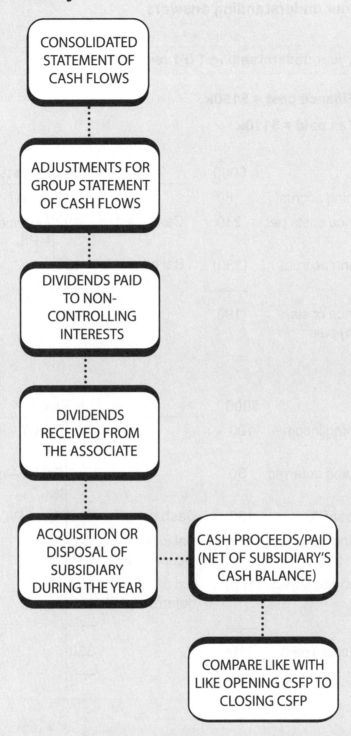

7 Chapter summary

Test your understanding answers

Test your understanding 1 (F1 revision)

(a) **Finance cost = $190k**

(b) **Tax paid = $110k**

	$000	Finance costs		
Opening accrual	80		Bal b/f	80
Finance costs per P/L	240	Cash paid	190	Finance costs – P/L	240
Closing accrual	(130)	Bal c/f	130		
	———		———		———
Finance costs (cash) paid	190		320		320
	———		———		———

	$000	Tax		
Opening income tax	100		Bal b/f – income tax	100
Opening deferred tax	50		Bal b/f – deferred tax	50
Tax per P/L	180	Cash paid	110	Tax – P/L	180
Closing income tax	(120)	Bal c/f – income tax	120		
Closing deferred tax	(100)	Bal c/f – deferred tax	100		
	———		———		———
Tax (cash) paid	110		330		330
	———		———		———

Test your understanding 2 (F1 revision)

Cash paid on PPE = $95k

	$000	Non-current assets			
Opening NBV	100	Bal b/f	100	Depreciation	20
Depreciation	(20)	Revaluation	60	Disposal	15
Revaluation surplus	60	Additions – leases	30		
Disposal	(15)	Additions – cash paid (β)	95		
Additions under leases	30			Bal c/f	250
Additions – cash paid (β)	95		285		285
Closing NBV	250				

Test your understanding 3 (F1 revision)

Consolidated statement of cash flows (extracts)

	$000
Cash flows from operating activities	
Adjustments for:	
Decrease in inventory (240 – 150)	90
Increase in receivables (275 – (200 + 35))	(40)
Increase in payables (180 – (90 + 18))	72

Test your understanding 4 (OTQ style)

Dividend paid to NCI = $360k

	$000	**Non-controlling interests**			
Opening NCI	440			Bal b/f	440
NCI share of TCI	500	Divs paid (β)	360	NCI share of TCI	500
Divi paid (bal)	(360)	Bal c/f	580		
	———		———		———
Closing NCI	580		940		940
	———		———		———

Test your understanding 5 (OTQ style)

Dividend paid to P = $500k

Retained earnings	$000	**Retained earnings**			
Op. bal	1,625			Bal b/f	1,625
Parent share of profit	3,200	Divs paid (β)	500	Parent share of profit	3,200
Divi paid (bal)	(500)	Bal c/f	4,325		
	———		———		———
Cl. bal	4,325		4,825		4,825
	———		———		———

NB The P's share of profit is taken to group RE's. Not P's share of total comprehensive income. Only profits impact RE's.

Test your understanding 6 (OTQ style)

Dividend received from associate = $475k

	$000	Investment in Associate			
Opening investment in associate	200	Bal b/f	200		
Share of profits	750	Share of profits	750	Divis received (β)	475
Share of OCI	25	Share of OCI	25		
Dividend received from assoc (bal)	475			Bal c/f	500
Closing investment in associate	500		975		975

Test your understanding 7 (OTQ style)

Cash spent on NCAs = $380k

	$000	Non-current assets			
		Bal b/f	150	Depreciation	50
Opening NBV	150	New sub	200	Disposal of sub	180
Depreciation	(50)	Additions – cash (β)	380		
Disposal of sub	(180)				
New sub	200			Bal c/f	500
Additions – cash (β)	380		730		730
Closing NBV	500				

Test your understanding 8 (integration question)

Extracts to be included within cash generated from operations (in $000's)

Decrease in inventory	**125**
Decrease in receivables	**55**
Increase in payables	**280**

	$000	**Inventory**			
Opening inventory	200	Bal b/f	200		
New sub	50	New sub	50	Disposal – sub	25
Disposal sub	(25)			Decrease (β)	125
				Bal c/f	100
Decrease (β)	(125)		——		——
	——		250		250
Closing inventory	100		——		——
	——				

	$000	**Receivables**			
Opening rec'bles	200	Bal b/f	200		
New sub	200	New sub	200	Disposal – sub	45
Disposal sub	(45)			Decrease (β)	55
				Bal c/f	300
Decrease (β)	(55)		——		——
	——		400		400
Closing rec'bles	300		——		——
	——				

	$000	Payables			
Opening payables	200			Bal b/f	200
New sub	40	Disposal – sub	20	New sub	40
Disposal sub	(20)				
		Bal c/f	500	Increase (β)	280
Increase (β)	280				
	———		520		520
Closing payables	500		———		———
	———				

Test your understanding 9 (integration question)

Group statement of cash flows for Linford for year ending 30 September 20X9

Cash flows from operating activities	$m	$m
Group profit before tax	123	
Adjustments for:		
Depreciation	58	
Goodwill impairment (W1)	10	
Profit on sale of property	(10)	
Share of associate's profit	(17)	
Finance costs	44	
	———	
	208	
Decrease in inventory ((105 – 90) – 30)	15	
Decrease in receivables ((120 – 100) – 25)	5	
Decrease in payables ((65 – 55) – 15)	(5)	
	———	
Cash generated from operations	223	
Finance costs paid	(44)	
Tax paid (W3)	(32)	
	———	
Net cash from operating activities		147

Cash flows from investing activities

Proceeds on disposal of property (90 + 10)	100	
Purchase of property, plant and equipment (W2)	(33)	
Dividends received from associate (W6)	7	
Acquisition of sub, net of cash balances (100 – 10)	(90)	
	——	
Net cash used in investing activities		(16)

Cash flows from financing activities

Repayment of loan – 12% loan stock	(90)	
Dividends paid to NCI (W5)	(1)	
Dividends paid to parent shareholders (W4)	(26)	(117)
	——	——
Increase in cash and cash equivalents		14
Brought forward cash and cash equivalents (75 – 85)		(10)
		——
Carried forward cash and cash equivalents (30 – 26)		4
		——

Workings

(W1) Goodwill

	$m
Bal b/f	19
Acquisition of sub (below)	16
	——
	35
Impairment (balance)	(10)
	——
Bal c/f	25
	——

Or

Goodwill

B/f	19	**Impairment (balance)**	10
Acquisition of subsidiary (below)	16	C/f	25
	35		35

Goodwill of acquired sub:

	$m
Fair value of P's investment	100
NCI at proportion of net assets (20% × 105)	21
Fair value of sub's net assets at acquisition	(105)
Goodwill at acquisition	16

(W2) PPE

	$m
Bal b/f	280
Revaluation	15
New subsidiary	60
Depreciation	(58)
Disposal	(90)
	207
Cash paid for new assets (balance)	33
Bal c/f	240

Or

PPE

B/f	280	Depreciation	58
Revaluation	15	Disposal	90
New sub	60	C/f	240
Bank (balance)	**33**		
	___		___
	388		388
	___		___

(W3) **Taxation**

	$m
Bal b/f (8 + 24)	32
SP/L charge	35
New subsidiary	5
	___
	72
Cash paid (balance)	(32)
	___
Bal c/f (10 + 30)	40
	___

Or

Taxation

Bal c/f (10 + 30)	40	Bal b/f (8 + 24)	32
		SP/L charge	35
		New sub	5
Bank (balance)	**32**		
	___		___
	72		72
	___		___

(W4) Dividends paid to parent shareholders

	$m
Bal b/f (on retained earning)	142
Profit for the period (attributable to parent)	78
	220
Cash paid (balance)	(26)
Bal c/f	194

Or

Retained earnings

C/f		194	B/f	142
			Profit	78
Divis paid (balance)	**26**			
		220		220

(W5) Non-controlling interests

	$m
Bal b/f	40
Comprehensive income per CSCI	12
New subsidiary (105 × 20%)	21
	73
Dividends paid (balance)	(1)
Bal c/f	72

Or

Non-controlling interests

C/f	72	B/f	40
		Comp income	12
		New sub	21
Bank (balance)	**1**	(105 × 20%)	
	—		—
	73		73
	—		—

(W6) **Investment in associate**

	$m
Bal b/f	70
Share of profits	17
	—
	87
Cash received (balance)	(7)
	—
Bal c/f	80
	—

Or

Investment in associate

B/f	70	C/f	80
Share of profit	17	**Bank (balance)**	**7**
	—		—
	87		87
	—		—

Test your understanding 10 (further OTQs)

(1) **Items A, D and E**

B is not a cash flow and will not appear anywhere in the consolidated statement of cash flows.

C and F would be adjustments to profit reflected in the cash flows from operating activities section of the statement.

(2) **Movement in receivables = $1,000,000 addition**

i.e positive adjustment in operating activities section

	$000
Bal b/f	5,300
Acquisition of subsidiary	2,200
	7,500
Decrease (balance)	(1,000)
Bal c/f	6,500

(3) **B Dividends received from associate = $450,000**
Positive figure in investing activities section

	$000
Bal b/f	1,200
Profit from associate	2,300
OCI from associate	150
	3,650
Dividends received (balance)	(450)
Bal c/f	3,200

Or

Associate

Bal b/f	1,200		
Profit from associate	2,300		
OCI from associate	150	**Dividends received – balance**	450
		Bal c/f	3,200
	3,650		3,650

(4) **B is incorrect**

NCI dividends are a cash outflow, not inflow.

(5) **Cash outflow from purchase of PPE = $400,000**

	$000
Bal b/f	9,500
Depreciation	(1,000)
	8,500
Cash paid (bal fig)	400
Bal c/f	8,900

There is no adjustment for the disposal of shares as a controlling interest remains and therefore XY will continue to consolidated ABC's property, plant and equipment.

Foreign currency translation

Chapter learning objectives

B2. Demonstrate the impact on the preparation of the consolidated financial statements of certain complex group scenarios.

(b) Demonstrate the impact on the group financial statements of consolidating a foreign subsidiary

1 Session content

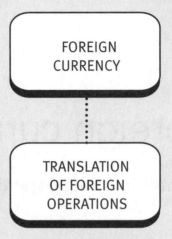

FOREIGN
CURRENCY

TRANSLATION
OF FOREIGN
OPERATIONS

2 IAS 21 The effects of changes in exchange rates

IAS 21 deals with:

- the definition of functional and presentation currencies
- accounting for individual transactions in a foreign currency
- translating the financial statements of a foreign operation

Accounting for individual transactions is now included in the F1 syllabus. The F2 syllabus focuses on the translation of the financial statements of a foreign operation, in the context of that operation being a subsidiary.

3 Functional and presentation currencies

The **functional currency** is the currency of the primary economic environment in which the entity operates. In most cases this will be the local currency.

An entity should consider the following when determining its functional currency:

- The currency that mainly influences sales prices for goods and services
- The currency of the country whose competitive forces and regulations mainly determine the sales prices of goods and services
- The currency that mainly influences labour, material and other costs of providing goods and services

The following factors may also be considered:

- The currency in which funding from issuing debt and equity is generated
- The currency in which receipts from operating activities are usually retained

The entity maintains its day-to-day financial records in its functional currency.

The **presentation currency** is the currency in which the entity presents its financial statements. This can be different from the functional currency, particularly if the entity in question is a foreign owned subsidiary. It may have to present its financial statements in the currency of its parent, even though that is different to its own functional currency.

4 Translation of foreign currency transactions

Where an entity enters into a transaction denominated in a currency other than its functional currency, that transaction must be translated into the functional currency before it is recorded.

Translation of foreign currency transactions in an individual entity set of financial statements is assessed in F1. See the expandable text below for detail.

Foreign currency transactions

Whenever a business enters into a contract where the consideration is expressed in a foreign currency, it is necessary to translate that foreign currency amount into the functional currency for inclusion in its own accounts. Examples include:

- imports of raw materials
- exports of finished goods
- importation of foreign manufactured non-current assets
- investments in foreign securities
- raising an overseas loan.

Initial recognition

- The transaction will initially be recorded by applying the spot exchange rate, i.e. the exchange rate at the date of the transaction.

> **Subsequent measurement – settled transactions**
>
> When cash settlement occurs, for example payment received from a foreign customer, the settled amount should be translated using the spot exchange rate on the settlement date.
>
> If this amount differs from that recorded when the transaction occurred, there will be an exchange difference which is taken to the statement of profit or loss in the period in which it arises.

Example 1

An entity based in the US sells goods to the UK for £200,000 on 28 February 20X3 when the exchange rate was £0.55: $1.

The customer pays in April 20X3 when the rate was £0.60:$1.

The functional currency of the entity is the $.

Required:
How does the US entity account for the transaction in its financial statements for the year ended 31 July 20X3?

Example 1 answer

On the sale:

Translate the sale at the spot rate prevailing on the transaction date.

£200,000/0.55 = $363,636

		$
Dr	Receivables	363,636
Cr	Sales	363,636

When the cash is received:

Dollar value of cash received = £200,000/0.60 = $333,333

Loss on transaction = 363,636 – 333,333 = 30,303

		$
Dr	Bank	333,333
Cr	Receivables	363,636
Dr	P/L (loss)	30,303

Unsettled transactions at the reporting date

Subsequent measurement – unsettled transactions

The treatment of any 'foreign' items remaining in the statement of financial position at the year end will depend on whether they are classified as monetary or non-monetary.

Monetary items

Currency held and assets or liabilities to be received or paid in currency.

E.g. cash, receivables, payables, loans

Treatment:
Retranslate using the closing rate (year end exchange rate)

Non-monetary items

Other items in the statement of financial position.

E.g. non-current assets, inventory, investments

Treatment:
Do not translate

i.e. leave at historic rate

Any exchange difference arising on the retranslation of monetary items must be taken to the statement of profit or loss in the period in which it arises.

Example 2

A US entity sells apples to an entity based in Moldovia where the currency is the Moldovian pound (Mol). The apples were sold on 1 October 20X1 for Mol 200,000 and were paid for in February 20X2.

The rate on 1 October 20X1 is US $1: Mol 1.55.

The rate on 31 December 20X1 (the reporting date) is US $1: Mol 1.34.

The functional currency of the entity is the $.

Required:

How does the US entity account for the transaction in its financial statements for the year ended 31 December 20X1?

Example 2 answer

On the sale:

Translate the sale at the spot rate prevailing on the transaction date.

Mol 200,000/1.55 = $129,032

		$
Dr	Receivables	129,032
Cr	Sales	129,032

At the reporting date:

The receivables balance is a monetary item and so must be retranslated using the closing rate.

Mol 200,000/1.34 = $149,254

Gain = 149,254 – 129,032 = 20,222

		$
Dr	Receivables	20,222
Cr	P/L (gain)	20,222

5 Translating the financial statements of a foreign operation

If the currency of a subsidiary is different to that of the parent entity, it will be necessary to translate the subsidiary's financial statements into the parent's presentation currency prior to consolidation.

This is done using the 'closing rate' or 'net investment' method and the following exchange rates should be used in the translation:

Statement of comprehensive income

- Income and expenses – average rate for the year

Statement of financial position

- Assets and liabilities – closing rate i.e. the rate at the reporting date
- Goodwill of subsidiary – closing rate

Exchange gains or losses on translation

Exchange differences arise upon translation of the subsidiary and can be separated into two main components:

- **Exchange difference on net assets** – arising as opening net assets are initially translated at the opening rate, the comprehensive income for the year (i.e. movement on net assets) will have been translated at average rate and the closing net assets on the statement of financial position are then translated at the closing rate

- **Exchange difference on goodwill** – will have been previously translated at the current year's opening rate (the previous year's closing rate), any impairment in the year will be translated at average rate in the statement of profit or loss and the year end goodwill is then translated at closing rate in the statement of financial position

The sum of these two exchange differences is recognised **within other comprehensive income**. The group share of these foreign exchange differences would be held in a separate reserve within equity in the statement of financial position. Upon disposal of the subsidiary, the balance on this reserve would be recycled through profit or loss to form part of the total gain or loss on disposal of the subsidiary.

The exchange difference on net assets is always split between parent and NCI based on the group shareholdings.

The treatment of the goodwill exchange difference depends upon the method used for valuing the NCI and therefore should be considered separately.

Illustration 1 – Exchange difference on translation of subsidiary

To help understand the exchange difference consider the following scenario.

A subsidiary, whose functional currency is the Dit (D), prepares its financial statements for the year ended 31 December 20X1 and the movement on net assets is as follows:

	D000
Opening net assets at 1 January 20X1	15,000
Comprehensive income for the year ended 31 December 20X1	1,750
Closing net assets at 31 December 20X1	16,750

The parent's presentation currency is the dollar ($) and exchange rates were as follows:

At 1 January 20X1	5 Dits = $1
At 31 December 20X1	7 Dits = $1
Average rate for the year ended 31 December 20X1	6.2 Dits = $1

The brought forward net assets were translated at last year's closing rate (= this year's opening rate) in last year's consolidated financial statements. The comprehensive income has been translated at average rate for inclusion in the consolidated statement of comprehensive income for the year. The closing net assets have been translated at this year's closing rate for inclusion in the consolidated statement of financial position.

This gives rise to the following exchange difference:

	D000	Exchange rate	$000
Opening net assets	15,000	5	3,000
Comprehensive income	1,750	6.2	282
Exchange difference (bal)			(889)
Closing net assets	16,750	7	2,393

Another way of presenting this calculation is:

	D000	Exchange rate	$000
Closing net assets at closing rate	16,750	7	2,393
Less opening net assets at opening rate	(15,000)	5	(3,000)
Less comprehensive income for the year at average rate	(1,750)	6.2	(282)
Exchange difference arising on translation of subsidiary			(889)

A further exchange difference then arises upon consolidation as goodwill is recognised at the closing rate in the consolidated statement of financial position each year and therefore is re-translated from opening to closing rate.

6 Approach to a question

Assessment questions are likely to focus on the calculation and accounting treatment of the exchange differences however you may also be tested on the impact of translation on individual figures from the consolidated statement of comprehensive income and statement of financial position.

The key things to remember are:

- Profit or loss and other comprehensive income items are translated at average rate each year

- Assets and liabilities are translated at closing rate each year

- Exchange differences arising on the retranslation of the operation (on net assets and goodwill) are recognised within other comprehensive income.

- The exchange difference on net assets is attributed between parent shareholders and NCI based on their percentage holdings

- The exchange difference on goodwill be attributed as follows:
  - All to parent shareholders, if NCI is measured using proportion of net assets method

  - Between parent shareholders and NCI (based on their percentage holdings) if the NCI is measured using the fair value method

  - Note that this is consistent with the treatment of goodwill impairment.

To calculate the exchange differences, the following proformas can be used.

Exchange difference on net assets for the year

	A$
Closing net assets at closing rate	X
Less opening net assets at opening rate	(X)
Less comprehensive income for the year at average rate	(X)
	X/(X)

Exchange difference on goodwill for the year

	A$
Closing goodwill at closing rate	X
Less opening goodwill at opening rate	(X)
Add back impairment for the year at relevant rate (question should provide guidance on the rate used to translate impairment)	X
	X/(X)

Example 3

This example walks you through the entire process of preparing a set of consolidated financial statements with a foreign subsidiary. Note that you will not be asked to do this in full in your assessment, but understanding the process will help you to answer any questions that arise.

P acquired 75% of the share capital of S on 1 January 20X5 for 500,000Fr, when the retained earnings of S were 120,000Fr. The functional currency of S is Fr. The functional currency and presentation currency of P is $.

Statements of financial position at 31 December 20X6

	P	S
	$000	Fr000
Non-current assets	1,250	850
Investment in S	100	–
Current assets	325	150
	1,675	1,000
Share capital	700	250
Reserves	675	350
Liabilities	300	400
	1,675	1,000

Statements of comprehensive income for the year ended 31 December 20X6 (summarised)

	P	S
	$000	Fr000
Revenue	600	150
Expenses	(475)	(90)
Profit for the year	125	60
Other comprehensive income	–	–
Total comprehensive income	125	60

Exchange rates:

1 January 20X5	$1 = 5.0Fr
31 December 20X5	$1 = 4.2Fr
31 December 20X6	$1 = 4.5Fr
Average for the year ended 31 December 20X5	$1 = 4.6Fr
Average for the year ended 31 December 20X6	$1 = 4.4Fr

P has a policy of measuring NCI at acquisition at fair value. The fair value of the NCI holding in S at acquisition was 160,000Fr. The goodwill has been impaired by 10% in the year ended 31 December 20X5 and a further 10% of its book value in the current year. The impairment each year has been translated at the average rate for the year.

Required:

Prepare the consolidated statement of financial position and consolidated statement of comprehensive income for the year ended 31 December 20X6.

Note: Work to the nearest $1,000.

Example 3 answer (the basics)

A good starting point is to translate the basic financial statements of the subsidiary so that the figures are in the presentation currency of the parent ready for adding across on the face of the main statements.

(W1) Translation of S's statement of financial position at 31 December 20X6

Using closing rate of 4.5	$000
Non-current assets (850/4.5)	189
Current assets (150/4.5)	33
Liabilities (400/4.5)	89

Translation of S's statement of comprehensive income for the year ended 31 December 20X6

Using average rate of 4.4	$000
Revenue (150/4.4)	34
Expenses (90/4.4)	(20)
	——
Profit/TCI for year (60/4.4)	14
	——

To complete the consolidated statement of financial position the usual workings should then be prepared: net assets, goodwill, NCI reserve and group (consolidated) reserves.

When preparing the net assets working, translate the net assets at acquisition using the acquisition rate and the net assets at the reporting date using the closing rate.

The difference between the two will reflect the translated post-acquisition reserves (for inclusion in both the NCI reserve and group reserve workings). This figure includes both the movement in post-acquisition reserves and the cumulative exchange difference to date on the net assets of the subsidiary. The detailed answer that follows this solution demonstrates this point.

(W2) **Net assets of subsidiary**

	Acquisition date	Reporting date
	Fr000	Fr000
Share capital	250	250
Reserves	120	350
	370	600
Translation rate	Acquisition rate = 5	Closing rate = 4.5
Translated net assets ($000)	74	133

Post-acquisition reserves = 59 ($000)

When calculating goodwill, start in the **functional currency of the subsidiary and then translate** into the presentation of the parent using three different rates: acquisition rate, opening rate and closing rate.

The difference between opening and closing rate will be part of the exchange difference to be recognised within other comprehensive income for the year.

The difference between acquisition and closing rate will be part of the foreign currency translation reserve that has arisen since the subsidiary was acquired and should be included in the group reserves working.

(W3) **Goodwill**

	Fr000
Fair value of Ps investment	500
NCI at fair value	160
Fair value of sub's net assets at acquisition (W2)	(370)
Goodwill at acquisition	290
Impairment year ended 31 Dec 20X5 (10% × 290)	(29)
Gross goodwill at 31 December 20X5	261
Impairment year ended 31 Dec 20X6 (10% × 261)	(26)
Goodwill at reporting date	235

Translation of goodwill:

	$000
At acquisition date (290/5)	58
Less impairment in y/e 31 Dec 05 at average rate (29/4.6)	(6)
Exchange difference y/e 31 Dec 05 (balancing figure)	10
	___
At 31 Dec 05 (261/4.2)	62
Less impairment in y/e 31 Dec 06 at average rate (26/4.4)	(6)
Exchange difference y/e 31 Dec 06 (balancing figure)	(4)
	___
At 31 Dec 06 (235/4.5)	52
	___

When preparing the non-controlling interests working, remember that this is a reserve and builds up over time.

- The value at acquisition should be translated at the acquisition rate

- The post-acquisition reserves have already been translated in the net assets working

- Any impairment will also have been translated in the goodwill working

- Remember to include the NCI's share of any cumulative exchange difference on goodwill if NCI is measured using the fair value method at acquisition. This exchange difference has already been calculated in the goodwill working.

(W4) Non-controlling interests in the CSFP

	$000
NCI at acquisition (160/5)	32
NCI% x post acquisition reserves (25% × 59 (W2))	15
NCI% x cumulative impairment loss (25% × (6 + 6 (W3)))	(3)
NCI% x cumulative exchange diff on goodwill (25% × (10 – 4) (W3))	1
	___
	45
	___

The group reserves working then follows on from the NCI reserve as usual. The first figure to include is the parent's reserves (already in the parent's presentation currency). The group reserves then include the remaining (parent's) share of the figures partly included in the NCI reserve working.

(W5) Group reserves

	$000
P	675
S: (75% × 59)	44
Impairment (75% × (6 + 6))	(9)
Exchange difference on goodwill (75% × (10 – 4))	5
	715

Note: By using the translated post-acquisition reserves both the group and NCI reserve reflects both the actual movement on the post-acquisition reserves and the share of the exchange differences that have arisen on the subsidiary's net assets.

The consolidated statement of financial position can now be completed.

P Group consolidated statement of financial position at 31 December 20X6

	$000
Goodwill (W3)	52
Non-current assets (1,250 + 189 (W1))	1,439
Current assets (325 + 33 (W1))	358
	1,849
Share capital	700
Reserves (W5)	715
Non-controlling interests (W4)	45
Payables (300 + 89 (W1))	389
	1,849

Finally, to complete the consolidated statement of comprehensive income for the year, we need to calculate the current year exchange difference on net assets. (We already have the figure for goodwill from our goodwill working.)

(W6) Exchange difference for the year

	$000
Closing net assets at closing rate (W2)	133
Less opening net assets at opening rate (600 – 60)/4.2	(129)
Less comprehensive income for the year at average rate (W1)	(14)
Exchange difference on net assets for the year	(10)
Current year exchange difference on goodwill (W3)	(4)
Total exchange difference for the year	(14)

The exchange difference on net assets is split between parent and NCI based on the percentage holdings.

As the NCI has been measured using the fair value method, the exchange difference on goodwill should also be allocated between parent and NCI.

We can now complete the consolidated statement of comprehensive income, including the above exchange difference for the year within other comprehensive income.

P Group consolidated statement of comprehensive income for the year ended 31 December 20X6

	$000
Revenue (600 + 34 (W1))	634
Expenses (475 + 20 (W1) + 6 impairment (W3))	(501)
Profit for the year	133
Other comprehensive income	
Items that may be reclassified subsequently to profit or loss:	
Foreign exchange difference (W6)	(14)
Total comprehensive income	119
Profit for the year attributable to:	
Parent shareholders (balance)	131
Non-controlling interest (25% × (14 (W1) – 6 (W3)))	2
	133

	$000
Total comprehensive income attributable to:	
Non-controlling interest (2 (above) – (25% × 14 (W6))	(2)
Parent shareholders (balance)	121
	119

Example 3 answer (detailed)

In the net assets working (W2), the movement in post-acquisition reserves each year can be analysed further. This will enable us to accurately calculate the foreign currency translation reserve.

To analyse the movement we firstly need to calculate the comprehensive income of the subsidiary for the year ended 31 December 20X5:

Movement on net assets of subsidiary

	Fr000
Net assets at acquisition (1 Jan X5)	370
Comprehensive income for y/e 31 Dec X5 (bal fig)	170
Comprehensive income for y/e 31 Dec X6 (S's SCI)	60
Net assets at 31 Dec X6	600

Now consider the movements each year, including the exchange difference that arises when the closing net assets are translated at closing rate for the consolidated statement of financial position.

Movement on post-acquisition reserves

	$000
Net assets at acquisition (1 Jan X5) at acquisition rate (370/5)	74
Comprehensive income for y/e 31 Dec X5 at average rate (170/4.6)	37
Exchange difference for y/e 31 Dec X5 (bal fig)	18
Net assets at 31 Dec X5 at closing rate (370 + 170)/4.2	129
Comprehensive income for y/e 31 Dec X6 at average rate (60/4.4)	14
Exchange difference for y/e 31 Dec X6 (bal fig)	(10)
Net assets at 31 Dec X6 at closing rate (600/4.5)	133

Therefore the post-acquisition reserves of 59 ($000) shown in W2 is:

	$000
Movement in post-acquisition reserves (37 + 14)	51
Foreign exchange differences (18 – 10)	8
	59

In the basic approach above, a combined reserves working was presented in working 5. However in practice all the exchange differences arising on translation of the subsidiary are held in a separate foreign currency translation reserve. The retained earnings reserve and foreign currency reserve in the above example would therefore be:

(W5a) Group retained earnings

	$000
P	675
S: 75% × 51 (movement on reserves excl. exchange diffs)	38
Impairment (75% × (6 + 6) (W3))	(9)
	704

(W5b) Group foreign currency translation reserve

	$000
Exchange differences on net assets of subsidiary since acquisition (75% × 8)	6
Exchange difference on goodwill since acquisition (75% × (10 – 4))	5
	11

Group retained earnings plus foreign currency translation reserve = 704 + 11 = 715 as shown in W5 using the combined approach.

Test your understanding 1 (Further practice integration question)

Paul is an entity whose functional and presentational currency is the dollar ($). On 1 January 20X7, Paul acquired 80% of the share capital of Simon, an entity whose functional currency is the Franc. Simon's reserves at this date showed a balance of Fr4,000. Paul paid Fr21,000 for the investment in Simon.

Below are the financial statements of Paul and Simon for the year ended 31 December 20X8.

Statements of financial position at 31 December 20X8

	Paul	Simon
	$	Fr
Non-current assets	60,000	25,000
Investment in Simon	4,200	
Current assets	35,800	15,000
	100,000	40,000
Equity		
Share capital	50,000	15,000
Reserves	20,000	14,000
	70,000	29,000
Current liabilities	30,000	11,000
	100,000	40,000

Statements of comprehensive income for the year ended 31 December 20X8

	Paul	Simon
	$	Fr
Revenue	25,000	10,000
Operating expenses	(10,000)	(4,000)
Profit from operations	15,000	6,000
Finance costs	(5,000)	(1,500)
Profit before tax	10,000	4,500
Tax	(3,000)	(1,000)
Profit for the year	7,000	3,500
Other comprehensive income	–	–
Total comprehensive income	7,000	3,500

Exchanges rates have been as follows:

	Fr: $1
1 January 20X7	5
31 December 20X7	3
31 December 20X8	2
Average for the year ended 31 December 20X8	2.5

It is Paul's policy to measure NCI at fair value at the date of acquisition and the fair value of the non-controlling interest in Simon was deemed to be Fr4,500 at this date. Goodwill had been reviewed for impairment as at 31 December 20X7 but none had arisen. At 31 December 20X8, it was determined that goodwill should be impaired by Fr1,000.

Required:

Prepare the consolidated statement of financial position and the consolidated statement of comprehensive income for the year ended 31 December 20X8.

Fair value adjustments in a foreign subsidiary

To deal with fair value adjustments in a foreign subsidiary, apply the following rules:

- On the face of the consolidated statement of financial position, translate the fair value adjustment using the closing rate

- In the statement of profit or loss, translate any fair value depreciation adjustment relating to the current year using the average rate

The impact of the fair value adjustment would then need to be carefully considered when calculating the exchange difference for the year on the net assets:

- The comprehensive income for the year should be adjusted for the current year fair value depreciation

- The opening and closing net assets should be adjusted for the fair value adjustment less accumulated depreciation at that point in time

Example 4 below demonstrates how a the fair value adjustment would affect the exchange difference calculation.

Example 4

In Example 3, P acquired 75% of the share capital of S on 1 January 20X5 for Fr 500,000 when the reserves of S were Fr 120,000. S's total share capital was Fr 250,000 and the reserves at the current reporting date of 31 December 20X6 were Fr 350,000. The fair value of the NCI at the date of acquisition was Fr 160,000 and it was group policy to measure NCI at fair value at acquisition.

S's total comprehensive income for the year ended 31 December 20X6 was Fr 60,000.

Relevant exchange rates were as follows:

1 January 20X5	$1 = 5Fr
31 December 20X5	$1 = 4.2Fr
31 December 20X6	$1 = 4.5Fr
Average for the year ended 31 December 20X5	$1 = 4.6Fr
Average for the year ended 31 December 20X6	$1 = 4.4Fr

Let's now assume that, at the date of acquisition, the fair value of S's net assets equalled book value with the exception of an item of plant whose fair value exceeded book value by Fr 200,000. The plant had a remaining useful life at the date of acquisition of 10 years.

The book values of property, plant and equipment of P and S at 31 December 20X6 were $1,250,000 and Fr 850,000 respectively.

In a change to the scenario in Example 3, let's also assume that goodwill has not been impaired.

Required:

Calculate the following amounts that would appear in the consolidated financial statements of the P group for the year ended 31 December 20X6 (work to the nearest $):

(1) Carrying value of property, plant and equipment at 31 December 20X6

(2) Total exchange difference arising on translation of S that would be recognised in other comprehensive income for the year.

Example 4 answer

In Example 3, the first step was to translate the financial statements of S. If there is a fair value adjustment then this can be built into this translation.

(W1) Translation of S's net assets at 31 December 20X6

	$000
Using closing rate of 4.5	
Non-current assets (850 + 200 FV – 40 dep)/4.5	224
(Note: FV depreciation = 200 × 2/10)	

We can then answer the first requirement - as all that is left is to add the translated figure to the parent's property, plant and equipment.

(1) **Carrying value of property, plant and equipment at 31 December 20X6 = $1,474,000**

	$000
PPE	
(1,250 + 224 (W1))	1,474

To calculate the exchange difference for the year we need to perform the goodwill calculation and we also need to consider the movement on net assets for the year.

(W2) **Goodwill**

	Fr000
Fair value of Ps investment	500
NCI at fair value	160
Fair value of sub's net assets at acquisition (250 + 120 + 200 FV)	(570)
Goodwill at acquisition and reporting date (no impairment)	90

Translation of goodwill:

	$000
At acquisition date (90/5)	18
Exchange difference y/e 31 Dec 05 (balancing figure)	3
At 31 Dec 05 (90/4.2)	21
Exchange difference y/e 31 Dec 06 (balancing figure)	(1)
At 31 Dec 06 (90/4.5)	20

In Example 3, to calculate the exchange difference arising on net assets we started with the closing net assets and worked backwards. An alternative is to work forwards and leave a line for the exchange difference (a balancing figure) before calculating the closing position. This can be useful in determining the opening net assets position of the subsidiary, which is the closing position less the comprehensive income for the year.

As you can see below, the fair value adjustments are then built into the calculation prior to translation. The fair value adjustment less cumulative depreciation is added to the closing net assets and the current year fair value depreciation is deducted from S's total comprehensive income for the year.

(W3) **Net assets**	Fr000	Rate	$000
Opening net assets (Closing less CI for year)	720	4.2	171
Comprehensive income for year (60 – 20 FV dep'n)	40	4.4	9
Exchange difference (bal fig)			(11)
Closing net assets (250 + 350 + 200 – 40) (SC + reserves + FV adjustment)	760	4.5	169

We now have the figures to answer requirement 2.

(2) **Total exchange difference for year = $12,000 loss**
Exchange difference in OCI:

	$000
Exchange loss on goodwill (W2)	(1)
Exchange loss on net assets (W3)	(11)
Total exchange loss for the year	(12)

Test your understanding 2 (integration question)

Upper acquired 85% of the equity shares of Lower, an entity whose functional and presentation currency is the Dinar (D), on 1 January 20X1 for cash consideration of D750,000. The book value of the net assets of Lower at the date of acquisition were D500,000 and this equated to fair value with the exception of an item of plant whose fair value was D120,000 higher than book value. The asset had a remaining useful life of 5 years at the date of acquisition and depreciation is charged on a straight line basis.

It is group policy to measure non-controlling interest at fair value at the date of acquisition and the fair value of the non-controlling interest in Lower on 1 January 20X1 was D150,000.

At the 31 December 20X4, the book values of Upper's and Lower's property, plant and equipment were $950,000 and D440,000 respectively. The book value of Lower's net assets at 31 December 20X4 was D620,000 and its total comprehensive income for the year ended 31 December 20X4 was D75,000.

Goodwill is tested for impairment annually but none was considered to have arisen as at 31 December 20X4.

The Upper group's presentation currency is the $.

Relevant exchange rates are:

Date	D to $1
1 January 20X1	7.8
31 December 20X3	9.0
31 December 20X4	8.2
Average rate for year ended 31 December 20X4	8.6

Required:

Calculate the following amounts that would be presented in the consolidated financial statements of the Upper group for the year ended 31 December 20X4:

(a) Property, plant and equipment as at 31 December 20X4

(b) Total exchange difference arising on the translation of Lower that would be presented in other comprehensive income for the year ended 31 December 20X4

State your answer to the nearest $.

(1) IAS 21 provides guidance on how to account for foreign currency transactions and operations.

Which of the following statements are TRUE? Select all that apply.

A The functional currency is the currency in which an entity must present its financial statements.

B Subsidiaries must present their financial statements in the presentation currency of their parent.

C When determining functional currency, entities should select the currency in which the majority of its purchases are made.

D When translating a foreign operation, the exchange difference should be recognised in profit.

E When translating a foreign operation, the exchange difference should be recognised as other comprehensive income.

F The presentation currency is decided by the directors.

(2) P owns 80% of the equity share capital of its foreign subsidiary F. F prepares financial statements in groats. Both entities have a reporting date of 31 March. At 1 April 20X3 the net assets of F were 20 million groats. The total comprehensive income of F for the year ended 31 March 20X4 was 2,200,000 groats. F does not pay dividends and goodwill was fully written off prior to 31 March 20X3. The presentation currency of P is the dollar, $.

Relevant exchange rates are:

Date	Groats to $1
31 March 20X3	2.5
31 March 20X4	2.0
Average rate for year ended 31 March 20X4	2.2

Calculate the exchange gain that would be recorded in other comprehensive income in the consolidated financial statements of the P group for the year ended 31 March 20X4 in respect of its subsidiary F (state your answer to the nearest $).

(3) North acquired 75% of the equity shares of South on 1 October 20X1 for Fr180,000. The book value of the net assets of South at the date of acquisition was Fr98,000 and this was considered to be the same as fair value.

It is group policy to measure non-controlling interest at fair value at the date of acquisition and the fair value of the non-controlling interest in South on 1 October 20X1 was Fr45,000.

Goodwill is tested for impairment annually. There was no impairment in the year ended 30 September 20X2 however goodwill was considered to have been impaired by 20% in the year ended 30 September 20X3. The impairment was translated at average rate for inclusion in the statement of consolidated profit or loss.

The North group's presentation currency is the $.

Exchange rates are:

Date	Fr to $1
1 October 20X1	3.0
30 September 20X2	2.7
30 September 20X3	2.4
Average rate for year ended 30 September 20X3	2.5

Calculate the exchange gain on goodwill in the year ended 30 September 20X3 that would be recognised in other comprehensive income. Give your answer to the nearest $.

(4) **Complete the sentences below by placing one of the options in each of the spaces (you may need to use the same option more than once).**

When a foreign operation is included in a consolidated set of financial statements, the assets and liabilities of the operation will be translated at _____ rate in the statement of financial position and the income and expenses will be translated at _____ rate in the consolidated statement of profit or loss and other comprehensive income.

An exchange difference arises on net assets and goodwill and this should be recognised each year in the statement of _____.

The exchange difference is calculated by translating the opening position at the _____ rate, the closing position at the _____ rate and any movements in the year (typically) at the _____ rate.

Options:

acquisition; average; closing; opening; other comprehensive income; profit or loss

(5) Yorkshire holds an 80% holding in Humber, an overseas entity. The Yorkshire group's presentation currency is $ and Humber's presentation currency is the Groat (Gr). The carrying value of property, plant and equipment (PPE) in Yorkshire's statement of financial position at the reporting date is $1,700,000. Humber's PPE at the same date has a carrying value of Gr 800,000.

Yorkshire acquired Humber 3 years ago and, at the date of acquisition, the fair value of Humber's PPE exceeded book value by Gr 250,000. The PPE had a remaining useful life at this date of 10 years.

Humber is the only subsidiary in the Yorkshire group.

Exchange rates are:

Date	Gr to $1
Acquisition (3 years ago)	7.5
Reporting date	6.2
Average rate for year	6.4

Calculate the carrying value of property, plant and equipment that would be recognised in the consolidated statement of financial position of the Yorkshire Group at the reporting date. Give your answer to the nearest $.

7 Chapter summary

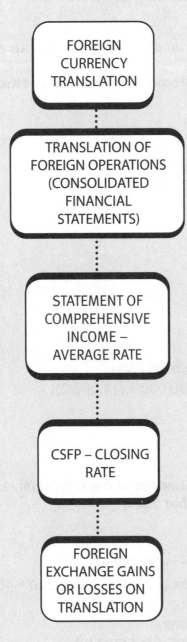

FOREIGN CURRENCY TRANSLATION

TRANSLATION OF FOREIGN OPERATIONS (CONSOLIDATED FINANCIAL STATEMENTS)

STATEMENT OF COMPREHENSIVE INCOME – AVERAGE RATE

CSFP – CLOSING RATE

FOREIGN EXCHANGE GAINS OR LOSSES ON TRANSLATION

Test your understanding answers

Consolidated statement of financial position at 31 December 20X8

	$
Goodwill (W3)	2,750
Non-current assets (60,000 + (25,000/2))	72,500
Current assets (35,800 + (15,000/2))	43,300
	118,550
Equity	
Share capital	50,000
Reserves (W5)	29,720
	79,720
Non-controlling interests (W4)	3,330
Current liabilities (30,000 + (11,000/2))	35,500
	118,550

Consolidated statement of comprehensive income for the year ended 31 December 20X8

	$
Revenue (25,000 + (10,000/2.5))	29,000
Operating expenses (10,000 + (4,000/2.5) + 400 (W3))	(12,000)
Profit from operations	17,000
Finance costs (5,000 + (1,500/2.5))	(5,600)
Profit before tax	11,400
Tax (3,000 + (1,000/2.5))	(3,400)
Profit for the year	8,000

Other comprehensive income
Items that may be reclassified subsequently to profit or loss:

Foreign exchange gains (W7)	5,583
Total comprehensive income	13,583

Profit attributable to:

Parent shareholders (balance)	7,800
NCI shareholders (W6)	200
	8,000

Total comprehensive income attributable to:

Parent shareholders (balance)	12,266
NCI shareholders (200 + (5,583 × 20% (W7))	1,317
	13,583

Workings

(W1) Group structure

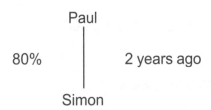

Paul

80%   2 years ago

Simon

(W2) Net assets of subsidiary

	Acquisition date	Reporting date
	Fr	Fr
Share capital	15,000	15,000
Retained earnings	4,000	14,000
	19,000	29,000
Translation	Acq'n rate = 5	Closing rate = 2
Translated net asset ($000)	3,800	14,500
Post-acq'n reserves (incl. exchange diff)	10,700	

(W3) Goodwill

	Fr
Fair value of P's investment	21,000
NCI at fair value	4,500
Fair value of sub's net assets at acquisition (W2)	(19,000)
Goodwill at acquisition/start of the year	6,500
Impairment	(1,000)
Goodwill at reporting date	5,500

	$
Translation of goodwill:	
At acquisition (6,500/5)	1,300
Exchange difference prior to current year (bal fig)	867
Opening goodwill at opening rate (6,500/3)	2,167
Impairment in current year at average rate (1,000/2.5)	(400)
Exchange difference current year (bal fig)	983
Goodwill at reporting date (5,500/2)	2,750

(W4) Non-controlling interests

	$
NCI at acquisition (4,500/5)	900
NCI% x post acquisition reserves (20% × 10,700 (W2))	2,140
NCI% x impairment (20% × 400)	(80)
NCI% x exchange diff on goodwill (20% × (867 + 983)(W3))	370
	3,330

(W5) Reserves

	$
Paul	20,000
Simon: (80% × 10,700 (W2))	8,560
Impairment (80% × 400)	(320)
Exchange difference on goodwill (80% × (867 + 983) (W3))	1,480
	29,720

(W6) **NCI share of profits**

	Fr
S's profit for the year	3,500
Impairment (fair value method)	(1,000)
Equity b/f per individual SOCIE	2,500
× 20%	500
Translated at average rate (500 @ 2.5)	$200

(W7) **Foreign exchange difference for OCI**

	$
Closing net assets at closing rate (W2)	14,500
Less opening net assets at opening rate (29,000 – 3,500)/3	(8,500)
Less comprehensive income for the year at average rate (3,500/2.5)	(1,400)
Exchange difference on net assets	4,600
Exchange difference on goodwill (W3)	983
Total exchange difference for the year	5,583

Test your understanding 2 (integration question)

(a) **Property, plant and equipment**

	$
Upper	950,000
Lower (440,000 + 120,000(FV) – 96,000(below))/8.2	56,585
CV of consolidated PPE	1,006,585

Working – FV depreciation

	D
FV depreciation (120,000 × 4/5)	96,000

(b) Total exchange difference for year (for OCI)

	$
Exchange difference on goodwill (W1)	3,035
Exchange difference on net assets (W2)	6,718
Total exchange difference	9,753

(W1) Goodwill

	D
Fair value of Upper's investment	750,000
NCI at fair value at acquisition	150,000
Fair value of Lower's net assets at acquisition (500,000 + 120,000)	(620,000)
Goodwill at acquisition and reporting date (no impairment)	280,000

Translation:	$
At opening rate (280,000/9.0)	31,111
At closing rate (280,000/8.2)	34,146
Exchange gain for year	3,035

(W2) Net assets

	D	Rate	$
Opening net assets (Closing less CI for year)	593,000	9.0	65,889
Comprehensive income for year (75,000 – 24,000 FV dep)	51,000	8.6	5,930
Exchange difference (bal fig)			6,718
Closing net assets (620,000 + 120,000 – 96,000) (Net assets + FV adj – FV dep of 120 ×4/5)	644,000	8.2	78,537

Test your understanding 3 (OTQ style qns)

(1) **E and F are the true statements.**

A is incorrect. An entity can choose a presentation currency that differs to its functional currency.

B is incorrect. Subsidiaries may choose to present their financial statements in the presentation currency of the parent (and may be under pressure to do so) but there is no regulatory requirement to do so.

C is incorrect. When determining functional currency, the currency that mainly influences sales prices and the currency that mainly influences labour, material and other costs should be considered. Costs are not given preference over sales prices.

D is incorrect. The exchange difference arising on translation of a foreign operation is recognised as other comprehensive income.

(2) **Exchange difference = $2,100,000**

	$000
Closing net assets at closing rate (20m + 2.2m)/2.0	11,100
Less opening net assets at opening rate 20m/2.5	(8,000)
Less comprehensive income for the year at average rate 2.2m/2.2	(1,000)
Exchange difference on net assets	2,100
No exchange difference on goodwill as fully written off	–
Total exchange difference for the year	2,100

(3) **Exchange gain on goodwill for year ended 30 September 20X3 = $5,456**

	Fr
Fair value of parent's investment	180,000
NCI at fair value at acquisition	45,000
Less fair value of net assets at acquisition	(98,000)
Goodwill at acquisition/start of the year	127,000
Impairment (20% × 127,000)	(25,400)
Goodwill at reporting date	101,600

Translation of goodwill:	$
Opening goodwill at opening rate (127,000/2.7)	47,037
Impairment in current year at average rate (25,400/2.5)	(10,160)
Exchange difference current year (bal fig)	5,456
	————
Goodwill at reporting date (101,600/2.4)	42,333
	————

(4) When a foreign operation is included in a consolidated set of financial statements, the assets and liabilities of the operation will be translated at **closing** rate in the statement of financial position and the income and expenses will be translated at **average** rate in the consolidated statement of profit or loss and other comprehensive income.

An exchange difference arises on net assets and goodwill and this should be recognised each year in the statement of **other comprehensive income.**

The exchange difference is calculated by translating the opening position at the **opening** rate, the closing position at the **closing** rate and any movements in the year (typically) at the **average** rate.

(5) **Property, plant and equipment = $1,857,258**

Property, plant and equipment

	$
Yorkshire	1,700,000
Humber (800,000 + 250,000 (FV) − 75,000 (below))/6.2	157,258
	————
CV of consolidated PPE	1,857,258
	————

Working – FV depreciation

	Gr
FV depreciation (250,000 × 3/10)	75,000

Analysis of financial performance and position

Chapter learning objectives

C1. Evaluate the financial performance, financial position and financial adaptability of an incorporated entity.

(a) Calculate ratios relevant for the assessment of an entity's profitability, financial performance, financial position and financial adaptability:

- – Ratios for profitability, performance, efficiency, activity, liquidity and gearing.

(b) Evaluate the financial performance, financial position and financial adaptability of an entity based on the information contained in the financial statements provided

(c) Advise on action that could be taken to improve an entity's financial performance and financial position.

C2. Discuss the limitations of ratio analysis.

(a) Discuss the limitations of ratio analysis based on financial statements that can be caused by internal and external factors:

- – Inter-segment comparisons
- – International comparisons.

1 Session content

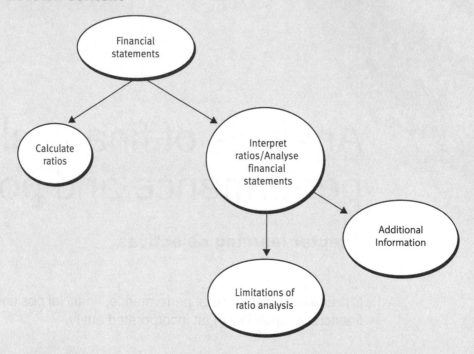

2 Introduction

The IASB's conceptual framework states:

The objective of financial reporting is to provide financial information about the reporting entity that is useful to existing and potential investors, lenders and other creditors in making decisions about providing resources to the entity.

Interpretation and analysis of the financial statements is the process of arranging, examining and comparing the results in order that users are equipped to make such decisions. This process is assisted by adopting an analytical approach. The main components of an appropriate approach are:

- identification of the user of the analysis
- an understanding of the nature of the business, industry and organisation
- identification of relevant sources of data for analysis
- numerical analysis of the data available
- interpretation of the results of the analysis.

3 Users of the analysis

It is important to identify the type of user for whom an analysis is being prepared, as different users have different needs. It is important that any analysis exercise is oriented towards the needs of the particular user who requires the analysis.

There is a wide range of user groups that may be interested in an entity's financial statements. Historically the financial statements have been prepared for investors. However, other users will also be interested in them.

Users of financial statements

Present and potential investors

Both present and potential investors are interested in information that is useful in making buy/sell/hold decisions. Will the entity be able to generate cash in the future? How risky is the investment? Does its financial performance exceed that of other potential investee entities? How much is the investment likely to yield in capital growth and/or dividend? Analysis of the financial statements can help to answer these questions. There is a range of ratios of particular interest to the investor group; these are examined in detail later in this chapter. In addition, return on capital employed (ROCE) and related performance and asset management ratios are likely to be of interest to this group of users.

Lenders and potential lenders

Lenders are principally interested in assessing whether or not the loans that they have made are likely to be repaid, and whether or not the related interest charge will be paid in full and on time. Potential lenders require analysis of financial statements in order to assist them in deciding whether or not to lend. Lender groups are likely to be particularly interested in ratios such as interest cover and gearing, and will be interested in the nature and longevity of other categories of loan to the entity.

Suppliers and other creditors

This group is interested in information that helps them to decide whether or not to supply goods or services to an entity. Availability of cash will be of particular interest, together with such evidence as is available in general-purpose financial statements about the entity's record in paying its creditors on time. Working capital ratios and the working capital cycle may be appropriate calculations to undertake when analysing financial statements for the benefit of this class of user.

Employees

In large organisations employees are likely to be particularly interested in one part of the entity's operations. They may, therefore, find segmental information to be useful. More generally, they need to be able to assess the stability and performance of the entity in order to gauge how reliable it is likely to be as a source of employment in the longer term. Employees are likely to be interested in disclosures about retirement benefits and remuneration.

Customers

Customers may be in a vulnerable position if there are few potential suppliers in a market for goods. They may therefore be interested in assessing the risks which threaten their supplier. Potentially they may be interested in takeover opportunities in order to ensure the continuing supply of a particular raw material.

Governments and their agencies

The governmental group is in a position to require special-purpose reports. Tax computations would fall into this category. However, general-purpose reports may also be of use, for example in gathering statistics on particular industries.

The general public

Members of the public may have special interests in the activities of certain entities, especially where, say, an individual entity dominates the local employment market. Pressure groups and their members would also fall under the umbrella category of 'general public', and their needs will vary according to their special interest. Environmental issues are of increasing concern to many people, and it is likely that pressure groups will take a particular interest in firms that are perceived as polluters. Analysis of the financial statements for this type of user would tend to focus on any additional voluntary disclosures made about the entity's environmental policies, on provisions and contingent liabilities related to environmental damage, and on capital investment (e.g. investment in new plant).

4 Understanding the entity

It is often thought that financial analysis involves purely the application of a standard set of numerical calculations to a set of published accounts. This is only one part of the task. In order to interpret those calculations it is important to understand the entity's current position.

The history of the entity underlies the current position and future outlook. Furthermore, the owners and their individual characteristics will influence factors such as the level of risk in the entity and dividend policy. Knowledge of the quality, qualifications and experience of management will assist in evaluating the performance and position of the entity.

Financial analysis requires an understanding of the products, services and operating characteristics of the entity. This will assist in understanding data such as revenue, profitability, inventories and working capital.

The entity operates within an industry consisting of entities with similar operating characteristics. If the analysis requires comparison of the entity with the industry norms, it is important to identify the key characteristics of the industry and to establish benchmarks such as gross profit ratios, receivables collection days etc.

5 Relevant sources of data

In practice, the analyst needs to consider carefully the possible sources of information available about an entity, starting with the annual report. This will contain financial information but there may be additional voluntary disclosures that will be helpful to the analyst, such as the entity's environmental impact, employment reports, graphs, pie charts and ratio calculations.

In the management level case study, pre-seen material will be provided in advance of the assessment and it will be important to consider how this information might be helpful in performing any analysis requirements that appear in the assessment.

6 Calculation and interpretation of ratios

There are a variety of ratios that can be used when assessing an entity's financial statements and they fall into four broad categories:

- Profitability/performance ratios
    - Gross profit margin, operating profit margin, net profit margin
    - Return on capital employed
- Liquidity ratios
    - Current and quick (acid test) ratios
- Efficiency/activity ratios
    - Working capital ratios
    - Asset turnover ratios
- Capital structure ratios
    - Gearing
    - Interest cover

The financial statements provided below will be used to demonstrate how to calculate and interpret these ratios across test your understandings (TYUs) 1 to 4.

Financial information for TYUs 1 to 4

Below are the financial statements for T for the years ended 30 June 20X5 and 20X6:

Statement of profit and loss and other comprehensive income

	20X6	20X5
	$000	$000
Revenue	180	150
Cost of sales	(65)	(60)
Gross profit	115	90
Operating expenses	(40)	(29)
Share of profit of associate	59	–
Finance costs	(24)	(10)
Profit before tax	110	51
Tax	(14)	(13)
Profit for the year	96	38
Other comprehensive income:		
Items that may be reclassified subsequently to profit or loss:		
AFS gains	14	5
Items that will not be reclassified to profit or loss:		
Revaluation of PPE	30	–
Total comprehensive income	140	43

Summarised statements of changes in equity

	20X6	20X5
	$000	$000
Opening balance	100	82
Issue of shares	3	–
Total comprehensive income for the year	140	43
Dividends	(25)	(25)
Closing balance	218	100

Statements of financial position

	20X6	20X5
Non-current assets	$000	$000
Property, plant and equipment	266	190
Investment in associate	250	–
Other financial assets	31	17
	547	207

	20X6		20X5	
Current assets				
Inventory	15		12	
Receivables	49		37	
Cash and cash equivalents	–		1	
		64		50
		611		257

	20X6	20X5
Equity		
Share capital	12	10
Share premium	5	4
Revaluation reserve	30	–
Available for sale reserve	21	7
Retained earnings	150	79
Total equity	218	100

	20X6	20X5
Non-current liabilities		
Long term borrowings	335	110
Deferred tax	14	15
	349	125

	20X6	20X5
Current liabilities		
Trade payables	12	11
Overdraft	9	–
Taxation	13	11
Provisions	10	10
	44	32
	611	257

Test your understanding 1 (integration question) – Profitability

Required:

For each of the two years, calculate the following ratios for T and suggest reasons why the ratios have changed.

	20X6	20X5

Gross profit margin

$$\frac{\text{Gross profit}}{\text{Revenue}} \times 100\%$$

Operating profit margin

$$\frac{\text{Operating profit}}{\text{Revenue}} \times 100\%$$

Profit before tax margin

$$\frac{\text{Profit before tax}}{\text{Revenue}} \times 100\%$$

Effective tax rate

$$\frac{\text{Tax expense}}{\text{Profit before tax*}} \times 100\%$$

* Share of profit of associate should be excluded from profit, as it is already net of tax

Return on capital employed

$$\frac{\text{Operating profit}}{\text{Capital employed}} \times 100\%$$

Operating profit = Gross profit less operating (admin and distribution) expenses

Capital employed = equity (share capital plus reserves) + interest bearing borrowings – non-current assets that do not contribute to operating profit (such as financial assets and investments in associates)

Analysing profitability ratios and data

Start by looking at the first line in the statement of comprehensive income: *revenue*. Has it gone up or down and what is the percentage increase or decrease? A change in revenue may be due to a change in selling price or sales volume or both.

Gross profit margin is the percentage of revenue retained after costs of sale are deducted. Entities will aim to sell many products with a low margin or potentially fewer products with a high margin. A change in gross profit margin may be due to a change in product mix, for example selling more of a product with a higher margin or conversely bringing a new product to market with a low margin to gain market share.

The *operating profit margin* is the trading or operating profit in relation to revenue, expressed as a percentage. The difference between gross profit margin and operating profit margin is the operating costs of the entity such as administration costs, telephone costs and advertising costs. You need to use any background information provided to assess how these expenses may differ to the prior year or to another entity.

Profit before tax margin expresses the relationship between profit before tax and sales. Profit for this purpose would be after deduction of finance costs. An alternative is to calculate profit after tax margin.

Non-current asset policies (see Illustration 1) can have a substantial effect on ratios and comparison between entities. For example, there may be differences in whether an entity owns or leases assets and whether assets are measured at historical cost or are revalued. Depreciation charges will be higher for revalued assets. Depreciation may be categorised as a cost of sale or operating expense.

Exceptional items such as a profit on disposal of a non-current asset should be removed from the analysis to enable comparisons to be made.

Effective tax rate assesses the extent of the impact that tax has on the entity's profit.

Return on capital employed (ROCE) is a very useful measure when analysing performance. It assesses the efficiency with which the entity uses its assets to produce profit. You should consider any changes in capital employed and, for example, whether an increase occurred towards the end of an accounting period and hence there has not yet been an opportunity for the entity to use the capital to generate increased profit.

Further analysis of profitability

Revenue

Problems can arise in making a valid interpretation of movements in revenue. For example:

- Accounting policies on revenue recognition may vary between entities. There may be inconsistencies between accounting periods, especially where the entity derives some or all of its revenue from long-term contracts.

- Inflation may account for some of the increase in price.

- A detailed breakdown of revenue for the entity may not be available. To some extent IFRS 8 Operating Segments (see later in the chapter for more details) requires revenue details for different segments of the entity. However there are problems in using segmental data, for example, segments may not be consistently defined.

Understanding the reasons for movements in revenue may help to explain movements in costs such as cost of sales, advertising, selling and distribution costs and telephone charges. If revenue increases, then a similar increase in these revenue-related costs could be expected. Conversely, an increase in, say, marketing and advertising expenditure might help to explain an increase in revenue.

Gross profit margin

This ratio is expected to be more or less constant from one year to the next within an entity. Even if there is an increase in direct costs, an efficient entity could be expected to pass on the increases in the form of increased sales prices. However, this may not be the case in reality.

The gross profit margin requires a detailed breakdown in order to gain an understanding of movements. Ideally, the analyst requires information relating to opening and closing inventories, purchases, direct wages and overheads. Further information as to the following items would be required in order to evaluate gross profit margin fully:

- breakdown by product, geographical area or other segment

- inventory valuation policies

- overhead allocation methods

- purchasing details such as bulk discounts, purchasing errors, wastage or theft

- selling prices of different products over the period.

Obviously, much of this information is not available from an entity's annual report. Some entities do not even report gross profits.

Operating profit margin

Operating profit is the profit from the trading activities of the business; it comprises profits after operating costs, but before finance costs, tax, investment income and any share of profits from an associate. Note that IAS 1 revised does not encourage the reporting of operating profit as a separate line item, although there is nothing to prevent entities providing additional information.

Profit before/after tax margin

Where comparing profit year on year, it is important to allow for any exceptional charges or credits. Also, it would be sensible when calculating profit after tax margin to take into account any large adjustments in respect of under- or over-provided tax provisions.

Effective tax rate

This will help to understand the impact that tax has on the overall profit for the year. Tax is a consequence of being profitable and, to a certain extent, the impact of tax on profits is outside the control of the entity, however it should be considered when making investment decisions.

Return on capital employed

Return on capital employed (ROCE) is a measurement that is frequently used in the analysis of financial statements. This shows the overall performance of the entity, expressed as a percentage return on the total investment. It measures management's efficiency in generating profits from the resources available.

Consistency of numerator and denominator is important in this ratio. Therefore, in calculating ROCE, the numerator should include profit before any deductions for finance costs. If capital employed includes a bank overdraft, the profit figure used in the calculation should exclude interest paid and payable on the overdraft.

The basic capital employed figure (the denominator) is equity (including share capital, reserves and NCI) and interest bearing borrowings. An adjustment should then be made to remove the carrying value of any non-current asset that does not contribute to operating profit (the numerator) in order to provide consistency. A classic example of this is an investment in associate. The share of associate profit is presented in the statement of profit or loss below operating profit, therefore the value of the investment in associate should be deducted from the capital employed figure.

EBITDA

EBITDA is an acronym for earnings before interest, tax, depreciation and amortisation.

In recent years many large entities have adopted EBITDA as a key measure of financial performance. Sceptics suggest that they do this in order to publicise a higher measure of earnings than profit from operations (this type of measurement is sometimes cynically referred to as EBB – earnings before the bad bits).

However, it does make some sense to measure EBITDA, provided that the user fully understands what is included and what is left out. Depreciation and amortisation are accounting adjustments, not representing cash flows, that are determined by management. It can therefore be argued that excluding these items in assessing earnings eliminates a major area where management bias can operate.

Unfortunately, EBITDA is consequently often misunderstood as being a measurement of cash flow, which of course it is not. Even though two categories of non-cash adjustment are eliminated, financial statements are prepared on an accruals basis. EBITDA makes no adjustments in respect of accruals or working capital movements, and so is emphatically not a cash flow measurement.

Test your understanding 2

Requirement

Using the financial information for TYU 1 – 4, calculate the EBITDA for 20X6 and 20X5.

The following further information is also available:

	20X6	20X5
Depreciation	6	3

Illustration 1 – Effect of non-current asset policies on ratios

The following information has been extracted from the financial statements of A, B and C for the year ended 30 September 20X4:

	A	B	C
Statement of profit or loss	$000	$000	$000
Revenue	200	200	200
Operating costs	(160)	(190)	(170)
Profit from operations	40	10	30
Statement of financial position			
Share capital	50	50	50
Retained earnings	90	60	50
Revaluation reserve		210	
Capital employed	140	320	100
Operating profit margin	20%	5%	15%
Return on capital employed	28.6%	3.1%	30%

Entity A

A had purchased an asset costing $200,000 4 years ago. The asset is being depreciated on the straight-line basis over 10 years. Therefore, $20,000 of depreciation has been charged to this year's statement of profit and loss and the asset has a carrying value of $120,000 in the statement of financial position.

B and C as entities hold a similar asset to A but have adopted the following treatments in their financial statements. They are identical to A in all other respects.

Entity B

B revalued the asset to its current value of $350,000 at the start of the current year. As a result a revaluation gain of $210,000 has been recognised and depreciation has been increased to $50,000 per annum, i.e. additional depreciation of $30,000 has been charged to the statement of profit and loss in the current year.

The revaluation has caused the operating profit margin to fall due to the extra depreciation. Return on capital employed has also fallen due to the revaluation reserve being included in capital employed.

Hence the entity looks to be generating a lower return.

Entity C

C has been leasing the asset under an operating lease agreement, paying an annual rental of $30,000 which has been charged to operating expenses.

This causes the operating profit margin to fall due to the lease payments being higher than depreciation. However, the return on capital employed is higher than A since the asset is not included on the statement of financial position but is still being used by the business to generate sales.

Test your understanding 3 (integration question) – Liquidity

Required:

Using the financial statements provided for T, calculate the following ratios for T and suggest why the ratios may have changed.

	20X6	20X5

Current ratio

$$\frac{\text{Current assets}}{\text{Current liabilities}}$$

Quick ratio

$$\frac{(\text{Current assets} - \text{Inventory})}{\text{Current liabilities}}$$

Test your understanding 4 (integration question) – Efficiency

Required:

Using the financial statements provided for T, calculate the following ratios for T and suggest why the ratios may have changed.

	20X6	20X5

Inventory holding period

$$\frac{\text{Inventory}}{\text{Cost of sales}} \times 365 \text{ days}$$

Receivables collection period

$$\frac{\text{Receivables}}{\text{Revenue}} \times 365 \text{ days}$$

Payables payment period

$$\frac{\text{Trade payables}}{\text{Cost of Sales}} \times 365 \text{ days}$$

Asset turnover

$$\frac{\text{Revenue}}{\text{Capital employed}}$$

Non-current asset turnover

$$\frac{\text{Revenue}}{\text{Non-current assets (that contribute to revenue)}}$$

Analysing liquidity

The analysis of the liquidity of an entity should start with a review of the actual *bank balance* in absolute terms. Has the bank balance increased or decreased significantly? It could be that the overdraft is near to its permitted limit or that high cash resources indicate a good takeover prospect.

The *current ratio* compares current assets to current liabilities. A ratio greater than 1 indicates there are more current assets than current liabilities. The current ratio guides us to the extent the entity is able to meet its current liabilities as they fall due.

The *quick ratio* compares current assets, excluding inventory, to current liabilities. The quick ratio gives a better indicator of liquidity if the inventory of an entity is difficult to realise into cash, for example, a whisky distillery that requires a number of months to mature before being sold.

Analysing efficiency/activity

The *inventory holding period* indicates how much working capital is tied up in goods in the warehouse by giving an average number of days that inventory is held before being sold. An entity must balance the need to supply goods on time to customers with the risk of obsolescence.

The *receivables collection period* tells us the number of days it takes on average to receive payment from credit customers. It should be based on the credit agreement with customers. Cash should be collected efficiently whilst bearing in mind customers in a strong negotiating position.

The *payables payment period* is the length of time it takes to pay suppliers for goods bought on credit. This is effectively a free source of finance but the business should make sure suppliers are paid on a timely basis to avoid the risk of stock-outs.

Asset turnover measures how much revenue is being generated from the overall capital invested. It is a measure of the efficiency/activity of the capital.

Non-current asset turnover is a similar calculation but measuring the efficiency/activity of non-current assets only. There are many variations of this ratio that can provide useful information, such as total asset turnover and working capital turnover.

Over-trading

When an entity grows rapidly there is a risk of *over-trading*, i.e. expanding the entity without adequate long term or short term finance. Inventory, receivables and payables increase but there is a decline in cash and the entity may be unable to pay its suppliers as debts fall due.

Entities in this position should look to raise long-term finance. This will enable the entity to improve its inventory and credit control and, by reducing its inventory and receivable days, improve its cash-flow.

Other options include factoring of receivables or invoice discounting facilities.

Further analysis of liquidity and efficiency/activity

Short term liquidity

The quick ratio recognises that the time taken to convert inventory into cash in many entities is significantly longer than other current assets and so gives a more conservative view of liquidity. However, it is important to select ratios suitable for the circumstances of the entity. If inventory is an insignificant amount (as it would be, for example, in most service entities), there is little point in calculating the quick ratio.

There is no standard number that should be expected in these calculations; it should depend on the industry and should be linked to other areas of the analysis. The higher the ratio, the more liquid the entity, but high liquidity can itself be a problem. It may mean that the entity is unable to utilise cash effectively by investing it profitably.

The working capital cycle

The length of the working capital cycle can assist in determining the immediate effects of the financial position on the bank balance.

The working capital cycle comprises cash, receivables, inventory and payables. The entity uses cash to buy inventory. Additional inventory may be purchased on credit.

Inventories are sold and become receivables. Receivables pay and then the entity has cash available to repay payables or buy further inventory.

The total length of the working capital cycle is the inventory holding period plus the receivables days less the payables days, which approximates to the total time it takes to purchase the inventory, sell the inventory and receive cash.

Inventory holding period

The ratio gives the number of days that inventory, on average, has remained in the warehouse. If only a closing figure is available for inventory, then that can be used. However, the result must be treated with some caution, as the closing figure may be unrepresentative, particularly if the nature of the entity's business is seasonal. An average stock level should be used if the closing stock figure is deemed not representative.

Receivables days

A retail or cash-based entity may have zero or very low receivables days. Note that, where an entity sells for both cash and on credit, it will be necessary to split revenue into the two types.

Payables days

Current payables comprise a form of finance which is free, or almost free. However, there may be costs in terms of loss of prompt payment discount, and loss of supplier goodwill where excessive time is taken to pay. Efficiency is measured relative to industry norms, receivables days and supplier terms.

To calculate the working capital cycle, if figures are not available for credit sales and credit purchases (as may well be the case if the data source is a set of published accounts), an approximation may be obtained by using total revenue and cost of sales respectively, but the results of such ratio calculations must be treated with caution.

Asset turnover/utilisation

This calculation shows how much revenue is produced per unit of capital invested.

This ratio shows the productivity of assets in generating sales. It should be noted that this ratio is not always useful or informative. Where an entity is using assets that are nearing the end of their useful lives, having been subject to annual depreciation charges over a relatively long period, the ratio is likely to be rather high. Similarly, where an entity uses the historical cost convention, unmodified by revaluation, asset values are also likely to be relatively low, an effect which is more intrusive as the assets age. Also, in labour-intensive entities, where the non-current asset base is low, the ratio tends to lack significance.

Note that, where possible, the average asset figure over the year should be used in the denominator of the fraction. This is likely to give a more consistent and representative result. External users of annual reports do not have access to monthly information with which to calculate an average, but opening and closing figures often give a reasonable approximation.

The denominator should exclude any assets that do not contribute to revenue as these would distort the ratio.

Test your understanding 5 (integration question) – Gearing

Required:

Using the financial statements provided for T in TYU 1, calculate the following ratios for T and suggest why the ratios may have changed.

	20X6	20X5

Gearing

$$\frac{\text{Debt}}{\text{Debt} + \text{Equity}}$$

Gearing (alternative)

$$\frac{\text{Debt}}{\text{Equity}}$$

Interest cover

$$\frac{\text{Operating profit}}{\text{Finance costs}}$$

Average rate of borrowing

$$\frac{\text{Finance costs}}{\text{Borrowings}}$$

Dividend cover

$$\frac{\text{Profit for the year}}{\text{Dividends}}$$

Analysing capital structure ratios and data

Gearing is an important measure of risk and a guide to the long term solvency of the entity. It is calculated by taking long term debt as a percentage of total capital employed, i.e. long term debt plus shareholders' funds. Alternatively it can be calculated by taking debt as a percentage of equity, or shareholders' funds. Make your calculation clear in the exam.

It is important to assess the gearing ratio against the *industry average* and to ensure that the debt finance is put to good use to generate revenue and profits.

The interest charged on debt finance should be compared to *interest rates* available to the entity from other sources. Also, debt is often *secured on assets* for security so there needs to be sufficient assets for this to be possible.

Interest cover indicates the number of times profits will cover the interest charge; the higher the ratio, the better. When looking at interest cover, the *stability of profits* is important as the interest must be paid consistently out of available profits otherwise the entity may default on its debt and may have to repay it at short notice.

Average rate of borrowings indicates the typical interest rate that the entity pays on its debt finance. A high rate would suggest that lenders consider the entity to be a relatively high risk.

Dividend cover indicates the number of times profits will cover the dividend; the higher the ratio the better as shareholders may expect a sustainable dividend payment.

Further analysis of capital structure

The gearing (or leverage) ratio is an important measure of risk.

It is important to analyse, particularly for users such as shareholders and creditors, the ability to satisfy debts falling due after one year. There are two elements to consider: repayment of capital and payment of interest. The statement of financial position shows the current liquidity and capital structure of the entity, that is the short-term liquidity and the level of fixed prior charge capital.

The statement of profit or loss shows the profitability of the business generally, indicating its ability to generate cash, some of which may be available to repay debt.

The capital structure of the entity provides information about the relative risk that is accepted by shareholders and creditors. As long-term debt increases relative to shareholders' funds, then more risk is assumed by long-term creditors and so they would require higher rewards, thereby decreasing resources available for the shareholders. As risk increases, creditors require higher interest in order to compensate for the higher risk.

However, the use of debt by management in their capital structure can assist in increasing profits available to shareholders. Cash received into the entity from lenders will be used to generate revenue and profits. As interest costs are fixed, any profits generated in excess of the interest costs will accrue to the shareholders. There is, however, a negative side to the use of debt in the entity. If the cash from the debt does not raise sufficient profits then the fixed interest cost must be paid first and so profits available to shareholders are decreased, and may be extinguished completely.

Gearing

Gearing is calculated by taking long term debt as a percentage of total capital employed, i.e. long term debt plus shareholders' funds. Long-term debt includes debentures, mortgages and other long-term debt, including redeemable preference shares. Any bank overdraft would be included to the extent that it is actually a source of long-term finance. Whether overdrafts are deemed long-term (therefore used in gearing) or short-term (not used in gearing) would be explicitly stated within any exam question. Shareholders' funds comprises equity share capital and reserves.

Interest cover

Although the use of debt may generate higher profits for shareholders there is a limit to its use. This may be gauged from the statement of profit or loss by focusing on the profitability and interest repayments in the interest cover ratio.

Illustration 2 – High gearing can be beneficial to shareholders

	Alpha		Beta	
	20X1	20X2	20X1	20X2
Statements of profit or loss	$	$	$	$
Profit from operations	20,000	25,000	20,000	25,000
Finance cost	(1,000)	(1,000)	(4,000)	(4,000)
Profit before tax	19,000	24,000	16,000	21,000
Income tax	(5,700)	(7,200)	(4,800)	(6,300)
Profit for the year	13,300	16,800	11,200	14,700
Dividends paid (5c per share)	2,000	2,000	500	500
Statements of financial position				
10% Loan notes	10,000	10,000	40,000	40,000
Share capital $1 ordinary shares	40,000	40,000	10,000	10,000
Reserves	50,000	53,500	50,000	53,500
Capital employed	100,000	103,500	100,000	103,500

Beta is more highly geared than Alpha in 20X1, but both companies have the same amount of capital employed in total and generate the same returns overall:

	Alpha	Beta
	20X1	20X1
Gearing (Debt/ debt + equity)	10%	40%
ROCE (Operating profit/debt + equity)	20%	20%

In 20X2 there is a 25% increase in the operating profits of both companies. However the shareholders of Beta benefit more than the shareholders of Alpha:

	Alpha		Beta	
	20X1	20X2	20X1	20X2
Return on equity	14.8%	18.0%	18.7%	23.1%
(Profit for year/equity)				
Increase on prior year		+21.6%		+23.5%
Earnings per share	33.25c	42c	112c	147c
(Profit for year/no. of shares)				
Increase on prior year		+26.3%		+31.25%

Test your understanding 6 (OTQ style)

The return on capital employed of YK has increased from 12.5% to 16.4% in the year to 31 December 20X4.

Required:

Which one of the following would be a valid reason for this increase?

A   YK has acquired a significant amount of property, plant and equipment close to the year end.

B   YK has revalued its land and buildings for the first time this year, resulting in an increase in carrying value.

C   YK raised long-term borrowings to finance the payment of a significant dividend.

D   A significant number of YK's assets were fully written down at the previous year end.

Test your understanding 7 (integration question)

The financial statements of DFG for the year ended 31 December 20X1 are provided below:

Statements of financial position at 31 December

	20X1		20X0	
	$m	$m	$m	$m
Non-current assets				
Property, plant and equipment	254		198	
Investment in associate	24		–	
		278		198
Current assets				
Inventories	106		89	
Receivables	72		48	
Cash and cash equivalents	–		6	
		178		143
Total assets		456		341

Equity

Share capital ($1 equity shares)	45	45
Retained earnings	146	139
Revaluation reserve	40	–
	231	184

Non-current liabilities

Long-term borrowings	91	91

Current liabilities

Trade and other payables	95	66
Short-term borrowings	39	–
	134	66
	456	341

Statement of comprehensive income for the year ended 31 December

	20X1	20X0
	$m	$m
Revenue	252	248
Cost of sales	(203)	(223)
Gross profit	49	25
Distribution costs	(18)	(13)
Administrative expenses	(16)	(11)
Share of profit of associate	7	–
Finance costs	(12)	(8)
Profit before tax	10	(7)
Income tax expense	(3)	2
Profit for the year	7	(5)
Other comprehensive income:		
Items that will not be reclassified to profit and loss		
Revaluation gain on PPE	40	–
Total comprehensive income for the year	47	(5)

Required:

Calculate the following ratios for DFG for the year ended 31 December 20X1 and its comparative period:

- Gross profit margin

- Operating profit margin

- Profit for the year margin

- Gearing (debt/equity)

- Current ratio

- Quick ratio

- Receivables collection period

- Payables payment period

- Inventory holding period

- Return on capital employed

- Non-current asset turnover

- Interest cover

Test your understanding 8 (case style)

You work as an accountant for XYZ. The finance director has asked you to analyse the financial statements of DFG, the entity whose financial statements are included in TYU 6 above, as the board of directors are considering acquiring the business. DFG supplies the building trade. The finance director commented that he had reviewed the information on DFG's website and there were lots of positive messages about the entity's future, including how it had secured a new supplier relationship in 20X1 resulting in a significant improvement in margins.

In addition to the financial statements, he has obtained the following information about DFG:

(1) **Long term borrowings**

The long term borrowings are repayable in 20X3.

(2) Contingent liability

The notes to the financial statements include details of a contingent liability of $30 million. A major customer, a house builder, is suing DFG, claiming that it supplied faulty goods. The customer had to rectify some of its building work when investigations discovered that a building material, which had recently been supplied by DFG, was found to contain a hazardous substance. The initial assessment from the lawyer is that DFG is likely to lose the case although the amount of potential damages could not be measured with sufficient reliability at the year-end date.

(3) Revaluation

DFG decided on a change of accounting policy in the year and now includes its land and buildings at their revalued amount. The valuation was performed by an employee of DFG who is a qualified valuer.

Required:

Using the financial information from TYU 6 and the additional information above, analyse the financial performance of DFG for the year to 31 December 20X1 and its financial position at that date to assess its suitability as an acquisition target for XYZ. Discuss your findings in a report address to the Board of Directors.

7 Limitations of analysis of financial statements

Financial statements analysis has its limitations and it may be necessary to highlight limitations in your assessment (or discuss them in the case study).

It is important to answer the question requirement carefully, i.e. are you asked for limitations of financial information or the limitations of using ratios for analysis? It is also important to make your answer specific to the entity in question, if you are provided with one.

Limitations of financial reporting information

- Only provide historic data.
- Only provide financial information.
- Filed at least 3 months after reporting date reducing its relevance.
- Limited information to be able to identify trends over time.
- Lack of detailed information.
- Historic cost accounting does not take into account inflation.

Difficulties in drawing comparisons between different entities

- Comparisons affected by changes in the entity's business, for example selling an operation.
- Different accounting policies between different entities, e.g. revaluations.
- Different accounting practices between different entities, e.g. debt factoring, lease v buy decisions.
- Different entities within the same industry may have different activities.
- Non co-terminous accounting periods.
- Different entities may not be comparable in terms of size.
- Comparisons between entities operating in different countries will be influenced by different legal and regulatory systems, the relative strength and weakness of the national economy and exchange rate fluctuations.

Limitations of ratio analysis

- Where ratios have been provided, there may be discrepancies between how they have been calculated for each entity/period, e.g. gearing.
- Distortions when using year-end figures, particularly in seasonal industries and when entities have different accounting dates.
- Distortions due to not being able to use most appropriate figures, e.g. total sales revenue rather than credit sales when calculating receivables days.
- It is difficult to identify reasons behind ratio movements without significant additional information.

Creative accounting

- Timing of transactions may be delayed/speeded up to improve results, e.g. not investing in non-current assets to ensure ROCE does not fall.

- Profit smoothing using choices allowed, e.g. inventory valuation method.

- Classification of items, e.g. expenses v non-current assets; ordinary v exceptional.

- Off-balance sheet financing to improve gearing and ROCE.

- Revenue recognition policies.

- Managing market expectations.

These are, of course, generic limitations that are not necessarily applicable to all entities in all circumstances. If asked to discuss limitations (in the case study) or when attempting a F2 examination question, your discussion or answer must be applied to the unique traits of an entity, for example: if you have been asked to compare two entities it makes sense to consider whether they use the same accounting policies (e.g. depreciation rates) and business methods (e.g. acquiring or leasing assets). Please refer to the following expandable text sections for further guidance on these areas.

Limitations of financial reporting information

The objective of financial statements is set out in the IASB's Conceptual Framework for Financial Reporting, published in September 2010:

"The objective of general purpose financial reporting is to provide financial information about the reporting entity that is useful to existing and potential investors, lenders and other creditors in making decisions about providing resources to the entity."

A rather substantial limitation of financial statements, is, however, then explained in the following paragraphs:

"... general purpose financial reports do not and cannot provide all of the information that existing and potential investors, lenders and other creditors need. Those users need to consider pertinent information from other sources, for example, general economic conditions and expectations, political events and political climate, and industry and company outlooks.

Other parties, such as regulators and members of the public other than investors, lenders and other creditors, may also find general purpose financial reports useful. However, those reports are not primarily directed to these other groups."

It appears that although financial statements may be useful to a wide range of users, their usefulness is limited. The principal drawback is the fact that financial statements are oriented towards events that have already taken place. However, there are other significant limitations of the information contained in a set of financial statements. These can be summarised under the following principal headings.

Timeliness

By the time financial statements are received by users, 2 or 3 months or longer may have elapsed since the year end date. The earliest of the transactions that contribute to the income and expense items accumulated in the statement of profit or loss will have taken place probably 15 or more months previously.

In some jurisdictions there may be a requirement for large, listed entities to produce half-yearly or even quarterly financial statements. Where these are available, the timeliness problem is reduced. However, the comprehensiveness of the information may be limited in comparison to what is produced in the annual report. For example, quarterly statements may include only a statement of profit or loss without a statement of financial position or statement of changes in equity. Also, it is possible that they will have not been subject to verification in the form of audit.

Comparability

Comparisons over time for one entity

Comparisons over time between the financial statements of the same entity may prove to be invalid, or only partially valid, because significant changes have taken place in the entity. The disclosure provisions of IFRS 5 Non-current Assets Held for Sale and Discontinued Operations may assist the analyst if the entity plans to sell an operation. However, it may not be possible to discern the effect of other significant changes. For example, an entity that makes an investment in a new non-current item, say a major addition to its production facilities coupled with a significant increase in working capital, is not obliged to disclose any information about how well or badly the new investment has performed.

The analyst may, for example, be able to see that the entity's profitability overall has decreased, but the explanations could be as follows:

- The investment has proved to be very successful, but its success is offset by the rapidly declining profitability of other parts of the entity's productive capacity. As these elements are gradually replaced over the next 2 or 3 years, profitability is likely to increase overall.

- The investment has proved to be less successful than expected and is producing no better a return than the worn-out machinery it replaced.

- Although productive capacity has increased, the quality of goods overall has declined, and the entity has not been able to maintain its margins.

Financial statements simply do not provide sufficient information to permit the analyst to see these finer points of detail.

Comparisons over time and inflation

Comparability over time is often threatened by the effects of price inflation. This can, paradoxically, be particularly insidious where the general rate of inflation in the economy is comparatively low because analysts and others are not conscious of the effect. For example, suppose that the rate of price inflation applicable to a particular entity has been around 2.5 per cent per year over a 5-year period. Sales in 20X3 were reported at $100,000. A directly comparable level of sales in 20X4 would be $102,500 ($100,000 × 1.025). Therefore, sales in 20X4 would have to have increased to more than $102,500 before any real increase could be claimed. However, the analyst, seeing the two figures alongside each other on the statement of profit or loss, and knowing that inflation is running at a low level, may very well not take this factor into account.

Differences in accounting policy and accounting practices

Changes in accounting policy and accounting practices may affect comparability over time in the same entity. Also, when comparing the financial statements of two or more entities, it is really quite likely that there will be some differences in accounting policy and/or practice between them.

The type of differences which make comparisons difficult include the following:

- Different approaches to valuation of non-current assets, as permitted under IAS 16 Property, Plant and Equipment. An entity that revalues its non-current assets on a regular basis, as permitted by that standard, is likely to have higher carrying values for its assets than an entity that carries non-current assets at depreciated historical cost. Also, the depreciation charges of the revaluing entity are likely to be higher. The two entities are therefore not strictly comparable.

- Different classifications of expenses in the statement of profit or loss. It is not always easy to decide whether or not expenses should be classified as part of cost of sales or operating expenses. If entities classify similar expenses under the different headings their gross profit margins will not be comparable.

- More or less conservative approaches to judgements about the impairment of assets. Impairment review inevitably involves some degree of estimation.

Only the first of these three items relates, strictly speaking, to an accounting policy difference. The other two relate to variations in respect of judgemental issues. Where there is a difference in formal accounting policies adopted it is, at least, possible to discern this from the financial statements and to make some kind of adjustment to achieve comparability. However, judgemental matters are almost impossible to adjust for.

Entities in the same sector

Entities may appear to be comparable in that they operate in the same business sector. However, each entity has unique features, and a particular entity may not be strictly comparable with any other. Segment disclosure does allow for a more detailed approach to comparisons, although as we will see later in the chapter:

- Not all entities are required by accounting standards to make segment disclosures.

- Identifying segments is, necessarily, a judgemental matter. It is quite possible that one entity would identify a particular part of its business as a reportable segment, whereas another would not make the same judgement.

Non co-terminous accounting periods

Financial statements are prepared to a particular date annually. The annual financial statements of an entity with a year end of 31 December are not strictly comparable with those of an entity with a June year end. The difference is only 6 months, but significant events may have occurred in the industry or the economy as a whole that affect the statements prepared to the later date but not those prepared to the earlier date.

Size of the entity

It may be inappropriate to compare two entities of very different sizes, or to compare a listed with a non-listed entity. A large entity may be able to take advantage of economies of scale that are unavailable to the small entity, but that is not to say that the smaller entity is inefficient. It may, relatively speaking, be a better manager of the resources available to it. Conversely, a smaller entity may be able to react more rapidly to changes in economic conditions, because it can be easier to effect radical change in that environment.

Listed entities are subject to a great deal of additional regulation and their activities are far more likely than those of an unlisted entity to attract media coverage. Their share prices are widely advertised and are sensitive to alterations in market perceptions. It can be less acceptable for a listed entity to take risks or any course of action that might affect a regular flow of dividends to shareholders. By contrast, an unlisted entity whose shares are held by a limited number of people may be able to make investment decisions that result in a curtailment of dividends in the short term in exchange for projected higher returns in the long-term. So, operational flexibility varies between entities, and this may mean that their financial statements are not really comparable, or at least, that comparisons must be treated with caution.

Verification

Although regulations relating to audit vary from one country to another, it is likely that, in most jurisdictions, the financial statements of larger entities are audited. However, smaller entities' financial statements may not be subject to audit, and so the analyst has no external report on their validity or the fairness of their presentation.

International issues

Where the financial statements of entities based in different countries are being compared, there may be further sources of difference in addition to those already covered in this section.

- The entities may be subject to differing tax regimes.

- The financial statements may be based on different legal and regulatory systems. For example, traditionally, German, French and Spanish financial statements have been prepared in accordance with tax regulation (so, e.g. the depreciation allowances provided for in the financial statements are exactly those allowable for tax purposes). The preparation of British and Irish financial statements, by contrast, is focused much more upon the objective of achieving a true and fair view, and the link between accounts for tax purposes and accounts for filing and presentation purposes has been relatively weak.

- The relative strengths and weaknesses of a national economy, and of the exchange rate relating to its national currency, may produce cyclical differences in the profitability of business entities. These effects may have the result of reducing comparability of the financial statements of two entities located in different countries.

Provision of non-financial information

It was noted earlier in this section: '… financial reports do not and cannot provide all the information that existing and potential investors, lenders and other creditors need to make decisions' (the IASB's Conceptual Framework for Financial Reporting). Major listed entities have tended, in recent years, to provide more non-financial information in their financial statements, and it is increasingly common to find disclosures relating to, for example, environmental issues. However, there is a dearth of regulation relating to non-financial disclosure, and users cannot rely on finding a consistent level of high quality information in annual reports.

Limitations of ratio analysis

Calculation method

The only accounting ratio to have a prescribed method of calculation is earnings per share which is regulated through IAS 33 Earnings per share (see chapter 5). In respect of some of the other accounting ratios, there may be more than one valid method of calculation. There are, for example, two perfectly valid approaches to the calculation of gearing. When making comparisons between financial statements it is important to ensure that the same method of calculation is used consistently, otherwise the comparison will not be valid.

Reliability

Many ratios are calculated using average figures. Often the average is based on only two figures: the opening and closing. However, these may not be representative of a true average figure, and so any ratios calculated on the basis of such a figure will be unreliable. This effect is noticeable in entities with seasonal operations. For example, suppose that an artificial Christmas tree business starts building up its inventory from a low point at the beginning of February, gradually accumulating in order to build up to a maximum level at the beginning of November. Eighty-five per cent of its annual sales total is made in November and December.

If the entity has an accounting year end of 31 January (which would make sense as there's not much going on at the time of year), inventory will be at its lowest level. (Opening inventory + closing inventory)/2 will certainly produce an average inventory figure but it will not be representative of the entity's level of activity in the intervening months.

The idea of the norm

Sometimes we attempt to set norms for ratios: for example, that the current ratio should ideally be around 2, or 1.5 or 2.5. However, setting norms is both unrealistic and unhelpful. Some entities can, and do, operate successfully with a substantial excess of current liabilities over current assets. Such entities typically sell for cash, so don't have receivables, turn over their inventory very quickly (perhaps because it's perishable) but manage to take the maximum amounts of credit from their suppliers.

Inappropriate use of ratios

Not all ratios are useful or applicable in all business situations and the analyst must take care over the selection of ratios to use. For example, an entity may have a mixture of cash and credit sales, but it would normally not be possible to distinguish between them armed only with the information included in the annual financial statements. However, seeing a line for revenue and a line for receivables, the analyst (or student) might assume that it was therefore sensible to work out the number of days sales represented by receivables. The ratio would be inaccurate and the analyst could be seriously misled by it.

Limited usefulness of ratios

Ratios, and more importantly their analysis, may contribute to an understanding of an entity's business operations but quite often they simply lead to more questions that cannot be answered due to lack of available information.

A related point is that stand-alone ratios are generally of very limited use. The analyst may be able to calculate that a business's gross profit percentage is 14.3 per cent for a particular year. In isolation, that piece of information is really quite useless. It's reassuring to know that the entity has actually made a positive gross profit, but without comparators, it's hard to say much more than that.

Creative accounting

Defining the nature and scope of creative accounting is not straightforward. Despite the best efforts of accounting regulators there remains wide scope for the use of judgement in matters such as the determination of useful lives of assets and allowances for irrecoverable receivables.

The term 'creative accounting' is commonly used to suggest a rather suspicious approach to accounting. It carries connotations of manipulation of figures, deliberate structuring of series of transactions and exploitation of loopholes in the rules.

It should be noted that the directors have a legal responsibility to ensure that the financial statements reflect a fair presentation of the performance and position of the entity over the reporting period. Any creative accounting techniques would be likely to contravene this rule and would be considered highly unethical.

In addition, the auditors will consider the possibility of creative accounting carefully when forming their opinion on the financial statements. If they believe that a fair presentation is not reflected they will ask the directors to make amendments and, in the event that the directors refuse to do so, the auditors would be required to amend their opinion accordingly.

Methods employed by creative accountants

Financial statements can be manipulated in many ways, some more acceptable than others. Methods include the following:

Altering the timing of transactions

For example, the despatch of sales orders could be hurried up or delayed just before the year end to either increase or decrease sales for the reporting period. Other examples include delaying sales of non-current assets and the timing of research and development expenditure. If an entity needs to improve its results it may decide upon a lower level of research and development activity in the short term in order to reduce costs. Delaying the replacement of worn-out assets falls into the same category. Some people would regard this type of 'manipulation' as falling outside the definition of creative accounting.

Artificial smoothing

This approach involves the exploitation of the elements of choice that exist in accounting regulation. Although the IASB has worked hard to reduce the number of allowed alternative treatments, there remains some scope for artificial adjustments in respect of, for example, the choice of inventory valuation method, the estimated useful lives of non-current assets, and the choice between valuation of non-current assets at revalued amounts or depreciated historical cost that is permitted by IAS 16 Property, Plant and Equipment.

A change in accounting policy would, of course, have to be noted in the year in which it occurs, but its effects are not so easily discernible after that first year.

Classification

One of the grey areas that persists in accounting is the classification of debit items as either expenses of the current year or as non-current assets. If items are classified as non-current assets they do not impact (unless they are depreciated) on the reported income for the period.

One of the best known cases of mis-classification in recent years occurred in the US long-distance phone company WorldCom. Over a 3-year period the entity improperly reported $3.8 billion of expenses as non-current assets, thus providing a considerable boost to reported earnings. The entity is also reported as having manipulated provisions in order to increase reported earnings. In this particular case, the scale of the irregularities has been such that senior officers are currently being prosecuted for fraud.

Other areas of the financial statements which provide opportunities for creative accounting via classification include the categorisation of expenses and income as exceptional and the decisions about classification as reportable segments where the entity is required to undertake segment reporting.

Exclusion of liabilities

Under-reporting liabilities in the statement of financial position can help to improve accounting ratios. For example, the calculation of gearing would be affected and total capital employed would be reduced, so that return on total capital employed would appear to be higher. Entities have sometimes been able to take advantage of loopholes in accounting regulation to arrange off-balance sheet financing in the form of subsidiary undertakings that are technically excluded from consolidation. This was demonstrated in the Enron case, where so-called Special Purpose Entities were set up to provide finance to the business; these SPEs were, however, excluded from consolidation so that their liabilities did not appear in the group financial statements. Regulations have been revised to make this more difficult, with the recent introduction of IFRS 10: *Consolidated Financial Statements* being an example. However, off-balance sheet financing remains a problem.

The analyst must read the notes to the financial statements carefully to be aware of any contingencies. A contingent liability is where the probability of occurrence is less than 50% but it is not remote. Where an item is noted as a contingent liability together with a note of the estimated financial impact, it may be useful to calculate the impact on the entity's liquidity and to work out accounting ratios both with and without the item.

Recognition of revenue

Aggressive accounting often exploits revenue recognition rules. Some examples of inappropriate revenue recognition include:

- recognising revenue from sales that are made conditionally (i.e. where the purchaser has the right to return the goods for an extended period, or where experience shows that returns are likely);
- failing to apportion subscription revenue over the appropriate accounting periods but instead recognising it immediately;
- recognising revenue on goods shipped to agents employed by the entity;
- recognising the full amount of revenue when only partial shipments of goods have been made.

Managing market expectations

This final category of manipulation has nothing to do with massaging an entity's figures, but it does involve the way the entity presents itself to the world. Reporting by listed entities, especially in the US market, is driven very much by analysts' expectations. It may be easier to massage their expectations rather than to improve the reported results by use of creative accounting techniques. Directors of listed entities meet analysts in briefing meetings where they have the opportunity to influence analysts' expectations by forecasting fairly poor figures. When the entity then proceeds to turn in a better result than expected, the market's view of the shares may be enhanced. This is a psychological game of bluffing which may backfire on the reporting entity if analysts become aware of what it is doing.

The motivation to use creative accounting

Various research studies have examined the issue of managerial motivation to use creative accounting. The following have been identified as significant factors:

Tax avoidance

If income can be understated or expenses overstated, then it may be possible to avoid tax.

Increasing shareholder confidence

Creative accounting can be used to ensure an appropriate level of profits over a long period. Ideally, this would show a steady upward trajectory without nasty surprises for the shareholders, and so would help to avoid volatility in share prices, and would make it easier to raise further capital via share issues.

Personal gain

Where managerial bonuses are linked to profitability there is a clear motivation for managers to ensure that profits hit the necessary threshold to trigger a bonus payment.

Indirect personal gain

There is a market in managerial expertise in which demand often appears to outstrip supply. A manager's personal reputation in the marketplace will almost certainly be enhanced by association with entities that have strong earnings records. So, although the pay-off may not be either immediate or obvious, there is likely over the longer term to be a reward in terms of enhanced reputation and consequent higher earning power.

Following the pack

If managers perceive that every other entity in their sector is adopting creative accounting practices, they may feel obliged to do the same.

Meeting covenants

Sometimes, lenders insist on special covenant arrangements as a condition of making a loan: for example, they may stipulate that an entity's current ratio should not fall below 1.5:1, or that gearing never exceeds 35 per cent. In such cases, if the entity cannot meet those covenants that it has agreed to, the lender may be able to insist upon immediate repayment or to put the entity into liquidation. Where an entity is in danger of failing to meet its covenants, there is an obvious incentive for managers (especially if they genuinely feel that the difficulty is short-term in nature) to massage the figures so that the covenant is, apparently, satisfied.

8 Additional information

In practice, and in your assessment, it is likely that the information available in the financial statements is not enough to produce a detailed and thorough analysis of the entity. This is particularly the case given the limitations of financial reporting information discussed in the previous section.

You may require additional information, financial and non-financial, to develop a better understanding of the entity's business and its industry. In the assessment it is imperative that you relate any additional information requested to the entity in the question and to the user for whom the report is being prepared. You should ensure that the information you are suggesting would be reasonably available to the user (i.e. don't suggest that a minority shareholder would be able to access board minutes).

Some examples of additional information are listed below.

You may require additional *financial* information such as:

- budgeted figures
- other management information
- industry averages
- figures for a similar entity
- figures for the entity over a longer period of time.

You may also require other *non-financial* information such as:

- market share
- key employee information
- sales mix information
- product range information
- the size of the order book
- the long-term plans of management.

Test your understanding 9 (OTQ style)

A colleague is looking to invest some surplus cash and has identified an entity that she believes has a promising future. However, having reviewed the financial statements she is a little concerned by the profit before tax margin which has fallen in the most recent financial year due to a significant increase in administrative expenses. She is also concerned that the cash position has worsened.

Which three of the following options would be considered realistic next steps for your colleague to take prior to making an investment decision?

A   Write to the Chief Financial Officer and request a breakdown of administrative expenses to understand the cause of the increase.

B   Review the narrative reports published alongside the financial statements to see whether they provide an explanation of the fall in margin.

C   Obtain a copy of any interim financial statements published since the previous year end to check whether the fall in profit is temporary.

D   Review the financial press for any recent articles concerning the future prospects of the business.

E   Review the cash flow forecasts of the business.

F   Obtain confirmation from the entity's bank that it will continue to support the business.

Information for TYUs 10 and 11

MLR prepares its financial statements in accordance with International Financial Reporting Standards and is listed on its local stock exchange. It is considering the acquisition of an overseas operation. Two geographical areas have been targeted, A-land and B-land. Entity A operates in A-land and entity B operates in B-land. Each entity is listed on its local stock exchange.

The most recent financial statements of entities A and B have been converted into MLR's currency for ease of comparison. The financial indicators from these financial statements and those of MLR are provided below.

	MLR	A	B
Revenue	$600m	$210m	$400m
Gross profit margin	32%	28%	19%
Profit before tax/revenue × 100	18%	10%	11%
Gearing	37%	66%	26%
Approx rate of borrowings	8%	5%	10%

Test your understanding 10 (OTQ style)

Which one of the following statements is NOT a realistic conclusion that could be drawn from the above information?

A   A's higher gross profit margin suggests that it is benefiting from greater economies of scale than B.

B   A and B have similar profit before tax margins but different gross margins, which could be due to different classification of expenses.

C   A's high gearing may be a consequence of relatively low interest rates available.

D   B's approximate rate of borrowings suggest that lenders consider it to be higher risk than either MLR or A.

Test your understanding 11 (OTQ style)

Which one of the following statements concerning the use of ratio analysis to make a decision about investing in A or B is false?

A   The entities are listed on different stock exchanges and may be using different accounting standards. This will reduce the comparability of the financial indicators.

B   The entities may use different accounting policies and this could affect comparison of specific ratios (i.e. cost model v revaluation model for property, plant and equipment would affect comparison of gearing)

C   Using only one year's worth of data gives no indication of whether the entities are growing or in decline

D   As A and B operate in differ geographical locations, they may pay different rates of tax and this will affect comparison of the margin ratios presented.

9 Investor ratios

Analysing investor ratios and data

When appraising an entity as a potential investment, all the ratios discussed above may be used. This information may be supplemented by further ratios specifically for investors.

The market price of an ordinary share is often used in this analysis.

Price earnings ratio

A common benchmark for investors analysing different entities is the use of the price/earnings (P/E) ratio:

$$\frac{\text{Current market price per share}}{\text{Earnings per share}}$$

Earnings per share is basically the earnings available for distribution divided by the number of ordinary shares in issue. The calculation of earnings per share is governed by IAS 33 *Earnings per* share and the rules of this accounting standard are covered in an earlier chapter of this text. The P/E ratio calculation produces a number which can be useful for assessing the relative risk of an investment.

Illustration 3 – P/E ratios

	V	W
Current market price per share	396c	288c
Most recent earnings per share	13.4c	35.6c
P/E ratio	29.6	8.1

W has much higher earnings per share than V, but the price of one share in W is lower than one share in V, giving rise to two very different P/E ratios. Generally, the lower the P/E ratio the greater the indication of risk for the investor.

The rational expectations of buyers and sellers in the stock market tend to be incorporated in the price of the share. The P/E ratios of these entities tend to suggest that the market considers investment in W to be riskier than investment in V.

There may be reasons to account for this difference, for example:

- The numerator of the fraction is current (an up-to-date market price can be obtained easily during the market's opening hours), but the EPS figure is the latest available which, for a listed entity in many markets, can be up to 6 months old. The EPS of either entity may therefore be quite significantly out of date.

- W may have issued a profits warning, or might have suffered adverse events, such as, for example, the loss of a major contract or the resignation of a key director. These events may have depressed the share price.

- W may be in a sector which is unfashionable or relatively undervalued.

- W may have had a difficult recent history with a volatile pattern of earnings. On the whole, markets prefer companies with a smooth profit record.

As usual, the process of analysis leads to demands for more information. A better picture could be obtained of V and W if share price graphs for the last year, for example, were available, so that the analyst could see whether the share prices quoted above are near to average or not.

Test your understanding 12 (OTQ style)

AB has 3 million $1 ordinary shares in issue throughout the year ended 31 October 20X3. It reported a profit for the year of $1,125,000 and its share price at the close of business on 31 October 20X3 was $3.75.

Required:

Calculate the price/earnings (P/E) ratio at 31 October 20X3.Give your answer to the nearest whole number.

Test your understanding 13 (OTQ style)

GH has a P/E ratio of 12.8 and its competitor has a P/E ratio of 18.9.

Required:

Complete the following sentences by placing one of the options in each of the spaces.

The market has _____ confidence in the future performance of GH than its competitor. Investing in GH is likely to be _____ than investing in its competitor.

Options: greater, lower, less risky, more risky

Dividend related ratios

Growth potential and the ability to generate future wealth in the entity may depend on the amount of profits retained. This relationship may be measured using the *profit retention ratio*:

$$\frac{\text{Profit after dividends}}{\text{Profit before dividends}} \times 100$$

The higher the proportion of earnings retained, the higher the growth potential. Cash is retained in the entity for growth as opposed to being paid to shareholders. The ratio is expressed in percentage terms.

When analysing financial statements from an investor's point of view it is important to identify the objectives of the investor. Does the investor require high capital growth, usually associated with high risk, or a lower risk fixed dividend payment and low capital growth?

Dividend yield will indicate the return on capital investment, relative to market price:

$$\frac{\text{Dividend per share}}{\text{Market price per share}} \times 100$$

Dividend yield is expressed as a percentage.

Dividend cover measures the ability of the entity to maintain the existing level of dividend and is used in conjunction with the dividend yield:

$$\frac{\text{Earnings per share}}{\text{Dividends per share}}$$

The higher the dividend cover, the more likely it is that the dividend yield can be maintained. Dividend cover will be expressed in terms of how many times the dividend can be paid e.g. 10 times.

Test your understanding 14 (OTQ style)

KL has paid a dividend of $25 million relating to the year ended 31 May 20X4. The weighted average number of shares for the year ended 31 May 20X4 was 50 million and the share price at 31 May 20X4 was $8.75.

Required:

Calculate the dividend yield for the year ended 31 May 20X4. Give your answer to one decimal place.

10 Analysis of the statement of cash flows

The cash flow of an entity is regarded by many users as being of primary importance in understanding its operations. After all, an entity that cannot generate sufficient cash will, sooner or later, fail.

The statement of cash flows provides valuable information for the analysis of an entity's operations and position. Students should note that the analysis of statements of cash flow is examinable in Financial Management.

The statement of cash flows prepared in accordance with IAS 7 categorises cash flow under three principal headings: cash flows from operating activities, cash flows from investing activities and cash flows from financing activities. As well as comparing these totals from year to year, cash flows in the following areas should be reviewed:

- cash generation from trading operations
- dividend and interest payments
- investing activities
- financing activities
- net cash flow

There are also useful ratios that can be calculated - see expandable text below.

Cash generation from trading operations

The figure should be compared to the profit from operations. The reconciliation note to the statement of cash flows is useful in this regard. Overtrading may be indicated by:

- high profits and low cash generation
- large increases in inventory, receivables and payables.

Dividend and interest payments

These can be compared to cash generated from trading operations to see whether the normal operations can sustain such payments. In most years they should.

Investing activities

The nature and scale of an entity's investment in non-current assets is clearly shown.

A simple test may be to compare investment and depreciation.

- If investment > depreciation, the entity is investing at a greater rate than its current assets are wearing out – this suggests expansion.
- If investment = depreciation, the entity is investing in new assets as existing ones wear out. The entity appears stable.
- If investment < depreciation the non-current asset base of the entity is not being maintained. This is potentially worrying as non-current assets are generators of profit.

Financing activities

The changes in financing (in pure cash terms) are clearly shown. Gearing can be considered at this point. It would be useful to comment on the impact that such changes will have on the gearing ratio.

Cash flow

The statement clearly shows the end result in cash terms of the entity's operations in the year. Do not overstate the importance of this figure alone, however. A decrease in cash in the year may be for very sound reasons (e.g. there was surplus cash last year) or may be mainly the result of timing (e.g. a new loan was raised just after the end of the accounting period).

Cash flow ratios

Return on capital employed: cash

$$\frac{\text{Cash generated from operations}}{\text{Capital employed}} \times 100$$

For many external users, cash is a more significant indicator than profit and this ratio should be calculated where the information is available.

Cash generated from operations to total debt

$$\frac{\text{Cash generated from operations}}{\text{Total long term borrowings}}$$

This gives an indication of an entity's ability to meet its long-term obligations. The inverse ratio can also be calculated:

$$\frac{\text{Total long-term borrowings}}{\text{Cash generated from operations}}$$

This provides an indication of how many years it would take to repay the long-term borrowings if all of the cash generated from operations were to be used for this purpose.

Net cash from operating activities to capital expenditure

$$\frac{\text{Net cash from operating activities}}{\text{Net capital expenditure}} \times 100$$

This gives some idea of the extent to which the entity can finance its capital expenditure out of cash flows from operating activities. If it cannot meet its capital expenditure from this source, then some kind of longer-term financing is likely to be required. However, this ratio could be misleading unless calculated and compared for several years.

Test your understanding 15 (case style)

SCF is considering the acquisition of FGH, one of its suppliers. SCF always look carefully at the liquidity position of potential acquirees having been exposed to cash flow problems in earlier acquisitions. If acquired, SCF would like to retain the existing management team of FGH.

You work as an accountant for SCF and the Managing Director has asked you to perform an analysis of FGH's most recent statement of cash flows to determine how well the management team is controlling cash.

FGH has been trading for a number of years and is currently going through a period of expansion of its core business area.

The statement of cash flows for the most recent year ended 31 December 20X0 for FGH is presented below.

	$000	$000
Cash flows from operating activities		
Profit before tax	2,200	
Adjustments for:		
Depreciation	380	
Gain on sale of investments	(50)	
Loss on sale of property, plant and equipment	45	
Investment income	(180)	
Interest costs	420	
	———	
	2,815	

Increase in trade receivables	(400)
Increase in inventories	(390)
Increase in payables	550
	———
Cash generated from operations	2,575
Interest paid	(400)
Income taxes paid	(760)
	———
Net cash from operating activities	1,415

Cash flows from investing activities

Acquisition of subsidiary, net of cash acquired	(800)
Acquisition of property, plant and equipment	(340)
Proceeds from sale of equipment	70
Proceeds from sale of investments	150
Interest received	100
Dividends received	80
	———
Net cash used in investing activities	(740)

Cash flows from financing activities

Proceeds of share issue	300
Proceeds from long term borrowings	300
Dividend paid to equity shareholders of the parent	(1,000)
	———
Net cash used in financing activities	(400)
	———
Net increase in cash and cash equivalents	275
Cash and cash equivalents at the beginning of the period	110
	———
Cash and cash equivalents at the end of the period	385
	———

Required:

Prepare a memo to the Managing Director assessing the cash management of FGH based on your analysis of the statement of cash flows.

11 Segmental analysis

One of the limitations mentioned above is that different entities may have different segments to their business. Comparing entities as a whole may not be appropriate if the segments account for different proportions of the overall business and the activities of each segment are not similar.

It is also beneficial for users to be aware of how the individual segments of an entity contribute to its overall financial performance and position and how changes in its segments may impact on the business as whole.

IFRS 8 *Operating Segments* addresses these issues and requires entities to disclose certain segmental information.

The requirements of IFRS 8 only apply to publicly listed entities, although non-listed entities are encouraged to comply.

Benefits of segmental information

More appropriate assessment of performance of entity

Separate segments may have wide ranges of profitability, cash flows, growth, future prospects and risks. Without information on these segments, users would not be able to identify these differences and it would be impossible to properly assess performance and future prospects of the entity.

IFRS 8 requires information to be provided on the revenue, expenses, profits, assets and liabilities of each segment. With this information, users can calculate the profit margins, asset utilisation and return on net assets of each segment and so further analyse the performance of each segment.

IFRS 8 is designed to allow users to see the type and categories of information that are used at the highest levels in the entity for decision-making. There is the further advantage that disclosure, while in many cases extensive, should not be excessively costly because it is based upon information reported and used within the entity.

Limitations of segmental information

Defining segments

One of the criticisms of IFRS 8 is that it allows an entity's managers to determine what is a reportable segment. Managers, therefore, are potentially able to conceal information by judicious selection of segments. A further, related, criticism is that comparability of segment information between entities suffers because segment identification is likely to differ between entities. However, it should be recognised that comparability between entities is often problematic, and users should in any case be very cautious when comparing entities even if they appear, superficially, to be quite similar in their operations.

Measurement of segment information

IFRS 8 also does not define segment revenue, segment expenses, segment result, segment assets or segment liabilities, but does require an explanation of how segment profit or loss, segment assets and segment liabilities are measured for each operating segment.

As a consequence, entities will have more discretion in determining what is included in segment profit or loss under IFRS 8, limited only by their internal reporting practices.

Apportionment of 'common' items

Allocations of revenues, expenses, gains and losses are only applied if the same allocation is included when the chief operating decision maker reviews the information. The same goes for assets and liabilities which can be difficult to apportion.

IFRS 8 does not prescribe how centrally incurred expenses should be allocated or whether they should be allocated at all. IFRS 8 simply states that amounts should be allocated on a reasonable basis.

This results in increased subjectivity and these allocations can significantly affect segment results.

Test your understanding 16 (OTQ style)

Which three of the following statements are considered to be benefits of using segmental analysis disclosures prepared in accordance with IFRS 8 *Operating Segments* when analysing performance and position of an entity?

A Directors can use their judgement when defining reportable segments.

B By reviewing segmental analysis, users can better assess the different types of risk facing the business and the extent of these risks on the business overall.

C The disclosures reflect the information reviewed regularly by the chief operating decision maker and therefore provide users with an 'inside view' of management accounting information.

D The operating segments note will be of particular use when comparing different entities.

E Users can assess which components of the business contribute the most to profit and revenue.

F Directors can leave certain items unallocated if they cannot reasonably allocate them to a particular segment.

Test your understanding 17 (further OTQs)

Note: there are TYUs earlier in the chapter that assess the calculation of ratios. This section concentrates on interpretation.

(1) Anderson has a bank overdraft and a current ratio of 1:1.

Which ONE of the following actions would increase the current ratio?

A Offering cash discounts to customers to encourage speedier payment

B Paying suppliers ahead of schedule to obtain cash discounts

C Selling inventory on credit at book value

D Increasing the allowance for doubtful receivables

(2) The Port Erin fishmonger and the Port Erin bookseller both operate on a 50% mark-up on cost. However, their gross profit margins are:

Fishmonger 25%

Bookseller 33%

Which one of the following statements would validly explain the higher gross profit margin of the bookseller?

A There is more wastage with inventories of fish than inventories of books

B The fishmonger has a substantial bank loan whereas the bookseller's business in entirely financed by family

C The fishmonger has expensive high street premises whereas the bookseller has cheaper back street premises

D The fishmonger's sales revenue is declining whereas the bookseller's is increasing

(3) The following statements allegedly refer to the conclusions to be drawn when using ratio analysis to interpret the financial statements of an entity.

Which two of the following statements are TRUE?

A An entity can only increase its gross profit margin by increasing its selling prices or reducing its costs per unit of production.

B With other things remaining equal, an upwards revaluation of non-current assets would lead to a reduction in the return on capital employed.

C An entity can increase its return on capital employed in the short term by postponing replacement of aged non-current assets.

D An upwards revaluation of non-current assets will result in an increase in the gearing of an entity.

(4) ST, UV and WX are listed entities operating in the same business sector. At 31 October 20X6, their P/E ratios were reported as follows:

ST 16.2

UV 12.7

WX 8.4

Which ONE of the following statements, based on the above P/E ratios, are TRUE?

A   ST is regarded by the market as the riskiest of the three entities.

B   ST has the highest earnings per share of the three entities.

C   UV represents the safest investment because its P/E lies approximately midway between the other two.

D   WX's share price may be relatively lower than that of ST and UV because of an adverse effect such as a profit warning.

(5) JA and GB operate in the same industry and are of a similar size. The non-current asset turnover ratios of the two entities are as follows:

JA 2.5

GB 1.7

Which of the following statements would be VALID explanations of the differences in the non-current asset ratio of the two entities? Select all that apply.

A   JA has a policy of revaluing its non-current assets whereas GB uses the cost model. The revaluations normally reflect an increase in value.

B   JA's non-current assets are older than GB's.

C   GB's non-current assets are under-utilised at present.

D   GB has acquired non-current assets in the final month of the accounting period, whereas JA last purchased significant non-current assets in the previous accounting period.

(6) The following information has been obtained for two potential acquisition targets, A and B, who operate in the same industry.

	A	B
Revenue	$160m	$300m
Gross profit margin	26%	17%
Profit before interest and tax margin	9%	11%

Which two of the following statements are VALID conclusions that could be drawn from the above information?

A   A's gross profit margin is higher as A would be expected to have achieved more economies of scale than B.

B   The difference between gross profit margins could be due to the entities classifying their costs differently between cost of sales and operating expenses.

C   The difference between profit before interest and tax margins could be due to the entities classifying their costs differently between cost of sales and operating expenses.

D   A has lower operating expenses than B.

E   B has lower operating expenses than A.

12 Chapter summary

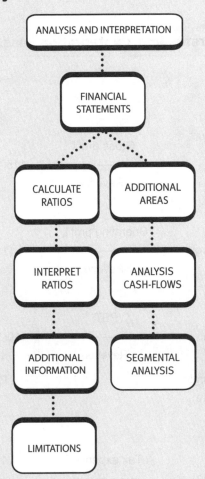

Test your understanding answers

Test your understanding 1 (integration question) – Profitability

Profitability:

		20X6	20X5
Gross profit margin	$\dfrac{\text{Gross profit}}{\text{Revenue}}$	115/180 = 63.9%	90/150 = 60%
Operating profit margin	$\dfrac{\text{Operating profit}}{\text{Revenue}}$	(115-40)/180 = 41.7%	(90-29)/150 = 40.7%
Profit before tax margin	$\dfrac{\text{PBT}}{\text{Revenue}}$	110/180 = 61.1%	51/150 = 34%
Profit before tax margin (excluding Associate)		(110-59)/180 = 28.3%	
Effective tax rate (excluding Associate)	$\dfrac{\text{Tax expense}}{\text{PBT} - \text{Assoc}}$	14/(110-59) = 27.5%	13/51 = 25.5%
Return on capital employed	$\dfrac{\text{Operating profit}}{\text{Capital Employed}}$	(115–40)/(218+335+9–250) = 24.0%	(90–29)/(100+110) = 29.0%

(Note: CV of Associate is deducted from capital employed)

Possible reasons why T's ratios have changed:

Gross profit margin increased:

- Increase in sales due to increasing volume sold and so economies of scale result in lower costs per unit sold;
- Increase in sales price per unit;
- Changes in product mix.

Operating profit margin smaller increase (than GPM):

- Increase in expenses such as advertising to boost revenue
- Increased depreciation charges following acquisitions of non-current assets
- Poor control of costs since revenue increased by 20% but operating expenses increased by 38%

Profit before tax margin significant increase:

- Due to share of profit of associate
- Removing this shows an actual reduction in margin
- Increased borrowing to fund expansion has resulted in 140% increase finance costs

Effective tax rate increase:

- Effect of change in legislation
- Under-provision in previous year

Return on capital employed:

- Fall due to significant increase in capital employed, not generating as significant an improvement in operating profit
- Large increase in long term borrowings to fund investment in non-current assets during year. If acquired near year-end, will not have generated returns yet.
- Non-current assets also revalued – this increases capital employed but will not lead to an improvement in profit (it distorts the ratio)

Test your understanding 2

EBITDA = Earnings before interest, tax, depreciation and amortisation.

	20X6	20X5
Profit for the year (PAT)	96	38
Add back		
Tax	14	13
Interest (finance costs)	24	10
Depreciation	6	3
	140	**64**

Test your understanding 3 (integration question) – Liquidity

Liquidity ratios:

		20X6	20X5
Current ratio	$\dfrac{\text{Current assets}}{\text{Current liabilities}}$	64/44 = 1.5:1	50/32 = 1.6:1
Quick ratio	$\dfrac{(\text{Current assets} - \text{Inventory})}{\text{Current liabilities}}$	49/44 = 1.1:1	38/32 = 1.2:1

Overall liquidity situation has deteriorated:

- Current and quick ratios have both fallen slightly but not yet at levels that give cause for concern. The main reason for the reduction is the cash balance changing from positive to negative in 20X6.

- The increasing inventory holding and receivables collection periods (see efficiency ratios below) have been funded by an overdraft rather than an equivalent increase in the payables payment period.

Test your understanding 4 (integration question) – Efficiency

Efficiency/activity ratios:

		20X6	20X5
Inventory holding period	$\dfrac{\text{Inventory}}{\text{Cost of sales}} \times 365$ days	15/65 × 365 = 84 days	12/60 × 365 = 73 days
Receivables collection period	$\dfrac{\text{Receivables}}{\text{Revenue}} \times 365$ days	49/180 × 365 = 99 days	37/150 × 365 = 90 days
Payables payment period	$\dfrac{\text{Trade payables}}{\text{Cost of Sales}} \times 365$ days	12/65 × 365 = 67 days	11/60 × 365 = 67 days
Asset turnover	$\dfrac{\text{Revenue}}{\text{Capital Employed}}$	180/(218+335+9−250) = 0.58 times	150/(100+110) = 0.71 times
Non-current asset turnover	$\dfrac{\text{Revenue}}{\text{NCAs (that cont. to revenue)}}$	180/266 = 0.68 times	150/190 = 0.79 times

Possible reasons why T's ratios have changed:

Inventory holding period increased:

- Build up of inventory levels as a result of increased capacity following expansion of non-current assets
- Increasing inventory levels in response to increased demand for product
- Expectation of higher demand after year end
- Lack of control over inventory

Receivables collection period increased:

- Deliberate policy to attract customers
- Poor credit control procedures

Payables payment period unchanged.

Asset/non-current asset turnover:

- Revaluation of non-current assets will reduce asset turnover but not a "real" deterioration in efficiency

- Significant increase in non-current assets during year. If acquired near year-end, will not have generated returns/revenue for full year yet.

Test your understanding 5 (integration question) – Gearing

Capital structure

		20X6	20X5
Gearing	$\dfrac{\text{Debt}}{\text{Debt + Equity}}$	(335+9)/ (335+9+218) = 61.2%	110/ (110+100) = 52.4%
Gearing (alternative)	$\dfrac{\text{Debt}}{\text{Equity}}$	(335+9)/218 = 1.6:1	110/100 = 1.1:1

NB. Gearing may be shown as a % or a ratio. The exam question make it explicit regarding how to present your answer.

		20X6	20X5
Interest cover	$\dfrac{\text{Operating profit}}{\text{Finance costs}}$	(115-40)/24 = 3.1 times	(90-29)/10 = 6.1 times
Average rate of borrowing	$\dfrac{\text{Finance costs}}{\text{Borrowings}}$	24/(335+9) = 7.0%	10/110 = 9.1%
Dividend cover	$\dfrac{\text{Profit for year}}{\text{Dividends}}$	96/25 = 3.8 times	38/25 = 1.5 times

Gearing increase and interest cover reduction:

- Significant increase in long-term borrowings – to finance acquisition of associate/PPE

- Increase in loan significantly greater than increase in equity finance

- Gearing ratio appears quite high and interest cover falling creates concern

- Interest cover may increase next year when full year's impact of investment reflected

Average rate of borrowing has fallen:

- New borrowings at lower rate

- Loans taken out mid-way through year, so full year's cost not yet reflected

Dividend cover significant increase, principally due to associate profit.

Test your understanding 6 (OTQ style)

D is the valid reason.

A is incorrect. A significant investment close to the year end would result in a large increase in capital employed with little increase in profit, therefore ROCE would reduce.

B is incorrect. A revaluation increases equity and therefore capital employed with no corresponding increase in profit.

C is incorrect. The reduction in retained earnings would be netted off against the increase in long-term borrowings so capital employed would not be affected.

Test your understanding 7 (integration question)

	20X1	20X0
Gross profit margin	49/252 × 100 = 19.4%	25/248 × 100 = 10.1%
Operating profit margin	(49 – 18 – 16)/252 × 100 = 6.0%	(25 – 13 – 11)/248 x 100 = 0.4%
Profit for year margin	7/252 × 100 = 2.8%	(5)/248 × 100 = (2.0)%
Gearing	(91+39)/231 × 100 = 56.3%	91/184 × 100 = 49.5%
Current ratio	178/134 = 1.3:1	143/66 = 2.2:1
Quick ratio	(178 – 106)/134 = 0.5:1	(143 – 89)/66 = 0.8:1
Receivable days	72/252 × 365 days = 104 days	48/248 × 365 days = 71 days
Payable days	95/203 × 365 days = 171 days	66/223 × 365 days = 108 days
Inventories days	106/203 × 365 days = 191 days	89/223 × 365 days = 146 days
Return on capital employed	(49 – 18 – 16)/(231+91 – 24) = 15/298 × 100 = 5.0%	(25 – 13 – 11)/(184+91) = 1/275 × 100 = 0.4%
Non-current asset turnover	252/254 = 0.99	248/198 = 1.3
Interest cover	(10 + 12)/12 = 1.8 times	((7) + 8)/8 = 0.1 times

Test your understanding 8 (case style)

To: Board of Directors of XYZ

From: Accountant

Subject: Report on financial performance and position of DFG

The revenue of DFG has only marginally increased in the year by 1.6%, however profit margins have all increased significantly. In particular the gross profit margin has increased from 10% to 19%, which is likely to be as a result of reduced purchase prices from the new supplier contract that was secured in the year. Whilst this is a very positive and important step for DFG (given its low margin in the previous year) it will be important to establish whether this reduced cost also means a reduced level of quality. If quality is being compromised then this increase in margin may be short-lived as customers may be driven away in the longer term.

In addition, the switch in supplier may be responsible for the lawsuit. It is a risky strategy for DFG to pursue aggressive revenue and margin targets at the expense of supplying good quality products. Although a contingent liability of $30 million is included in the notes, the lawyer's assessment is that DFG is likely to lose the court case and the payout may be more. There is already serious pressure on DFG's finances and it may not survive if the payout is any more or if other customers decide to sue. There is therefore a significant risk to the going concern of the entity.

Both administration and distribution costs have increased significantly when compared to a 1.6% increase in revenue. Whilst these costs are not that large in relation to revenues, it may suggest that management do not have good control of overheads. The impact of legal fees as a result of the court case may also be seen with the increase of expenses.

ROCE has increased overall due to the increases in operating margins described above. However, revaluation reserve recorded during the year would reduce ROCE. The increase in ROCE would be greater if the impact of the revaluation where to be removed. ROCE without the revaluation is calculated as 15/(298 − 40) × 100 = 5.8% compared to last years ROCE of 0.4%.

The increase in total comprehensive income is largely due to the revaluation gain reported within other comprehensive income. The valuation was performed by an internal member of staff, which is perhaps not as ideal as someone external, however the financial statements have been finalised and so I assume they have been audited and that the valuations are fair. We should consider why the directors have chosen this year to change the policy - as it could be an attempt to boost income and reduce gearing to make further borrowing easier, especially as the long term borrowings will need to be repaid or re-negotiated relatively soon. However, it maybe shows good commercial sense to ensure that assets that are to be used as security for finance are at the most up-to-date valuation.

The overall liquidity of DFG is on the low side at 1.3:1 and has fallen significantly from 20X0. One contributing factor to the worsening liquidity is the significant increase in inventories in the year. This could be as a result of bad publicity about below standard goods and customer orders being cancelled. There is then an increased risk of obsolete inventories. This is reinforced by the inventories days which have increased from146 days to 191 days. Receivables days have also increased from 71 days to 104 days, and this could be as a result of disputed invoices. DFG may then have a problem with slow/non-payment of these debts. Payables days have increased from 108 days to 171 days and this could be resulting from a deliberate attempt by DFG to improve cash flow by delaying payment, particularly in response to the struggle to recover cash from their customers, or extended credit terms given by the new supplier to attract DFG's business.

The cash position of DFG is clearly a concern as the cash has moved from a positive balance to an overdraft and the long term borrowings are soon to be repaid or re-negotiated. This coupled with the poor working capital management would indicate that DFG must raise some additional funding if it is to survive. The gearing ratio shows deterioration on the previous year, despite an increase in equity from the revaluation. However, it is likely to be the lack of interest cover that would put lenders off. It is unlikely that DFG could afford to pay interest on any additional funding.

Recommendation

I would recommend that you do not consider investing in DFG at this time. If they lose the court case and have a large settlement to pay this could result in the entity collapsing and despite the fact that details of this are only in the notes, the seriousness of it should not be overlooked. The entity may struggle to survive anyway as there is a lack of cash and funding options (and it should be noted that DFG did not pay a dividend in 20X1). The increases in profitability are not enough of an indicator of a stable/growing entity – especially an entity involved in the building trade which is known for its sensitivity to the economy around it.

Test your understanding 9 (OTQ style)

Realistic next steps are B, C and D.

Options A, E and F are not available to minority shareholders.

Test your understanding 10 (OTQ style)

A is not a realistic conclusion.

A has much lower revenue than B and therefore B should be achieving more economies of scale than A.

Test your understanding 11 (OTQ style)

D is false.

The tax rate will have no effect on the ratios presented. The profits used in the margin calculations are **before** tax.

Test your understanding 12 (OTQ style)

EPS = $1,125,000/3 million = 37.5 cents

P/E ratio = 3.75/0.375 = 10

Test your understanding 13 (OTQ style)

The market has **lower** confidence in the future performance of GH than its competitor. Investing in GH is likely to be **more risky** than investing in its competitor.

Test your understanding 14 (OTQ style)

Dividend per share = $25 million/50 million = $0.50

Dividend yield = 0.50/8.75 = 5.7%

Test your understanding 15 (case style)

Memo to Managing Director

Firstly, FGH has managed to generate significant cash from operating activities which is a positive sign for any business wishing to be a going concern, particularly since it appears that FGH is expanding. In addition to the inflow of cash from trading, the directors have clearly made some good investment decisions as investment income of $180,000 has been included in the year and also profit of $50,000 has been earned from the sale of these investments.

It does look as if FGH needs to improve working capital as receivables have increased in the year and it looks like the entity has in turn withheld payment to payables with an increase of $550,000. The increase in receivables may be a deliberate attempt to secure new customers by offering them favourable credit terms but it is essential that good working capital management is not compromised. We may also wish to compare our existing credit terms with FGH with those that they are offering to their other customers.

The increase in inventories has probably arisen in order to meet future expected demand from the expansion. It should be noted that FGH has acquired a subsidiary during the year, although the effect of the subsidiary on the working capital balances will have been adjusted for in the completion of the statement of cash flows.

The expansion is shown in two areas of investment, with the acquisition of a subsidiary and in the purchase of property, plant and equipment. The sale of property, plant and equipment for $70,000 resulted in a loss of $45,000. It's possible that the expansion has resulted in the need for new equipment and hence management have taken the view to sell some of the old equipment whilst there is still a second hand market for it. The sale of investments for $150,000 has probably been undertaken in order to generate funds for the expansion. The only note of caution is that these investments seem to be profitable and hence given that a proportion has been sold during the year, future income from investments will be reduced.

A significant dividend has been paid out. The existing shareholders may be stripping cash out of the business prior to selling their shares to us. A good sign however is that FGH has managed to fund its expansion without increasing the overall gearing of the business, as equal amounts of debt and equity have been raised as new finance. It indicates good stewardship of assets when long term expansion is financed by long term financing. FGH appears to have used a mixture of long term financing and retained earnings generated in the year, together with the sale of some investments to fund the expansion. However, this is not to the detriment of shareholders as they have still received a significant dividend during the year and it's possible that the new investments in a subsidiary and PPE will generate greater returns in the future than the investments which have been sold. In times of expansion, however, a more modest dividend may have negated the need for long term financing and the interest costs associated with it.

Overall, the cash position of the business has improved by $110,000 over the course of the year and therefore, even taking into account the expansion and significant dividend, FGH do not appear to have any significant liquidity issues.

Test your understanding 16 (OTQ style)

B, C and E are considered benefits.

A gives the directors the scope to manipulate the disclosures to present the information that they want users to see.

D is incorrect. Segmental disclosures have limited use when comparing different entities as they are not likely to have defined their segments in the same way, even if the businesses are similar in nature.

F again gives directors the scope to manipulate results by leaving certain expenses/assets as unallocated (and therefore making margins and return on assets look better).

Test your understanding 17 (further OTQs)

(1) **B**

By paying suppliers ahead of schedule there would be a reduction in payables and a smaller increase in the overdraft (as the payment would be reduced by the discount). Therefore liabilities in total would decrease (by the amount of the discount) and the current ratio would increase.

A is not correct. The reduction in the overdraft would be lower that the reduction in the receivables and therefore the current ratio would decrease.

C is not correct. There would be a reduction in inventory and increase in liabilities therefore the current ratio would decrease.

D is not correct. This would reduce receivables and therefore the current ratio would decrease.

(2) **A is correct.**

The fishmonger's inventories are perishable and some will therefore be written off, creating an additional expense within cost of sales and reducing the gross profit margin.

B is not correct. The bank loan would create finance costs but these are not expensed within gross profit.

C is not correct. The costs of the premises would be charged within operating expenses rather than cost of sales (they are selling expenses).

D is not correct. Regardless of sales volumes, if the mark up is 50% then a change in volume would not affect the gross profit margin.

(3) **B and C are correct.**

An upwards revaluation of non-current assets increases equity and therefore capital employed. It is also likely to reduce profit (if the assets are depreciable) as it will lead to higher depreciation charges.

When an entity continues to use fully depreciated assets there will be a positive effect on return on capital employed, as there will be no further depreciation charged but the assets and they will have nil carrying value, but they will continue to generate profits.

A is not correct. An entity can improve its gross profit margin by changing its sales mix and selling more high margin products.

D is not correct. Revaluation would increase equity and therefore reduce gearing.

(4) **D is correct.**

The P/E ratio measures the market price of a share relative to its earnings per share, with market price as the numerator. WX has the lowest P/E ratio and a low share price would therefore be a valid explanation.

A is not correct. As a general rule, the higher the P/E ratio, the less risky the investment. Therefore ST is likely to be the least risky of the three entities.

B is not correct. Earnings per share is the denominator of the P/E ratio and therefore ST has the lowest earnings per share relative to market price of the three entities.

C is not correct. See explanation of A above.

(5) **B, C and D are correct.**

Old non-current assets inflate the ratio as the carrying value is low and is included in the denominator.

A relatively low asset turnover also suggests that the assets are not generating sufficient revenue, hence they are under-utilised.

An alternative answer however would be if the assets have been acquired towards the end of the financial period, as the full cost would be included in the denominator but there wouldn't yet be a year's worth of revenue in the numerator.

A is incorrect. An upward revaluation would increase non-current assets and, as this is the denominator, this would make non-current assets relatively low.

(6) **B and E are correct.**

Difference classification of expenses of two entities will affect any comparison of gross profit.

The operating expenses of both entities can be calculated from the information provided.

	A $m	B $m
Gross profit (gross profit margin × revenue)		
(26% × $160m)	41.6	
(17% × $300m)		51
Operating profit (operating profit margin × revenue)		
(9% × $160m)	14.4	
(11% × $300m)		33
Therefore operating expenses	27.2	18

A is incorrect. Economies of scale would not be a valid conclusion for A having the better gross margin as it is the smaller entity - its revenue is only 53% of B's and the two entities operate in the same sector.

C is incorrect. Different classification of expenses between cost of sales and operating expenses should have no effect on profit before tax (which includes both categories). It only affects gross profit.

D is incorrect. See above calculation.

Index

Index